RELATIONAL PATTERNS,
THERAPEUTIC PRESENCE

RELATIONAL PATTERNS, THERAPEUTIC PRESENCE
Concepts and Practice of Integrative Psychotherapy

Richard G. Erskine

Routledge
Taylor & Francis Group

LONDON AND NEW YORK

First published 2015 by Karnac Books Ltd.

Published 2018 by Routledge
2 Park Square, Milton Park, Abingdon, Oxon OX14 4RN
711 Third Avenue, New York, NY 10017, USA

Routledge is an imprint of the Taylor & Francis Group, an informa business

British Library Cataloguing in Publication Data

A C.I.P. for this book is available from the British Library

ISBN-13: 9781782201908 (pbk)

Typeset by V Publishing Solutions Pvt Ltd., Chennai, India

*To my grandchildren who have a constant excitement for life,
and to Karen for her editing skills and enthusiasm*

CONTENTS

ACKNOWLEDGEMENTS

I should like to express my thanks for permission to reprint in this book the following material.

Chapter One

Copyright (1993) by the Institute for Integrative Psychotherapy and Richard G. Erskine, Ph.D. This chapter was originally co-presented with Rebecca L. Trautmann as a training workshop entitled "The Process of Integrative Psychotherapy" at the 1993 Eastern Regional Transactional Analysis Association Conference, Atlantic City, NJ, May 20–21, 1993. The citation for the original article is: Erskine, R. G. & Trautmann, R. L. (1993). The process of integrative psychotherapy. In: B. Loria (Ed.), The Boardwalk Papers: Selections from the 1993 Eastern Regional Transactional Analysis Association Conference. Madison, WI: Omnipress.

Chapter Two

This chapter was co-authored with Janet Moursund and served as a basis for a workshop entitled "Beyond Empathy: A Therapy of Contact in Relationship" presented by Richard Erskine at the British Institute for Transactional Analysis National Conference. Swansea, Wales, April

9–12, 2003. Copyright 1998 by the Institute for Integrative Psychotherapy. The citation for the original article is: Erskine, R. G. (2003). Beyond Empathy: A Therapy of Contact-in-Relationship. In: K. Leech (Ed.), ITA Conference Papers, Expanding Perspectives in Transactional Analysis, VII (pp. 28–51). Marlborough, UK: Institute for Transactional Analysis.

Chapter Three

This paper was presented as a keynote speech entitled "A Therapeutic Relationship?" at the 1st Congress of the World Council for Psychotherapy, Vienna, Austria, June 30 to July 6, 1996. Portions of this paper were also included in a closing address, "The Psychotherapy Relationship", at the 7th Annual Conference of the European Association for Psychotherapy, Rome, Italy, June 26–29, 1997. Copyright (1998) European Association for Psychotherapy. Reprint by permission from the editor, *International Journal of Psychotherapy*. The citation for the original article is: Erskine, R. G. (1998). Attunement and Involvement: Therapeutic Responses *to* Relational Needs. *International Journal of Psychotherapy*, 3(3): 235–244.

Chapter Four

Portions of this paper were presented as the keynote address entitled "Unconscious Processes: The Intimate Connection between Client and Therapist" at the International Integrative Psychotherapy Association conference, April 12–15, 2007 in Rome, Italy. The author thanks members of the Professional Development Seminar of the Institute for Integrative Psychotherapy for their valuable contributions in formulating the concepts in this article. His heartfelt gratitude also goes to "Kay" and "Andrew" for providing him with the opportunity to enhance his learning about psychotherapy through their work together. Copyright (2008) by the International Transactional Analysis Association. Reprinted by permission of the International Transactional Analysis Association and SAGE Publications. The citation for the original article is: Erskine, R. G. (2008). Psychotherapy of Unconscious Experience. *Transactional Analysis Journal*, 38(2): 128–138.

Chapter Five

Copyright (2009) by the International Transactional Analysis Association. Reprinted by permission of the International Transactional

Analysis Association and SAGE Publications. The citation for the original article is: Erskine, R. G. (2009). Life Scripts and Attachment Patterns: Theoretical Integration and Therapeutic Involvement. *Transactional Analysis Journal, 39*(3): 207–218.

Chapter Six

Copyright 2010 by Karnac Books, London. Reprint by permission of Karnac Books. The citation for the original chapter is: Erskine, R. G. (2010). Life Scripts: Unconscious Relational Patterns and Psychotherapeutic Involvement. In: R. G. Erskine (Ed.), Life Scripts: A Transactional Analysis of Unconscious Relational Patterns (pp. 1–28). London: Karnac.

Chapter Seven

This chapter was coauthored with Marye O'Reilly-Knapp, Ph.D. Copyright (2010) by Karnac Books, London. Reprint by permission of Karnac Books. The citation for the original chapter is: O'Reilly-Knapp, M. & Erskine, R. G. (2010). The Script System: An Unconscious Organization of Experience. In: R. G. Erskine (Ed.), Life Scripts: A Transactional Analysis of Unconscious Relational Patterns (pp. 291–308). London: Karnac.

Chapter Eight

This chapter was originally presented as a lecture entitled "Psychological Functions of Life Scripts" in Kent, CT on August 3, 2008 at the ten-day psychotherapy training workshop of the Institute for Integrative Psychotherapy.

Chapter Nine

Copyright 2010 by Institute for Integrative Psychotherapy and Richard G. Erskine Consulting, Inc. Reprint with the approval of the *International Journal of Integrative Psychotherapy* and the International Integrative Psychotherapy Association. The citation for the original article is: Erskine, R. G. (2010). Integrating Expressive Methods in a Relational-Psychotherapy. *International Journal of Integrative Psychotherapy, 1*(2): 55–80.

Chapter Ten

I want to express a special thank you to Stanley (a pseudonym) for allowing me to write about our therapeutic journey together. This article is an excerpt of the closing keynote speech on Sunday, July 7, 2002 at the World TA Congress 2002. The theme of the conference was "Violence: Let's Talk". Copyright (2008) by the International Transactional Analysis Association. Reprinted by permission of the International Transactional Analysis Association and SAGE Publications. The citation of the original article is: Erskine, R. G. (2002). Bonding in Relationship: A Solution to Violence?. *Transactional Analysis Journal, 32*: 256–260.

Chapter Eleven

The author gratefully acknowledges the members of the Professional Development Seminars of the Institute for Integrative Psychotherapy for sharing personal experiences and for their professional involvement in formulating the ideas in this article. Portions of this article were presented at the Symposium on the Treatment of Shame, Minneapolis, MN, October, 1993. Copyright 1993 by the Institute for Integrative Psychotherapy and Richard G. Erskine, Ph.D., all rights reserved. The citation for the original article is: Erskine, R. G. (1995). A Gestalt Therapy Approach to Shame and Self-righteousness: Theory and Methods. *British Gestalt Journal, 4*(2): 108–117.

Chapter Twelve

This chapter was originally presented as the introduction to the continuing education symposium on "The Schizoid Process" held on August 20, 1999 during the International Transactional Analysis Association annual conference in San Francisco. Dr. Erskine served as the symposium moderator. Copyright (2001) by the International Transactional Analysis Association. Reprinted by permission of the International Transactional Analysis Association and SAGE Publications. The citation of the original article is: Erskine, R. G. (2001). The Schizoid Process. *Transactional Analysis Journal, 31*(1): 4–6.

Chapter Thirteen

Copyright 2011 by Institute for Integrative Psychotherapy and Richard G. Erskine Consulting, Inc. Reprinted with the approval of the *International Journal of Integrative Psychotherapy* and the International Integrative Psychotherapy Association. The citation for the original article is:

Erskine, R. G. (2012). Early Affect-Confusion: The "Borderline" Between Despair and Rage. Part 1 of a Case Study Trilogy. *International Journal of Integrative Psychotherapy*, 3(2): 3–14.

Chapter Fourteen

Chapter Fifteen

Chapter Sixteen

Chapter Seventeen

Intrapsychic Conflict: Psychotherapy of Parent Ego States. In: C. Sills & H. Hargaden (Eds.), Ego States: Key Concepts in Transactional Analysis, Contemporary Views (pp. 109–134). London: Worth.

Chapter Eighteen

This chapter was originally presented as a workshop entitled "Working with the Traumatic Elements of Bereavement in an Integrative-Relational Perspective" at the International Integrative Psychotherapy Association Conference, July 12, 2013, Belton Woods, Grantham, UK. Portions of this chapter are the copyright (2014) of the International Transactional Analysis Association. Reprinted by permission of the International Transactional Analysis Association and SAGE Publications. The citation of the original article is: Erskine, R. G. (2014). What Do You Say Before You Say Goodbye?: Psychotherapy of Grief. *Transactional Analysis Journal*, 44(4). Other portions of this chapter are the copyright of the Institute for Integrative Psychotherapy and Richard G. Erskine Consulting, Inc. (2013). Reprinted with permission from the editor, *International Journal of Psychotherapy*.

Chapter Nineteen

Copyright 2014 by Institute for Integrative Psychotherapy and Richard G. Erskine Consulting, Inc. Reprint with the approval of the *International Journal of Integrative Psychotherapy* and the International Integrative Psychotherapy Association. The citation for the original article is: Erskine, R. G. (2014). Nonverbal stories: The body in psychotherapy. *International Journal of Integrative Psychotherapy*, 5: 21–33.

Chapter Twenty

Copyright 2013, American Academy of Psychotherapists (AAP). All rights reserved. Reprinted with permission of *Voices*, the journal of the American Academy of Psychotherapists. The citation for the original article is: Erskine, R. G. (2013). Narcissism or The Therapist's Error?. *Voices: The Art and Science of Psychotherapy*, 49: 27–33.

ABOUT THE AUTHOR

Richard G. Erskine, Ph.D., has conducted a full-time psychotherapy practice and has served as training director at the Institute for Integrative Psychotherapy in New York City since 1976. He is a licensed clinical psychologist, licensed psychoanalyst, certified clinical transactional analyst, a certified group psychotherapist, and a UKCP and EAPA certified psychotherapist. His professional background includes: training in Gestalt therapy with both Fritz and Laura Perls, client-centered therapy, emotional and cognitive development, body oriented psychotherapy, British object relations therapy, and psychoanalytic self psychology.

This collection of essays on *Relational Patterns, Therapeutic Presence* presents a comprehensive integrative theory and style of therapeutic involvement that reflects a relational and non-pathological perspective. The various sets of methods described are contact-based, profoundly respectful, developmentally attuned, co-constructive, and intersubjective.

FOREWORD

When Dr. Richard Erskine asked me to write the foreword to this latest collection of articles, I was both honored and uncertain. I was honored by being asked to write something for a man I've known, admired, learned from, and worked with since the 1970s and I was uncertain about what perspective I might add. I decided I would say something about how I came to know Richard and why, after all of the other trainings, therapies, and professional experiences that I've had in my life as a clinical psychologist, I have continued to attend his seminars and to learn from him.

As fate would have it, learning how to type when I was eleven years old led me to meeting Richard in San Francisco in the summer of 1976. When I was twenty-four, I moved to San Francisco from Cambridge, Massachusetts. In Cambridge, I had been waiting tables and bartending, writing short stories and songs, and engaging in a very valuable three years of psychodynamic therapy (with another Richard). Although I had been an English major in college, this post-college therapy experience had begun to spark my interest in psychotherapy as a possible career. Once I moved to San Francisco my interest in psychotherapy took off after a simple walk down Union Street.

In San Francisco in the mid-'70s one could walk along Union Street and stop at the offices of the Gestalt Institute, the Bioenergetics Institute, the Esalen Institute, the Humanistic Psychology center, a Primal Scream office, yoga centers, and the storefront offices of a number of New Age therapies. Just a few blocks away was the headquarters for the International Transactional Analysis Association. I collected brochures from all of them and attended various experiential workshops that included Gestalt therapy and bioenergetics. To pay for the workshops I dusted off my typing skills and obtained work with a local secretarial agency called Kelly Girl.

One of my Kelly Girl jobs was at the home of a woman who needed me to type her doctoral dissertation in psychology and, fortuitously for me, happened to be the wife of the president of the International Transactional Analysis Association. It was at their house that I discovered the *Transactional Analysis Journal* which included a recent article by a psychologist named Richard Erskine on "The ABC's of Effective Psychotherapy" (April, 1975). My interest in this article motivated me to attend the 1976 ITAA conference to specifically seek out Richard Erskine's workshop and learn more about "The ABC's."

What was it about Richard's article that drew me to hear him speak? Having already experienced the benefits of some vastly different therapy approaches—each of which brought me to different depths of self-understanding and feeling—I was immediately drawn to his view of personality and behavior as an *interaction of the affective, behavioral, and cognitive*—the ABC's of psychotherapy. In subsequent writings he would elaborate more on the role of the *physiological* and *relational* as the fourth and fifth dimensions of integration (Erskine & Moursund, 1988; Erskine, Moursund, & Trautmann, 1999; Erskine & Trautmann, 1993). In his view each of the ABC's are equally important, each one influencing the other, and each a possible, or even necessary, avenue for therapeutic intervention. The notion that focusing on multiple dimensions of the whole person and using a variety of therapeutic methods made immediate sense to me.

However, if it was the ABC's perspective of Richard's article that brought me to his workshop, it was the subsequent clarity with which he explained and elaborated on his ideas in person, and the apparent ease and sensitivity with which he talked about clinical issues, that made me think I'd like to learn more from him and continue my own professional growth with him. I remember approaching him after the workshop and awkwardly saying something about wanting to join his training program if I moved to New York in the future. I don't believe he thought much of it at the time—for which I can't blame him—but the desire stuck with me nonetheless.

Three years later when I was back living in New York City where I had grown up, was bartending at a local French restaurant to pay the bills, and had already completed my first year of a Ph.D. program in clinical psychology at the New School for Social Research, I contacted Richard and he did, in fact, welcome me into his training program. (At the time I believe he thought he was taking a chance on a "bartender.") I joined his clinical training program and, some years later, the advanced Professional Development Seminar where I continued until the Seminar disbanded in 2010.

Why did I stay so long? I was impressed with the inseparable combination of Richard as a theorist, teacher, clinician, and person. Richard lives an ongoing commitment to his own personal and professional growth. He has always invited, and often challenged, those around him to do the same—to learn, to grow, to be sensitive—to be courageous. Put another way, there was always something new to learn by studying with him, by attending his workshops and Professional Development Seminars, and by reading his latest articles and books.

I believe what the reader of this current volume of articles will find— especially if you have some familiarity with his earlier writings—is that these articles are the product of his steadfast quest to keep developing his ideas on theory, clinical practice, and human relationships. His 1975 "ABC's" article began as an exploration of the "integrative nature of an effective psychotherapy." Although his original ideas were rooted in the theory of transactional analysis, Gestalt therapy, and his background in child development, his theory and practice have evolved into an even richer, in-depth, "relationally based integrative psychotherapy"—a comprehensive system of therapy that reflects his own additional understanding and integration of British object relations theory, psychoanalytic self psychology, body therapy, and recent advances in neuropsychology and child development.

As early as 1972, in his lectures at the University of Illinois and his training programs at the Institute for Integrative Psychotherapy, Richard was emphasizing the process of an integrative psychotherapy. At the time, the word "integrative" was not used to describe any known approach to psychotherapy, and had—and still has—very specific meanings in

Richard's work (Erskine & Moursund, 1988). Now the term "integrative psychotherapy" is used by many, with the definitions and the practices having different meanings for different individuals.

Richard has always spotlighted the importance of the internal integration within the person—the integration of each person's affect, physiology, and cognition so that behavior is by choice in the current context and not activated by compulsion or fear. However, the current overuse of the term "integrative" generally veers miles away from the kind of integration Richard has been talking about and developing all these years. Most "integrations" pull one or two approaches to therapy together and call it a new theory, or they eclectically mix techniques from multiple schools based on the "whatever works" principle without a clear foundation in underlying theory.

I believe that Richard, however, has been doing something quite different in his approach to integrative psychotherapy. He has created a comprehensive and internally consistent system of psychotherapy integration. I have Dr. Mary Henle, one of my first professors in graduate school, to thank for giving me a critical lens through which I could evaluate and appreciate what Richard the theoretician was already doing in the 1970s and continues to do right through his current set of articles, almost forty years later. He was taking theory building seriously, deciphering which theories congruently integrate within relational perspectives of motivation, personality formation, and clinical method.

Dr. Henle taught the course in "Systems of Psychology" and she was very strongly opposed to any theory-making that hinted at eclecticism. Dr. Henle had studied and worked with some of the pioneers of Gestalt psychology who were scientific and rigorous in their approach to theory (e.g., Kohler, Lewin). She taught us that a true paradigm of psychology had to have an internal consistency that explained human motivation and personality development. Piecing together a variety of eclectic ideas and methods and calling it a theory because something seemed to "work," was anathema to her. (Unlike me in 1976, I don't think she would have been impressed by the psychotherapy shops on Union Street.)

The paradigm lens which Dr. Henle provided has helped me appreciate something that I believe Richard has carefully and methodically done over these many years, and is still part of the answer to why I appreciate Richard as a theoretician and teacher to this day. He has never stopped challenging himself—and the clinicians he teaches or the people who read his collected writings—to think about a relational integrative psychotherapy that is based on an internally consistent framework and that addresses the core questions of human motivation and personality development. Recognizing the importance of sound theory building, Richard wrote:

> Theories of motivation provide a metaperspective that encompasses theories of personality. A theory of motivation determines which theories of personality can be integrated and which are conceptually inconsistent and do not integrate into a unified, comprehensive theory of human functioning. When theories of motivation and personality have an internal validity and consistency, they work together as a conceptual organization for a unified theory of method. (1997b, p. 8)

While fully acknowledging the influence of many schools of psychology and therapy in his thinking and practice, Richard has set a goal never to put together an eclectic blend of theoretical ideas or of therapeutic techniques. Rather, beyond eclecticism (to paraphrase his book title *Beyond Empathy*) what you'll find in this current set of writings are articles that continue to refine his view of human motivation as a balance between stimulus processing, structure making, and relationship seeking. His articles contain two main focal points: he articulates several theories of personality and how personality becomes structured (not always for the best) based on patterns of early relationship-seeking experiences; and he describes a theory of therapeutic intervention that emphasizes a relationship-oriented approach to psychotherapy. Both of these focal points are based not on an unrelated eclectic assortment of techniques, but on theory-consistent methods of helping people to heal the unfinished issues in their lives.

I hope you enjoy and learn from these latest writings as I have and will continue to do so.

Dr. Joshua Zavin, President,
International Integrative Psychotherapy Association,
Morristown, New Jersey

PREFACE

The winter sun is bright, the rivers frozen solid, and all is white in the arctic landscape below my airplane window. It is January, 2014, and I am on my way from Vancouver to France, Spain, and the UK to facilitate several training workshops and supervision groups. As I sit on this airplane I am looking at the landscape below and reminiscing about my first trip to Europe in 1974. On that first trip I had been invited to give a series of lectures at both the University of Munich in Germany and Aarhus University in Denmark. I remember that flight very well. I was scared and unsure of myself. I studied on the plane even though I knew the material well. In those days I struggled to intellectualize my fears; it distracted me from my uncertainties. Little did I know that I would have such a welcoming reception and professional support that would result in numerous invitations over the next forty years to return to various countries in Europe to teach, supervise, and facilitate experiential workshops.

So much has changed since that first eventful trip to teach integrative psychotherapy in Europe. Then I was a professor at the University of Illinois in Urbana-Champaign where I was exploring how to teach the integration of various schools of psychotherapy to master's and doctoral students. The students already had several courses in behavioral therapy, some client-centered therapy, and a smattering of psychoanalytic concepts. I was excited about introducing them to the theory and methods of transactional analysis and Gestalt therapy, the concepts of Heinz Kohut's psychoanalytic self psychology, and psychotherapy from a child developmental perspective.

I sought supervision with Herman Eisen, a retired psychology professor, to whom I lamented about the vast amount of material I wanted to teach. Dr. Eisen said, "Teach your own integration. Use what you know well. Keep it simple." His wisdom has been the basis of my professional practice and goals ever since: to teach and write about my own understanding of psychotherapy; to describe my own repertoire of therapeutic contact; and to emphasize the centrality of a respectful therapeutic relationship.

This collection of twenty essays reflects some of what I have written and taught in the past twenty years, from 1993 to 2014. The articles cover a wide range of topics that include a discussion of various psychotherapy theories and methods, the significance of attachment and developmental processes, and the implications and magnitude of an involved therapeutic-relationship. Included in this book are a number of clinical case examples that give a realistic account of how I apply a relationally based integrative psychotherapy in actual practice with my clients.

I have chosen to write from an integrative frame of reference that melds the ideas and concepts of Carl Rogers's client-centered therapy, Eric Berne's transactional analysis, Fritz and Laura Perls's Gestalt therapy, Heinz Kohut's psychoanalytic self psychology, various writers from the British object relations school of psychoanalysis, the intersubjective viewpoint in psychoanalysis, and the theories and research in human development. My first years in this profession were spent working with emotionally disturbed children; my Ph.D. is in emotional and cognitive development. Those educational and therapeutic experiences have left me sensitive to the needs and reactions of the young child who has experienced neglect, abuse, criticism, and distain; this sensitivity furnishes the backdrop in most of my writings. My professional quest has been to define and refine a developmentally and relationally based theory and practice that leads to the healing of our clients' old emotional wounds and neglects.

In a previous book, *Theories and Methods of an Integrative Transactional Analysis: A Volume of Selected Articles* (1997), the twenty-seven chapters span a wide variety of subjects. Even though I primarily wrote in the voice of a transactional analyst, my predominant focus was, and is, *relational*. This current volume entitled *Relational Patterns, Therapeutic Presence* emphasizes the significance and centrality of human relationships.

Relational Patterns shape our internal and external life. They form our unconscious systems of mental organization—systems composed of physiological survival reactions, internal working models, implicit and procedural memories, and the influences of significant others—what I refer to in several chapters as a *Life Script* (Erskine, 2010a, 2010b). *Therapeutic Presence* is provided through the psychotherapist's sustained attuned responses to both the verbal and nonverbal expressions of the client. It occurs when the behavior and communication of the psychotherapist at all times respect and enhance the integrity of the client. My premise is that "healing of emotional and relational wounds occurs through a contactful therapeutic relationship."

This book is written in an integrative voice—a voice that draws from a number of therapeutic perspectives, each of which focuses on the significance of interpersonal relationship. The book focuses primarily on relationships: the relational needs that are an essential part of life, what happens when there are repeated disruptions in significant relationships, how to identify both internal and external relational disruptions, and the attitude and methods that are essential in creating a healing relationship.

The twenty chapters in this book reflect an extension and further development of the theories and methods written in three previous books: *Beyond Empathy: A Therapy of Contact-in-Relationship* (1999); *Integrative Psychotherapy: The Art and Science of Relationship* (2003); and *Integrative Psychotherapy in Action* (1988 & 2011).

Each of the chapters in this book began with my struggle to master a theoretical concept or evaluate the effectiveness of a method and therapeutic approach. When I was perplexed about a theory or uncertain about a method I would read the relevant liturature intensely, make numerous therapy notes, and discuss my muddle with colleagues. As I became clearer about a concept or theory I would introduce it into the supervision sessions I was conducting. My supervisees and I would explore and experiment with the concepts. Inevitably, the topic would emerge in various lectures to training groups and seminars. Eventually, after teaching the topic for a while, I would write about the concepts in a formal way to convey the ideas to a broader range of professional colleagues.

There are a number of training groups and seminars that have been influential and crucial in the development and refinement of concepts and practice described in this book. Importantly, I want to thank the many members of the Professional Development Seminars and Training Programs of the Institute for Integrative Psychotherapy in New York City, Kent (Connecticut), and Vancouver (British Columbia). Without their input, discussions, arguments, and encouragement many concepts would not have been developed or refined. Before a final writing many of these articles were originally taught and discussed in the Chicago Training Group; the training groups at the Ohio Counseling Center and the Indianapolis Gestalt Institute; and further developed in the training programs in Nottingham and Manchester, England; the training programs in Lyon, Montpellier, and Valence, France; in Rome, Italy; and in Asturias, Barcelona, Bilbao, and Madrid, Spain.

I want to express my gratitude to three co-authors who have been valued partners in my attempts to put these complex ideas into clear English: Janet P. Moursund, Ph.D.; Rebecca L. Trautmann, RN, MSW; and Marye O'Reilly-Knapp, Ph.D. They have each helped me find a vocabulary and style of communication. Also, there have been several individuals who have been instrumental in my personal and professional development. I want to take this opportunity to honor a few:

- Robert Neville, Ph.D., client-centered therapist extraordinaire, who provided me with two years of daily supervision when I was treating the survivors of a mass murder
- David Kuffer, Ph.D., who introduced me to the subtleties and depth of a clinical transactional analysis
- Fritz Perls, M.D., Ph.D., who challenged me to be excited about the practice of Gestalt therapy, and Laura Perls, Ph.D., who encouraged and supported me in my own integration of theory and practice
- Robert Melnicker, Ph.D., for our ten years of psychoanalysis and his loving attention to my personal development
- and the many unnamed others who have nurtured, supported, and encouraged me over the past fifty years in this profession.

I invite you, the reader, to join with me in the further development and refinement of a developmentally based and relationally focused integrative psychotherapy. I hope that the chapters in this book stimulate your thinking about your clients and offer a refreshing perspective on your therapeutic practice. May we each expand and fine-tune our capacity for a psychotherapy of contact-in-relationship.

Philosophical principles of integrative psychotherapy

As we begin, I want to articulate some of the philosophical principles that influence my therapeutic outlook, attitude, and interactions with clients. These are the principles inherent in a respectful, co-constructed, and interpersonally focused integrative psychotherapy. The philosophical principles described here are the foundation for our therapeutic approach when we engage in a developmentally based and relationally focused psychotherapy—a psychotherapy that holds the relationship between the therapist and client as central to a process of healing and personal growth.

Unlike the introductions to many books, I do not intend to summarize each chapter. Instead, I want to describe eight principles that form the foundation of the theory and methods articulated throughout this book. These principles reflect my value system and personal attitudes toward the practice of psychotherapy and express the esteem with which I regard my clients. Although I do not describe these philosophical principles in any formal manner in the various chapters, each of these principles forms the underlying themes that determine which concepts and theories can be effectively integrated and how we can sculpt our practice of psychotherapy. Most likely this list is not complete and there may be other important principles that you want to add. However, the eight philosophical principles listed here may provide you with both an orientation to the various chapters in this book and a template for applying a relationally focused integrative psychotherapy in actual practice.

All people are equally valuable: This seems like such a simple statement yet the concept is profound. Many of our clients have grown up in homes and school systems where they were treated as though they had no value as a human being. They, like us, attempt to protect themselves from being vulnerable in the presence of neglect, humiliation, or physical abuse. It is our therapeutic responsibility to find ways to value every client even if we do not understand their behavior or what motivates them. This involves respecting their vulnerability, as well as their attempts at being invulnerable, while we maintain a therapeutic relationship that fosters a sense of security. We manifest this principle of equality when we treat our clients with kindness, when we provide them with options and choices, when we create security, and when we accept them as they present themselves rather than looking for a possible ulterior agenda.

All human experience is organized physiologically, affectively and/or cognitively: Our biological imperatives require that we make meaning of our phenomenological experiences and that we share those meanings with others. People are always communicating a story about their life either consciously or unconsciously. Our clients' unconscious communication is embodied in their physical tensions, entrenched in their emotional reactions, and encoded in the way they make visceral and cognitive sense of their current and past situations. Therefore, our therapeutic task is to observe, inquire, listen, and decode our clients' many unconscious attempts to communicate their life story and to seek a healing relationship. This requires us to decenter from our own perspective and to experience the client through his or her own way of being in the world. In so doing we provide a relationship that allows each client to fully express their life story to a respectful and involved other person.

All human behavior has meaning in some context: It is our therapeutic task to help our clients become aware of and appreciate the various meanings of their behaviors and fantasies. This includes a therapeutic involvement of normalizing their behaviors by helping them understand the contexts in which their behaviors, beliefs, or fantasies were derived. All problematic behaviors and interruptions to internal and external contact serve some psychological function such as reparation, prediction, identity, continuity, stability, or enhancement.

Before focusing on behavioral change in therapy it is essential to know and appreciate our clients' phenomenological experiences and various psychological functions. Resolution of both current and archaic conflicts occurs when the client becomes conscious of implicit relational patterns, the psychological function of those patterns, and how those implicit and procedural memories affect current relationships.

All people are relationship-seeking and interdependent throughout life: Many of the difficulties that our clients describe are based on repeated disruptions in their relational systems and their resulting inability to depend on significant others when it was developmentally necessary. As a result, they are unconsciously inhibited by archaic internal working models of relationship that influence the development of a sense of self and the quality of interpersonal relationships. Through psychotherapy we provide the intersubjective contact that may challenge our clients' old script beliefs and dysfunctional patterns of behavior. We offer a new intersubjective relationship that provides emotional security, validation, and dependability.

As we effect a change in one aspect of our clients' relational systems we influence their other relationships as well. When we affectively, rhythmically, and developmentally attune to our clients, consistently inquire about our clients' experience, and when we are authentically involved with our clients, we change their perspectives of what is possible in intersubjective contact thereby opening new possibilities to being vulnerable and authentic with other people in their lives.

Humans have an innate thrust to grow: The ancient Greeks used the term *physis* to describe the vitality and psychic energy that is invested in health, creativity, and the expansion of our personal horizons. *Physis* is the source of our internal thrust to challenge acquiescence, to explore different ways of doing and being, to have aspirations, and to develop our full potential. As a psychotherapist, it is my commitment to engage each client in a contactful relationship that vitalizes this innate thrust to grow.

Such a therapeutic relationship:

- enhances each client's understanding of his or her history and inner experience
- furnishes each client with a sense that his or her behavior has an important psychological function

- fosters the capacity for full internal and external contact
- provides the opportunity for each client to experience being seen as a unique and valuable human being
- explores creative options and outlets, and
- nourishes the possibility of pleasure in relationships.

Humans suffer from relational disruptions not "psychopathology": A relationally focused integrative psychotherapy emphasizes a non-pathological perspective in understanding people's behavior. Discomforting physiological and emotional symptoms, entrenched belief systems, obsessions and compulsive behaviors, aggression or social withdrawal are all examples of creative attempts to satisfy relational needs and resolve disruptions in interpersonal contact.

When we view someone as "pathological" we lose our awareness of the person's unique creative accommodation and their attempts to manage situations of neglect, ridicule, and/or abuse. We also lose a valuable opportunity for interpersonal contact when we mistakenly focus on an individual as a "personality disorder," or view people as either passive or manipulative, or even define them as playing psychological games. Yes, people can be passive-aggressive, manipulative, game playing; they can be cruel; they can lie and cheat—we would be foolish not to recognize such behavior—but our therapeutic advantage is in our understanding of our client's creative accommodation, their internal working models, core beliefs, and their desperate attempts to resolve intrapsychic conflicts. It is in recognizing and authentically appreciating the other person's emotional vulnerability, relational needs, and desperate attempts at self-reparation, self-regulation, or self-enhancement that we create the possibility for full intersubjective contact—a contact that heals old psychological wounds.

The intersubjective process of psychotherapy is more important than the content of the psychotherapy: Intersubjectivity refers to the synthesis of two people sharing an experience together. Each person brings to any interpersonal encounter his or her own phenomenological experience. The intersubjective process involves the melding together of each person's subjective experience, his or her affects, belief systems, internal relational models, implicit and explicit memories, and relational needs. Effective psychotherapy emerges in the creation of a new perspective and understanding—a unique synthesis. A new psychological synthesis occurs when there is authentic and open contact between two people. Each is influenced by the other; the therapy process is co-created. Therefore, no two psychotherapists will ever do the same psychotherapy—each of us is idiosyncratic in how we interact with our clients.

The important aspects of the psychotherapy are embedded in the distinctiveness of each interpersonal relationship, not in what we consciously do as a psychotherapist, but in the quality of how we are in relationship with the other person. The therapist's attitudes and demeanor, the quality of interpersonal relationship and involvement, are just as important, sometimes even more so, than any specific theory or method. An effective healing of psychological distress and relational neglect occurs through a contactful therapeutic relationship—a relationship in which the psychotherapist values and supports vulnerability, authenticity, and intersubjective contact.

Conclusion

These eight philosophical principles serve as the foundation stones on which we build the theories and methods of a relationally focused integrative psychotherapy. These philosophical principles provide the basis for deciding which specific concepts and ideas can be integrated with the core relational theories of motivation, personality function, and methods. For a theory to be thoroughly integrative each theory, concept, and set of methods must dovetail with the fundamental philosophical principles. As you read each chapter please keep these principles in mind. Use them to question and evaluate the various concepts and how those concepts are applied in actual clinical practice.

CHAPTER ONE

Integrative psychotherapy: theory, process, and relationship

J ust as relationships between people are dynamic processes, so is the development of theory, originating as it does from the dynamic process of the individual theorist(s) and from the dynamic process of each therapeutic relationship which guides and informs that theory. Thus I would like to take the opportunity in this opening chapter to talk about how a relationally focused integrative psychotherapy has developed and how I think about it and practice it today.

The term "integrative" of integrative psychotherapy has a number of meanings. The original and primary meaning of "integrative psychotherapy" refers to the process of integrating the personality: helping the client to assimilate and harmonize the contents of his or her ego states, relax the defense mechanisms, relinquish the life script, and reengage the world with full contact. It is the process of making whole: taking disowned, unaware, unresolved aspects of the ego and making them part of a cohesive self. Through integration, it becomes possible for people to have the courage to face each moment openly and freshly, without the protection of a preformed opinion, position, attitude, or expectation.

"Integrative" also refers to the integration of theory, the bringing together of affective, cognitive, behavioral, physiological, and systems approaches to psychotherapy. The concepts are utilized within a perspective of human development in which each phase of life presents heightened developmental tasks, need sensitivities, crises, and opportunities for new learning. Integrative psychotherapy takes into account many views of human functioning: psychodynamic, client centered, behaviorist, family therapy, Gestalt therapy, neo-Reichian, object relations theories, psychoanalytic self psychology, and transactional analysis. Each provides a valid explanation of behavior, and each is enhanced when selectively integrated with the others. The psychotherapeutic interventions are based on research-validated knowledge of normal developmental process and the theories describing the self-protective defensive processes used when there are interruptions in normal development.

The ABC's and P

I presented the preliminary ideas of integrative psychotherapy in a series of lectures at the University of Illinois in 1972. A brief outline of these ideas was published in 1975 and then elaborated upon in 1980. Many of the ideas that my colleagues and I have written about have emerged from the case presentations, research, and discussions in the Professional Development Seminars of the Institute for Integrative Psychotherapy. I have an immense gratitude to this group of knowledgeable and curious psychotherapists who have helped me develop and refine the theories and methods of a relationally oriented integrative psychotherapy. Some of the clinical methods that will be briefly described in this and the following chapters are presented transaction-by-transaction in *Integrative Psychotherapy in Action* (Erskine & Moursund, 1988). In three subsequent books we elaborated on both the theory and methods of integrative psychotherapy. The books are: 1) *Beyond Empathy: A Therapy of Contact-in-Relationship* (Erskine, Moursund, & Trautmann, 1999); 2) *Integrative Psychotherapy: The Art and Science of Relationship* (Moursund & Erskine, 2004); and 3) *Theories and Methods of an Integrative Transactional Analysis* (Erskine, 1997c).

Our focus of integration is on five primary dimensions of human functioning and therefore our psychotherapeutic focus: *cognitive, behavioral, affective,* and *physiological*; each within a *relational system*. Simply put, the cognitive theories stress the mental processes of a person and focus on the question, "Why?" The cognitive approach explains and provides a model of understanding. Why do we have the problems that we have? Why does our mind work the way it does? It assumes that psychotherapy is an intellectual process and when the client comes to understand why he or she behaves and thinks in a particular manner, he or she will solve the conflicts involved.

Significantly different from the cognitive is the behavioral approach which deals with the question of "What?" Behavioral therapy describes what exists and attempts to shape appropriate behavior. What is the specific problem? What contingencies shaped and now maintain the behavior? What changes are necessary in the reward system to produce new behavior? And since behavioral therapy emerged out of experimental psychology, there is a great deal of attention given to what measures are to be applied to evaluate the changes made. The application of behavioral therapy involves a shift away from the question of "Why?" and instead is focused on "What?" The goal of behavioral therapy is to identify and reinforce desired behaviors.

Both cognitive and behavioral therapy are significantly different from an affective psychotherapy. An affective approach deals with the question "How?" How does a person feel? Here the focus is on the internal experiential process: how each person phenomenologically experiences what has happened. The major focus is not on the *why* of cognitive therapy or the *what* of behavioral therapy, but on *how* we emotionally experience ourselves in the here and now. A basic premise in affective therapy is that people are out of touch with their feelings and internal processes. It is assumed that removing blocks to emotions and fully expressing repressed affect will produce an emotional closure and provide for a fuller range of affective experiences.

In addition to the dimensions of affect, behavior, and cognition, we include the physiological dimension. As many of the mind/body theories and modalities have developed, including the research on psychoneuroimmunology, it became imperative to include a focus on the body as an integral aspect of psychotherapy. Disturbances in affect or cognition can adversely affect the body as physiological dysfunction can impact changes in behavior, affect, and cognition.

The affective, behavioral, cognitive, and physiological foundations of the human organism are viewed from a systems perspective—a cybernetic model wherein any dimension has an interrelated effect on the

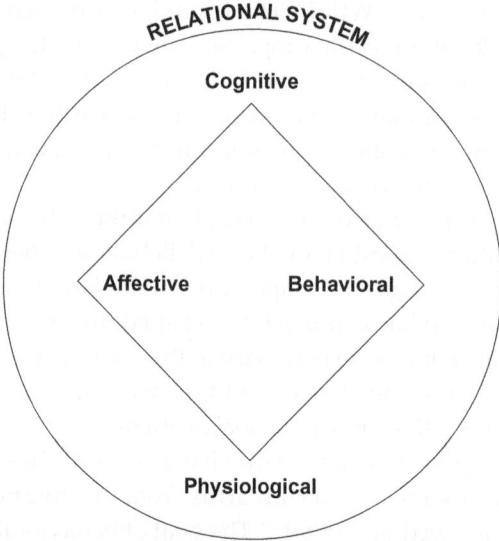

Figure 1. The self-in-relationship system.

other dimensions. Just as the individual is affected by others in a family or work system, he in turn contributes to the uniqueness of the system. In a similar systemic way the intrapsychic and observable dimensions of an individual are inherently influenced in the psychological function of the individual. The systems perspective leads to the question, "What is the function of a particular behavior, affect, belief, or body gesture on the human organism as a whole?" A major focus of an integrative psychotherapy is on assessing whether each of these domains—affective, behavioral, cognitive, and physiological—are open or closed to contact and in the application of methods that enhance full contact.

Contact

A major premise of integrative psychotherapy is that contact constitutes the primary motivating experience of human behavior. Contact is simultaneously internal and external: it involves the full awareness of sensations, feelings, needs, sensorimotor activity, thought, and memories that occur within the individual, and a shift to full awareness of external events as registered by each of the sensory organs. With full internal and external contact, experiences are continually integrated. To the degree that the individual is involved in full contact needs will arise, be experienced, and be acted upon in relation to the environment in a way that is organically healthy. When a need arises, is met, and is let go, the person moves on to the next experience. When contact is disrupted, however, needs are not met. If the experience of need arousal is not closed naturally, it must find an artificial closure. These artificial closures are the substance of physiological survival reactions and script decisions that may become fixated. They are evident in the disavowal of affect, habitual behavior patterns, neurological inhibitions within the body, and the beliefs that limit spontaneity and flexibility in problem solving and relating to people. Each defensive interruption to contact impedes full awareness. It is the fixation of interruptions in contact, internally and externally, that is the concern of integrative psychotherapy.

Relationships

Contact also refers to the quality of the transactions between two people: the full awareness of both one's self and the other, a sensitive meeting of the other and an authentic acknowledgement of one's self. Relationships between people are built on contact. Both internal and interpersonal contact are necessary for establishing and maintaining relationships. Integrative psychotherapy makes use of many perspectives on human functioning. For a theory to be integrative it must also separate out those concepts and ideas that are not theoretically consistent in order to form a cohesive core of constructs that inform and guide the psychotherapeutic process.

The single most consistent concept in the psychology and psychotherapy literature is that of relationship. From the inception of a theory of contact by Laura and Frederick Perls (Perls, 1944; Perls, Hefferline, & Goodman, 1951) to Fairbairn's (1952) premise that people are relationship-seeking from the beginning and throughout life, to Sullivan's (1953) emphasis on interpersonal contact, to Guntrip's (1971) and Winnicott's (1965) relationship theories and corresponding clinical applications, to Berne's (1961, 1972) theories of ego states and script, to Rogers's (1951) focus on client-centered therapy, to Kohut (1971, 1977) and his followers' (Stolorow, Brandschaft, & Atwood, 1987) application of "sustained empathic inquiry," (p. 10) to the feminist and relationship theories developed by the Stone Center (Bergman, 1991; Miller, 1986; Surrey, 1985), there has been a succession of teachers, writers, and therapists who have emphasized that relationship—both in the early stages of life as well as throughout adulthood—are the source of that which gives meaning and validation to the self.

The literature on human development also leads to the premise that the sense of self and self-esteem emerge out of contact-in-relationship. Erikson's (1950) stages of human development over the entire life cycle describe the formation of identity (ego) as an outgrowth of interpersonal relations (trust vs. mistrust, autonomy vs. shame and doubt, etc.). Mahler's (Mahler, 1968; Mahler, Pine, & Bergman, 1975) descriptions of the stages of early child development place importance on the relationship between mother and infant. Bowlby (1969, 1973, 1980) has emphasized the significance of early as well as prolonged physical bonding in the creation of a visceral core from which all experiences of self and other emerge. When such contact does not occur in accordance with the child's needs there is a physiological defense against the loss of contact, poignantly described by Fraiberg in "Pathological Defenses in Infancy" (1982).

From a theoretical foundation of contact-in-relationship coupled with Berne's concept of ego states (particularly Child ego state) comes a natural focus on child development. The works of Daniel Stern (1985) and John Bowlby (1969, 1973, 1980) are presently most influential, largely because of their emphasis on early attachment and the natural, lifelong need for relationship. Based on his research of infants, Stern delineates a system for understanding the development of the sense of self which emerges out of four domains of relatedness: emergent relatedness, core relatedness, intersubjective relatedness, and verbal relatedness. As we take this view of the developing person into our psychotherapy practice, we have a deep appreciation for the vitality and active constructing that is so much a part of who our client is. By looking at the client from a simultaneous perspective of what a child needs and how he or she processes experiences as well as these being ongoing life processes, we use our self in a directed way to assist the process of developing and integrating.

What is frequently very significant in the psychotherapy is the process of attunement, not just to discrete thoughts, feelings, behaviors, or physical sensations, but also to what Stern terms "vitality affects," such that we try to create an experience of unbroken feeling-connectedness.

The sense of self and the sense of relatedness that develop seem crucial to the process of healing, particularly when there have been specific traumas in the client's life, and to the process of integration and wholeness when aspects of the self have been disavowed or denied because of the failures of contact-in-relationship.

Psychological constructs

Integrative psychotherapy correlates constructs from many different theoretical schools resulting in a unique organization of theoretical ideas and corresponding methods of clinical intervention. The concepts of contact-in-relationship, ego states, and life script are central to our integrative theory.

Ego states and transference

Eric Berne's (1961) original concept of ego states provides an overall construct that unifies many theoretical ideas (Erskine, 1987, 1988). Berne defined the Child ego states as an archaic ego consisting of fixations of earlier developmental stages; as "relics of the individual's own childhood" (1961, p. 77). The Child ego states are the entire personality of the person as he or she was in a previous developmental period (Berne, 1961, 1964). When functioning in a Child ego state the person perceives the internal needs and sensations and the external world as he or she did in a previous developmental age. This includes the needs, desires, urges, and sensations; the defense mechanisms; and the thought processes, perceptions, feelings, and behaviors of the developmental phase when fixation occurred. The Child ego state fixations occurred when critical childhood needs for contact were repeatedly not met and the child's use of defenses against the discomfort of the unmet needs became habitual.

The Parent ego states are the manifestations of introjections of the personalities of actual people as perceived by the child at the time of introjection (Loria, 1988). Introjection is a self-stabilizing defense mechanism (including disavowal, denial, and repression) frequently used when there is a lack of full psychological contact between a child and the adults responsible for his or her psychological needs. By internalizing the parent with whom there is conflict, the conflict is made part of the self and experienced internally, rather than with that much-needed parent. *The function of introjection is in providing the illusion of maintaining relationship, but at the expense of a loss of self.*

Parent ego state contents may be introjected at any point throughout life and, if not reexamined in the process of later development, remain unassimilated or not integrated into the Adult ego state. The Parent ego states constitute an alien chunk of personality, imbedded within the ego and experienced phenomenologically as if they were one's own, but, in reality, they form a borrowed personality, potentially in the position of producing intrapsychic influences on the Child ego states.

The Adult ego consists of current age-consistent emotional, cognitive, and moral development; the ability to be creative; and the capacity for full contactful engagement in meaningful relationships. The Adult ego accounts for and integrates what is occurring moment-by-moment internally and externally, past experiences and their resulting effects, and the psychological influences and identifications with significant people in one's life.

The object relations theories of attachment, regression, and internalized object (Bollas, 1979, 1987; Fairbairn, 1952; Guntrip, 1971; Winnicott, 1965) become more significant when integrated with the concepts of the Child ego states as fixations of an earlier developmental period and the Parent ego states as manifestations of introjections of the personality of actual people as perceived by the child at the time of introjection (Erskine, 1987, 1988, 1991).

The psychoanalytic self psychology concept of selfobject function (Kohut, 1971, 1977) and the Gestalt therapy concept of defensive interruptions to contact (Perls, Hefferline, & Goodman, 1951) can be combined within a theory of ego states to explain the continued presence of separate states of the ego that do not become integrated into the Adult ego (Erskine, 1991).

Ego state theory also serves to define and unify the traditional psychoanalytic concepts of transference (Brenner, 1979; Friedman, 1969; Langs, 1976) and non-transferential transactions (Berne, 1961; Greenson, 1967; Lipton, 1977).

Transference within an integrative psychotherapy perspective of ego states can be viewed as:

1. the means whereby the client can describe his past, the developmental needs which have been thwarted, and the defenses which were erected to compensate

2. the resistance to full remembering and, paradoxically, an unaware enactment of childhood experiences
3. the expression of an intrapsychic conflict and the desire to achieve intimacy in relationships, or
4. the expression of the universal psychological striving to organize experience and create meaning.

This integrative view of transference provides the basis for a continual honoring of the inherent communication in transference as well as a recognition and respect that transactions may be non-transferential (Erskine, 1991).

Script

The concept of script serves as the third unifying construct and describes how as infants and small children we begin to develop the reactions and expectations that define for us the kind of world we live in and the kind of people we are. Encoded physically in body tissues and biochemical events, emotionally, and cognitively in the form of beliefs, attitudes, and values, these responses form a blueprint that guides the way we live our lives (Erskine, 1980, 2010a).

Eric Berne termed this blueprint a "script" (1961, 1972) and Fritz Perls, innovator of Gestalt therapy, described a self-fulfilling, repetitive pattern (1944) and called it "life script" (Perls & Baumgardner, 1975). Alfred Adler referred to this as "life style" (Ansbacher & Ansbacher, 1956); Sigmund Freud used the term "repetition compulsion" to describe similar phenomena (1920g); and recent psychoanalytic writers have referred to a developmentally preformed pattern as "unconscious fantasy" (Arlow, 1969b, p. 8) and as "schemata" (Arlow, 1969a, p. 29; Slap, 1987). In psychoanalytic self psychology the phrase "self system" is used to refer to recurring patterns of low self-esteem and self-defeating interactions (Basch, 1988, p. 100) that are the result of "unconscious organizing principles" termed "pre-reflexive unconscious" (Stolorow & Atwood, 1989, p. 373). Stern (1985), in analyzing research on infant and toddler development, conceptualizes these learned patterns as "representations of interactions that have been generalized (RIGs)" (p. 97).

The psychotherapy literature has described such blueprints as "self-confirmation theory" (Andrews, 1988, 1989) and as a self-reinforcing system or "a self-protection plan" referred to as the "script system"

(Erskine & Moursund, 1988; O'Reilly-Knapp & Erskine, 2010). The script system is divided into three primary components: script beliefs, script manifestations, and reinforcing experiences.

Script beliefs. In essence, the script answers the question, "What does a person like me do in a world like this with people like you?" Both the conscious and unconscious answers to this question form the script beliefs—the compilation of the survival reactions, implicit experiential conclusions, procedural schema, explicit decisions, self-protective measures, and reinforcements that occurred, when under stress, during the process of growing up. Script beliefs may be described in three categories: beliefs about self, beliefs about others, and beliefs about the quality of life. Once adopted, script beliefs influence what stimuli (internal and external) are attended to, how they are interpreted, and whether or not they are acted upon. They become the self-fulfilling prophecy through which the person's expectations are inevitably proven to be true (Erskine & Zalcman, 1979).

The script beliefs are maintained in order (a) to avoid re-experiencing unmet needs and the corresponding feelings suppressed at the time of script formation, and (b) to provide a predictive model of life and interpersonal relationships (Erskine & Moursund, 1988). Prediction is important, particularly when there is a crisis or trauma. Although the script is often personally destructive, it does provide psychological balance or homeostasis: it gives the illusion of predictability (Bary & Hufford, 1990; Perls, 1944). Any disruption in the predictive model produces anxiety: to avoid such discomfort, we organize our perceptions and experiences so as to maintain our script beliefs (Erskine, 1981).

Script manifestation. When under stress or when current needs are not met in adult life, a person is likely to engage in behaviors that verify script beliefs. These behaviors are referred to as the script manifestations and may include any observable behaviors (choice of words, sentence patterns, tone of voice, displays of emotion, gestures and body movements) that are the direct displays of the script beliefs and the repressed needs and feelings (the intrapsychic process). A person may act in a way defined by script beliefs, such as saying "I don't know" when believing "I'm dumb." Or he may act in a way that socially covers up the script beliefs, as, for example, excelling in school and acquiring numerous degrees as a way of keeping the "I'm dumb" belief from being discovered by others.

As part of the script display, individuals often have physiological reactions in addition to or in place of the overt behaviors. These internal experiences are not readily observable; nevertheless, the person can give a self-report: fluttering in the stomach, muscle tension, headaches, colitis, or any of a myriad of somatic responses to the script beliefs. Persons who have many somatic complaints or illnesses frequently believe that "something is wrong with me" and use physical symptoms to reinforce the belief—a cognitive defense that serves to keep the script system intact.

Script display also includes fantasies in which the individual imagines behaviors, either his or her own or someone else's, that lend support to script beliefs. These fantasized behaviors function as effectively as overt behaviors in reinforcing script beliefs/feelings—in some instances, even more effectively. They act on the system exactly as though they were events that had actually occurred.

Reinforcing experiences. Any script display can result in a reinforcing experience—a subsequent happening that "proves" that the script belief is valid and thus justifies the behavior of the script display. Reinforcing experiences are a collection of emotion-laden memories, real or imagined, of other people's or one's own behavior; a recall of internal bodily experiences; or the retained remnants of fantasies, dreams, or hallucinations. Reinforcing experiences serve as a feedback mechanism to reinforce script beliefs. Only those memories that support the script belief are readily accepted and retained. Memories that negate script beliefs tend to be rejected or forgotten because they would challenge the belief and the whole defensive process.

Each person's script beliefs provide an egocentric framework for viewing self, others, and the quality of life. In order to engage in script display, individuals must discount other options; they frequently will maintain that their behavior is the "natural" or "only" way they can respond. When used socially, script displays are likely to produce interpersonal experiences that, in turn, are governed by and contribute to the reinforcement of script beliefs.

Thus each person's script system is distorted and self-reinforcing through the operation of its three interrelated and interdependent subsystems: script beliefs/feelings, script displays, and reinforcing experiences. The script system serves as a distraction against awareness of past experiences, needs, and related emotions while simultaneously being a repetition of the past.

Principles and domains

Two principles guide all integrative psychotherapy. The first is our commitment to positive life change. Integrative psychotherapy is intended to do more than teach a client some new behaviors or a handful of coping skills designed to get him through today's crisis. It must somehow affect the client's life script. Without script change, therapy affords only temporary relief. We wish to help each client integrate his fixed perspectives into a flexible and open acceptance of learning and growing from each experience.

The second guiding principle is that of respecting the integrity of the client. Through respect, kindness, compassion, and maintaining contact we establish a personal presence and allow for an interpersonal relationship that provides affirmation of the client's integrity. This respectfulness may be best described as a consistent invitation to interpersonal contact between client and therapist, with simultaneous support for the client to contact his internal experience and receive recognition for that experience.

The four dimensions of human functioning that were outlined above—affective, behavioral, cognitive, and physiological—also indicate the domains in which therapeutic work occurs. Cognitive work takes place primarily through the therapeutic alliance between the client's Adult ego and the therapist. It includes such things as contracting for change, planning strategies for change, and searching for insight into old patterns.

Behavioral work involves engaging the client in new behaviors that run counter to the old script system and that will evoke responses from others inconsistent with the collection of script-reinforcing memories. We sometimes assign "homework" so that the therapeutic experience can be extended beyond formal therapy sessions and during sessions invite the client to behave differently with us, with group members, and in fantasy with those people who helped him or her build and maintain the life script through the years.

Affective work, while it may involve current feelings, is more likely to involve archaic and/or introjected experiences. This is often experienced as going back to an age when the original introjects were taken on or physiological survival reactions and life script decisions were made, or when those introjections or decisions were strongly reinforced. In this regressed state clients feel and think like a younger version of themselves, exhibiting many of the attitudes and decisions that went into the creation of their life scripts. In this supported regression there is an opportunity to express the feelings, needs, and desires that had been repressed and to experiment with contact that might not before have been possible. The inhibiting decisions of years before are vividly recalled and can be reevaluated and redecided (Erskine & Moursund, 1988).

The fourth major avenue into the client's life script is the physical: working directly with body structures. As Wilhelm Reich (1945) pointed out, people live out their character structures in their physical bodies.

Life script conclusions, decisions, and physiological reactions inevitably involve some distortion of contact and such distortions often carry with them a degree of muscular tension. Over time the tension becomes habitual and is eventually reflected in actual body structure. Working directly with this structure through muscle massage, altering breathing patterns, and/or encouraging or inhibiting movements, we can often help the client to access old memories and patterns and experience the possibility of new options.

We seldom limit a piece of work to a single domain; most work eventually involves several or all of them. This is another aspect of the integrative nature of our work. When a person is not defended against his own inner experience, he is able to integrate psychological functioning in all domains, taking in, processing, and sending out messages through each avenue and translating information easily from one to another internally.

Another way of looking at integrative psychotherapy is in terms of the primary ego state focus of the work. A given segment may deal primarily with a specific Child ego sate, a Parent ego state, with Child–Parent dialogue, or with the Adult ego. Work with Child ego states usually opens with some sort of invitation to the client either to remember or to relive an old experience from childhood. In the Child ego state the client has direct access to old experiences and is able to relive those memories, which may be actual or representative. Through the process of remembering, reexperiencing the needs and feelings from that time, sometimes by expressing what was unexpressed, and having those needs and feelings responded to, the early fixated experience can become integrated. The invitation may be something like, "Go back to a time when you felt this way before," or it may involve invoking visual, auditory, and kinesthetic cues that assist the client in moving into old memories unavailable to Adult ego state awareness. Sometimes physical movement or massage work will stimulate the cathexis of earlier experiences. The therapist often paces and leads the client into childhood experiences through a series of verbal interchanges during which the Child ego state is increasingly elicited. Occasionally a structured relaxation exercise might be used.

Once the client is into the necessary experience, the therapist is then able to help the Child (with the Adult ego observing) to uncover the way in which the life script was formed and lived out through the years. The client vividly remembers the early trauma, the early unmet needs, and reexperiences the process of reaction or decision through which he or she created a defensive artificial closure to deal with those needs. This recreation of an old scene is both the same as the original experience (the feelings, wants, and needs are felt again, along with the constraints that led to that early resolution) and different from the original, in that the presence of the observing Adult ego state and the supportive therapist create new resources and options that were not available before. It is these new resources that make possible a different decision this time (Erskine & Moursund, 1988; Goulding & Goulding, 1979).

Because the self-in-the-world is literally experienced in a different way in the therapeutic regression, making a change in the archaic physiological survival reaction, relational schema, or decision can break the old life script pattern. The client sees, hears, and feels self and the world in a new way and therefore can respond to self and others in new ways. The Child ego state's experience is integrated into an Adult ego through ongoing, consistent contact with the attuned therapist who responds to the client's needs in an acknowledging, validating, and normalizing manner. Such contact-in-relationship provides a therapeutic space for the client to drop the contact interrupting defenses and relinquish life script beliefs. This is the essence of the integration of the Child ego state into the Adult ego state.

When the script pattern is primarily linked to an internally influencing Parent ego state (introject), the client might be invited to cathect that Parent ego state: to "be" Mom or Dad and to enter into a conversation with the therapist as Mom or Dad might have done (Erskine, 2003; Erskine & Trautmann, 2003; McNeel, 1976). The therapist first gets acquainted with the introjected Parent much as if a new and unknown person had actually come into the room. As the Parent ego state begins to experience and respond to the therapist's joining, the quality of the interaction gradually shifts into a more therapeutic mode and the Parent is encouraged to deal with his own issues. This is working through the life script issues of the parenting person that the client has taken on as his own. Many of the methods used to treat the Child ego state may be used here if the Parent needs to deal with repressed experiences. Or the therapist may intervene on behalf of the child involved—the client—to advocate for and provide protection if the introjected Parent is unyielding or continues to be destructive in some way. As the Parent begins to respond to challenges to his life script pattern, the introject loses its compulsive, binding quality. The thinking patterns, attitudes, emotional responses, defenses, and behavioral patterns that were introjected from significant others no longer remain as an unassimilated or exteropsychic state of the ego but are decommissioned as a separate ego state and integrated into an aware neopsychic or Adult ego (Erskine & Moursund, 1988; Moursund & Erskine, 2004).

Most enduring and problem-creating life script patterns are maintained by both Parent and Child ego states—that is, they contain elements of both Child decisions and Parent introjects. To facilitate full integration, a given piece of therapeutic work may involve both Parent and Child ego states, either in sequence (as the therapist deals first with the Parent, brings that segment to closure, and then helps the Child to explore and respond to the new information) or in the form of a dialogue between Parent and Child ego states.

Our work also incorporates direct interaction with the client's Adult ego. This is particularly important for making contact, clarifying goals, and to serve as an observer and ally when working with the Child or Parent ego states. For some clients psychotherapy requires neither focus on fixated defense mechanisms or regression to childhood traumas that have been unresolved, nor a decommission of introjections, but rather to the concerns of the adult life cycle. We evaluate what the client presents in light of developmental transitions, crises, age-related tasks, and existential experiences. When life cycle transitions and existential crises are respected as significant and the client has an opportunity to explore his emotions, thought, ideals, and borrowed opinions and to talk out possibilities, there emerges a sense of meaningfulness or purpose in life and its events.

Methods

Inquiry

Inquiry is a continual focus in contact-oriented, relationship-based psychotherapy. It begins with the assumption that the therapist knows nothing about the client's experience and therefore must continually strive to understand the subjective meaning of the client's behavior and intrapsychic process. Through respectful investigation of the client's phenomenological experience the client becomes increasingly aware of current and archaic needs, feelings, and behavior. It is with full awareness and the absence of internal defenses that needs and feelings which are fixated due to past experiences can be integrated into a fully functioning Adult ego.

It should be stressed that the process of inquiring is as important, if not more so, than the content. The therapist's inquiry must be empathetic with the client's subjective experience to be effective in discovering and revealing the internal phenomena (physical sensations, feelings, thoughts, meanings, beliefs, decisions, hopes, and memories) and uncovering the internal and external interruptions to contact.

Inquiry begins with a genuine interest in the client's subjective experiences and construction of meanings. It proceeds with questions from the therapist as to what the client is feeling, how he experiences both himself and others (including the psychotherapist) and what conclusions he makes. It may continue with historical questions as to when an experience occurred and who was significant in the person's life. Inquiry is used in the preparatory phase of therapy to increase the client's awareness of when and how he interrupts contact.

It is essential that the therapist understand each client's unique need for a stabilizing, validating, and reparative other person to take on some of the relationship functions that the client is attempting to manage alone. A contact-oriented relationship therapy requires that the therapist be attuned to these relationship needs and be involved, through empathetic validation of feelings and needs and by providing safety and support.

Attunement

Attunement is a two-part process: the sense of being fully aware of the other person's sensations, needs, or feelings and the communication of that awareness to the other person. Yet more than just understanding, attunement is a kinesthetic and emotional sensing of the other; knowing his experience by metaphorically being in his skin. Effective attunement also requires that the therapist simultaneously remain aware of the boundary between client and therapist.

The communication of attunement validates the client's needs and feelings and lays the foundation for repairing the failures of previous relationships. Attunement is demonstrated by what we say, such as "That hurt," "You seemed frightened," or "You needed someone to be there with you." It is more frequently communicated by the therapist's facial or body movements that signal to the client that his affect exists, is perceived by the therapist, that it is significant, and that it makes an impact on the therapist.

Attunement is often experienced by the client as the therapist gently moving through the defenses that have protected him or her from the awareness of relationship failures and the related needs and feelings, making contact with the long-forgotten parts of Child ego states. Over time, this results in a lessening of external interruptions to contact and a corresponding dissolving of internal defenses. Needs and feelings can then be increasingly expressed with the comfort and assurance that they will be met with an empathetic response. Frequently the attunement provides a sense of safety and stability which enables the client to begin to remember and to endure regressing into childhood experience, becoming fully aware of the pain of traumas, the failure of relationship(s), and the lost self.

It is not unusual, however, for the communication of attunement by the therapist to be met with a reaction of intense anger, withdrawal, or even further dissociation. The *juxtaposition* of the attunement by the therapist and the memory of the lack of attunement in previous significant relationships produce intense emotional memories of needs not being met. Rather than experience those feelings clients may react defensively with fear or anger at the contact offered by the therapist. The contrast between the contact available with the therapist and the lack of contact in their early life is often more than clients can bear, so they defend against the present contact to avoid the emotional memories (Erskine, 1993).

It is important for the therapist to work sensitively with juxtaposition. The affect and behavior expressed by the client are an attempt to disavow the emotional memories. Therapists who do not account for the defensive reactions may misidentify the juxtaposition reaction as negative transference and/or experience intense countertransference feelings in response to the client's avoidance of interpersonal contact. This concept helps therapists to understand the intense difficulty the client has in contrasting the current contact offered by the therapist with the awareness that needs for contactful relationship were unfulfilled in the past.

Juxtaposition reactions may signal that the therapist is proceeding more rapidly than the client can assimilate. Frequently it is wise to return to the therapeutic contract and clarify the purpose of the therapy. Explaining the concept of juxtaposition has been beneficial in some situations. Most often a careful inquiry into the phenomenological experience of the current interruption to contact will reveal the emotional memories of disappointment and painful relationships.

With the dissolution of the interruptions to contact, the relationship offered by the therapist provides the client with a sense of validation, care, support and understanding—"someone is there for me." This involvement by the therapist is an essential feature in the total dissolving of the defenses and a resolution and integration of traumas and unrequited relationships.

Involvement

Involvement is best understood through the client's perception—a sense that the therapist is contactful. It evolves from the therapist's empathetic inquiry into the client's experience and is developed through the therapist's attunement with the client's affect and validation of his needs. Involvement is the result of the therapist being fully present, with and for the person, in a way that is appropriate to the client's developmental level of functioning. It includes a genuine interest in the client's intrapsychic and interpersonal world and a communication of that interest through attentiveness, inquiry, and patience.

Involvement begins with the therapist's commitment to the client's welfare and a respect for his phenomenological experiences. Full contact becomes possible when the client experiences that the therapist 1) respects each defense; 2) stays attuned to his affect and needs; 3) is sensitive to the psychological functioning at the relevant developmental ages; and 4) is interested in understanding his way of constructing meaning.

Therapeutic involvement that emphasizes acknowledgement, validation, normalization, and presence diminishes the internal discounting that is part of an archaic self-protective process. These engagements allow previously disavowed feelings and denied experiences to come to full awareness. The therapist's *acknowledgement* of the client's feelings begins with an attunement to his affect, even if it is unexpressed. Through sensitivity to the physiological expression of emotions the therapist can guide the client to express his feelings or to acknowledge that feelings or physical sensations may be the memory—the only memory available. In some situations the child may have been too young for the availability of linguistic and retrievable memory. In many cases of relationship failure the person's feelings were not acknowledged and it may be necessary in psychotherapy to help the person gain a vocabulary and to voice those feelings. Acknowledgement of physical sensations and affect helps the client claim his own phenomenological experience. Acknowledgement includes a receptive other who knows and communicates about the existence of nonverbal movements, tensing of muscles, affect, or even fantasy.

There are times in clients' lives when their feelings were acknowledged but were not validated. *Validation* communicates to the client that his affect or physical sensations are related to something significant in his experiences. Validation is making a link between cause and effect. Validation diminishes the possibility of the client internally discounting the significance of affect, physical sensation, memory, or dreams. It provides the client with an enhanced value of his phenomenological experience and therefore an increased sense of self-esteem.

Normalization means to depathologize the client's or others' categorization or definition of their internal experience or their behavioral attempts at coping. It may be essential for the therapist to counter societal or parental messages such as, "You're crazy for feeling scared," with "Anyone would be scared in that situation." Many flashbacks, bizarre fantasies, nightmares, confusion, panic, defensiveness, are all normal coping phenomena in abnormal situations. It is imperative that the therapist communicates that the client's experience is a normal defensive reaction, not pathological.

Presence is provided through the psychotherapist's sustained empathetic responses to both the verbal and nonverbal expressions of the client. It occurs when the behavior and communication of the psychotherapist, at all times, respects and enhances the integrity of the client. Presence includes the therapist's receptivity to the client's affect—to be impacted by his emotions, to be moved and yet to stay present with the impact of his emotions, not to become anxious, depressed, or angry. Presence is an expression of the psychotherapist's full internal and external contact. It communicates the psychotherapist's responsibility, dependability, and reliability.

Therapeutic involvement is maintained by the therapist's constant vigilance to providing an environment and relationship of safety and security. It is necessary that the therapist be constantly attuned to the client's ability to tolerate the emerging awareness of past experiences so that he is not overwhelmed once again in the therapy as he may have been in a previous experience. When the inquiring of the client's phenomenological experiences and the therapeutic regressions occur in a surround that is calming and containing, the fixated defenses are further relaxed and the needs and feelings of the past experience(s) can be integrated.

The psychotherapist's involvement through transactions that acknowledge, validate, and normalize the client's phenomenological experiences and sustain an empathetic presence fosters a *therapeutic potency* that allows for the client to safely depend on the relationship with the psychotherapist. Potency is the result of engagements that communicate to the client that the therapist is fully invested in his welfare. Acknowledgement, validation, and normalization provide the client with permission to know his own feelings, value the significance of his affects, and relate them to actual or anticipated events. Therefore such *therapeutic permission* to diminish defenses, to know his physical sensations, feelings, and memories and to reveal them must come only after the client experiences protection within the therapeutic environment. Such *therapeutic protection* can be adequately provided only after there is a thorough assessment of the intrapsychic punishment and the client has a sense of safety that the therapist is consistently invested in his welfare. *Intrapsychic punishment* involves the child's perceived loss of bonding or attachment, shame, or threat of retribution. Protective interventions may include supporting a regressive dependency, providing a reliable and safe environment wherein the client can rediscover what has been lost to awareness, and pacing the therapy so the experiences may be fully integrated.

There are times when a client will attempt to elicit attunement and understanding by *acting out* a problem that he cannot talk about or express in any other way. Such acting out expressions are simultaneously both an archaic self-stabilizing deflection of the emotional memories and also an attempt to communicate his internal conflicts. Confrontations or explanations can intensify the use of archaic self-stabilizing behaviors making the awareness of needs and feelings less accessible to awareness. Involvement includes a gentle, respectful inquiring into the internal experience of the "acting out." The therapist's genuine interest in and honoring of the communication, which often may be without language, is an essential aspect of therapeutic involvement. Involvement may include the therapist being active in facilitating the client's undoing repressive retroflections and activating responses that were inhibited, such as screaming for help or fighting back.

The therapist's considered revealing of her internal reactions or showing compassion are further expressions of involvement. It may also include responding to earlier developmental needs in a way that symbolically represents need fulfillment, but the goal of a contact-oriented therapy is not in the satisfaction of archaic needs. This is an unnecessary and impossible task. Rather, the goal is the dissolving of fixated contact-interrupting defenses that interfere with the satisfaction of current needs and with full contact with self and others in life today. This is often accomplished by working within the transference to allow the intrapsychic conflict to be expressed within the therapeutic relationship and to be responded to with appropriate empathetic transactions.

A contact-oriented psychotherapy through inquiry, attunement, and involvement responds to the client's current needs for an emotionally nurturing relationship that is reparative and sustaining. The aim of this kind of therapy is the integration of the affect-laden experiences and an intrapsychic reorganization of the client's beliefs about self, others, and the quality of life.

Conclusion

Contact facilitates the dissolving of defenses and the integration of the disowned parts of the personality. Through contact the disowned, unaware, unresolved experiences are made part of a cohesive self. In integrative psychotherapy the concept of contact is the theoretical basis from which clinical interventions are derived. Transference, ego state regression, activation of the intrapsychic influence of introjection, the presence of defense mechanisms, are all understood as indications of previous contact deficits. The four dimensions of human functioning—affective, behavioral, cognitive, and physiological—are an important guide in determining where someone is open or closed to contact and therefore of our therapeutic direction. A major goal of integrative psychotherapy is to use the therapist-client relationship—the ability to create full contact in the present—as a stepping stone to healthier relationships with other people and a satisfying sense of self. With integration it becomes possible for the person to face each moment with spontaneity and flexibility in solving life's problems and in relating to people.

CHAPTER TWO

A therapy of contact-in-relationship

In *Beyond Empathy: A Therapy of Contact-in-Relationship* (Erskine, Moursund, & Trautmann, 1999), we have characterized the skills of inquiry and the qualities of attunement and involvement as central to effective psychotherapy. Empathy is the foundation for inquiry, attunement, and involvement. Each of the three, however, goes "beyond empathy" in some way—or, at least, beyond the definitions of empathy that one finds in the general psychotherapy literature. It is likely that truly empathetic therapists are also skilled inquirers, sensitively attuned to their clients, and appropriately involved in the therapeutic process. If so, then attunement and inquiry and involvement are not extensions of empathy so much as subdivisions: aspects or facets of the overall empathetic frame within which change and growth are nurtured.

Whichever they are, extensions or subdivisions, attunement and inquiry and involvement are central to the therapeutic process. To the degree that we can provide them, our therapy is likely to be more effective and satisfying to both our clients and ourselves. As is true for nearly every other effort to describe or define some important aspect of psychotherapy, discussing attunement or inquiry or involvement alone requires an artificial and unrealistic teasing apart of what is essentially indivisible. Inquiry without attunement and involvement is sterile and inquisitorial; involvement and attunement without inquiry have no sense of direction or purpose. All three, moreover, are useful only when they are guided by therapeutic intent: a commitment that the client's growth and healing take priority over anything else that may happen in the therapy session.

Of all the things that therapists do, asking questions and listening to the answers is probably the most common. Questions are asked at all stages of therapy, from initial diagnosis to the final termination process. By "questions," we do not refer just to those sentences which end in a question mark; questions include any sort of intervention that requests the client to search internally to discover his self. Replying with an "Oh?" or a "Hmm," repeating what the client has just said, lifting an eyebrow, or smiling encouragingly, even waiting patiently for what may come next—all of these are forms of inquiry. Indeed, insofar as the essence of therapy is to help the client explore his internal world and reestablish contact with self and others, most of what we do as therapists can be seen as a kind of inquiry.

Asking questions is easy. Questions occur naturally in conversations between friends, in consultations with professionals, in the classroom, and in the workplace. Children learn to ask questions as soon as they learn to talk, as anyone who has faced the endless "why" of a preschooler can tell you. Inquiring therapeutically, on the other hand, requires skill. It requires, among other things, that we know—and remember—the purpose of our inquiry. Questions can be asked for a variety of reasons: in order to provide the questioner with some information ("Where do you keep the napkins?"), to continue an argument ("Why won't you let me have the car tonight?"), as an implied criticism ("Why are you watching TV when you have homework?"), or simply to demand attention ("What are you doing, Mommy?"). In a relationship-focused integrative psychotherapy, inquiry has but one purpose: to assist the client in expanding his awareness, increasing internal and external contact, and enhancing the sense of self-in-relationship.

If the purpose of inquiry is to expand the client's awareness, it follows that what the therapist may learn from the client's answer is secondary. While we certainly listen to the answers to our questions (verbal and nonverbal), and learn from those answers, what the client learns is much more important. Part of the skill involved in therapeutic inquiry is that of getting out of the client's way, postponing our need to understand fully in order not to interrupt his process of discovery. It also follows that the easily answered question, the question to which the client already knows the answer, is generally less valuable than the question that requires him to search for a response. Clients don't learn much from stating what they already know; they learn by being challenged to discover something new or something that has been forgotten. Uncertainty and ambiguity stimulate people to learn more, to solve the problem and clarify what is happening. Questions that ask about what is not yet known tend to invite the client into his areas of uncertainty and ambiguity, and challenge him to explore those areas. Well-executed inquiry is a spiral process, with each response leading to a new question, and each question opening the door to a previously out-of-awareness response.

Characteristics of effective inquiry

The most basic characteristic of therapeutic inquiry is that of respect. The questions the therapist asks, and the way in which she asks them, must be respectful—respectful of the client's needs, of his problem-solving efforts, of his internal wisdom. Her respect springs from what Rogers (1951) has termed "unconditional positive regard," a fundamental conviction that every client is doing, and has done, the best he is capable of at any given moment. Without this kind of respect, inquiry is likely to turn into interrogation, the therapist becomes "she-who-knows-better," and the whole process can disintegrate into advice-giving or sermonizing. Respecting the client's wisdom and intentions, in contrast, leads to genuine interest and healthy curiosity about how the client experiences his world. Interest and curiosity, in turn, are vital in helping the therapist to frame the sorts of questions that will further the client's explorations.

Inquiry should be open-ended. The therapist's questions, and her questioning behaviors, invite the client to search for answers; they do not restrict him or demand that the answer meet the therapist's expectations. Indeed, willingness to abandon expectations and let go of preconceived ideas is another hallmark of successful inquiry. Even though the therapist's theoretical training and clinical experience may lead her to expect a certain kind of answer (and may have suggested her question or comment in the first place), she is glad to be surprised. Getting a response that she did not expect whets her curiosity, pops her out of the rut of the conventional, allows her as well as her client to discover something new.

Neimeyer (1995) recommends "… a willingness to use the client's personal knowledge system, to see the problem and the world through his or her eyes, though not necessarily to be encapsulated by it. To this is added … a curiosity or fascination with the client's perspective and its implications" (p. 114). The therapist's theoretical and clinical expectations provide a background for this fascination, but must not blind her to what the client is really telling her. Open-ended questions help to keep the therapist open to learning something new from the client, something not predicted by her past experience.

What does a therapist do when the client tells her something that she finds difficult to believe? When he changes the subject, insists on telling long, rambling stories, or simply says "I don't know" and then waits? These sorts of behavior suggest that the client may be retreating into an old defensive system, rather than being honest with himself. The first rule of good inquiry is: don't argue. The therapist should never try to persuade the client that his answer is wrong. How could it be "wrong" when it came from him? It is his response, and the therapist's job is to help him understand it. She may express curiosity, or confusion; she may ask him about what he means or what lies behind his response. "You surprised me; help me to understand how you came to that conclusion," "What happened inside, just before you said that?" "How is this story related to the problems you were talking about earlier?"

Inquiry grows out of a constant attention to contact. Its goal is contact-enhancement; all the therapist's questions are designed to help the client establish and maintain contact of some sort. The focus at one point may be on his internal contact ("What are you experiencing?") or at another on his external contact ("Tell me what you are noticing and attending to right now"); often we deal with the contact between therapist and client ("What's it like for you to hear me say that?"). Contact leads to health and growth, and lack of contact to fragmentation and constriction and shutting down. To the degree that our inquiry promotes the former, and moves away from the latter, it will be therapeutic.

Areas of inquiry

Attending to contact, and remembering that her purpose is to enhance it, helps the therapist to construct and frame her inquiry. She must be careful, though, not to neglect one aspect of contact as she pursues another. Therapeutic inquiry is like a web, spun out of many strands; the therapist follows first this strand, then that, but eventually all must be woven into the pattern. Let's look, for a moment, at these strands.

One of the most obvious strands is that of affect: therapists are used to asking clients about their feelings, helping clients to explore and deepen their emotional responses. Many clients, though, are relatively closed to affect. They don't know what they are feeling; they have learned to disavow or close off their awareness of painful emotions and don't know how to open those doors. For such clients, inquiring about physical sensations and reactions can be useful. The therapist can invite her client to be aware of his body, and of what his body is doing. Is he breathing shallowly, and what does that shallow breathing feel like? Is he aware of a swinging foot or a balled fist? Simply noticing, and talking about physical experiences is a first step toward increased contact with self.

Cognition is another natural area of inquiry. What is the client thinking? What are those thoughts connected to, and how does he get from one thought to another? What is he remembering? What decisions is he making, and how is he making them? Thoughts and memories and decisions (past and present) often weave back into affect, just as affect can take him into thinking and remembering.

Inquiry about fantasies provides another window into the client's phenomenological world. Fantasies involve thinking, feeling, sensation. They are not only the client's daydreams and night dreams; they also include the client's hopes and fears and expectations. They are his imaginings about what has happened in the past and about what is yet to come. Because they are built upon past experience, experience that has often been blocked from awareness, they can help him reconnect with himself, with long-buried thoughts and feelings. Fantasies and expectations determine the way in which he makes and maintains relationships with others and they shape the therapeutic relationship as well. Clients use fantasy to transform painful internal experiencing into that which can be borne; to provide substitute gratification of needs that cannot be met in reality; to manage behaviors that they fear may run out of control. It is a rich vein of information, and mining it can lead to rich rewards.

Inquiry is a basis for forming a therapeutic relationship. The experience of being in a relationship that is qualitatively different from past, script-forming relationships is a key factor in dissolving that script. The impact of this relationship experience is heightened when relational inquiry is used to call attention to it. Questions like "What are you wanting from me right now?" or "How do you feel about what I just said?" or "What do you think my response would be if you told me the whole story?" invite the client to explore his reactions to what the therapist is offering. Is he defending against a level of contact that would be too threatening? He and the therapist can talk about the threat, and the means of defense as well. Does he disagree, disbelieve, or discount what the therapist says? The therapist asks about his disagreement or disbelief or discounting. She is open to the client's criticism, cares about his disbelief, is interested in the ways in which he supports the discount. She is also interested in how the client experiences her support and concern. She asks about it all.

As the therapist improves her inquiry skills, learns to gather up the various strands of experiencing and help the client to explore their interrelationships, she is guided by attunement. She notices the client's rhythms, his thinking and feeling, his developmental level, his moment-to-moment relational needs; and what she notices directs what she asks about and how she does the asking. But there is another element at work here. Therapists are not simply skilled machines, taking in information and forming interventions. The therapeutic process is a relationship, formed in the in-between of two living, thinking, feeling human beings.

Attunement

Attunement involves sensitizing oneself to the client, and responding accordingly. Kohut (1977) defined empathy as a kind of "vicarious introspection," in which the therapist understands the client by finding something akin to the client's responses within himself. Attunement involves using both conscious and out-of-awareness synchronizing of therapist and client process, so that the therapist's interventions fit the ongoing, moment-to-moment needs and processes of the client. It is more than simply feeling what the client feels: it includes recognizing the client's experience, and moving—cognitively, affectively, and physically—so as to complement that experience in a contact-enhancing way (Erskine & Moursund, 1988). In this sense, attunement is not a subdivision of empathy but does extend the concept.

Attunement goes beyond empathy: it is a process of communion and unity of interpersonal contact. It is a two-part process that begins with empathy—being sensitive to and identifying with the other person's sensations, needs, or feelings; and includes the communication of that sensitivity to the other person. More than just understanding or vicarious introspection, attunement is a kinesthetic and emotional sensing of the other—knowing their rhythm, affect, and experience by metaphorically being in their skin, and going beyond empathy to create a two-person experience of unbroken feeling connectedness by providing a reciprocal affect and/or resonating response (Erskine, 1998a, p. 236).

The attuned therapist leads by following. Her interventions often feel, to the client, more like confirmations than questions: they direct his attention to what he is ready to know but has not yet quite realized. She anticipates and observes the effects of her behavior on the client; she decenters from her own experience in order to focus on the client's process. Yet she also is aware of her own internal responses, her thoughts and feelings and associations. She is "multi-tasking," simultaneously following both the client and herself, as well as noting the intricate interactions between self and other. And she communicates this synchrony: with body language and voice tone as much as (or more than) with words, she weaves a fabric of understanding and concern, and at the same time conveys her belief in the client's ability to grow and change. "I know where you are," she seems to be saying, "and we will travel from there together."

To the degree that the therapist is attuned to the client and conveys that attunement, the client feels respected. "This therapist not only understands me—she's really with me! Maybe the things I'm thinking/feeling/doing/wanting aren't so hopeless after all." Attunement conveys interest, as well: one of the ways we know if someone is interested in us is by their curiosity and understanding and involvement, their close attention to our story, and their acknowledgement of our needs and wants.

Respect and interest, in turn, create a climate of safety. The therapist who respects me won't turn on me, laugh at me, be disgusted by me. She is interested enough to take the time and make the effort to understand, all the way through, what I am trying to say; she won't leap to the wrong conclusions and steer me in a wrong direction. It's OK to be here, OK to be who I am, OK to (maybe, just a little) let the defenses down and peek at the things I really haven't wanted to see.

A client who feels respected and secure in the presence of his therapist can get on with the primary aim of therapy: reclaiming that which has been closed off, healing that which has been fragmented, making both internal and external contact where contact has been interrupted. Attunement reaches beyond the client's concern with an immediate problem, down into the hopes and fears and beliefs that keep the problem from being fully solved. Attunement encourages the client to come to grips with those deep hopes and fears and beliefs, to explore them and update them in the light of more recent learnings. And attunement provides a constant invitation to contact, a gentle but firm and dependable "I'm here" when the client is feeling overwhelmed and hopeless.

One last benefit of attunement: when the therapist does get it wrong and makes that inevitable error, her previous level of attunement will ease the process of resynchronizing and reestablishing a climate of trust. The general level of attunement sensitizes the therapist to the client's reaction to having been missed, and allows her to catch her error quickly, acknowledge it, and request clarification. Acknowledging and apologizing for an error are usually, in fact, another demonstration of attunement; when the therapist goes off the track, what the client most needs and wants is that the therapist admit it, apologize, and reestablish contact (Guistolese, 1997).

Affective attunement

Most therapists are trained to be aware of, and even encourage, clients' affect. We learn to be comfortable with our clients' tears, anger, fear, and joy. We help clients to deepen their affect (or heighten it, depending on whose vocabulary is being used), and to access emotional responses that they had previously closed off and hidden from others and even from themselves. The therapist's ability to respond empathetically helps clients to do this affective work. We've considered a lot about empathy already—so what does affective attunement add?

In an empathetic response, the therapist feels what the client is feeling. She metaphorically crawls inside the client's skin and shares the client's affective experience. The affectively attuned therapist goes beyond empathy, meeting the client's affect with her own personal and genuine affective response (Erskine, Moursund, & Trautmann, 1999).

Moreover, affective attunement requires that the therapist attend not only to the emotion itself, but also to the message being sent by the emotional display. Emotion is a two-person phenomenon; it is a way of communicating with others who are present physically or in fantasy. Attunement—being in resonance with the client—allows us to distinguish between, for example, tears that plead "Please take care of me and make things better," and tears that say "I'm ashamed to be so upset about this," and to respond appropriately.

An attuned response, by the way, is really a three-stage phenomenon—although the stages may follow each other so rapidly that they are difficult to distinguish. The first stage of an attuned response is that of noticing, recognizing, and empathizing with the client's affect: the client's eyes fill with tears, for example, and the therapist recognizes and sympathizes with the client's sadness. The second stage involves the therapist's internal reaction: perhaps first one of vicariously feeling the client's emotion, or a less intense echo of it, and then moving to her uniquely personal response to that emotion. Recognizing that the client is sad, the therapist finds herself feeling compassionate, wishing she could make things better, and at the same time glad that the client's sadness is finally breaking through the defensive barrier that has kept him stuck and miserable for so long. Finally, the third stage of the therapist's response is what she communicates to the client. She may simply reflect that the client looks sad, or she may share some of her own feelings—or she may simply wait quietly, or hold out her hand in a gesture of comfort.

Affective attunement is achieved in a variety of ways. The first of these is simply attending to the cues that signal an emotional response in our clients. It is easy to get so caught up in the content of the client's story, or in our eagerness to find a solution to his problem, that we fail to notice the tiny facial, gestural, or voice tone changes that often accompany a feeling response. It is equally easy to attend just to the display of affect and ignore the message that the emotion is sending. When we make either of these errors, the usual result is that the affect goes underground: the client either decides that it was inappropriate (because we didn't validate it), or that the therapist is insensitive and therefore not safe to be emotionally vulnerable with. Not only is the current opportunity lost, but the therapist may have to prove herself all over again before regaining the client's trust.

Lee (1998) has suggested that emotional tuning in between two individuals involves one person unconsciously imitating the other's facial expression and in so doing setting up a similar affective response in himself. Affectively attuned therapists probably do some of this sort of unconscious imitation, but the imitation quickly gives way to a more authentic and personal response to what has been sensed in the client. Tuning in to oneself is as important as tuning in to the client; internal contact combines with external contact to take affective attunement an important step beyond empathy.

Some internal responses to someone else's feelings, of course, may not be therapeutic. Partners who become enraged at each other, or parents who are either overcritical or overprotective of their children, may be observing the other person's emotion quite accurately and responding to it quite authentically—and hurting the other person in doing so. In order for affective attunement to be therapeutically useful, it must be combined with therapeutic intent and with clinical competence. Therapeutic intent keeps us focused on the client's welfare, and competence helps us to understand what sorts of things the client may need from us at any given moment and how to create a response to that need. Together, therapeutic intent and clinical competence provide a framework for our internal response to the client, ensuring (in most cases) that that response will be helpful—or at least not destructive.

Each general class of affect seems to call for a certain kind of reciprocal response, whether the responder be a therapist or someone else in close relationship to the "sender" of the emotional message. Sadness, for example, requires compassion—not a gushy, "Oh you poor thing" sort of sympathy, but a genuine sorrow that the other person is in pain. Anger involves a request to be taken seriously: the attuned therapist will attend, will be respectful, will not make light of or try to diffuse or explain things away. Anger is a serious thing, and in order to take it seriously the therapist must see the world from the perspective of the angry client and allow herself to be impacted by his anger. It is not necessary that she too feel angry, but it is certainly unhelpful (and relationally destructive) to be amused by or frightened of what the client is experiencing.

The most appropriately attuned therapeutic response to a client's fear is a sense of protectiveness. This does not mean that the therapist acts so as to protect the client—in most cases, such behavior would get in the way of the client's working through his fear—but rather that the impulse to protect is stirred in her. The impulse to protect stems from the therapist's sensitivity to the nuances of the client's feelings. Taking those feelings seriously, she is roused to activate her clinical skills, to figure out what sort of intervention will be most useful in helping the client deal with his fear; her efforts also convey to him that she is contact-available, that she has received and is responding to his message.

We've considered the three most common uncomfortable affects—what about the pleasant ones? How do we appropriately attune ourselves to a client's feelings of happiness, joy, triumph? Here the answer is simple: share them. Feel the joy ourselves—but slightly less intensely than the client does. It's the client's joy, not ours; the client leads and we follow (Erskine, 1998b).

Cognitive attunement

Humans are thinking creatures. How we experience our world is largely determined by how we think about it, by what meanings we make of it. A given event can be experienced as amusing, frightening, boring, or exciting—watch people emerging from a carnival "fun house" and you will see variants of all of those reactions. Our emotions do affect how we think, to be sure, but equally strong is the effect of our thoughts on how we feel. Cognitions, says Lee, interact with affects so as to magnify or attenuate the affective processes (1998, p. 145). We can talk ourselves out of experiencing a strong emotion ("I just won't think about it; it really isn't so bad; I'll feel better in the morning") or, as Ellis and the rational-emotive therapists (Ellis, 1997) are fond of pointing out, we can "awfulize" a situation and make ourselves feel intensely bad about it.

Cognitive attunement involves understanding and temporarily borrowing the process by which a client makes meaning—not only as those meanings affect his emotions, but as they affect his whole way of making internal and external contact. How does he "sort out" his world? How clearly does he distinguish between his various perceptions, suppositions, and memories? How does he go about solving problems—or avoiding them? What are the rules that determine what he allows himself to think about, and what is forbidden ground? In *Beyond Empathy: A Therapy of Contact-in-Relationship* (Erskine, Moursund, & Trautmann, 1999), we described cognitive attunement in this way:

> Cognitive attunement is more than simply attending to content. It is not the same as "understanding the client's cognitions" because it goes beyond simple understanding. It involves attending to the client's logic, to the process of stringing ideas together, to the kinds of reasoning that the client uses in order to create meaning out of

> raw experience. It's about what the client is thinking; but more importantly, about how the client is thinking it. As we attune to the client's cognitions, we enter the client's cognitive space, moving into a kind of resonance with the client and using our own thoughts and responses as a sounding board to amplify the tiny cues that the client is giving. We bring the client's words and nonverbal expressions into ourselves; take on their meanings, implications, connections; experience this way of thinking ourselves in a kind of internal "as if." (p. 54)

Just as affective attunement requires a kind of alternation between attending to the client's affect and attending to our own affective response, so cognitive attunement requires that we alternate between the client's way of thinking and our own. We adopt the client's thought process, as closely as we are able, in order to see the world through his eyes, experience its events as he does, discover what it is like to live with his blind spots and his defenses. But we cannot allow ourselves to stay in that place; it is the contrast between his cognitive process and our own that allows us to note those distortions and defenses. Without such a contrast, we would be as blind to his process as he is, and as unable to imagine any other way of thinking. We move back and forth, thinking about the client's frame of reference, then thinking within that frame of reference, then thinking about what it was like to be within it.

Because we are attuned to the client's cognitive process, we can better understand and respond to what he is trying to tell us. Indeed, sometimes we will understand even before he spells it out: thinking in the same way, we often know where he is going and what conclusions he may reach. With the trust and the sense of safety that comes from being understood in this way, the client is increasingly open to pushing the boundaries, both by exploring new areas on his own and through our invitations and suggestions that he review a memory, consider a possibility, examine an interaction.

Sometimes, of course, we will be wrong. Cognitive attunement can never be perfect; we can never fully enter into another person's stream of thought. We must constantly remind ourselves that our understanding of the client's cognitive world is a hypothesis, not a fact, and that our trying on of his meaning-making process is an experiment that requires validation from the client himself before it can be fully trusted. If we do get it wrong, the most important thing we can do is acknowledge our error and ask the client to help us get back on track. Sometimes these sorts of error-and-correction sequences are extraordinarily helpful: they signal the therapist's willingness to respect the client's wisdom and to admit her own fallibility, and they invite the client into a process of shared exploration in which he and the therapist each make a uniquely valuable contribution (Guistolese, 1997).

Developmental attunement

"In all therapies, including psychoanalysis and psychodrama," write James and Goulding (1998), "regression occurs whether it is planned by the therapist or client or whether it is spontaneous" (p. 16). Regression has been defined in a variety of ways; for our purposes we shall define it as a return to patterns of thinking, feeling, and/or behaving that were present for the client at an earlier time in his life. It occurs not only in psychotherapy, but in daily life: whenever we find ourselves responding as we did in a previous developmental period, we have regressed. Regression is a common phenomenon; it occurs most often under stress but may also be observed during states of childlike joy or excitement.

Psychotherapeutically, regression is of interest when it represents a fallback to old patterns of dealing with the world, patterns which were learned earlier in life and remain available to us when our current strategies are not working. The therapist may invite a client to regress ("Take yourself back to a time when ...") in order to facilitate discovering what those old patterns are and how they relate to the client's current difficulties. Other therapeutic regressions may be spontaneous, a response to the "safe emergency" (Perls, 1973) of the therapy session. The client may be aware that he has regressed, and indeed be actively cooperating in achieving and maintaining the regression, or may be quite unaware of it. In either case, it is important that the therapist be attuned to the level of regression and respond accordingly. We refer to this sort of attunement as "developmental attunement" because it requires sensitivity to the developmental level to which the client has returned, cognitively or emotionally or behaviorally.

Depending upon one's theory of psychotherapy, regression may be seen as useful, as irrelevant, or as an impediment to achieving the client's goals. Therapists who take a strict behavioral or cognitive-behavioral position are likely to discourage regression, seeing it as interfering with the client's ability to evaluate, problem-solve, and follow through on a plan for change. Others, more psychodynamically oriented, believe that regression is useful in that it allows clients to access defended memories and experience otherwise forbidden affect. We believe that the value of regression depends upon when and how it occurs, and how the therapist chooses to use it. Contact is the key here: a regression in which contact between client and therapist is lost (usually because the therapist is still responding to a here-and-now adult client, rather than to a psychologically younger person), is likely to interfere with the therapeutic process. In contrast, the client who experiences the therapist's contactfulness throughout a regression is likely to feel deeply understood. Developmental attunement helps us to maintain contact with a regressed client, and either invite him back to a more here-and-now appropriate level of functioning or support his continuing regressive experience.

Recognizing that a client has regressed, and identifying the level to which that regression has taken him, is essential for maintaining contact. Using adult language with and expecting adult responses from someone who is experiencing the world the way a four or eight or twelve year old does, is not likely to enhance the client's sense of connectedness or trust. Children, like adults, yearn to be understood; the phenomenological child that is the product of a client's regression wants to be seen and heard and respected, not ignored or missed altogether. How, then, can we recognize and identify a client's level of regression? How can we keep ourselves developmentally attuned?

Obviously, in order to attune oneself to a client's developmental level, one must have a sense of what that level is. Eric Berne (1961) has suggested four ways in which a therapist can assess the client's developmental level of functioning. The first of these is the client's own phenomenology. We may ask the client how old he is feeling at this moment, or the client may spontaneously report a regression: "I feel like a five-year-old," or "I'm scared, just like when my Dad used to come home drunk." A second aid to identifying regression and maintaining developmental attunement is the therapist's awareness of the client's unique developmental history. If we know that the client was raped when he was in high school, or that he was sent to live with his grandmother when he was ten years old, it can help us to interpret the meaning of verbal and nonverbal communications, and of the developmental level from which they spring. We can also call upon our general understanding of child development to relate the client's current behavior to behaviors typical of a younger stage or—and it behooves us to have a good knowledge of the typical stages and phases through which young children move. This is particularly important when the client is regressing to a relatively early stage of life, and his ability (and desire) to communicate verbally may be limited.

Probably the most important set of guidelines, though, comes from our own intuitive, emotional response to the client's behavior. How old does the client feel to us? What sort of younger person seems to be looking out of his eyes? If we put to one side the adult body in front of us, what seems to be the most natural way of responding to what he is doing and saying? We are often able to pick up tiny cues, cues of which we are consciously unaware, from the nonverbal behavior of our clients; such cues can aggregate out of our awareness and make themselves known as a general hunch about how to respond most effectively. Spending time with children, learning to interact with them at their level and sensitizing oneself to one's own reactions to them, is a good way to hone one's ability to attune in this way.

Developmental attunement, if it is to be useful, must be communicated. You may know that your client is, at this moment, seeing the world and responding to it as he did when he was a toddler; but this knowledge will be of little use unless the client feels your understanding and your support. At the same time, the client also needs to know that you are aware of the adult, here-and-now self who is also participating in the process. Maintaining attunement with a regressed client requires a kind of therapeutic "double vision," an ability to recognize and acknowledge both the regressed-to-childhood (or adolescence, or young adulthood) person and the self-observing adult. Both are present, both require contact, and both play an important part in the client's growth.

One of the most potent ways to maintain developmental attunement is to use the client's own language and language patterns. As he regresses, his vocabulary is likely to shift too—the developmentally attuned therapist shifts with him. If the therapist senses that the client is moving into the psychological world of a six year old, she talks to him as she would to a six year old. Her own body language is keyed to his: not imitating it, but responding to it as an adult responds physically to a child. The therapist can facilitate a client's regression by encouraging childlike gestures and movements; conversely, she can invite him out of the regression by requesting that he assume a more adult posture and by using adult language and phrasing in her responses to him.

We have found, over years of working with clients, that therapeutic regression is a powerful tool in enhancing contact with self and, eventually, with others as well. It is useful in overcoming the unconscious defenses which prevent full awareness of thoughts and feelings and memories. Developmental attunement is the single most vital factor in developing and therapeutically facilitating a client's regression. Without developmental attunement, regressions are likely to be short-lived and therapeutically sterile; with it, they can lead to the corrective emotional experience that lies at the heart of a relationship-focused integrative psychotherapy.

Rhythmic attunement

In a sense, it is odd to give rhythmic attunement a special section of its own, since attuning to the client's rhythm is an essential aspect of cognitive, affective, and developmental attunement. When we are out of synch with the client's rhythm and timing, he will not experience us as being attuned in any other way. But there are some particularly interesting aspects of rhythmic attunement, and dealing with it as a separate topic is one way to make sure we remain sensitive to those aspects.

The term "rhythmic attunement" really defines itself: being sensitive to and responding within the client's rhythmic patterns. Rhythm is one of the primary ways in which people, out of awareness, assess the quality of their contact with each other. When two people are rhythmically attuned, their transactions mesh together easily. Their silences are comfortable; there is no competition for who will speak when. Even when they interrupt each other, it is as if one of them is stimulated by the other's thought, and the interruption does not jar or derail their process. In contrast, when they are not attuned rhythmically, their conversation is jerky and their silences strained. Neither is likely to feel at ease with the other, though they often cannot explain their discomfort.

In ordinary conversations, each person is responsible for adapting to the other's rhythm, maintaining a pace and style that is comfortable for both. In therapy, the primary responsibility for attunement falls to the therapist. The therapist must attune to the client, not the other way around; expecting the client to match the therapist's rhythm will force him into an artificial way of speaking and thinking and feeling that will interfere with the client's work. Tuning in to and matching a client's rhythm requires, first, that the therapist attend to that rhythm and how it may differ from her own. Does he use long pauses to collect his thoughts, and is the therapist impatient with those pauses? Or does he jump from idea to idea, illustrating his words with quick gestures, and appearing uneasy if the therapist speaks slowly or has to search for words?

It is relatively easy (at least in theory) to slow oneself down in order to attune to the rhythm of a client who is processing his experience more slowly than we ordinarily do. Speeding oneself up to match a rhythmically rapid client is more difficult: how can a therapist think and feel faster, without losing important information? Rather than try to push herself to keep up, and risk distorting or disrupting contact with herself and/or the client, it is best for the therapist to acknowledge the differences, and openly request time to digest what the client has been telling her: "You are moving through these ideas very quickly, and I don't want to miss anything. Give me a moment to think about what you've been telling me …"

While each person does develop his or her own unique rhythm, there are some general rhythmic patterns which seem to hold for nearly everyone. Most of these involve slowing down, rather than speeding up. A major goal of therapy is to attend to what has been overlooked, to explore what has been defended against, and this generally requires that we move more slowly than usual; indeed, racing along from one association to the next is a way to not notice things, and not feel one's feelings. One of the paradoxes of our work is that slowing down is likely to speed up the therapeutic process, while going too fast is likely to slow the client's overall progress.

Affective work, in general, proceeds at a slower pace than cognitive work. It is not that we experience emotions more slowly than we think—quite the contrary; emotions spring up quickly and can shift and move with lightning speed. A loud, unexpected noise can create an immediate startle-scare feeling; it takes no time at all to experience tenderness and love when we look at our infant grandchild; but putting those feelings into words can be a slow and laborious process. Talking about feelings requires translation, from a global, wordless experience, mediated primarily through body chemistry, to a linear, verbal process. Moreover, many clients have trained themselves not to attend to their feelings, and they accomplish this by rushing past them, moving on to a new thought. Giving such clients permission to slow down, so that they can feel and think and talk about their internal experience, will further their ability to make and maintain full contact with themselves and with others.

Developmental level regression also affects one's rhythm, and developmentally attuned therapists recognize that as clients move to younger and younger psychological levels, their rhythms tend to slow. Indeed, a slowing of rhythm may be a major indicator that the client is regressing. Just as we tend to talk more slowly to a young child, the therapist needs to attune herself to the slower rhythm of the client who is at this moment experiencing the world from a younger, less verbally sophisticated place.

It is easier to review what we already know than to explore what is unknown; clients who exhibit a quite rapid pace when sharing well-rehearsed material are likely to slow down as they begin to explore new thoughts and previously walled-off emotions. Like someone feeling their way around a dark and unfamiliar (and often frightening) room, they need to take time to find out what is there, to examine it fully. They need time to integrate the new with the old, to figure out how their discoveries fit with the familiar and comfortable parts of themselves that they've known about all along.

For all these reasons, errors in rhythmic attunement are much more likely to involve going too fast rather than going too slowly. As therapists, we pride ourselves on being quick to understand, being good at putting things together; we've been rewarded throughout our schooling for coming up with right answers quickly. Now we need to put that skill to one side, slow ourselves down, slip gently into the client's rhythm of speaking and moving. When we do so, the client is likely to feel joined, met, in contact. Our matched rhythms will create a sense of moving together; the need for lengthy explanations will decrease; the client will feel protected by our willingness to be together in his way.

Rhythmic attunement extends beyond the sort of transaction-by-transaction rhythms that we have been discussing. People differ in the length of time they are comfortable in spending on one topic, one idea, before moving on to the next. They differ in the amount of "warm up" time they need at the beginning of a session before moving into full contact with themselves and with the therapist. There are even differences in rhythm over much longer periods of time: clients often differ in the length of time they need between sessions to process their work. Some do best with shorter sessions, more frequently spaced; others prefer longer sessions at greater intervals. The weekly, fifty-minute session is convenient for the therapist, but it may not match the client's rhythm (Efran, Lukens, & Lukens, 1990). If a client would benefit by changing the length or frequency of his sessions, it is advisable to do so; when such changes are not possible, one can at least acknowledge his need. If the therapist lets the client know that she recognizes his preferred rhythm, and shares her reasons for not adapting to that preference, the absence of attunement here will be less jarring.

As stated at the beginning of this section, rhythmic attunement flows through all the other aspects of attunement. In order for the client to experience cognitive or developmental or affective attunement, the therapist must be operating within that client's rhythm—his rhythm is a part of his cognition, his affect, his developmental level.

Attunement errors

Verbal and nonverbal messages sent by the therapist are like the instrumental voices of a symphony. When one or more of those voices is off tempo, the whole performance sounds wrong. Moreover, just as we respond to one piece of music or another depending on the state or mood we find ourselves in, so the client will respond differently to different therapist "symphonies" depending on his or her own state—dealing with affect or cognition, regressed or not, energized or fatigued, and so on. It is no accident that a musical metaphor like this fits with the notion of "attunement." Hearing all of the nuances of the client's melody and rhythm, and responding from and with the harmony of one's whole therapeutic orchestra, verbally and nonverbally, is what attunement is all about (Erskine, Moursund, & Trautmann, 1999).

A client's affect, mood, and behavior shifts from moment to moment. Being attuned to these shifts requires close attention to the client's responses to the therapist's behavior. What begins as an attuned response to, say, either a developmental level or the need for self-definition, can change into the therapist's failure to deal with the need for security. Because therapists are human, and imperfect, such misses are inevitable; when they occur, one simply goes back and talks about the miss. "Go back and talk about it" is good advice for failures in every facet of attunement. Missing an affective shift, not understanding a cognitive process, misjudging the client's psychological level of development, moving too quickly or too slowly—all are bound to occur sooner or later.

The therapist who castigates herself internally for her error, or tries to gloss over it so the client won't notice that it happened, takes herself away from the client and distorts the contact between them. This sort of contact distortion, in turn, is likely to create a repeat for him of the very kinds of relational experience that support his script and have gotten him into the situation that brought him to therapy in the first place. In contrast, the therapist's acknowledgement of what has happened and reattuning (to herself and to him) allow the therapeutic process to move on.

CHAPTER THREE

Attunement and involvement: therapeutic responses to relational needs

Standardized protocols or treatment manuals define the practice of psychotherapy from either a quantitative research-based behavioral model or symptom-focused medical model (Erskine, 1998b). The therapeutic relationship is not considered central in such practice manuals. In this era of industrialization of psychotherapy it is essential for psychotherapists to remain mindful of the unique interpersonal relationship between therapist and client as the central and significant factor in psychotherapy. This chapter outlines several dimensions of the therapeutic relationship that have emerged from a qualitative evaluation of the practice of psychotherapy conducted at the Institute for Integrative Psychotherapy in New York City.

A major premise of a relationship-oriented psychotherapy is that the need for relationship constitutes a primary motivation of human behavior (Fairbairn, 1952). Contact is the means by which the need for relationship is met. In colloquial language, "contact" refers to the quality of the transactions between two people: the awareness of both one's self and the other, a sensitive meeting of the other, and an authentic acknowledgement of one's self. In a more theoretically exact meaning, "contact" refers to the full awareness of sensations, feelings, needs, sensorimotor processes, thought, and memories that occur within the individual, and a shift to full awareness of external events as registered by each sensory organ. With the capacity to oscillate between internal and external contact, experiences are continually integrated into a sense of self (Perls, Hefferline, & Goodman, 1951).

When contact is disrupted, needs are not satisfied. If the experience of need arousal is not satisfied or closed naturally, it must find an artificial closure that distracts from the discomfort of unmet needs. These artificial closures are the substance of survival reactions that become fixated defensive patterns, or habitual behaviors that result from rigidly held beliefs about self, others, or the quality of life. They are evident in the disavowal of affect, the loss of either internal or external awareness, neurological inhibitions within the body, or a lack of spontaneity and flexibility in problem-solving, health maintenance, or relating to people. The defensive interruptions to contact impede the fulfillment of current needs (Erskine, 1980).

The literature on human development also leads to the understanding that the sense of self and self-esteem emerge out of contact-in-relationship (Stern, 1985). Erikson's (1950) stages of development over the entire life cycle describe the formation of identity as an outgrowth of interpersonal relations (trust vs. mistrust, autonomy vs. shame and doubt, etc.). Mahler's (1968; Mahler, Pine, & Bergman, 1975) descriptions of the stages of early child development place importance on the relationship between mother and infant. Bowlby (1969, 1973, 1980) has emphasized the significance of early as well as prolonged physical bonding in the creation of a visceral core from which all experiences of self and other emerge. When such contact does not occur in accordance with the child's relational needs, there is a physiological defense against the loss of contact—poignantly described by Fraiberg in "Pathological Defenses of Infancy" (1982). These developmental perspectives foster a deep appreciation for the need for interpersonal connection and active construction of meaning that is so much a part of who the client is.

In a relationship-oriented psychotherapy the psychotherapist's self is used in a directed, involved way to assist the client's process of developing and integrating full contact and the satisfaction of relational needs. Of central significance is the process of attunement, not just to thoughts, feelings, behaviors, or physical sensations, but also to what Stern terms "vitality affects," such that an experience of unbroken feeling-connectedness is created (1985, p. 156).

The client's sense of self and sense of relatedness that develop are crucial to the process of healing and growth, particularly when there have been specific traumas in the client's life and when aspects of the self have been disavowed or denied because of the cumulative failure of contact-in-relationship (Erskine, 1997a).

Attunement

Attunement goes beyond empathy: it is a process of communion and unity of interpersonal contact. It is a two-part process that begins with empathy—being sensitive to and identifying with the other person's sensations, needs, or feelings; and includes the communication of that sensitivity to the other person. More than just understanding (Rogers, 1951) or vicarious introspection (Kohut, 1971), attunement is a kinesthetic and emotional sensing of others knowing their rhythm, affect, and experience by metaphorically being in their skin, and going beyond empathy to create a two-person experience of unbroken feeling connectedness by providing a reciprocal affect and/or resonating response. Attunement is communicated by what is said as well as by the therapist's facial or body movements that signal to the client that his affect and needs are perceived, are significant and make an impact on the therapist. It is facilitated by the therapist's capacity to anticipate and observe the effects of her behavior on the client and to decenter from her own experience to focus extensively on the client's process. Yet, effective attunement also requires that the therapist simultaneously remains aware of the boundary between client and therapist as well as her own internal processes.

The communication of attunement validates the client's needs and feelings and lays the foundation for repairing the failures of previous relationships (Erskine, 1998a). *Affective attunement*, for example, provides an interpersonal contact essential to human relationship. It involves the resonance of one person's affect to the other's affect. Affective attunement begins with valuing the other person's affect as an extremely important form of communication, being willing to be affectively aroused by the other person and responding with the reciprocal affect. When a client feels sad, the therapist's reciprocal affect of compassion and compassionate acts complete the interpersonal contact. Relationally, anger requires the reciprocal affects related to attentiveness, seriousness, and responsibility, with possible acts of correction.

The client who is afraid requires that the therapist respond with affect and action that convey security and protection. When clients express joy, the response from the therapist that completes the unity of interpersonal contact is the reciprocal vitality and expression of pleasure. Symbolically, attunement may be pictured as one person's yin to the other's yang that together form a unity in the relationship.

Attunement is often experienced by the client as the therapist gently moving through the defenses that have prevented the awareness of relationship failures and related needs and feelings. Over time this results in a lessening of internal interruptions to contact and a corresponding dissolving of external defenses. Needs and feelings can increasingly be expressed with comfort and assurance that they will receive a connecting and caring response. Frequently, the process of attunement provides a sense of safety and stability that enables the client to begin to remember and endure regressing into childhood experiences. This may bring a fuller awareness of the pain of past traumas, shaming experiences, past failures of relationship(s), and loss of aspects of self (Erskine, 1994).

Relational needs

Attunement also includes responding to relational needs as they emerge in the therapeutic relationship. Relational needs are the needs unique to interpersonal contact. They are not the basic needs of life such as food, air, or proper temperature, but are the essential elements that enhance the quality of life and a sense of self-in-relationship. Relational needs are the component parts of a universal human desire for relationship.

The relational needs described in this chapter have emerged from a study of transference and a qualitative investigation of the crucial factors in significant relationships conducted at the Institute for Integrative Psychotherapy in New York City. Although there may be an infinite number of relational needs the eight described in this chapter represent those needs that, in my experience, clients most frequently describe as they talk about significant relationships. Other client-therapist intersubjective experiences may reveal a different cluster of relational needs beyond the eight described here. This further illustrates that the client-therapist relationship is irreproducible. No two therapists will produce the same therapeutic process. Some of the relational needs described here are also described in the psychotherapy literature as fixated needs of early childhood, indicators of psychopathology or problematic transference. While the tendency to pathologize dependence or transference does exist in the psychotherapy literature, in the context of the time and theoretical milieu, Kohut in 1971 and 1977 made strides to connect transference to developmental needs. Kohut distinguishes relational, developmental needs that have suffered disruption or rupture from the classical transference based on a drive model of psychoanalysis. Although he identifies mirroring, twinship, and idealization as problematic transferences, he also relates them to essential needs. However, his methods remain psychoanalytic and do not make full use of a relationship-oriented integrative model of psychotherapy. Bach (1985), Basch (1988), Stolorow, Brandschaft, & Atwood (1987), and Wolf (1988) have expanded on Kohut's concepts, each emphasizing the importance of a relational perspective in understanding transference. Clark's (1991) integrative perspective on empathetic transactions bridges the concepts of transference and relational needs and emphasizes a therapy of involvement.

Relational needs are present throughout the entire life cycle from early infancy through old age. Although present in early childhood, relational needs are not only needs of childhood or needs that emerge in a developmental hierarchy: they are the actual components of relationship that are present each day of our lives. Each relational need may become figural or conscious as a longing or desire while the others remain out of consciousness or as background. A satisfying response by another person to an individual's relational need allows the pressing need to recede to ground and another relational need to become figural as a new interest or desire. Often it is in the absence of need satisfaction that an individual becomes most aware of the presence of relational needs. When relational needs are not satisfied the need becomes more intense and is phenomenologically experienced as longing, emptiness, a nagging loneliness, or an intense urge often accompanied by nervousness. The continued absence of satisfaction of relational needs may be manifested as frustration, aggression, or anger. When disruptions in relationship are prolonged the lack of need satisfaction is manifested as a loss of energy or hope and shows up in *script beliefs* such as "No one is there for me" or "What's the use?" (Erskine & Moursund, 1988). These script beliefs are the cognitive defense against the awareness of needs and the feelings present when needs do not get a satisfying response from another person (Erskine, 1980).

The satisfaction of relational needs requires a contactful presence of another who is sensitive and attuned to the relational needs and who also provides a reciprocal response to each need. *Security* is the visceral experience of having our physical and emotional vulnerabilities protected. It involves the experience that our variety of needs and feelings are human and natural. Security is a sense of simultaneously being vulnerable and in harmony with another.

Attunement involves the empathetic awareness of the other's need for security within the relationship plus a reciprocal response to that need. It includes respectful transactions that are non-shaming and the absence of actual or anticipated impingement or danger. The needed response is the provision of physical and affective security where the individual's vulnerability is honored and preserved. It communicates, often nonverbally, "Your needs and feelings are normal and acceptable to me." Therapeutic attunement to the relational need for security has been described by clients as "total acceptance and protection," as a communication of "unconditional positive regard" or "I'm OK in this relationship." Attunement to the need for security involves the therapist being sensitive to the importance of this need and conducting herself both emotionally and behaviorally in a way that provides acceptance and protection in the relationship.

Relational needs include the need *to feel validated, affirmed and significant* within a relationship. It is the need to have the other person validate the significance and function of our intrapsychic processes of affect, fantasy, and constructing of meaning, and to validate that our emotions are a significant intrapsychic and interpersonal communication. It includes the need to have all our relational needs affirmed and accepted as natural. This need is a relational request for the other person to be involved through providing a quality of interpersonal contact that validates the legitimacy of relational needs, the significance of affect, and the function of intrapsychic processes.

Attunement with a client's need for validation is conveyed through the psychotherapist's phenomenological inquiry and contactful presence. The therapist's affective reciprocity with the client's feelings validates the client's affect and provides affirmation and normalization of the client's relational needs. The psychotherapist's focus on the psychological function—stability, continuity, identity, predictability—of rigidly held beliefs or behaviors lessens the likelihood of the client experiencing shame while validating the psychological significance of the beliefs or behaviors. Such validation is a necessary prerequisite to lasting cognitive or behavioral change.

Acceptance by a stable, dependable, and protective other person is an essential relational need. Each of us as children had the need to look up to and rely on our parents, elders, teachers, and mentors. We need to have significant others from whom we gain protection, encouragement, and information. The relational need for acceptance by a consistent, reliable, and dependable other person is the search for protection and guidance that may be manifested as an idealization of the other. In psychotherapy, such idealization is also the search for protection from a controlling, humiliating introjected ego's intrapsychic effect on the vulnerability of Child ego states (Erskine & Moursund, 1988; Fairbairn, 1952; Guntrip, 1971). It can also be the search for protection from one's own escalations of affect or exaggerations of fantasies. The therapist protects and facilitates integration of affect by providing an opportunity to express, contain, and/or understand the function of such dynamics.

The degree to which an individual looks to someone and hopes that he or she is reliable, consistent, and dependable is directly proportional to the quest for intrapsychic protection, safe expression, containment, or beneficial insight. Idealizing or depending on someone is not necessarily pathological as implied in the popular psychology term, "co-dependent," or when misinterpreted as "idealizing transference" (Kohut, 1977), or as Berne's psychological game of "Gee, you're wonderful, professor" (1964). When we refer to some clients' expressions of this need to be accepted and protected as "a victim looking for a rescuer," we depreciate or even pathologize an essential human need for relationship that provides a sense of stability, reliability, and dependability.

In psychotherapy, attunement involves the therapist's recognition of the importance and necessity of idealizing as an unaware request for intrapsychic protection. Such recognition and attunement by the therapist to the client's relational need most often occurs in the accepting and respecting nature of the interpersonal contact and therapeutic involvement and may not necessarily be spoken about directly. Such a therapeutic involvement includes both the client's sense of the psychotherapist's interest in the client's welfare and the use of the therapist's integrated sense of self as the most effective therapeutic tool (Erskine, 1993; Erskine & Moursund, 1988). It is this relational need to be accepted by a stable, dependable, and protective other person that provides a client-centered reason to conduct our lives and psychotherapy practice ethically and morally.

The *confirmation of personal experience* is also an essential relational need. The need to have experience confirmed is manifested through the desire to be in the presence of someone who is similar, who understands because he or she has had a like experience, and whose shared experience is confirming. It is the quest for mutuality, a sense of walking the same path in life together with a companion who is "like me." It is the need to have someone appreciate and value our experience because they phenomenologically know what that experience is like.

Affirmation of the client's experience may include the therapist joining in or valuing the client's fantasies. Rather than define a client's internal storytelling as "just a fantasy," it is essential to engage the client in the expression of the needs, hopes, relational conflicts, and protective strategies that may constitute the core of the fantasies. Attunement to the need for affirmation of experience may be achieved by the therapist accepting everything said by the client, even when fantasy and reality are intertwined, much like the telling of a dream reveals the intrapsychic process. Fantasy images or symbols have a significant intrapsychic and interpersonal function. When the *function* of the fantasy is acknowledged, appreciated, and valued the person feels affirmed in his experience.

When the relational need for confirmation of personal experience is present in a client's communication, he may be longing for a model with a similar experience. An attuned psychotherapy may include the sharing of the therapist's own experiences: telling how she solved a conflict similar to the client's and providing a sense of mutuality with the client. Attunement is provided by the therapist valuing the need for confirmation by revealing carefully selected personal experiences, mindfully (i.e., client-focused), sharing vulnerabilities or similar feelings and fantasies, and by the therapist's personal presence and vitality. The client who needs confirmation of personal experience requires a uniquely different reciprocal response than the client who needs validation of affect or who needs to be accepted by a dependable and protective other. In neither of these latter two relational needs is the sharing of personal experience or the creating of an atmosphere of mutuality an attuned response to the client's need.

Self-definition is the relational need to know and express one's own uniqueness and to receive acknowledgement and acceptance by the other. Self-definition is the communication of one's self-chosen identity through the expression of preferences, interests, and ideas without humiliation or rejection.

In the absence of satisfying acknowledgement and acceptance, the expression of self-definition may take unconscious adversarial forms such as the person who begins his or her sentences with "No" even when agreeing, or who constantly engages in arguments or competition. People often compete to define themselves as distinct from others. The more alike people are the greater the thrust for self-defining competition.

Attunement begins with the therapist's sensitivity to and understanding that adversity and competition in relationships may be an expression of the need for self-definition with acknowledgement and acceptance by the other. Therapeutic attunement is in the therapist's consistent support for the client's expression of identity and in the therapist's normalization of the need for self-definition. It requires the therapist's consistent presence, contactfulness, and respect even in the face of disagreement.

Another essential relational need is *to have an impact on the other person*. Impact refers to having an influence that affects the other in some desired way. An individual's sense of competency in a relationship emerges from agency and efficacy—attracting the other's attention and interest, influencing what may be of interest to the other person, and affecting a change of affect or behavior in the other.

Attunement to the client's need to have an impact occurs when the psychotherapist allows herself to be emotionally impacted by the client and to respond with compassion when the client is sad, to provide an affect of security when the client is scared, to take the client seriously when he is angry, and to be excited when the client is joyful. Attunement may include soliciting the client's criticism of the therapist's behavior and making the necessary changes so the client has a sense of impact within the therapeutic relationship.

Relationships become more personally meaningful and fulfilling when the need *to have the other initiate* is satisfied. Initiation refers to the impetus for making interpersonal contact with another person. It is the reaching out to the other in some way that acknowledges and validates the importance of him or her in the relationship.

The psychotherapist may be subject to a theory-induced countertransference when she universally applies the theoretical concepts of non-gratification, rescuing, or refraining from doing more than 50% of the therapeutic work. While waiting for the client to initiate the psychotherapist may not be accounting for the fact that some behavior that appears passive may actually be an expression of the relational need to have the other initiate.

The therapist's attunement to this relational need requires a sensitivity to the client's non-action and the therapist's initiation of interpersonal contact. To respond to the client's need it may be necessary for the therapist to initiate a dialogue, to move out of her chair and sit near the client, or to make a phone call to the client between sessions. The therapist's willingness to initiate interpersonal contact or to take responsibility for a major share of the therapeutic work normalizes the client's relational need to have someone else put energy into reaching out to him. Such action communicates to the client that the therapist is involved in the relationship.

The need to *express love* is an important component of relationships. Love is often expressed through quiet gratitude, thankfulness, giving affection, or doing something for the other person. The importance of the relational need to give love—whether it be from children to parents, sibling, or teacher, or from a client to a therapist—is often overlooked in the practice of psychotherapy. When the expression of love is stymied, the expression of self-in-relationship is thwarted. Too often psychotherapists have treated clients' expression of affection as a manipulation, transference, or a violation of a neutral therapeutic boundary.

Attunement to the client's relational need to express love is in the therapist's gracious acceptance of the client's gratitude and expressions of affection, and in acknowledging the normal function of love in maintaining a meaningful relationship.

Those clients for whom the absence of satisfaction of relational needs is cumulative require a consistent and dependable attunement and involvement by the psychotherapist that acknowledges, validates, and normalizes relational needs and related affect. It is through the psychotherapist's sustained contactful presence that the cumulative trauma (Khan, 1963; Lourie, 1996) of the lack of need satisfaction can now be addressed and the needs responded to within the therapeutic relationship.

Involvement

Involvement is best understood through the client's perception— a sense that the therapist is contactful and is truly invested in the client's welfare. It evolves from the therapist's respectful inquiry into the client's experience and is developed through the therapist's attunement to the client's affect and rhythm and to the validation of his needs. Involvement includes being fully present with and for the person in a way that is appropriate to the client's developmental level of functioning and current need for relationship. It includes a genuine interest in the client's intrapsychic and interpersonal world and a communication of that interest through attentiveness, inquiry, and patience.

Therapeutic involvement is maintained by the therapist's constant vigilance to providing an environment and relationship of safety and security. It is necessary that the therapist be constantly attuned to the client's ability to tolerate the emerging awareness of past experiences so that he is not overwhelmed once again in the therapy as he may have been in a previous experience. Therapeutic involvement that emphasizes acknowledgement, validation, normalization, and presence diminishes the internal defensive process.

The therapist's *acknowledgement* of the client begins with an attunement to his affect, relational needs, rhythm, and developmental level of functioning. Through sensitivity to the relational needs or physiological expression of emotions the therapist can guide the client to become aware and to express needs and feelings or to acknowledge that feelings or physical sensations may be memory—the only way of remembering that may be available. In many cases of relationship failure the person's relational needs or feelings were not acknowledged and it may be necessary in psychotherapy to help the client gain a vocabulary and learn to voice those feelings and needs. Acknowledgement of physical sensations, relational needs, and affect helps the client claim his own phenomenological experience. It includes a receptive other who knows and communicates about the existence of nonverbal movements, tensing of muscles, affect, or even fantasy.

There may have been times in a client's life when feelings or relational needs were acknowledged but were not validated. *Validation* communicates to the client that his affect, defenses, physical sensations, or behavioral patterns are related to something significant in his experiences. Validation makes a link between cause and effect; it values the individual's idiosyncrasies and way of being in relationship. It diminishes the possibility of the client internally disavowing or denying the significance of affect, physical sensation, memory, or dreams; and it supports the client in valuing his phenomenological experience and transferential communication of the needed relationship, thereby increasing self-esteem.

The intent of *normalization* is to influence the way clients or others may categorize or define their internal experience or their behavioral attempts at coping from a pathological or "something's-wrong-with-me" perspective to one that respects the archaic attempts at resolution of conflicts. It may be essential for the therapist to counter societal or parental messages such as "You're stupid for feeling scared" with "Anyone would be scared in that situation." Many flashbacks, bizarre fantasies, nightmares, confusion, panic, and defensiveness are all normal coping phenomena in abnormal situations. It is imperative that the therapist communicates that the client's experience is a normal defensive reaction—a reaction that many people would have if they encountered similar life experiences.

Presence is provided through the psychotherapist's sustained attuned responses to both the verbal and nonverbal expressions of the client. It occurs when the behavior and communication of the psychotherapist at all times respects and enhances the integrity of the client. Presence includes the therapist's receptivity to the client's affect—to be impacted by his emotions; to be moved and yet to stay responsive to the impact of his emotions and not to become anxious, depressed, or angry. Presence is an expression of the psychotherapist's full internal and external contact. It communicates the psychotherapist's responsibility, dependability, and reliability. Through the therapist's full presence the transformative potential of a relationship-oriented psychotherapy is possible. Presence describes the therapist's provision of a safe interpersonal connection. More than just verbal communication, presence is a communion between client and therapist.

Presence is enhanced when the therapist de-centers from her own needs, feelings, fantasies, or hopes and centers instead on the client's process. Presence also includes the converse of de-centering; that is, the therapist being fully contactful with her own internal process and reactions. The therapist's history, relational needs, sensitivities, theories, professional experience, own psychotherapy, and reading interests all shape unique reactions to the client. Each of these thoughts and feelings within the therapist are an essential part of therapeutic presence. The therapist's repertoire of knowledge and experience is a rich resource for attunement and understanding. Presence involves bringing the richness of the therapist's experiences to the therapeutic relationship as well as de-centering from the self of the therapist and centering on the client's process.

Presence also includes allowing oneself to be manipulated and shaped by the client in a way that provides for the client's self-expression. As effective psychotherapists we are played with and genuinely become the clay that is molded and shaped to fit the client's expression of their intrapsychic world towards the creation of a new sense of self and self-in-relationship (Winnicott, 1965). The dependable, attuned presence of the therapist counters the client's sense of shame and discounting his self-worth. The quality of presence creates a psychotherapy that is unique with each client: attuned to and involved with the client's emerging relational needs.

What gives psychotherapy its transformative effect in people's lives is the psychotherapist's focus on the client's relational needs and the relationship between client and therapist. Such a relationship can never be standardized or prescribed or even quantified by research. The uniqueness of each therapeutic relationship emerges out of the therapist's attunement and involvement that is responsive to the client's cluster of relational needs—a therapy of contact-in-relationship.

CHAPTER FOUR

Psychotherapy of unconscious experience

Sigmund Freud's theoretical formulation that the unconscious determines motivation and behavior was revolutionary a century ago. Today that same theoretical formulation may be equally accurate in understanding motivation and behavior, but contemporary conceptualizations of the dynamics of "unconscious" experience have changed the focus from one emphasizing defensive repression to a developmental and neurological perspective. In response to current neurological research and contemporary psychological theory, I no longer think of a dynamic unconscious as formed exclusively from defensive repression; rather, I view it as an expression of developmental and neurological processing of significant experiences (Bucci, 1997; Fosshage, 2005; Howell, 2005; Kihlstrom, 1984; Lyons-Ruth, 1999; Orange, Atwood, & Stolorow, 1997; Siegel, 2003).

Freud postulated that "the unconscious" was like a vault in the mind where emotionally conflictual experiences were stored and forgotten. Such a "dynamic unconscious" was the result of the defensive activity of repression (Freud, 1900a, 1915e). Ian Suttie (1935), an early psychoanalytic object relations theorist, described such repression as an "entirely unconscious process" and distinguished it from "suppression," which is a conscious reaction to coercion (p. 97). With repression, particularly uncomfortable affect-laden or traumatic experiences of self with others are psychologically prevented from coming to awareness. Other self-protective and defensive reactions—such as desensitization, disavowal, dissociation, and psychological splitting—may accompany and reinforce repression.

In working with many clients in psychotherapy, especially those who have experienced acute or cumulative trauma, it has become clear to me that particular memories, fantasies, feelings, and physical reactions may be repressed because they may bring to awareness relational experiences in which physical and relational needs were repeatedly unmet and related affect cannot be integrated because there was (or is) a failure in the significant other person's attuned responsiveness (Erskine, 1993; Erskine, Moursund, & Trautmann, 1999; Lourie, 1996; Stolorow & Atwood, 1989; Wallin, 2007).

Winnicott (1974), in writing about clients' "fear of breakdown" and their potential regression to early childhood emotionally charged experiences, departed from classical psychoanalytic theory which postulated that the dynamic unconscious was composed of repressed drives and conflictual experience. He described the unconscious as the ego's inability to encompass intense emotional experience. In light of current findings in neurology and child development, Winnicott's premise about the formation of unconscious experience appears accurate. It is now evident that the brain's frontal cortex may not process intense emotional and physiological reactions that are occurring in the ascending reticular formation (Cozolino, 2006; Damasio, 1999; Siegel, 2007), and that consciousness is directly the result of the brain's ability to symbolize experience (Bucci, 2001; Lyons-Ruth, 2000).

Gestalt therapy (Perls, Hefferline, & Goodman, 1951) theory dispensed with the psychoanalytic concept of "unconscious" and replaced it with the concept of "loss of awareness." In Gestalt therapy, "unconscious" became a process rather than a place in the mind. A person's loss of awareness was the result of having fixed perceptions (gestalten) that inhibit or prevent alternative ways of perceiving experience. The loss of awareness is maintained by the contact interrupting mechanisms of retroflection, confluence, introjection, projection, and egotism. Gestalt therapy postulates that through the integration of here-and-now awareness, fixed gestalten are dissolved and the person is conscious of his current experience.

Although most of the transactional analysis literature does not address the "unconscious" per se, Berne made several references to unconscious process with little reference to the term or concept of "unconscious." In his original conceptualization of ego states, both the formation and influence of Child and Parent ego states are not conscious to the Adult ego state (1961). He borrowed the psychoanalytic concept of unconscious but changed the terminology. In his writings about psychological cathexis, he referred to unconscious, subconscious, and conscious as bound, unbound, and free energy. In the "monkey in the tree" metaphor, it is clear that Berne's description of bound energy refers to emotional experience that is locked away and excluded from awareness, similar to Freud's repression. Unbound energy refers to experience that is subconscious or preconscious and with the right stimulus is available to awareness. And, free energy refers to experience that is conscious (pp. 40–41).

In Berne's description of ulterior transactions, he referred to them as coming from the psychological level rather than the social level. In the case of ulterior transactions from Child or Parent ego states, the individual's Adult ego state may not be aware of the psychological communication—an unaware or unconscious communication. Here, psychological level seems to be equated with unconscious (ibid., pp. 103–105, 124). Perhaps the clearest examples in Berne's writing of the concept of unconscious process are in his description of script protocol and palimpsests. Script protocol and palimpsests refer to the presymbolic, sub-symbolic, and procedural forms of memory that form the unconscious relational patterns and implicit experiential conclusions that are the core of life scripts (pp. 116–126).

Berne specifically addressed unconscious experience in his description of the client's "primal judgments" and "primal images": "It appears that the most important and influential judgments which human beings make concerning each other are the products of preverbal processes— cognition without insight—which function almost automatically below the level of consciousness" (1955, p. 72). He went on to describe the therapist's symbolic-nonverbal processes in connection with the client's unconscious expression of experience and referred to it as the therapist's "ego image"—the image in the psychotherapist's mind when she envisions the troubled child that the client once was (1957b). Berne also used the term "intuition" to describe the therapist's unconscious connecting with the client's unconscious communication: "Intuition is subconscious knowledge without words, based on subconscious observations without words" (1947, p. 35).

Rogers (1951) emphasized the importance of empathy—feeling what the client feels—as a nonverbal yet significant form of connecting with the client's unconscious communication. Reik (1948) and Heimann (1950) were two of the early psychoanalytic writers who emphasized the psychotherapist's emotional response to the client as one of the most important instruments of research into the client's unconscious experience. Later, Kohut (1977) described empathy as a vicarious introspection, a way of knowing the client's unconscious thought processes by imagining being in his affective and relational experience. Over the past several years, the transactional analysis literature has increasingly focused on the significance of both the client's and the therapist's unconscious process as being central to the therapeutic relationship (Erskine & Trautmann, 1996; Hargaden & Sills, 2002; Novellino, 1984, 2003).

In-depth psychotherapy

When there is a therapeutic contract for in-depth psychotherapy aimed at fundamental change in the client's script, deconfusion and resolution of Child ego state conflicts, and decommissioning of influencing Parent ego states, the therapeutic goal is to facilitate making conscious what has been unconscious. This involves bringing to the client's awareness the memories, feelings, thoughts, sensations, and associations that were previously not conscious. Such a recovery of consciousness allows the client to be aware of his motivation, personal history, coping style, and relational needs, thus providing the opportunity for behavior to be determined by current choice rather than by compulsion, fear, or programmed obedience.

In practicing in-depth psychotherapy, I find it essential to take into account that specific memories of experiences, relationships, feelings, or fantasies may be actively repressed because they bring to awareness emotionally painful relational conflicts and unmet needs. This is in accordance with Freud's original premise. Such unconscious functioning is maintained by cognitive denial, emotional disavowal, physiological desensitization, psychological dissociation, and schizoid distancing. These self-protective and defensive interruptions to contact contribute to making and keeping experience unconscious. However, experience that is unconscious is not only the result of psychological defenses. Experience that is unconscious may also result from a physiological survival reaction in response to trauma or may reflect fixated developmental levels of functioning. Trauma may be defined as the intense overstimulation of the amygdala and the limbic system of the brain such that the physiological centers of the brain are activated in the direction of flight, freeze, or fight. There is little activation of the frontal cortex or integration with the corpus callosum, so thought, time sequencing, language, concepts, narrative, and the capacity to calculate cause and effect are not formed (Cozolino, 2006; Damasio, 1999; Howell, 2005). Such trauma often results in dissociation and/or schizoid isolation (Erskine, 2001a).

Experience may be unconscious because both acute trauma and prolonged neglect are not recorded as explicit and symbolic memory but as physiological survival reactions, intense and undifferentiated affect, sub-symbolic memory, implicit memory, and procedural memory of relational patterns that may become manifested as avoidance, ambivalence, or aggression (Wallin, 2007). Most of what we colloquially refer to as "unconscious" may best be described as pre-symbolic, sub-symbolic, symbolic nonverbal, implicit, or procedural expressions of early childhood experiences that are significant forms of memory (Bucci, 2001; Kihlstrom, 1984; Lyons-Ruth, 2000; Schacter & Buckner, 1998). These forms of memory are not conscious in that they are not transposed to thought, concept, language, or narrative. Such sub-symbolic or implicit memories are phenomenologically communicated through physiological tensions, undifferentiated affects, longings and repulsions, tone of voice, and relational patterns that may stimulate physiological and affective resonance in the psychotherapist. The transference-countertransference dyad is an unconscious unfolding of two intersubjective life stories and a window of opportunity into both the client's and the therapist's unconscious experience.

It is our task as psychotherapists to be attuned to the client's affect, rhythm, developmental level of functioning, and relational needs while inquiring about the client's phenomenological experience. Phenomenological inquiry provides an opportunity for the client's affectively and physiologically charged memories to be put into dialogue with an interested and involved person—perhaps for the very first time. What was never "conscious" has an opportunity to become conscious through an involved therapeutic relationship.

I find it important to think not only in terms of unconscious process as reflecting either trauma or repression, but also to think developmentally. I generally conceptualize sub-symbolic or implicit memory as being composed of six developmental and experiential levels: preverbal, never verbalized, never acknowledged within the family, nonmemory, actively avoided verbalization, and pre-reflective relational patterns. I will briefly describe each type of sub-symbolic and implicit memory, but first, I offer a case example that illustrates how archaic and unconscious memory becomes conscious through an involved therapeutic relationship.

Kay's cumulative trauma

Kay was a fifty-four-year-old woman who worked as an accountant. She came to psychotherapy because of a deep sense of loneliness as well as her anger toward those she perceived to be controlling of her. She had never married and had never had a boyfriend, although in high school and colleges he had some secret crushes on a few young men. She had been in therapy with two previous therapists. The first therapist had helped her set some educational and career goals and to attain a good job, while the second therapy ended in a "disaster" because she experienced the therapist as "controlling" and "confronting."

In our early sessions, she was often very talkative about current events but would lapse into silence when I inquired about her phenomenological experience, such as her feelings, bodily sensations, fantasies, or hopes. I was attempting to connect with her deep sense of loneliness, which she frequently made passing reference to, but she often managed to distract me by talking about what was in the news or her job situation. The obvious transferences with me involved her constant fear that I would abandon her and also her constant anticipation that I would become controlling. She distrusted my phenomenological inquiry. It seemed that she often lacked the concepts, or even the vocabulary, to describe her feelings and internal experience. She had only vague memories of her early childhood and school years and most of those memories centered upon her family's religious activities.

In the second year of therapy a remarkable event occurred when a spider slowly descended from the ceiling on a long silvery strand and then proceeded to climb back up and drop down again over and over. She had a little girl's thrill and fascination, and I could feel myself emotionally moved in resonance with her excitement over the spider's activities. But, within about fifteen minutes, she became distant and silent. As I adjusted to her slow rhythm and psychic distancing, she commented that she had always liked spiders since she had been in the hospital. I was surprised, because in our intake interview and subsequent therapy sessions over the previous year she had never mentioned being hospitalized. Kay had never thought to tell me, or her two previous therapists, that she had spent two years in an iron lung recovering from polio between the ages of two and four. When I learned of her two-year hospital confinement, my heart went out to her. In subsequent sessions, I often imagined taking that young child out of the iron lung and holding her in my arms. Several times Kay described how her only "friend" during that time was a spider that had made its web on the ceiling above her iron lung, way out of touch. She spent hours being entertained by its movements, and I spent hours attuned to the importance that the spider had in this young girl's life.

Amid long silences, Kay eventually talked about how the nurses would come in and poke and prod her and how she hated being manipulated by them. Prior to each session, I found myself looking forward to talking to the little girl who was in the iron lung. We cried together about her loneliness. I took her anger seriously as she described being a "prisoner." Kay talked about how she would pass the hours of the day watching a large hospital clock tick the seconds away. In several sessions she described how the second hand makes a different clicking sound as it drops from twelve to six than it does when it ticks upward from six to twelve. She eventually remembered imagining that the hands of the clock were reaching down from the wall to stroke her head and face.

As the therapy progressed, she became less verbally descriptive of her hospital experience and had no vocabulary to express her affect or needs. There were long periods of silence and sadness. I sat closer to her where we could reach out and touch our fingers together. With finger-to-finger contact, she seemed more alive. We played the finger game of itsy-bitsy spider over and over. We laughed together at our silliness. Then she would cry as she experienced the juxtaposition between our playfulness and her years of loneliness.

Kay often used her fingers and face muscles to describe the agony of being confined to the iron lung. She would silently rage at me with her facial movements and hand gestures when I did not match her rhythm or respond with the appropriate affect. She was nonverbally telling me the story of her developmental needs, loneliness, and abandonment. Together we cocreated both a nonverbal and a verbal narrative of her experiences between ages two and four. My therapeutic involvement was to repeatedly validate her sadness, fear, anger, and sense of abandonment as affective expressions of real events. We developed a vocabulary and created meaning for the physiological and affective experience of her cumulative trauma. We normalized both her developmental and current needs and explored how she could have her adult relational needs responded to by people in her current life. My sense of personal presence was expressed in the combination of affective, rhythmic, and developmental attunement that was central to our relationship. In the ten years since the therapy, Kay has still not formed a romantic relationship with a man. But she reports that she is "in love with the children" at the hospital where she volunteers three days a week.

Forms of unconscious memory

Preverbal. Early childhood memory is pre-symbolic and nonlinguistic. It is not available to consciousness through language because the experience is preverbal. Such memory may be expressed in self-regulating patterns, emotional reactions, physiological inhibitions, and styles of attachment and relationships. Later in life, preverbal relational patterns are experienced but not usually thought about. The therapist's attunement to affect, rhythm, and developmental level are essential in forming an emotional connection that facilitates a communication of preverbal experience. The client's story may be expressed in nonverbal enactments and/or created by therapeutic inference. This is often the situation when dealing with the client's unconscious but felt experience about being an infant, toddler, or even preschool-age child. For example, in Kay's therapy, the three- and four-year-old child in the hospital was regressed to a much younger preverbal age wherein only her physical gestures and our finger-to-finger touch could express Kay's agony, loneliness, irritation, and longing for relationship. Both my constant attentiveness while she was silent and our finger-to-finger contact allowed the preverbal memory to be expressed.

Never verbalized. Pre-symbolic and implicit memory reflect childhood experiences that were not verbalized in the original situation. The child may have had some language, such as nouns and verbs, but lacked the concepts to describe feelings and needs and/or did not have a responsive other person who was interested in a way that gave significance and meaning to the child's experience. The narrative about the child's experience was never formed because there was no relationship that fostered the child's self-expression and concept formation.

When a child has the opportunity to talk about his or her experience, each experience takes on a vocabulary and description; it becomes understood because concepts are formed. It becomes conscious. When there is an absence of interpersonal dialogue, an experience is less likely to become conscious and form usable concepts and a self-expressive narrative. Phenomenological inquiry and affective attunement are important dynamics in a person expressing his emotional experience. The attuned, interested other helps to provide a dialogical language that allows the phenomenological experience to be formed, expressed, and have meaning as autobiographical memory. In Kay's case, she had never spoken to anyone, neither her friends nor her previous therapists, about her experience in the hospital. Together we cocreated a story that facilitated consciousness and provided meaning to her previously never-verbalized emotional experiences.

Unacknowledged. Some developmental experiences may be unconscious because the child's emotions, behaviors, or relational needs were never acknowledged within the family. When there is no conversation that gives meaning to the child's experience, the experience may remain without social language. Cozolino (2006) describes the effects of both acknowledgement and lack of acknowledgement of the child's experience:

> Parental concern and curiosity make children aware that they have an inner experience of their own. ... Because this inner experience can be understood, discussed and organized through a coconstructed narrative, it becomes available for conscious consideration. ... When a child is left in silence due to parental inability to verbalize internal experience, the child does not develop the capacity to understand and manage his or her world. ... When verbal interactions include references to sensations, feelings, behaviors, and thoughts, they provide a medium through which the child's brain is able to integrate the various aspects of experience in a coherent manner. (p. 232)

Psychotherapy provides the opportunity to address that which has never been acknowledged. For example, Kay's parents actively prayed for her recovery while she was in the hospital and, once she was home, continually thanked God that she did not die. But they never talked to her about her hospital experience of loneliness, physical agony, and intense fear. In the hospital there was almost no conversation with the nurses. She was alone in her experience. As a result, these unacknowledged memories unconsciously dominated her life.

If the spider had not descended from the ceiling of my consulting room, Kay might never have told me about her hospitalization. The spider provided a special, emotionally filled moment in which I resonated with vitality to Kay's excitement and then, with quiet patience, to her silence and distance. This was a crucial turning point in our therapeutic work together. I was finally able to form a developmental image (i.e., Berne's "ego image") of a hospitalized, and perhaps traumatized, little girl that enabled me to begin to communicate with both the hospitalized child of two to four years old, as well as that little girl who was regressed to an emotional state of infancy. Later, when we processed our therapeutic work about her regressive experience, Kay told me that she had never spoken to anyone about her hospitalization because she just assumed that "no one would be interested," a transferring of her parent's lack of acknowledgement onto all others, including all three of her therapists.

Non-memory. A lack of memory may seem unconscious because significant relational contact did not occur. When important relational experiences never occurred, it is impossible to be conscious of them. If kindness, respect, or gentleness were lacking, the client will have no memory; there will be a vacuum of experience. This is often the situation with childhood neglect. Lourie (1996) described the absence of memory in clients with cumulative trauma that reflects the absence of vital care and an ignoring of relational needs. Kay's story illustrates "unconscious" as non-memory—comforting touch, validation of her affective needs, clarifying explanations, and active companionship were all missing during Kay's hospital years. The juxtaposition between my providing touch, validation, explanations, and companionship, and the absence of these important relational elements, stimulated her awareness that they were absent in her early life and that her unconscious compensating reactions to missing relational connections dominated her current life.

Kay's story reflects four types of unconscious processes: never verbalized, unacknowledged, non-memory, and regression to a preverbal period. In Kay's psychotherapy, the resolution of her cumulative trauma is also an example of the therapist's provision of a relational psychotherapy that allows previously unconscious experiences to become conscious through an intersubjective and affective connection. For many years, Kay lived and acted out various unconscious sub-symbolic and implicit memories. The story of her therapeutic journey is one of her becoming conscious of preverbal and never verbalized but lived experiences. She was not conscious of the relationships that never occurred (the non-memory) yet needed to occur for healthy development, such as the need for a dependable and consistent other responsive to her feelings and needs. Much of the psychotherapy was aimed at helping her reflect on and appreciate her various archaic relational patterns and self-regulating behaviors as attempts to communicate and seek reparation for numerous unrequited relational needs. In addition to Freud's concept of an unconscious resulting from repression, I organize my therapy perspective to include the possibility that the client may have unconscious and unexpressed developmental experiences that are preverbal, never verbalized, unacknowledged, or non-memory—the basis for fixated relational patterns.

Avoided verbalization. When experience is actively devoid of conversation, it may become unconscious, that is, not remembered as a series of specific events and no longer available to narrative. This is similar to Freud's (1915e) dynamic unconscious, where shameful experiences or guilt become unconscious because the person is acutely uncomfortable in talking to someone about the experience. For example, Andrew came to therapy with a number of intense obsessions, including shame about obsessing. I focused on several dimensions of the treatment of obsession, including understanding the psychological functions, script beliefs, and, specifically, the ways his obsessions were an attempt to tell a lost but important story. We explored how his shame about obsessing was an avoidance of a deeper sense of shame. Eventually, Andrew was able to tell me about the wonderful summer he had had when he was twelve years old. His family spent the summer at a lakeside cottage; another boy his age lived nearby. The two boys spent their time playing ball, swimming, and riding their bicycles. But, the most exciting part of the summer was their sexual play with each other. They explored each other's penises and performed fellatio on each other. Andrew loved the sexual experience, and he loved the other boy, whom he missed intensely when the summer was over.

He was extremely afraid to tell anyone about his wonderful experience. The two boys had never spoken to each other about their sexual play or what they were feeling. Andrew silently relished in the pleasure, but he could not tell his parents because "Father would beat me if he knew and Mother would go hysterical." He could not tell the nuns or priests at school because he knew "it was a sin." And, importantly, he could not tell any of the other boys what he had experienced that summer because he was afraid they would call him a "homo." Andrew's exciting story was kept a secret for twenty-four years, a secret even unto himself. Yet, the actively avoided telling of his story was acted out in his intense and diverse obsessions, obsessions for which he was deeply ashamed and that seemed to distract him from the socially imposed shame about his sexual experience.

Pre-reflective patterns. Many psychodynamics operate outside of the individual's awareness. They are pre-reflective patterns of self in relationship (Stolorow & Atwood, 1989). The five pre-reflective patterns described here—attachment style, self-regulation, relational needs, script beliefs, and introjection—are not clearly conscious to most clients in the early phase of psychotherapy, even though they often talk about their script beliefs, self-regulation, and reactions to relationships. Rather, they are unconscious of the pervasive influence such patterns have in their lives. An important aspect of psychotherapy is creating the quality of relationship in the context of which these pre-reflective patterns become conscious, understood, and experienced as choice.

Attachment styles are unconscious pre-symbolic procedural forms of memory based on early relational patterns (Bowlby, 1988a). In in-depth psychotherapy I often talk with clients about their style of attachment, both with me and with significant other people. We examine whether their relationships are secure, ambivalent, avoidant, disorganized, or isolated and explore the early family dynamics and implicit experiential conclusions that led to these patterns. Clients' awareness of attachment styles and their resources for building meaningful relationships become an important aspect of our dialogue. For example, in Kay's psychotherapy, she eventually began to appreciate how her ambivalent attachment style was formed and how she was maintaining it in her adult life. Andrew's isolated attachment was compensated for with many forms of obsession. He was eventually able to identify how each obsession created isolation in relationship.

People are often not conscious of their patterns of self-stabilization and self-regulation, which were developed to reduce intense affect. Clients often engage in particular gestures, repetitive behaviors, or script beliefs to calm overstimulating emotional reactions in the absence of need-fulfilling relationships. It is imperative that the psychotherapist eventually bring these self-regulating patterns to the client's awareness and investigate what is happening phenomenologically within the client in response to the therapeutic relationship or within the client's memory in the moments prior to the self-regulating action. Such behaviors might take the form of stroking one's hair, wringing one's hands, or ending sentences with "you know."

Body language is an important conveyer of unconscious communication, and therefore it is essential in psychotherapy to focus on clients becoming aware of the communication inherent in their physical movements, gestures, and postures. For example, it took me almost two years to realize that Kay's constant movement of her fingers against each other was an unconscious attempt to tell the story of emotional and physical abandonment. In Andrew's case, he would momentarily, but frequently, turn his eyes away from me to regulate his affect when the contact between us was intense. Together we learned to use these moments of self-soothing withdrawal to understand his sense of isolation and my misattunement.

The concept of relational needs (Erskine & Trautmann, 1996) is usually not conscious to most clients. The lack of satisfaction of relational needs is expressed as nervousness, irritation, preoccupation, or prolonged discomfort. Such sensations then shape the interactions or avoidance of interactions with people. Relational needs are inherent, yet often unconscious, dynamics in the transferences of everyday life and in the intersubjective therapeutic engagements. It is the psychotherapist's task to help the client gain awareness of his or her need for security in relationship; a sense of validation of one's affect and internal experience; a sense of reliance, dependability, and consistency from a significant other; a shared experience; the opportunity for self-definition; the capacity to make an impact in relationship; the other to initiate; and an expression of one's appreciation and gratitude. In both Kay's and Andrew's therapy, the need for security, validation, and dependability of the other were extremely important. Neither client was aware of the significance of these needs when entering therapy.

Clients' script beliefs about self, others, and the quality of life (Erskine & Zalcman, 1979) are usually unconscious, although they are often evident in social conversation. These pre-reflective sets of script beliefs provide a self-regulating mental framework and represent implicit experiential conclusions that have been formulated over a number of developmental ages. Once formulated and adopted, script beliefs influence what stimuli (internal and external) are attended to, how they are interpreted, and whether or not they are acted on. Script beliefs serve to distract against awareness of past experiences, relational needs, and related emotions. At the beginning of therapy, neither Kay nor Andrew was conscious of her or his script beliefs and how those beliefs organized her or his experiences in life. Andrew's script beliefs were "Something is wrong with me," "No one is there for me," and "No one understands me." Kay's script beliefs were "I'm all alone in the world," "My feelings are unimportant," and "People will control me." Each of these script beliefs unconsciously determined their behaviors, fantasies, and quality of relationships.

Introjection, by definition, is an unconscious, defensive identification with elements of the personality of a significant other that occurs in the absence of full relational contact (Erskine, 2003). Clients, although often aware of an internal critical voice, are not aware of the pervasive influence of their Parent ego state. In in-depth, integrative psychotherapy, it may be essential to investigate and even decommission the introjection of the attitudes, behaviors, or emotions of significant others that have been unconsciously identified as one's own (Erskine & Trautmann, 2003). With Kay and Andrew, we did not focus on psychotherapy of the Parent ego state; it did not seem germane to the treatment. For other clients, affects, attitudes, bodily reactions, and/or defensive patterns introjected from significant others may internally influence or even dominate their lives. Awareness and resolution of introjections is an important aspect of in-depth, integrative psychotherapy.

The process of psychotherapy

Our psychotherapeutic task is to help clients make conscious what is "unconscious"! What most people generally consider "conscious memory" is usually composed of explicit memory—the type of memory that is described as symbolic: a photographic image, impressionistic painting, or audio recording of what was said in past events. Such explicit or declarative memory is usually anchored in the capacity to use social language and concepts to describe experience. Experience that is unconscious usually lacks explicit recall of an event because it is sub-symbolic or pre-symbolic, physiological or procedural, repressed or the result of trauma (Bucci, 2001; Fosshage, 2005; Howell, 2005; Lyons-Ruth, 1999). Such unconscious memory is potentially "felt" as physiological tensions, undifferentiated affect, longings, or repulsions and manifested as pre-reflective relational and self-regulating patterns. These are the symptoms that bring clients to psychotherapy.

Clients like Kay and Andrew require a psychotherapist who is aware of the various dimensions of implicit, pre- and sub-symbolic, and procedural memories. It is necessary in a relational and integrative psychotherapy that the therapist remain sensitive to the unconscious communication inherent in the transferential expressions both within the therapeutic relationship and, importantly, within the transferences of everyday life (Freud, 1912b). Affective escalations, relational conflicts, habitual worries and obsessions, absence of affect, and even some physical ailments may represent a form of unconscious expression of implicit and emotional memory. Unconscious procedural memory may be expressed in attachment styles marked by ambivalence, avoidance, or aggression (Main, 1995; Wallin, 2007).

It is through the psychotherapist's awareness of his or her own personal emotional reactions and associations to the client, together with an understanding of child development and self-protective reactions, that the therapist can sense the client's unconscious communication of relational conflicts or traumatic experiences of early childhood. Through affective and rhythmic attunement and an awareness of the importance of relational needs, the psychotherapist can create a sensitive phenomenological and historical inquiry that allows unconscious, pre- and sub-symbolic emotional memory to be symbolically communicated through a shared language with an attuned and involved listener (Erskine, Moursund, & Trautmann, 1999).

For example, Kay could not put her hospital experience into words with either her first therapist, who focused on educational and career goals, or her second therapist, whose methods emphasized confrontation and appropriate behavior. When a psychotherapist focuses primarily on behavioral change, providing explanations, and encouraging a redecision or is bound by a theoretical perspective, the opportunity for the client's unconscious process of communication to be received, understood, and processed into language may be overlooked in the psychotherapy. It is through our sustained affective and rhythmic attunement that we sense the unconscious developmental nature of the client's pre- and sub-symbolic experiences. Through our empathy, we sense what relational needs were unrequited and how to respond therapeutically to those unrequited needs and the client's resulting styles of compensation and attachment.

Kay required a psychotherapist who could be emotionally responsive to her fear of abandonment, her profound loneliness, and her anger at being controlled. She needed attunement to both the two- to four-year-old child's agony and that child's regression to a preverbal developmental level—a regression that was a desperate attempt at self-regulation. She needed a psychotherapist who would attune to her silence, rhythm, and despair; who would play with her; and who would help her put her preverbal, never verbalized, unacknowledged, and non-memory unconscious experiences into interactive communication and language. Kay required a therapist who could decode her nonverbal experiences through being sensitive to the underlying meaning in her distracting comments, her silences, her facial and hand gestures, and her developmental needs; a therapist who, through affective reciprocity and therapeutic inference, could supply the necessary words and concepts that would make it possible to put her experiences into words—to make the unconscious hospital experience conscious.

Andrew required a therapist who was sensitive to his overwhelming sense of shame and his terror about punishment as well as to the psychological functions and script beliefs underlying his numerous obsessions. He also needed a combination of therapeutic protection against punishment and an understanding of his previously unconscious pre-reflective patterns of attachment, self-regulation, and relational needs (Moursund & Erskine, 2004). Andrew's avoidance of telling about his sexual experience resulted in the experience becoming unconscious. In the psychotherapist's consistent use of phenomenological inquiry, Andrew's unconscious memories were formed into an explicit memory and symbolic narrative. He no longer obsessed to distract himself from his original fear of punishment.

The stories of Kay and Andrew reflect the importance of the psychotherapist's attunement and involvement in decoding the various aspects of pre-symbolic and sub-symbolic unconscious communication. The aim of an in-depth integrative psychotherapy is to provide the quality of therapeutic relationship, understanding, and skill that facilitates the client in becoming conscious of what was previously unconscious so that he can be intimate with others, maintain good health, and engage in the tasks of everyday life without preformed restrictions.

Life scripts and attachment patterns: theoretical integration and therapeutic involvement

Life scripts are unconscious systems of psychological organization and self-regulation developed as a result of the cumulative failures in significant, dependent relationships. Scripts are unconsciously formed by infants, young children, and even adolescents and adults as a creative strategy for coping with disruptions in relationships that repeatedly fail to satisfy crucial developmental and relational needs. The unconscious organizing patterns that compose a life script are often first established in infancy as sub-symbolic internal relational models based on the quality of the infant/caregiver relationship. These early models are then reinforced and elaborated during a number of developmental ages. The results are the unconscious relational patterns that constitute a life script.

Eric Berne (1961) originally described a script as an "extensive unconscious life plan" (p. 123) that reflects the "primal dramas of childhood" (p. 116). This life plan is formed from the "script protocol" and "palimpsests," the preverbal, sub-symbolic, and pre-symbolic procedural memories that form the unconscious relational patterns and implicit experiential conclusions that are the core of life scripts (Bucci, 2001; Erskine, 2008). The protocol and palimpsests are the preverbal, affectively charged physiological survival reactions. They are the earliest formations of unconscious relational patterns—the internal working models that are, by developmental nature, exclusively physiological and affective. Berne (1972) wrote, "The first script programming takes place during the nursing period, in the form of short protocols which can later be worked into complicated dramas" (p. 83).

Although Cornell and Landaiche (2006) have drawn attention to the clinical significance of the script protocol and the psychotherapeutic necessity for thinking and working developmentally, the transactional analysis literature has not sufficiently focused on the central role of the "primal dramas" that compose the script protocol—the parental misattunements and cumulative neglects of sub-symbolic/preverbal infancy and pre-symbolic early childhood. Rather, the literature has emphasized how scripts are formed from parental messages, explicit decisions, and significant stories during the kindergarten and elementary school years, at an age when the child has the capacity for symbolic mentalization (Berne, 1972; English, 1972; Goulding & Goulding, 1979; Steiner, 1971; Stuntz, 1972; Woolams, 1973).

This emphasis in the transactional analysis literature on script formation occurring between four years old and adolescence may, in part, be due to Berne's (1972) statement, published posthumously, in which he referred to script as "a life plan based on decisions made in childhood, reinforced by parents, justified by subsequent events and culminating in a chosen alternative" (p. 446). In this comment Berne implied that scripts are conscious decisions that occur once the child has reached an age of language development, when symbolic reasoning, concrete operations of cause and effect, and awareness of alternative choices are possible (Bucci, 2001; Piaget, 1954).

The emphasis in the transactional analysis literature on scripts being formed in middle childhood may also be due in part to the fact that, by this developmental stage, symbolic and explicit memory is possible, thereby making the memory of many script decisions, parental messages, and childhood struggles to adapt to family, peer, and school demands available to consciousness. Additionally, script decisions, parental messages, and behavioral patterns that are symbolic, conscious, and available to language are more amenable to cognitive explanation, behavior modification, and brief redecisional methods of psychotherapy.

The clinical transactional analysis literature has often neglected to emphasize the significance of infancy and early childhood subsymbolic, preverbal, physiological survival reactions and implicit experiential conclusions that form unconscious procedural maps or internal working models of self-in-relationship (Erskine, 2008). The recent literature on neuroscience, child development, and early child/ parent attachment research has been a siren call reemphasizing the importance of psychotherapists focusing the therapeutic relationship on the client's early childhood preverbal relational experiences (Beebe, 2005; Cozolino, 2006; Damasio, 1999; Hesse, 1999; LeDoux, 1994; Schore, 2002; Siegel, 1999; Weinberg & Tronick, 1998).

The infant's and young child's physiological survival reactions and affective/procedural experiences—the life script protocol and palimpsests that compose the primal dramas of childhood—form sub-symbolic internal working models of self-regulation and relational interaction (Bowlby, 1973). Later in life, these unconscious sub-symbolic memories of physiological reactions, affect, and procedural experiences are expressed through physiological discomforts, escalations or minimizations of affect, implicit knowing, and the transferences of everyday life. These unconscious relational patterns influence the reactions and expectations that define for us the kind of world we live in, the people we are, and the quality of interpersonal relationships we will have with others. Encoded physically in body tissues and biochemical events, affectively as subcortical brain stimulation, and cognitively in the form of beliefs, attitudes, and values, these responses form a blueprint that guides the way we live our lives.

Life scripts involve a complex network of neural pathways formed as thoughts, affects, biochemical and physiological reactions, fantasy, relational patterns, and the important process of homeostatic self-regulation of the organism. Scripts formed from physiological survival reactions, implicit experiential conclusions, relational failures, prolonged misattunements and neglects, as well as chronic shock and acute trauma, all require a developmentally focused psychotherapy wherein the therapeutic relationship is central and is evident through the respect, reliability, and the dependability of a caringly involved, skilled, real person (Erskine, 1993).

Overview of the literature

Fritz Perls described self-confirming, repetitive conclusions and patterns as a "life script" (Perls, 1944; Perls & Baumgardner, 1975) composed of both an "early scene" and a resulting "life plan" (Perls,

Hefferline, & Goodman, 1951, pp. 305–306). Alfred Adler referred to these recurring childhood patterns as "life style" (Ansbacher & Ansbacher, 1956), while Sigmund Freud (1920g) used the term "repetition compulsion" to describe similar phenomena. Contemporary psychoanalytic authors are referring to a similar phenomena when they write about the life-shaping influence of developmentally formed unconscious relational patterns, although they do not use the terms "script" or "life script" (Arlow, 1969a; Basch, 1988; Slap, 1987; Stolorow & Atwood, 1989).

The general psychology literature has described such unconscious relational systems as cognitive structures that represent an individual's organization of the world into a unified system of beliefs, concepts, attitudes, and expectations (Lewin, 1951) that reflect some aspect of unconscious relational patterns or life scripts (Andrews, 1988, 1989; Beitman, 1992; Kelly, 1955; Thelen & Smith, 1994).

The transactional analysis literature on scripts began with Berne (1961) describing the significance of the infant's primal or protocol experience with caregivers as the "earliest version of the script" (Berne, 1972, p. 447), the "original dramatic experiences upon which the script is based" (p. 446). He devoted only a few pages to this important topic, leaving it to other transactional analysts to research, refine, and expand the concepts and develop the clinical acumen for effective life script psychotherapy.

Steiner (1971) illustrated one aspect of the theory of scripts with his ego state matrix, which diagrammed parental influence. He put particular emphasis on the coercive power of the parents' overt and ulterior messages to gravely shape a child's life. Robert and Mary Goulding (1978) described another aspect of the theory with a list of injunctions that formed the basis of a child making script decisions. Their examples of script decisions are instances of explicit memories wherein an actual scene from childhood is consciously remembered, a corresponding parental injunction is identified, and the child's decision to comply with the injunction is articulated.

In his last writing, Berne (1972) emphasized three antecedents of a life script: parental programming, the child's decision, and the influence of stories. He described how children, particularly within the "magic years" of four and seven, will use fairytales and mythology as the inspiration on which to model their lives (Fraiberg, 1959). Such childhood stories are often a culmination and elaboration of parental messages, earlier childhood experiences, and life-determining decisions. They serve to provide a sense of meaning and definition about self, others, and the quality of life. In his 1972 book, written for popular rather than professional reading, Berne did not emphasize his view that the origin of life scripts was in the primal dramas, protocol, and palimpsests of very early childhood; rather, he provided only a partial definition of script: "A script is an ongoing program, developed in early childhood under parental influence, which directs the individual's behavior in the most important aspects of his life" (p. 418).

It was Cornell (1988) who emphasized the significance of the script protocol in infancy—the physiological survival reactions and "tissue level" of life scripts. Cornell's article raised the consciousness of transactional analysts to again think developmentally and to focus our psychotherapy on the fundamental importance of the earliest relationships in life.

Although Berne and other transactional analysis authors described various ways in which a life script may be formed, they did not provide a comprehensive definition. It was in a 1980 article entitled "Script Cure: Behavioral, Intrapsychic, and Physiological" that I provided the first operational definition. I defined script as a life plan based on decisions made at any developmental stage that inhibit spontaneity and limit flexibility in problem solving and in relating to people. Such script decisions are usually made when the person is under pressure and awareness of alternative choice is limited. The script decisions emerge later in life as constricting script beliefs about self, others, and the quality of life.

These script beliefs, along with the feelings repressed when the person was under pressure, are manifested in internal and external behavior and, together with selected memories, form a closed system of experiencing one's life. This closed system is the script (ibid., p. 102). This definition, like the descriptions of other transactional analysis authors, gives the impression that script is formed from conscious decisions, as if the child was aware of making a choice. If the term "decisions" refers to explicit experience and conscious choice, then the script-forming effects of the sub-symbolic and implicit primal dramas of childhood (the affectively and physiologically based protocol and palimpsest) are not part of an explicit decision because they occur prior to symbolic reasoning. If, however, we use a broader definition of "decisions" to include the sub-symbolic, pre-linguistic, and bodily reactions of infancy and early childhood that are not available to symbolic mentalization, then the term "decision" may include these early implicit and pre-symbolic self-regulating life experiences that are composed of undifferentiated affects, physiological reactions, and relational patterns.

Recently I elaborated on this earlier definition and provided a comprehensive definition of scripts that includes the profound influences of infancy and early childhood. "Life Scripts are a complex set of unconscious relational patterns based on physiological survival reactions, implicit experiential conclusions, explicit decisions, and/or self-regulating introjections, made under stress, at any developmental age, that inhibit spontaneity and limit flexibility in problem-solving, health maintenance and in relationship with people" (Erskine, 2007, p. 1). The physiological survival reactions and implicit experiential conclusions that I describe are the child's sub-symbolic and pre-symbolic attempts to manage the misattunements, cumulative neglects, traumas, and family dramas of infancy and pre-conceptual early childhood.

Bowlby (1969, 1973, 1980) also wrote about unconscious relational patterns and described the biological imperative of prolonged physical and affective bonding in the creation of a visceral core from which all experiences of self and others emerge. He referred to these patterns as "internal working models" that are generalized from experiences in infancy and early childhood. Bowlby proposed that healthy development emerged from the mutuality of both a child's and a caregiver's reciprocal enjoyment in their physical connection and affective relationship. His research collaborators (Ainsworth, Behar, Waters, & Wall, 1978) found that the mothers of secure infants were attuned to the affect and rhythms of their babies, sensitive to misattunements, and quick to correct their errors in attunement. It is these qualities of reparation, interpersonal contact, and communication of affect that are of utmost importance in forming secure relationships, a sense of mastery, and resilience in later life.

Bowlby went on to describe insecure attachments as the psychological result of disruptions in bonding within dependent relationships. His ideas influenced a number of researchers and developmentally focused writers who further identified specific patterns of insecure attachment that were the result of repeated disruptions in dependent relationships. They refer to these insecure patterns as ambivalent, avoidant, disorganized, or isolated attachment styles (Ainsworth, Behar, Waters, & Wall, 1978; Doctors, 2007; Main, 1995; O'Reilly-Knapp, 2001). Bowlby's theory provides an understanding of how an infant's or young child's physiological survival reactions and implicit experiential conclusions may form internal working models, the antecedents of an unconscious life script.

Each author just cited suggests a therapy that involves some combination of analysis, interpretation, explanation, interpersonal relatedness, and/or behavioral change. It is my opinion that to do a thorough life script cure, it is necessary to provide a developmentally focused relational psychotherapy that integrates affective, behavioral, cognitive, and physiological dimensions of psychotherapy while paying particular attention to the client's unconscious communication of sub-symbolic and pre-symbolic relational experiences that are revealed through their style of self-regulation, core beliefs, metaphors, avoidances, stories and narrative style, and transferences both with the psychotherapist and in everyday life. It is the therapist's task to decode the client's infant and early childhood physiological and affective experiences and to facilitate the client's becoming conscious of implicit relational patterns.

Attachment patterns

The literature on psychological attachment is relevant to understanding life scripts in that it provides an alternative perspective on how early childhood patterns of coping with relationships may be active years later in adult life (Hesse, 1999). Each person's internal working model of attachment (i.e., script pattern) is revealed in his characteristic patterns of behavior and transactions with others, core beliefs, fantasies, and personal narrative about his life. Bowlby (1973) described how a child's internal working model provides "a sense of how acceptable or unacceptable he himself is in the eyes of attachment figures" (p. 203). These internal working models determine anticipation, emotional and behavioral responses to others, the nature of fantasy, and the quality of interpersonal transactions. They are subtly evident in conversations and narrative, often as either prefix or suffix to a story or as a parenthetical phrase such as, "You won't believe me, but ..." or "There's no use trying ..." or "What can you expect from people?"

Fear-induced physiological survival reactions, prolonged neglect of relational needs, cumulative trauma, and unconscious conclusions are all recorded in the brainstem as procedural memories of self-in-relationship (Damasio, 1999). Attachment patterns—what Bowlby

(1973) referred to as internal working models—provide a reflection of the script protocol, the procedural memories that form the core of a life script: "Internal working models organize the child's cognitions, affects and expectations about attachment relationships" (Howell, 2005, p. 150). These internal working models emerge from a composite of implicit experiential conclusions, affective reactions, and unconscious procedures of relationship in response to repetitive interactions between child and caregiver(s). They are an adaptation and accommodation to the relational styles of significant others to ensure that a semblance of needs is met. Attachment patterns are composed of unconscious sub-symbolic procedural forms of memory based on early self-protective physiological and affective reactions (Bowlby, 1988a).

Secure attachment patterns provide affect regulation, reduce anxiety, and enhance feelings of well-being. They develop when caregivers are consistently attuned, available, and responsive to the young child (Doctors, 2007). Security is developed in the youngster through the caregivers' ongoing availability and emotional responsiveness, consistency, and dependability, where such caregivers are experienced as "stronger and/or wiser" (Bowlby, 1988a, p. 12). Securely attached children and adults deal with emotional disruption and distress by expressing and/or acknowledging it as it is emerging and then reaching out for comfort (Mikulincer, Florian, & Tolmatz, 1990). Securely attached children develop the ability to self-reflect, to remember their personal history, and to comment on their own process of thinking (Main, Kaplan, & Cassidy, 1985). Fonagy and his colleagues (1996) report that securely attached children make spontaneous, self-reflective comments and have complex and coherent narratives. They can judge their impact on others and evaluate their own behavior.

In summarizing their research on attachment patterns, Ainsworth and her colleagues (1978) concluded that the young child's security or lack thereof is generally determined by the quality of emotional, physical, and nonverbal communication in primary dependent relationships. Tasca, Balfour, Ritchie, and Bissada (2007) report that patterns of insecure anxious and avoidant attachment both develop in response to infant and childhood caregivers who are unavailable or insensitive. Children who develop anxious ambivalent attachment patterns usually have parents who were unpredictably responsive, whereas those with avoidant attachment patterns had parents who were predictably unresponsive (Main, 1995). Other authors indicate that avoidant attachment results when a child (and perhaps even an adolescent or an adult) perceives the primary attachment figure(s) as rejecting and punitive (Cozolino, 2006; Wallin, 2007). In each of these situations, it is the quality of the early childhood relationships that affects the person's capacity to reflect on life's experiences and to put such emotional experiences into a coherent narrative.

Anxiously ambivalent attached individuals express intense affect and distress in a hyper-vigilant and/or preoccupied manner. They tend to form dependent and clingy relationships and make unreasonable emotional demands for security, reassurance, and nurturance (Bartholomew & Horowitz, 1991) while also being either passive or overwhelmed in intimate relationships. If, in early development, significant others are experienced as inconsistent or unpredictably responsive, an excessive focus on clinging dependency and physical attachment may ensue. Their relationships may become overvalued, and the person may be overadapted to others as a result of an anxious ambivalent attachment pattern (Main, 1990). The life scripts of such individuals involve an unconscious escalating and/or minimizing of both awareness and expression of relational needs and feelings of attachment (Main, 1995).

Hesse's (1999) research revealed that adults with ambivalent attachment patterns may alternate between affective expressions of confused/passive and fearful/overwhelmed narratives about the course of their lives. They use psychological jargon, vague phrases, or irrelevancies to describe their life experiences. Hysteric or histrionic relational patterns reflect an ambivalent attachment style (Schore, 2002). In my clinical practice, I have found that clients with a life script based on ambivalent attachment patterns are highly adaptive within important relationships, such as in a marriage or a close friendship. They often feel unhappy with the other person's lack of emotional acknowledgement and care, yet they remain uncomfortably dependent in the relationship, always attached to the other's misattunements yet unable to separate. Perhaps rather than thinking of such individuals as "ambivalent," it would be useful to think of them as desperate for connection and anxious about loss. They have an implicit fear of abandonment.

Individuals with avoidant attachment patterns express their distress by dismissing or undervaluing the importance of relationships, either inhibiting or exaggerating emotional expression and avoiding intimacy (Kobak & Sceery, 1988; Main, 1990). They may be disdainful of vulnerability and tender expressions of affection and/or prone to anger. Main's (1995) research indicates that mothers of infants with an avoidant attachment style were emotionally unavailable; they tended to withdraw when the child was sad and were uncomfortable with physical touch. As an adaptive survival reaction to the caregiver's predictable unresponsiveness to the infant's affects and relational needs, the child learned to inhibit his communication of emotions, needs, and internal experiences. As a result, people with a history of avoidant attachment patterns unconsciously create a life script wherein they anticipate rejection. They form strategies of interpersonal relatedness in which they do not express, or may not even be conscious of, their attachment-related feelings and needs.

Hesse's (1999) Adult Attachment Interview reveals that avoidant patterns of attachment in adults (and therefore a possible indication of a troubling life script) are evident in adults' contradictory statements about their childhood experiences and the quality of contact with their parents or in other significant relationships. They engage in denial and disavowal of negative relational experiences, and they lack memory about dependent relational interactions. They diminish the significance of punishment and rejection in their lives and insist on the importance of self-reliance. In adulthood, they may express this avoidant attachment style by being dominant or cold in interpersonal relationships (Horowitz, Rosenberg, & Bartholomew, 1993).

Schore (2002) has suggested that avoidant attachment styles are evident in the quality of interpersonal contact made by people who engage in either obsession or narcissistic self-enhancement. People who obsess are deeply lonely because of their avoidant attachment patterns. They fill the relationship void with habitual worry and repetitive fantasizing. Those who are narcissistically self-aggrandizing or self-depreciating are also deeply lonely as a result of their avoidant attachment patterns, but they distract themselves temporarily through their self-focus and their demands for attention. In my own psychotherapy practice I have found that clients who operate primarily from an avoidant attachment pattern disavow their affect and are usually desensitized from their bodily sensations. They may focus on how their body looks from the outside, but they lack a sense of feeling internal sensations and internal physiological communication. Effective psychotherapy usually involves helping them to identify and own their body sensations and related affect. They have an implicit fear of vulnerability.

Disorganized attachment patterns reveal the profound psychological disorientation caused by unresolved trauma and significant loss of reparative relational contact. In response to a sense of relational disruption, young children will engage in the self-protective behaviors of freezing, flailing, turning away, and transposing affect (Fraiberg, 1982). With repeated use, these self-protective maneuvers may become fixated and form, in part, specific attachment patterns that contribute to the disorganization of the sense of self. Disorganized attachment patterns emerge when caregivers are experienced as the only source of needs satisfaction and simultaneously as a source of danger. Children with disorganized attachment patterns perceive their caregivers as predictably neglectful and/or punishing.

Infant disorganization is the result not only of profound psychological disruptions with parents whose anger or abuse is frightening, but also with parents who are themselves frightened. Disorganized relational patterns are thought also to arise and become fixated in response to repeated physical or sexual abuse or to caregivers who are themselves dissociated or having psychotic episodes (Bloom, 1997). When infants or young children are in the middle of ongoing violent arguments within a family, they become emotionally confused and their loyalties are torn; their affects and relational attachments may become disorganized. In my clinical experience I have found that clients with disorganized insecure attachment patterns may dissociate when under stress and may fragment into alter ego states or personalities. Each ego state or personality may express one of the other insecure attachment patterns, such as ambivalent, avoidant, or isolated (Doctors, 2007).

With many borderline individuals, their emotionally confused narratives about their early relational experiences reflect a history of disorganized attachment (Schore, 2002). In my experience, an empathetic way to understand borderline clients is to think of them as very young children suffering from an early relational and emotional confusion that is profoundly disorganizing. They lack the capacity to find consistent affect regulation, comfort, stabilization, or enhancement in intimate relationships. They require psychotherapy that provides a calming regulation of affect and consistency in relationship.

Some writers have demonstrated that disorganized attachment is a crucial factor in the development of dissociation in children and adults (Blizard, 2003; Liotti, 1999; Lyons-Ruth, Dutra, Schuder, & Bianchi, 2006; Muller, Sicoli, & Lemieux, 2000). Some clients with disorganized attachment patterns, when not using dissociation as a self-regulating process, seem overwhelmed by painful bodily reactions. This is particularly evident in my clients who have experienced physical and sexual trauma. Their emotional memories are conveyed by pain, physical tension, and intense restlessness. When these physiological memories are too intense, such clients may either desensitize their body or dissociate entirely as a way to escape the emotional and body memories. Putnam (1992) describes such dissociation as the "escape when there is no escape" (p. 104). Clients with disorganized attachment have a physiologically intense, implicit fear of violation.

Our therapeutic task is to provide a quality of professional involvement that gives such clients a sense of safety, stability, and dependability in relationship. Such consistency often helps the emotionally disorganized client to know the story that is being conveyed by the pain, tension, or restlessness. Disorganized attachment patterns can change as a result of an ongoing attuned and reliably involved therapeutic relationship (Cozolino, 2006).

Isolated attachment results from a series of experiences wherein the caregivers are experienced as repeatedly neglectful, untrustworthy, and/or invasive (O'Reilly-Knapp, 2001). The child's natural dependency on parents is met with an accumulation of rhythmic misattunements and, alternately, invasive and/or neglectful caregiving. To be vulnerable is sensed as dangerous. The child may then develop patterns of relationship marked by a social façade, psychological withdrawal, intense internal criticism, and the absence of emotional expression (Erskine, 2001a). An isolated attachment style is revealed in the quality of interpersonal contact made by individuals who use schizoid withdrawal to manage relationships. In my therapeutic practice I have found that clients who use emotional withdrawal to manage relationships report that significant caregivers were consistently misattuned to their physiological rhythms, misinterpreted their emotional expressions, and were controlling or invasive of the client's sense of identity. In some cases, their caregivers were themselves withdrawn and emotionally unavailable. Clients with an isolated attachment pattern have an implicit fear of invasion.

General considerations

Children may develop more than one attachment pattern. In the relationship with mothers, specific patterns of attachment may be formed that are uniquely different from patterns formed through interactions with fathers. If another dependent relationship is available to a child (such as a grandparent, aunt or uncle, older sibling, or nanny), alternative patterns of self-in-relationship may emerge and be significant in establishing and maintaining relationships throughout life. For example, individuals may have one relationship pattern with women and a distinctly different one with men. Or, a person may have one pattern with those who are in the same age range and a remarkably different pattern with someone who is much older. More than one relational or attachment pattern may be encoded in a client's stories or fantasies about family members, friends, or coworkers. These multiple patterns may also be enacted or engendered in the therapeutic relationship.

Throughout this chapter I have been using the generalizing term "attachment patterns." In both my clinical practice and in my teaching of psychotherapy, I make a distinction between attachment style, attachment patterns, and attachment disorder. I relate these three categories to the extent, pervasiveness, and quality of relational encounters inherent in a client's life script. I think of these three categories on a continuum from a mild to a moderate to a severe expression of an early childhood-influenced life script.

Attachment "style" refers to a general way in which an insecure attachment from early childhood may affect the client's way of being in the world. A "style" is not particularly problematic to the individual or to others except when that individual is under extreme stress and may revert to childlike patterns of self-regulation. Clients will reveal this level of their life script in their descriptions of how they managed a crisis or a family reunion, through dreams or an envisioned future, and through subtle transferential enactments.

Attachment "pattern" refers to a more problematic level of functioning on a day-by-day basis in relationships with others. An individual's repetitive attachment pattern is often more uncomfortable to family members and close associates than to the individual, who often sees his own behavior as natural and ordinary. As tiredness or stress increases, these individuals are likely to revert to archaic patterns of clinging, avoidance, disorganization, or isolation. When the internal stress becomes too great, they will seek psychotherapy in the hope of finding relief from the symptoms of depression, anxiety, relational conflicts and failures, low self-esteem, and physiological tensions. Attachment patterns become evident early in psychotherapy through the client's encoded stories, overt transferences enacted in both therapy and daily life, and the physiological and affective response engendered in the psychotherapist.

An attachment "disorder" refers to the continual reliance on early childhood internal working models of relationship and archaic methods of coping with relational disruptions. An individual's archaic form of self-regulation and coping is pervasive in nearly every relationship with people and in nearly every aspect of the person's life. Clients with an attachment disorder will often dramatically enact some element of their life script in their first and subsequent sessions. Evidence of the severity of the script may be embedded in their presenting problem, embodied in their physical gestures, and engendered in a strong physical and emotional reaction from the psychotherapist.

Therapeutic involvement

Each of the four insecure attachment patterns—ambivalent, avoidant, disorganized, and isolated—results in an accumulation of emotional experiences and the creation of script beliefs about self and others and the quality of life that serve to shape ensuing perceptions and affect about relationships. Siegel (1999) suggests that a child's attachment relationship to someone other than the parents—such as a grandparent, aunt, older sibling, teacher, or adult friend—provides an alternative attachment pattern to ones that may develop with parents who are frightening, neglecting, depressed, abusive, or invasive. An affectively and rhythmically attuned psychotherapist provides the person with that other who is sensitive, respectful, validating, consistent, and dependable. The psychotherapist's attunement provides the client with the security of affect-regulating transactions (Erskine, Moursund, & Trautmann, 1999). Such affect regulation is then within a sensitive, caring relationship rather than in the client's archaic attempts at self-regulation through clinging and over-adaptation, physical and emotional distancing, emotional confusion and fragmentation, or social façade and emotional withdrawal. Insecure attachment patterns can become secure through a caring therapeutic relationship.

While practicing psychotherapy, I often work through therapeutic inference, a decoding of the minute and subtle client/therapist transferential affects and enactments, interruptions to contact, and body sensations and movements as well as the client's reported stories that reflect his or her transferences with other people. A sensitive phenomenological and historical inquiry often reveals an outline of the client's early relational experiences. Examples of such an inquiry include:

"What was your experience when your mother or father tucked you in bed at night?" "Imagine what it was like for you to be spoon fed by your mother"; "What was the quality of care your received when you where sick or injured?" "What kind of greeting did you receive when you returned home from school?" Although this inquiry may not evoke explicit memories, almost every client has an emotional reaction that reveals procedural memories and provides some indication of the quality of his or her early relational experiences. The response to each inquiry may lead to further inquiry into the quality of the current relationship between the therapist and client and then return to further inquiry into the client's early physiological survival reactions and implicit procedural ways of relating.

Unconscious relational patterns may be "sensed" by the client as physiological tensions, confusing affects, longings, and repulsions. The unconscious memories of previous relationships may shape a person's interpretation of current events, orient or distract from what is occurring now, and form either anticipations or inhibitions of future events. The sub-symbolic procedural memories that form attachment patterns may be revealed either through exaggerations or minimizations of affect, in stories or metaphors, in fantasy and dreams, and/or in emotional responses in others. Each of these aspects of the transference/countertransference dyad is an unconscious unfolding of two intersubjective life stories and a window of opportunity into both the client's and the psychotherapist's unconscious experiences.

In an attempt to understand the script dynamics that are preverbal, sub-symbolic, and implicit, I attend to the various ways the infantile and early childhood dramas or script protocols are lived in current relationships. Each of the questions that follow here about the transference/countertransference relationship provides a window of opportunity to view the family interactions that may constitute the "primal dramas" and early emotional experiences of the client's life script. There are several ways in which the primal protocol is unconsciously expressed while involving intimate others, including the psychotherapist. I am continually curious as to what the client's unconscious early childhood story is.

1. *Enacted in the client's behavior*: What primal dramas of early childhood—such as emotional abandonment, neglect, abuse, ridicule, fear, rage, or despair—are possibly being lived out in the

client's behavior and transactions with the therapist and/or other people?

2. *Entrenched in the client's affect*: What deprivation of attunement is expressed in the client's escalation or immunization of emotions?

3. *Embodied in the client's physiology*: What is the client experiencing within his or her body? What is the client's body revealing about his or her relational history?

4. *Encoded in the client's stories and metaphors*: What relational experiences are being revealed through the content and style of the client's narrative?

5. *Envisioned in the client's fantasies, hopes, and dreams*: What developmental and relational needs were unrequited and may require therapeutic responsiveness and/or validation?

6. *Embedded in the client's internal and external interruptions to contact*: At what developmental stage would this interruption to contact be a "normal" way to manage the cumulative failures in significant, dependent relationships?

7. *Engendered in another's emotional response*: What physiological and affective responses, concordant or complementary, are stimulated within me or other people in this client's life?

Attachment patterns—the protocol and palimpsest of a life script—are not "conscious" in that they are not transposed to thought, concept, social language, or narrative and therefore remain as unformulated experiences. It is our task as psychotherapists to attune to the client's affects, rhythms, developmental levels of functioning, and relational needs while attending to the client's narrative. The client's narrative provides the basis for further inquiry about his or her phenomenological experiences. As psychotherapists, it is our skill and attunement in providing a new and reparative relationship that allows unconscious archaic insecure relational patterns to change.

In the psychotherapy of life scripts it is important that the psychotherapist understand and appreciate that attachment patterns, unconscious organizing principles, and life scripts are desperate and creative attempts to self-regulate while managing and adjusting to the failures that occurred in significant and dependent relationships throughout life; scripts are self-protective ways of compensating for what is/ was missing in relationship while ensuring a semblance of relationship. The process of script formation is relationally interactive and personally creative—an accommodation, assimilation, and adaptation (Piaget, 1954) to the neglects, misattunements, relational requirements, or even demands of significant others. It involves a neurologically based generalization of specific affect-laden experiences and an unconscious anticipation that these generalized experiences will be repeated throughout life (Stern, 1985).

The psychotherapy of life script necessitates an understanding and appreciation of each individual's unique temperament as well as these creative adjustments, coping and adaptive styles, and resulting internal and external interruptions to contact. The psychotherapist's sensitivity to and understanding of unconscious experiential conclusions, contact interruptions, and the unique relational nature of the therapeutic involvement is essential for an in-depth psychotherapy of archaic relational patterns, current relational disturbances, and fixated systems of psychological organization.

CHAPTER SIX

Life scripts: unconscious relational patterns and psychotherapeutic involvement

Life scripts are a complex set of unconscious relational patterns based on physiological survival reactions, implicit experiential conclusions, explicit decisions, and/or self-regulating introjections, made under stress, at any developmental age, that inhibit spontaneity and limit flexibility in problem-solving, health maintenance, and in relationship with people (Erskine, 1980).

Scripts are often developed by infants, young children, adolescents, and even adults as a means of coping with disruptions in significant dependent relationships that repeatedly failed to satisfy crucial developmentally based needs. These unconscious script patterns most likely have been formulated, reinforced, and elaborated over a number of developmental ages as a result of repeated ruptures in relationships with significant others. Life scripts are a result of the cumulative failures in significant, dependent relationships. Such life scripts are unconscious systems of psychological organization and self-regulation primarily formed from implicit memories (Erskine, 2008; Fosshage, 2005) and expressed through physiological discomforts, escalations or minimizations of affect, and the transferences that occur in everyday life.

These unconscious relational patterns, schemata, or life plans influence the reactions and expectations that define for us the kind of world we live in, the people we are, and the quality of interpersonal relationships we will have with others. Encoded physiologically in body tissues and biochemical events, affectively as sub-cortical brain stimulation and cognitively in the form of beliefs, attitudes, and values, these responses form a blueprint that guides the way we live our lives. Such scripts involve a complex network of neural pathways formed as thoughts, affects, biochemical and physiological reactions, fantasy, relational patterns, and the important process of homeostatic self-regulation of the organism. Scripts formed from physiological survival reactions, implicit experiential conclusions, relational failures, prolonged misattunements and neglects, as well as chronic shock and acute trauma, all require a psychotherapy wherein the therapeutic relationship is central and is evident through the respect, reliability, and the dependability of a caringly, involved, skilled real person (Erskine, 1993).

Literature review

Eric Berne, in articulating the theory of transactional analysis, termed these unconscious patterns, schemata, or archaic blueprints a "script" (1961). Berne originally defined a script as an "extensive unconscious life plan" (p. 23) that reflects the "primal dramas of childhood"; scripts "are derivatives, or more precisely, adaptations of infantile reactions and experiences" (p. 116). Later, he referred to a script as a "life plan based on decisions made in childhood, reinforced by parents, justified by subsequent events and culminating in a chosen alternative" (1972, p. 446).

Fritz Perls, who co-developed Gestalt therapy, also described such self-confirming, repetitive conclusions and patterns (1944) and called it a "life script" (Perls & Baumgardner, 1975) that was composed of both an "early scene" and a resulting "life plan" (Perls, Hefferline, & Goodman, 1951, pp. 305–306). Alfred Adler referred to these patterns or schemata as "life style" (Ansbacher & Ansbacher, 1956); Sigmund Freud used the term "repetition compulsion" to describe similar phenomena (1920g); and contemporary psychoanalytic writers have referred to a developmentally preformed pattern as "unconscious fantasy" (Arlow, 1969a, p. 8) and as "schemata" (Arlow, 1969b, p. 29; Slap, 1987). In psychoanalytic self psychology the phrase "self system" is used to refer to reoccurring patterns of low self-esteem and self-defeating interactions (Basch, 1988, p. 100) that are the result of "unconscious organizing principles" termed "pre-reflexive unconscious" (Stolorow & Atwood, 1989, p. 373). In dynamic systems theory, the term "preferred attractor states" is used to describe repetitive patterns of organizing affective and cognitive experiences and relating to others (Thelen & Smith, 1994).

John Bowlby (1969, 1973, 1980) also wrote about unconscious relational patterns and described the biological imperative of prolonged physical and affective bonding in the creation of a visceral core from which all experiences of self and others emerge. Bowlby referred to these patterns as internal working models that are generalized from past experiences. Bowlby's theory provides a model for understanding how an infant's or young child's physiological survival reactions and implicit experiential conclusions may form an "internal working model," the antecedents of an unconscious life script.

The general psychology literature has described such schemata, unconscious plans, or life scripts as "cognitive structures" that reflect an individual's organization of the world into a unified system of beliefs, concepts, attitudes, and expectations (Lewin, 1951); "personal constructs" (Kelly, 1955); "self-confirmation theory" (Andrews, 1988, 1989); "internalized relationship patterns" (Beitman, 1992); and as a self-reinforcing system or "a self-protection plan" referred to as both the "racket system" (Erskine & Zalcman, 1979) and the "script system" (Erskine & Moursund, 1988). Each of the authors cited above describes some aspect of unconscious relational patterns or life scripts. Each author suggests a therapy that involves some combination of analysis, interpretation, explanation, interpersonal relatedness, or behavioral change. It is my opinion that in order to do a thorough "script cure," it is necessary to provide a relational psychotherapy that integrates affective, behavioral, cognitive, and physiological dimensions of psychotherapy so that unconscious experience may become conscious (Erskine, 1980).

Unconscious processes

The purpose of a serious in-depth psychotherapy is the resolution of a client's unconscious script inhibitions or compulsions in relationship with people, inflexibility in problem-solving, and deficiencies in health care. Such a "script cure" involves an internal reorganization and new integration of affective and cognitive structures, undoing physiological retroflections, decommissioning introjections and consciously choosing behavior that is meaningful and appropriate in the current relationship or task rather than behavior that is determined by compulsion or fear or archaic coping reactions. The aim of an in-depth and integrative psychotherapy is to provide the quality of therapeutic relationship, understanding, and skill that facilitates the client becoming conscious of what was previously unconscious so that he can be intimate with others, maintain good health, and engage in the tasks of everyday life without preformed restrictions.

What most people generally consider as "conscious memory" is usually composed of explicit memory—the type of memory that is described as symbolic: a photographic image, impressionistic painting, or audio recording of what was said in past events. Such explicit or declarative memory is usually anchored in the capacity to use social language and concepts to describe experience. Experience that is "unconscious" usually lacks explicit recall of an event because it is sub-symbolic, implicit, and without language. Sub-symbolic or implicit memories, that are problematic or unresolved, are potentially "felt" as physiological tensions, undifferentiated affect, longings or repulsions, and pre-reflective relational and self-regulating patterns (Erskine, 2008; Fosshage, 2005; Kihlstrom, 1984). Bucci (2001) describes such physiological sensations as unconscious communication of emotional information processing. Such physiologically sensed affective memories are forms of experience that are neither linguistically descriptive nor verbally narrative. Physiological and affective experience may be revealed in body language that signals the person's unconscious story.

I find it important to think in developmental terms and concepts, not only in terms of unconscious process as reflecting either trauma or repression. I generally conceptualize unconscious process (pre-symbolic, sub-symbolic, procedural, or implicit memory) as being composed of several developmental and experiential levels: preverbal; never conceptualized; never acknowledged within the family; the absence of memory because significant relational experiences never occurred; actively avoided verbalization as a result of punishment, guilt, or shame; and pre-reflective patterns of self-in-relationship that are composed of attachment styles, strategies of self-regulation, relational needs, script beliefs, and introjections (Erskine, 2008).

When we define script as a complex set of unconscious relational patterns based on physiological survival reactions, implicit experiential conclusions, explicit decisions, and/or self-regulating introjections, made under stress, we are including script patterns that are formed from explicit memory embedded in conscious or preconscious decisions of a previous developmental period. We are also describing the structured result of pre-symbolic and implicit memory, as well as unconscious procedural ways of relating to others, unconscious bodily processes, the unconscious aspects of acute trauma and dissociation, the unconscious effects of cumulative misattunement and neglect, unconscious introjection and/or pre-reflective unconscious organization of attachment styles, relational needs, and self-regulation. Each of these antecedents of a life script requires a specific form of therapy to enable the unconscious experiences to become conscious and to facilitate the emergence of new patterns of thinking, feeling, body process, behavior, and interpersonal contact.

Injunctions and decisions: explicit memory

Berne (1972), English (1972), Steiner (1971), Stuntz (1972), and Woolams (1973) have each described script as being formed by parental injunctions and a child's acquiescence to the parents' messages. Their ideas vary in how injunctions are communicated, the critical developmental periods when a child is most susceptible to such messages, and the psychological severity of both injunctions and the resulting compliance. Each of these theorists basically views script as an interaction of injunctions, counterinjunctions, compliance, and early developmental protocol. Generally, therapy of these script dynamics is described by these authors as consisting of explanation, illustration, confirmation, and interpretation.

Steiner (1971) put particular emphasis on the coercive power of the parents' overt and ulterior messages to harmfully shape a child's life while Bob and Mary Goulding (1978) described a list of such injunctions that formed the basis of a child making script decisions. Their examples of script decisions are examples of explicit memories wherein an actual scene from childhood is consciously remembered, a corresponding parental injunction is identified, and the child's original decision to comply with the injunction is articulated. Because these memories and the resulting script decisions are explicit forms of memory they may be amenable to a redecision therapy. As a result of this conscious awareness of how the script was originally decided, with an awareness of the lifelong consequences, and with the therapist's support, a life changing redecision is possible (Erskine, 1974). Several examples of how redecisions are an effective form of script therapy when the script dynamics and decisions can be explicitly remembered are in Bob and Mary Goulding's book *Changing Lives Through Redecision Therapy* (1979) and their videotape *Redecision Therapy* (1987), as well as in Erskine and Moursund's *Integrative Psychotherapy in Action* (1988).

Allen and Allen (1972) suggested that the therapists' permissions to live differently than the parental injunctions dictate are an important element in counterbalancing or altering the effects of such script forming memory because the permissions provide new explicit memories of an involved other person who is invested in the client's welfare. In a 1980 article, I identified the behavioral, intrapsychic, and physiological dimensions of "script cure" and established the theoretical basis for the script system, originally referred to as the racket system (Erskine & Zalcman, 1979).

The script system provides a model of how a life script is formed from explicit decisions, implicit and pre-symbolic experiential conclusions, fixated patterns of self-regulation, and/or introjections. The script system is actually lived out in current life where it is expressed through behavior, the quality of relationships, fantasy, internal physical sensations, and selected explicit memories (Erskine & Moursund, 1988). The script system describes how the life script is operational in life today as core beliefs about self, others, and the quality of life. The script system is composed of internal experience, perception, imagination, and conceptualization that are augmented by generalizations and elaborations that construct a "reality" of ourselves, others, and the quality of life. It leads us to be afraid of or angry at what may never occur, to be deeply hurt by our anticipations, and to suffer unnecessarily in current relationships because of the self-reinforcing nature of script beliefs. Chapter Seven in this book, entitled "The script system: The unconscious organization of experience" explains the components of the script system, provides a useful diagram, and illustrates, through a case example, how an unconscious script was operational in a client's day-to-day life.

Implicit memory

Cumulative misattunements and experiential conclusions

Not all life scripts are based on parental injunctions or script decisions, contrary to what is emphasized in much of the literature on script theory. Unconscious conclusions based on lived experience account for a major portion of life scripts. Implicit experiential conclusions are composed of unconscious affect, physical and relational reactions that are without concept, language, sequencing of events, or conscious thought. Implicit script conclusions may represent early childhood preverbal or never-verbalized experiences that, because of the lack of relationship, concept and adequate language, remain unconscious (Erskine, 2008). Later in life these unconscious conclusions are experienced and expressed through a sense of unfulfilled longing or repulsion and unexpressed or undifferentiated affect. They may also be sensed as confusion, emptiness, uncomfortable body sensations, and/or a procedural knowledge for caution in relationships. These physiological sensations are sub-symbolic or pre-symbolic nonverbal affective memories.

In my clinical experience many clients' life scripts are an expression of procedural, sub-symbolic, and implicit memories of conditioned affective and sensorimotor responses, repetitive self-regulating behaviors, and preemptory, anticipatory, and inhibiting reactions that culminate in unconscious conclusions. Such implicit experiential conclusions provide a variety of psychological functions, such as orientation, self-protection, and a categorization of experiences. Implicit memory refers to the processing of subliminal stimuli, physiological sensations, and affect, as well as lived experience that, rather than becoming conscious as explicit memory, remain non-symbolized and therefore unconscious until there is an interested and involved other person who facilitates internal contact, concept formation, and linguistic expression.

Implicit script conclusions may unconsciously express developmental needs that were not satisfied, crucial relational interactions which never or seldom occurred, and the repeated failure of optimal responsiveness by primary caregivers. When primary caregivers are repeatedly distressed, anxious, or angry, crucial infancy and early childhood relational interactions may never have occurred. Examples of such crucial parent–child interactions are vital eye-to-eye contact, soothing touch, or the reflective mirroring on the parent's face as the child is either delighted or distressed (Beebe, 2005; Field, Diego, Hernandez-Reif, Schanberg, & Kuhn, 2003; Weinberg & Tronick, 1998). Such repeated parental failure to attune and respond to the developmental needs of the young child constitutes psychological neglect. These failures are not necessarily—or even usually—the result of deliberate and conscious choices on the part of caregivers. They are more often caused by parental ignorance, fatigue, or preoccupation with other concerns; or the parents may be depressed and tangled in script patterns of their own that are incompatible with meeting the child's needs. The child, however, is unlikely to understand adult preoccupation, depression, fatigue, or script manifestations and may well fantasize intentionality when none is present. "Mom has no time for me"; "I'm not important enough." "Dad doesn't even look at me; he must be really mad at me because I am so bad." Such implicit experiential conclusions, over time, form an unconscious life script.

Children who grow up with or go to school in an environment of psychological neglect, prolonged affective misattunements, or repetitive ridicule, often fail to develop a sense of competency, self-definition, or the capacity to make an impact on others. Their necessary sense of security, self-value, efficacy and agency, or self-definition, can be slowly and repeatedly undermined by disparaging comments, ridicule, or humiliating remarks from parents, teachers, siblings, and other children. The result may be a pervasive sense of shame and the conviction "something's wrong with me" (Erskine, 1994). In some situations, children and adolescents may unconsciously overcompensate by becoming extremely competent, demandingly self-definitive, or insistent on making an impact on others. The affective memories of such repetitive neglect, misattunement, or criticism (although implicit and/or procedural rather than explicit or conscious), shape conclusions about self and a style of relationship that may linger for many years. The result of such neglect is referred to as cumulative trauma. Cumulative trauma is a delayed reaction to scores of implicit and/or procedural memories of significant relational disruptions and repeated nonverbal conclusions about self, others, and the quality of life (Erskine, Moursund, & Trautmann, 1999; Lourie, 1996).

Many personally disturbing feelings and script beliefs about self-value, belonging within a group, or the capacity to learn have their origin in the unconscious physical and affective responses to the cumulative criticism, disregard, and rejections that may have occurred in school or on the playground. As well as the early child-parent-sibling interactions, the interpersonal dynamics between peers from preschool to university have a significant influence in forming unconscious procedural patterns and script beliefs about self, others, and the quality of membership in a group. The attitudes and behaviors of teachers may also be significant in shaping unconscious identification and/or experiential conclusions.

Cumulative trauma

Berne (1961) differentiated between "traumatic neurosis" caused by a specific trauma at a specific time in life, and "psychoneurosis," emerging from an ongoing series of misattunements over a long period of time. Khan (1963), who coined the term "cumulative trauma" to describe the unconscious effect of repetitive negative or neglectful events, recognized that relationship failure is the primary cause. He writes, "Cumulative trauma is the result of the breaches in the mother's role as a protective shield over the whole course of the child's development, from infancy to adolescence" (p. 290).

Even though it can lead to the same sort of script pattern typical in the cases of acute trauma, cumulative trauma is initially developed in a different way. Rather than protecting oneself from the pain of a specific incident, the person must deal with a slow but constant accumulation of tiny, almost insignificant misattunements, hurts, neglects, or criticisms. Over time, the person comes to accept this pattern as simply a part of the way he/others/life has to be. Like the slow drip of calcium-laden water that builds over the years into a stalactite or stalagmite, the drip of cumulative trauma results in the slow building up of script beliefs in the caverns of one's mind. There is often very little to point to in later life, no way to say "That is what happened to me, and this is how I reacted." Each early childhood neglect and misattunement in and of itself may not be traumatic, but they lead to script building consequences cumulatively and are recognized (if one eventually becomes conscious of the pattern and understands the influence) only in retrospect.

Lourie (1996) defines cumulative trauma as "the totality of the psychological failures, or misattunements, that a child endures from infancy through adolescence and beyond" (p. 277). When parents are not consistently contactful or do not resonate with the child's expression of affect, they fail to acknowledge or validate the child's relational needs. Children whose affective expressions and relational needs are not acknowledged and validated have no social mirror in which to view themselves and therefore lack the necessary relational partner whose mirroring response or explanation may provide an articulation and possible reversal of the emerging script conclusions. Cumulative misattunement to the child's emotional expressions, developmental needs, and emerging relational patterns and conclusions interferes with the child's opportunity to discover and create himself as a unique and emotionally supported individual within a matrix of social relationships (Trautmann & Erskine, 1999).

"A severe consequence of cumulative trauma," says Lourie (1996), "is the loss of trust in and knowledge of self resulting from the vast assortment of parental misattunements … that the child endures" (p. 277). These children may conclude that at their core they are inadequate and unlovable; they hide this conclusion and resulting belief from others—and from themselves—and the result may be an inability to form a lasting and satisfying intimate relationship. They may withdraw from the company of others or may chain themselves to a treadmill of endless and superficial social activities; they may constantly demand attention and care; or they may make themselves overresponsible for the needs of those around them. As a result, there is a loss of both internal and interpersonal contact (Erskine & Moursund, 1988; Perls, Hefferline & Goodman, 1951). The person may lose contact with his own sensations, feelings, needs, thoughts, or memories, as well as interrupting interpersonal contact with others.

All these contact interrupting cognitive and/or behavioral manifestations of the experiential conclusions serve to distract the person from the implicit memory of loneliness, emptiness, and misattunement that the child may have actually experienced. These script-based beliefs, fantasies, and behaviors do not satisfy the unrequited childhood relational needs—and, over the long run, actually prevent the satisfaction of current relational needs—but the internal and external interruptions to contact distract from an awareness of such needs for a time, dulling the pain and providing temporary relief (Moursund & Erskine, 2004).

Interruptions to contact (such as denial, disavowal, desensitization, retroflection, introjection, relational distancing) reduce the awareness and distress of relational failure. They may temporarily alleviate anxiety and the memory of neglectful or traumatic events while distracting from the sense of interpersonal loss. They are "normal" in that they are human, adaptive reactions to repeatedly unmet biological and relational needs. When used repeatedly, or to an extreme degree, contact interruptions interfere with the important integration of affect, physiology, and memory by creating perceptual distortion, emotional confusion, limitations in information processing, and a lack of awareness of relational needs.

Relational needs include many dimensions of interpersonal contact and attachment such as affective and rhythmic attunement, mutual influence and validation, and the shared use of language to communicate phenomenological experience. Some of the many dimensions of relational needs are: a sense of security in relationship; validation of one's affect and internal experience; a sense of reliance, dependability, and consistency from a significant other person; a shared experience; self-definition; the capacity for impact in relationship; to have the other initiate; and to express one's appreciation and gratitude (Erskine, 1998a; Erskine, Moursund, & Trautmann, 1999; Erskine & Trautmann, 1996). The experience of prolonged neglect of these relational needs interrupts internal contact and forms the core of implicit script conclusions.

Body script

Life scripts are often encoded biochemically within bodily tissue. In almost every case of script, whether formed by explicit decisions, unconscious experientially based conclusions, or survival reactions, there may be a corresponding biochemical and physiological response within the body. Because of the intense sub-cortical brain stimulation and biochemical activity at the time of script conclusion or decision, the person may be unable to freely express emotions and act in accordance with needs (Damasio, 1999). The amygdala and lymbic systems of the brain are overwhelmed and the natural physiological and affective expression may be turned inward—a physiological retroflection (Perls, Hefferline, & Goodman, 1951). This physiological retroflection that is paired with a lack of safety, an unexpressed protest, unexpressed fear, or a shutting down of the body's natural action, is often maintained years later as a physiological structure, habitual action, or inhibition of expression. When misattunement and neglect from significant others have persisted over time, these inhibiting retroflections actually become the person's physiological sense of "this is me." The stiff neck, the muscle pain in the shoulders, the grinding of teeth, the clenched fist, is what the client has always known. These manifestations of body scripts are encoded as physiological, as well as psychological, structures.

Life scripts that have an origin in either acute or chronic trauma, or even cumulative neglect, are almost always physiological—the script is within the body—as a result of the survival reactions within the hypothalamic-pituitary-adrenal axis of the brain and the corresponding muscular tension (Cozolino, 2006). These psychological survival reactions often reoccur as automatic and sudden responses that involve various organs, muscle groups, or even the total body, because of the brain's stimulation of neurotransmitters and hormones that affect every organ system (van der Kolk, 1994). The sudden reactivation of physiological survival reactions are not conscious (until after they have occurred) because the associational networks of the brain have become "fear conditioned" and are paired with other script dynamics such as core script beliefs, behavioral patterns, and a conglomerate of emotional memories (LeDoux, 1994).

When stress or neglect occurs early in life, is prolonged or extreme, brain functioning and behavior become organized around fear, rigidity, and an avoidance of stimulation and exploration (Cozolino, 2006). Several writings and research reports on early child development support the idea that script is formed by sub-symbolic physiological survival reactions, self-regulation patterns, and unconscious conclusions in response to the quality of both early and ongoing significant relationships (Beebe, 2005; Bloom, 1997; Field et al., 2003; Lyons-Ruth, Zoll, Connell, & Grunebaum, 1986; Tronick & Gianino, 1986; Weinberg & Tronick, 1998). The earlier the misattunement, neglect, or physical and emotional trauma, the more likely the script will be within the body and not accessible through language or a narrative form of therapy and, in many cases, not available to consciousness.

An effective and complete psychotherapy aimed at script cure must identify and ameliorate the physiological restrictions, inhibitions, and body tensions that interfere with affect, expression of current relational needs, or the maintenance of good health. When I engage in body script therapy, the treatment goal is to energize the body tissue that was inhibited and rigidified when developmentally based physical and relational needs were unsatisfied and primal feelings were repressed. Body script therapy may be the entrance into doing affective or cognitive therapy as a means of bringing unconscious experience to awareness, or it may be a concluding step in the treatment of specific script restrictions. Interventions at the level of body script include those approaches that lead to somatic change, such as attentive awareness to bodily process, gentle touch, deep massage work, tension relaxation, or proper diet, exercise, and recreational activities that enhance the flow of energy and movement of the body.

Script cure at the physiological level is a letting go of tensions, body armoring, and internal restrictions that inhibit the person from living life fully and easily within his or her own body. Changes in body script are often evident to an observer as a more relaxed appearance, freer movement, increased energy, and an established weight level that is appropriate for the person's frame. After experiencing an effective psychotherapy oriented to resolving physiological restrictions, inhibitions, and retroflection, people report having a greater sense of vitality, an ease of movement, and an increased sense of well-being.

A description of the methods that are useful in the cure of physiological aspects of life scripts is beyond the scope of this chapter. However, it is the responsibility of the psychotherapist to focus on bodily processes, retroflection, physiological survival-reactions, early childhood coping strategies (such as freezing, flailing, turning away), and even minute movements or silences. Each of these may be an expression of a physiological response to relational disruptions that are imbedded in a life script.

Introjection: Whose script is it?

Introjection is an unconscious self-protective identification with aspects of the personality of significant others that occurs in the absence of full contact, where crucial needs were unfilled in a dependent relationship. Introjection provides a psychological compensation for unsatisfied relational needs and disruptions in essential interpersonal contact. An external relational conflict is avoided but the conflict is, instead, internalized where it is seemingly easier to manage (L. Perls, 1978). Therefore, introjection is often accompanied by physiological survival reactions and retroflections (Perls, Hefferline, & Goodman, 1951).

Many aspects of a person's life script may actually be the result of introjecting parents', teachers', or significant others' feelings, bodily reactions, attitudes, script beliefs, behaviors, and relational patterns. It may be imperative in a thorough treatment of life script to identify the origin of the client's depression, disappointments, bitterness, spitefulness, or internal criticism. Are such attitudes, beliefs, anticipations, and behaviors the result of one's own life experiences, conclusions, and decisions? Or, are these the assumed thoughts, feelings, behaviors, and coping systems of a significant other that have been introjected? Is the script the result of a self-criticizing defense against awareness of the internal influence of an introjection (Erskine, 1988)? The therapeutic explanation and identification of the many aspects of introjection and the necessary psychotherapy are important in the treatment planning and selection of methods that lead to script cure. The specific methods in the treatment of introjection or vehement self-criticism and actual case examples are detailed in several other writings (Erskine, 2003; Erskine & Moursund, 1988; Erskine, Moursund, & Trautmann, 1999; Erskine & Trautmann, 2003; Moursund & Erskine, 2004). In a thorough psychotherapy aimed at script cure, it may be essential that the psychotherapist addresses the internalized elements of the personality of significant others and either provides a therapeutic interposition or a complete decommissioning of the introjection (Berne, 1961).

Transferences of everyday life

Although life scripts may be formed at any developmental age, in my clinical experience, tenacious life scripts are not formed by explicit decisions alone but are most commonly formed from a composite of implicit experiential conclusions, survival reactions, and introjections. The implicit memories of these script forming conclusions, survival reactions, and introjections are not directly available through the client's explicit memory or in any organized narrative about his early life experiences. Such early memories and implicit conclusions are revealed through bodily reactions, pre-reflective relational patterns, transference within the therapeutic relationship and, most commonly, through the transferences of everyday life (Freud, 1912b). The hurts and angers with family or friends or the fearfully anticipated reactions of coworkers, the disregard for one's health or general welfare, and the habitual worry, repetitive fantasies, or obsessions are examples of the unconscious transference of early emotional memory into the current events of everyday life.

Berne defines scripts as "transference phenomena" that may be reenacted over a lifetime and that are derived and adapted from "infantile reactions and experiences" and the "primal dramas of childhood" (1961, p. 116). In an effective psychotherapy, it is often necessary for the psychotherapist to help the client construct a narrative of his early emotional and relational experiences in order to gain an understanding and resolution of his transferential reactions. This is often accomplished through the therapeutic method of implication wherein the therapist co-constructs with the client meanings for his experience and provides both concepts and a sense of the significance to the affective and physiological memories. Transference both within the therapeutic relationship and the course of everyday life is often an expression of "the first traumatic experience, the protocol" and the cumulative "later versions or palimpsests" (ibid., p. 124) of the script—the unconscious experiential conclusions.

Transference within a therapy relationship, and even more commonly and frequently in the relationships and activities of everyday life, is an expression of the effects of previous relational disruptions and failures, as well as an expression of relational needs and a desire to achieve intimacy in relationships. It is an unconscious enactment of past affect-laden experiences and psychological functions such as self-regulation, compensation, or self-protection (Brenner, 1979; Erskine, 1993; Langs, 1976). Transference is a manifestation and expression of the unconscious dynamics of life scripts.

Elizabeth: an unconscious search for love

The following case example of Elizabeth's unconscious search for her mother's love is an illustration of how her life script was the result of implicit experiential conclusions, cumulative parental misattunement to her affect and relational needs, and an explicit script decision. In Elizabeth's psychotherapy we explored her bodily sensations and physiological survival reactions and how she may have introjected her mother's depression when she was an infant and preschool child. My phenomenological and historical inquiry, affective, developmental, and rhythmic attunement, and therapeutic inference revealed that the very young Elizabeth was deeply affected by her mother's depression. One of our therapeutic tasks was to separate her own unconscious reactive early childhood depression from the introjected depression of her mother and to provide a sensitive therapy to both aspects of the depression. Our psychotherapy focused on making her unconscious affect and physiological experience conscious and attending to her developmental needs for a dependable, consistent, and involved relationship. Interwoven through this case illustration are some examples of how the script was manifested in everyday life and the necessity for a relational and integrative psychotherapy aimed at achieving a script cure.

Elizabeth looked like a lost child when she began her psychotherapy. She described herself as "empty, lost and confused." In her initial sessions, she wondered if she had "inherited a depression" because she often felt "so empty inside." She dressed poorly, even though she had a well paying job. Her clothes neither fitted her well nor did the colors or patterns match. Her hair often looked uncombed and in need of a cut. My early impressions of Elizabeth were that she was a neglected and unloved child.

Elizabeth was married and described her relationship with her husband as "We mostly just live together" without much physical contact. She saw no problem with her marriage because she and her husband often did things together such as going to cinemas and she was pleased that he did the grocery shopping and all the cooking.

Elizabeth's father once angrily told her that Elizabeth's mother was "depressed" and that the depression was why her mother "abandoned" the family when Elizabeth was five years old. Her father would get angry and critical if Elizabeth ever asked any questions about her mother. There were no photos of Mother nor was there any contact with members of Mother's family. Mother ceased to exist. There was never any conversation between Elizabeth and her father about her mother's disappearance. Elizabeth's father never made any acknowledgement of Elizabeth's emotional loss of her mother and certainly no validation of her intense grief and need to be loved. She unconsciously concluded during her childhood years that her feelings, emptiness, and longings meant "I'm a bother to people."

Elizabeth could not consciously remember anything about her mother. She could not recall what her mother looked like. Father admitted that he had destroyed all the photographs of Mother, including wedding photos and photos of Elizabeth with her mother when she was a baby and preschooler. The result was that she walked the streets of New York City searching for a face that could be her mother's. Elizabeth's longing for love was unconscious. She was only aware of the emptiness inside and of a desperate "search."

She had no consciousness of her needs for mothering and loving. Whenever I inquired about any relational need Elizabeth might have, or about her mother, she would unconsciously stroke her lips or hair. I recognized these unconscious gestures as a need for security and early mothering even though she could neither think about nor verbalize her needs. Her self-soothing initially had no meaning to her until we talked about her lip and hair stroking many, many times and related the self-soothing to the need for mothering affection and soothing touch. Even though she had no consciousness for her need for mothering, she acted out her unconscious needs in the transference through her helplessness and demeanor of neglect.

Elizabeth found it incomprehensible that I would think about her between sessions. She had no sense that she could make an impact on me. Unlike other clients, Elizabeth never missed me when I traveled. She often said that she did not know what to talk about in our sessions. She expected me to be critical of her. In our early sessions, she was able to identify this expectation of my potential criticalness and related it to explicit memories of her father's "constant criticism of everyone." During this phase of therapy, she became conscious of having made an explicit script decision between the ages of ten and twelve to be cautious of everyone because "people are critical."

Elizabeth could recall some stories and explicit memories of interactions with her father, particularly about special events or vacations where they did activities together, such as going to football games or swimming. But Elizabeth had no capacity to either conceptualize or talk about feeling cared for in a relationship, nor did she have any awareness of her relational needs. During the psychotherapy, Elizabeth's implicit memories were transformed into explicit stories.

Elizabeth described how she would tighten her body in bed rather than snuggle into her husband. Through ongoing phenomenological inquiry about her sensations, affect, and internal images she eventually said, "I think I could not snuggle into my father. His embrace was hard and he was always in a hurry or critical." This comment was the opening in our examining several transferential reactions in her marriage and also to the realization of her disavowed anger at her father for the absence of loving in her family. She began to wonder about the cause of mother's alleged depression and why the mother might have left the family.

I never did any therapy with Elizabeth's possible introjection of her father's attitudes or feelings. If I had had the opportunity I would have investigated if it was also he who was depressed, particularly after his wife had left him when Elizabeth was five years old. It is possible that his "constant criticism of everyone," his destroying all the photographs, and his not ever speaking about Elizabeth's mother was an expression of either his depression or bitter resentment or both.

By the third year of therapy, I gently and persistently inquired about Elizabeth's early relationship with her depressed mother. I felt an intense tenderness for the little girl she once was and an attunement to the needs of a neglected baby and preschool child. I realize that I kept my eyes on her all the time, particularly on her eyes whenever I caught a glimpse of her downward or inward looking gaze. I experienced a simple innocence in her and a willingness to "please at any cost." My tender comments and reflections of her possible childhood needs were met with confusion and/or distracting comments—comments unrelated to her vulnerability, needs, or relationship with her mother. These juxtaposition reactions included Elizabeth's disregard of my caring gaze, words of tenderness, or descriptions of the relational needs of a young child—a juxtaposition between what she desperately needed from both parents and for which there were neither implicit nor explicit memories. Her deflection and distancing comments also expressed the unconscious script belief, "I don't need anything."

Elizabeth had neither explicit nor implicit memory of either Mother's or Father's vital eye contact, caring gestures or words, or any attention to her loss, vulnerability, or needs. Elizabeth had no concept of relational needs, only the longing, empty searching for "something." Her internal working model, an implicit memory—or, in this case, her non-memory because the events had never occurred—shaped her sense of confusion, distress, and emptiness in response to each of my caring comments. She could not be conscious of the cumulative trauma of what never happened but what should have happened in a loving family relationship. Instead, her unconscious conclusion built up over many years of neglect was "I'm not lovable."

My psychotherapy with Elizabeth often focused on her physical sensations as an unconscious expression of possible needs that were not responded to and remained unsatisfied while she was a child. I was particularly sensitive to her unconsciously expressed needs for security, validation, and to rely on someone who is consistent, dependable, and attuned to her affect. The relational need to make an impact on a significant other, or to have the other initiate any caring gestures, was conspicuously absent in her sparse narrative about her family life. Each of these needs became an integral part of our psychotherapy together. I repeatedly identified, validated, and appreciated these essential needs.

Interwoven in our therapy was a careful therapeutic attentiveness to Elizabeth's sense of shame—a shame she felt with her school peers about coming from a one-parent family and having a mother who had disappeared. Elizabeth described how she had often lied to the other kids by telling them about a dramatic childbirth in which her mother had died heroically.

Through a great deal of phenomenological inquiry and explanation of the normal needs of children—and by inference, her own needs— Elizabeth and I co-created a story that began to make sense to her of her longings and self-neglect, her frequent soothing gestures, her emotional discomfort with both eye contact and affectionate touch, and her endless search for a mother's love.

My affective and developmental attunement served to continually inform both of us of the unrequited needs of a young child. The tenderness, kindness, and gentleness that I strove to bring to the therapy provided an involved therapeutic relationship—a relationship that facilitated Elizabeth's valuing, for the first time in her life, of her vulnerability and needs. At the same time, I was facilitating her identification and understanding of the unconscious script conclusion that "life is an empty search." Putting this unconscious conclusion into words in a number of sessions became important to Elizabeth because it gave meaning to her longings, emptiness, and search for her mother. She slowly became secure enough in our therapeutic relationship to finally grieve for her lost mother and to acknowledge her anger at her father's criticalness and emotional distancing. Her appearance improved slowly over time. Periodically she was dressed in something new that fitted her attractively. One day, in the fifth year of therapy, she surprised me with a new stylish haircut and coloring—an adult form of self-soothing. She experimented in asking her husband to do things for her and to be more affectionate. As a result, she reported on an increased intimacy with her husband. She no longer searched for her lost mother's face on the streets of New York City; her unconscious search for love became conscious. She experienced being loved.

Psychotherapeutic involvement

For clients who are similar to Elizabeth, script cure necessitates a relational psychotherapy that addresses affect and cognition, developmental and current needs, the transferences in everyday life, behavior and fantasy, physiological reactions and health maintenance, and the psychological functions that perpetuate continual reinforcement of script beliefs. Throughout Elizabeth's psychotherapy I focused on many of her attempts at avoidance. We explored how each intrapersonal interruption to contact signaled a significant interruption to internal contact with feelings, bodily sensations, needs, memories, or longings. My therapeutic involvement included periodically identifying when and how I was misattuned to her. She was surprised when I took responsibility for my therapeutic errors (Guistolese, 1997). Both the content and affect of my communication were such juxtapositions with how her father related to her (Erskine, 1993).

My initial impression of Elizabeth as a neglected and unloved child, and her descriptions of the relationship with her husband, are only two examples of the unconscious communication of a life script through the transferences of everyday life. Her husband represented the longed for good mother who did all the grocery shopping and cooking while making no sexual demands. In the early phases of the psychotherapy there appeared to be no transference with me. She was not bothered when I went away. Yet the apparent absence of transference was the transference! Elizabeth's avoidance of interpersonal contact with me was a repeat of how she coped with the feelings, relational needs, and significant dialogue that was absent in her relationship with her father. Elizabeth required an involved psychotherapist who was sensitive, authentic, and fully present.

It is necessary in a relational and integrative psychotherapy that the psychotherapist provides an ongoing inquiry into the client's phenomenological experience of each developmentally dependent relationship, which includes the influence of parents, family members, teachers, and peers, on forming his relational patterns and script beliefs. Such a therapeutically useful phenomenological inquiry can only occur in an atmosphere of the psychotherapist's sustained attunement to the client's affect, rhythm, developmental level of functioning, cognitive style, and relational needs. In the case of Elizabeth, Father did not acknowledge or validate her grief of the loss of Mother. There was no conversation, no soothing gestures, no way for Elizabeth to resolve her grief and retain any precious memories of Mother. The photos were destroyed and there was no relationship with the mother's family. As a result of the unacknowledged mother–daughter relationship and resulting grief at the loss of the relationship, Elizabeth lost conscious memory of anything about her mother. In the psychotherapy, I continually brought up the absence of Mother and inquired about Elizabeth's grief and the missed opportunities between a mother and daughter. I often explained what a growing girl needs from a mother and would then inquire further about her feelings, bodily sensations, associations, and fantasies. We began to co-create a narrative about her previously unconscious and untold life story—a story that had been acted out by searching for Mother's face.

Conclusion

In the psychotherapy of life scripts it is important that the psychotherapist understand and appreciate that life scripts are a desperate and creative attempt to self-regulate while managing and adjusting to the failures that occurred in significant and dependent relationships throughout life. Scripts are a self-protective way of compensating for what was, and may still be, missing in relationship while ensuring a semblance of relationship. The process of script formation is relationally interactive and personally creative—an assimilation and accommodation (Piaget, 1954) to the neglects, misattunements, relational requirements, or even demands, of significant others (Block, 1982). It involves a generalization of specific experiences and an unconscious anticipation that these generalized experiences will be repeated throughout life.

The psychotherapy of life script necessitates an understanding and appreciation of each individual's unique temperament as well as these creative adjustments, coping and adaptive styles, and resulting internal and external interruptions to contact. The psychotherapist's sensitivity to and understanding of physiological survival reactions, unconscious experiential conclusions, contact interruptions, and the unique relational nature of the therapeutic involvement is essential for an in-depth psychotherapy that focuses on the resolution of archaic relational patterns, current relational disturbances, and fixated systems of psychological organization.

An effective relational psychotherapy includes the psychotherapist's acknowledgement of the client's psychological experiences, validation of his affect and attempts at meaning-making, and normalization of the client's developmental attempts to adapt and cope with family and school stressors. It also provides an interested, involved, and caring presence of a real person who communicates to the client that he is valued.

Script cure is the primary goal of an integrative psychotherapy. Script cure is the result of an integration of affect, cognition, and physiology so that important aspects of one's life are available to consciousness and that behavior, health maintenance, and relationships are the result of flexible choice rather than compulsion or inhibition. People who are no longer functioning in a restrictive life script report that they have the capacity to express themselves in a contactful way in relationship; internally they are emotionally stable because they are both unfettered by predetermined and restrictive script beliefs and they are aware of their current needs in relationship. They have a sense of self-definition, agency, and authenticity; their behavior is both contextual and sensitive to other people's relational needs. Interpersonally, they are conscientious, gracious, curious, personable, and intimate.

Life scripts formed from a composite of physiological survival reactions, implicit experiential conclusions, relational failures, prolonged misattunements, and neglects require a psychotherapy wherein the therapeutic relationship is central and is evident through the respect, reliability, and dependability of a caringly involved, skilled real person. Life scripts are the result of cumulative failures in significant and dependent relationships and, therefore, an involved relational psychotherapy is necessary for script cure.

CHAPTER SEVEN

The script system: an unconscious organization of experience

In early writings about life scripts, Berne (1958, 1961) describes the script as a complex set of transactions that determines the identity and destiny of the individual. He goes on to explain the script as similar to Freud's repetition compulsion and more like his destiny compulsion (Berne, 1966, p. 302). Most of the transactional analysis literature regarding scripts has focused on the historical perspective. The literature has addressed how scripts have been transmitted through parental messages and injunctions, and a child's reactions, such as unconscious conclusions and explicit decisions. Additionally, some contemporary transactional analysts have examined several processes such as early child–parent attachment, shared language acquisition, and the expression of narrative as central in the formation of scripts. Each of these historical perspectives has provided the clinician with theories and concepts that have guided a variety of clinical interventions.

The script system

The script system was designed to provide a way to analyze how the script is active in life today. Rather than taking an historical perspective, the script system identifies how the decisions, conclusions, reactions, and/or introjections are unconsciously expressed in current life as core beliefs, overt behaviors, fantasies and obsessions, internal physical sensations, and reinforcing memories. The intrapsychic dynamics of the script system serve to keep the original needs and feelings that were present at the time of script formation out of awareness while also maintaining a semblance of attachment with others. The script system categorizes human experience into four primary components: script beliefs; behavioral, fantasy, and physiological manifestations; reinforcing experiences; and the intrapsychic process of repressed needs and feelings (Erskine, 1982a; Erskine & Moursund, 1988; Erskine & Zalcman, 1979; Moursund & Erskine, 2004).

Script beliefs are the compilation of survival reactions, implicit experiential conclusions, explicit decisions, self-protective processes, self-regulating fantasies, relational coping strategies, and reinforcements that have occurred in the process of relating to others over the course of one's lifetime. Script beliefs are often a condensed expression of an unexpressed life story. They represent, in one phrase, an elaborate, often unexpressed, narrative. Script beliefs, which are usually not conscious, are the person's unique understandings and interpretations of the value of self, significant relationships, and life's events. Script beliefs, in and of themselves, are not pathological; rather, they represent a desperate, creative process of meaning-making. They function to provide a sense of self-regulation, compensation, orientation, self-protection, and an insuring prediction of future relational interactions. They also self-define one's integrity. In essence, script beliefs provide an unconscious organization of experience.

These beliefs may be described in three categories: beliefs about self, beliefs about others, and beliefs about the quality of life. Once formulated and adopted, script beliefs influence what stimuli (internal and external) are attended to, how they are interpreted and whether or not they are acted on. They become the self-fulfilling prophecy through which the person's expectations are inevitably proven to be true because they create a sequence of "repetitious relational experiences" (Fosshage, 1992, p. 34).

The script system is unconsciously maintained in order (a) to avoid reexperiencing unmet needs and the corresponding feelings suppressed at the time of script formation, (b) to generalize the unconscious experience of self in relationship with others, (c) to create a homeostatic self-regulation, (d) to provide a predictive model of life and interpersonal relationships (Erskine & Moursund, 1988; Moursund & Erskine, 2004). Suppression, generalization, self-regulation, and prediction are important psychological processes particularly relied upon when there is uncertainty, a crisis, or trauma. Although a previously created life script is often personally and relationally destructive, it does provide psychological balance and homeostasis; it maintains continuity with the past while it also provides the illusion of predictability (Bary & Hufford, 1990; Berne, 1964; Perls, 1944). Any disruption in self-regulation, interruptions in continuity, or change in the predictive model of the script system produces anxiety. To avoid such discomfort, people organize current perceptions and experiences so as to maintain a life script and to justify their behavior (Erskine, 1981; Erskine & Trautmann, 1993).

In the case example that follows, John´s life story illustrates how his script system was a repetition of his past and also how his script determined both his identity and his relationships with people. In addition, his story illuminates how the quality of interpersonal contact in the therapeutic relationship facilitated the client becoming conscious of his script beliefs and in making significant changes in his life. As John´s narrative unfolds, look for the various ways his five core script beliefs are portrayed in his behaviors, fantasies, body tension, transference, and reinforcing memories. Each of these expressions of a life script are often evident in the therapeutic relationship, either by

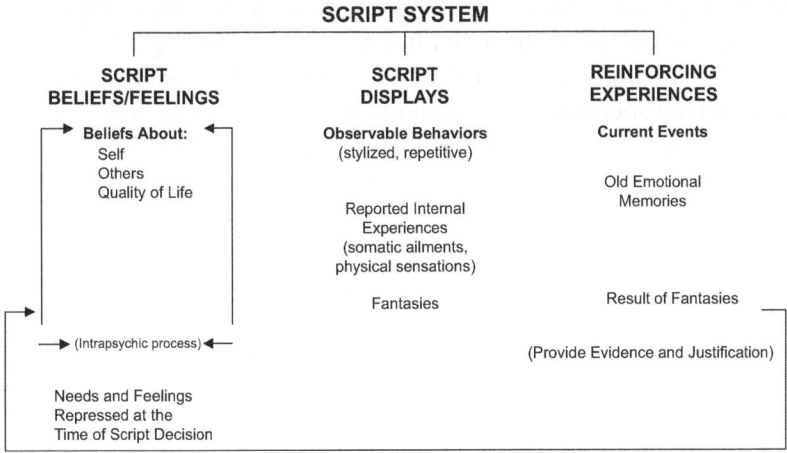

Figure 1. The script system.

observation or through transference, long before the actual words of the script beliefs are put into social language. Script beliefs are frequently expressed through the client's unaware prefixes, parenthetical phrases, or concluding statements to either a current or an old story. Unconscious script beliefs are often observable through various expressions, such as body posture and movement, forgotten appointments, misplaced objects, repeated physical injuries, or errors in reasonable judgement. It is an essential task of the psychotherapist to decode the behavioral, imaginative, transferential, and physiological expressions of a life script. The decoding is accomplished through phenomenological and historical inquiry, therapeutic inference within a developmental perspective, and a relational dialogue (Erskine, Moursund, & Trautmann, 1999). As the client's life narrative is revealed in the therapeutic relationship, the script beliefs are expressed, often without awareness, as a way to tell the condensed version of a significant emotion-filled story of personal relationships.

John's loneliness

When John first came to therapy, he had no knowledge of how pervasive his script system was in determining the course of his life. He was not particularly aware of his core beliefs, cognizant of his behavior and physiological reactions, or conscious of his feelings and needs. He had only a general knowledge of his experiences as a child. He remembered the house he lived in and the woods where he spent a lot of time playing with his dog. His father had been a caretaker on a large estate and his only time with other children was when he went to school. He remembered spending hours walking in the woods. The one feeling he could identify was that he was lonely a lot of the time. He said this as a factual statement with no apparent affect present. John could not remember sensitive family interactions such as gestures of caring, words of encouragement, or conversations about his feelings.

John had consulted with his primary care physician who referred him to psychotherapy. John's eyes focused either on the floor or the wall as he described the two major losses in the previous year—a divorce from his wife and the death of his father. He reported that he kept busy at work "in order not to have my imaginations—bad thoughts and feelings." "This is what I have always done my whole life, just to keep going," he told me. When I asked him about his reason for coming to see me he said it was because his doctor thought it might help him if he talked with someone about his losses. I asked John how he understood psychotherapy to work and John replied, "I have to build some strength to help myself." He went on to describe his father's motto as "Keep a stiff upper lip and just do it." Over several sessions it became evident that John, in the process of growing up, came to the decision that to do whatever it was he needed to get done, he had to be strong and follow his father's advice.

In the intake interview, I asked a number of questions about John's history and family relationships. His answers were simple and direct about his teenage years and either vague or nonexistent when I asked about his school and preschool years. Although his answers in the initial interview did not seem disorganized or contradictory, there appeared to be a significant lack in his ability to form a consistent narrative about his early life experiences and relationships. I wondered about the quality of his interpersonal relationships with each of his parents. I ended our initial session thinking about what internal images John may have of significant others, including extended family members and teachers and what internal influence those significant others may still have in his life.

In our second session I asked John to describe how he envisioned a therapeutic relationship with me. He talked about his mistrust of therapists in general and he wasn't sure that any professional person could help him. I inquired about how he experienced talking to me. He said that he thought that he "might be able to trust" me but that I probably could "not be helpful" for some things that had already happened. His body appeared very tense and he would look at me periodically and then quickly look away. I told him that I understood his reluctance to trust me and I assured him that, if he let me, I could most likely help him resolve the emotional losses of his wife and father.

I explained to John that, as he told me more about himself, the significance of his losses would become clear to both of us. In my own mind I raised several questions about what prior childhood losses may have occurred and may not yet be available to consciousness, either because they were so early or that they may never have been talked about with an interested and involved other. Later, as our psychotherapy progressed, I thoroughly inquired about his early childhood and the quality of his significant relationships.

In our first few sessions I realized the depth of John's loneliness that was portrayed in his descriptions of his childhood, his struggle to be with me, and by the fragmentary information he gave me about his family life during his school and preschool years. His lack of narrative about his family life left me feeling an emptiness and wondering about the emotional neglect that may have existed within his family. My countertransference was already forming and informing. Over the next several sessions we established our psychotherapy relationship. I focused on the qualities I could bring to our therapeutic work: my unconditional regard for John, my commitment to sustaining a relationship of quality between him and me, my sense of presence in helping him to regulate his affect, and my interest in the development of John's narrative of his life.

In subsequent sessions he then went on to talk about how difficult it was for him to understand that anyone could be interested in listening to him. He did not have a frame of reference that included someone being there for him and certainly not someone being interested and involved in his well-being. As I encouraged him to put words to his experiences with people he said, "People are only interested in themselves." Often as I sat and listened attentively, he would say that he could not comprehend how I could listen to his "rhetoric." My responses were to tell him that I wanted to listen to him, to everything he said, to his emotions, and even to his silences. I wanted to hear about his experiences. I wanted to be there with him and for him. In the following session I encouraged John to tell me more about his term "'rhetoric."

My phenomenological and historical inquiry guided him into a memory of being at the dinner table with his parents. John remembered that he had started to tell his parents about making a speech in his third grade class that day. His father responded with, "That's just a bunch of rhetoric," and his mother remained silent. He was devastated by his father's remarks as well as his mother's non-involvement. John, like his mother, went silent; he had never spoken to anyone about this memory. When I responded compassionately, John spontaneously remembered another time; when driving to his grandparents' house, he had started to tell his parents about a new friend he made that day in school. His father's immediate response was that "Friends don't stay around, so don't get too excited."

In both of these instances, John's experiences of excitement and joy were dismissed. As he finished these two stories, I inquired about what he was feeling. He gave what I later discovered to be his typical answer, an "OK." He said that his father's remarks didn't bother him. I told him that I was feeling sad for a little boy who compensated by saying it was "OK" when it was not. I reiterated that he had been excited about his third grade speech and about finding a new friend. I expressed that I was excited for him as that little boy. After a few minutes of silence, John responded with the wish that his mother could have said those words to him. He said, "No one is ever there for me." I again said that I was glad for him as a little boy who was excited about his speech and finding a new friend. I also told him that I was quite sad to hear that no one had been excited for him. In doing so, I identified the sadness about which John could not speak. Together we acknowledged his sense that in these two instances no one was emotionally present for him and that he was deeply sad.

In the last half of the session I had him imagine giving his third grade speech in front of the classroom. He described showing a picture of a bear to his class. He was again excited as he fantasized telling his fellow students about the way bears hibernate in the winter. This eight-year-old boy had interesting information about the habits of bears and he wanted to share it with the class. I also imagined being in his classroom listening with interest to his presentation, much as a proud parent or good teacher might do.

When he was finished, I voiced my excitement about his enthusiastic presentation. Although I could not satisfy his archaic needs to define himself, to make an impact on others, and to be acknowledged for his accomplishments, I did validate these as important relational needs of the eight-year-old boy as well as the current needs of a mature man.

He looked at me and smiled. His body posture relaxed as he sighed. Phenomenological inquiry, developmental attunement, and my emotional involvement were deepening our connection and providing an opportunity for him to talk about his memories, feelings, and physical sensations. I was forming an understanding of the meanings John made of these memories and how he unconsciously organized his life experiences.

During the next few sessions it became clear that John's childhood experiences were organized around his beliefs about self: "No one is ever there for me," "I have to do everything myself," and "My feelings don't matter." His motto, which he manifested in his day-to-day activities, was "Work hard and don't complain." I realized that this motto was a derivation of his father's "Keep a stiff upper lip and just do it." Together we continued to identify how active these three core beliefs were in determining his behaviors, both when he was alone and when he was with other people. In every situation he was convinced that he had to do things all by himself because no one would be there to help him; "People are only interested in themselves." His orientation of self-in-relationship-with-others, which originated in his relationships with his parents, was being repeated with everyone in his adult life.

I continually inquired about his life. Unemotionally, John talked about how his father never showed any interest in playing or talking with him. John had no siblings and the only children he spent time with were those at school. He spent a lot of time on his swings or with his dog. He reported spending hours alone in the woods on the estate. When asked about each of these experiences he could not identify any feelings. His affect was, at best, flat and often nonexistent. As he continued in therapy, John began to talk more frequently about his memories. He was able, through my phenomenological inquiry, to discover his feelings of sadness and loneliness.

Several times he was surprised at the extent of his feelings and that he was telling me about how he managed his loneliness. As a child he had never thought to go to his parents; he was certain that they would be neither emotionally present nor interested in him. He never got angry or complained. He repeatedly experienced that protest or complaints "only made matters worse." He had no memories of his mother ever complaining about his father's constant criticism of everyone or his lack of interest in either her or John. "She appeared sad a lot of the time," but neither she nor his father talked about what she was feeling. On many occasions he saw his father "shut down when any feelings started to surface," "Feelings were never talked about." He learned early on that any sadness he expressed was identified as tiredness by his mother. Anger was not to be voiced. Loneliness was his secret!

John recalled how even with his former wife he never talked about his loneliness. Several times I inquired about his experience in the marriage. He described how his wife was "only interested in herself" and repeated his belief, "My feelings don't matter." He later connected both of these script beliefs to his mother having told him that he was "a burden" when he was a young child. She never explained how he was a burden; that was left to his imagination. He fantasized that he had been too active and too emotional for her. He realized he had always expected that his wife would also say that he was too emotional for her, so he told her nothing of his feelings.

As John's therapy continued, I strove to establish an attuned and involved relationship that provided security for him to remember many never talked about childhood memories, to sense his physical tensions and related experiences, to identify relational needs, and express a whole range of feelings. I became the "one there" to counter his belief, "No one is ever there for me." In order to facilitate John's becoming conscious of his childhood experiences, he and I were engaged in a dialogue that gave validation of his feelings, reactions, and the coping skills he used as a child. As a preschool and school-age child he neither had the concepts and necessary language skills, nor parental encouragement to talk about his feelings. His mother and father did not engage him in dialogues wherein he could express himself. Because there was no relational language in the family, his emotional experiences were never acknowledged; they remained unconscious.

Prior to psychotherapy, John's explicit memories were few. His feelings, fantasies, bodily sensations, and significant experiences were not part of any conversation. In our psychotherapy, I continually inquired about John's bodily sensations and the extent of his beliefs about himself, others, and the quality of his life. I listened to the nuances of his sadness and comforted him with compassion and validation. I encouraged him to take deep breaths and to let out the sounds and tears of his sadness. He repeatedly cried about how "Life is lonely." When he was angry I maintained a space for him to talk about his anger and to seriously attend to how he both experienced it in his body and also attempted to "shut down" like his father.

As John struggled to articulate the narrative of his life he had my constant attention; he was validated and accepted by me. We often focused on how John used his script beliefs as an organizing schema both to create meaning and to reaffirm his childhood identity. We identified his repetitive behaviors, explored his fantasies, and clarified the function of his various script reinforcing experiences. As a result, John was increasingly able to own his feelings, identify his relational needs, and express his own uniqueness.

While spending many hours as a child without companionship, John fantasized himself doing things all alone but reaping appreciation from others for what he accomplished. In his play with toy soldiers, he imagined himself returning from war as a hero, greatly admired and cheered by all the people. As an adult, whenever he did something he waited for the cheers that never came. A frequently reoccurring dream involved scenes of John walking with his father on one side of him and his mother on the other. They are all holding hands and listening to

John as they walk together in the woods. The dream would abruptly end and he would be flooded with sadness. Each of these failed fantasies and interrupted dreams reinforced his script beliefs and childhood sense of being all alone.

As we discussed his loneliness and his mother's lack of emotional contact with him, John remembered a man who worked with his father. Ted had kind eyes and was interested in what John was doing. Ted would stop working and talk with John. Sometimes Ted would share his lunch with John and entertain him with stories about being in the army during the war. Then, one day, John found out that Ted had been seriously injured on the job and that he would not be coming back to work. He never saw Ted again. In response to John's missing Ted, his father gruffly told him that Ted was lazy and deserved to get hurt. John wept as he described how Ted would listen to him. He continued to weep while talking about the wooden gun that Ted had carved for him.

In the next session we explored how his earlier script conclusion made in reaction to his parents' behavior and lack of emotions had become reinforced when his friend Ted disappeared. That early childhood conclusion, "No one is EVER there for me," was cemented into a formidable life script with this reinforcing experience. I challenged the "No one will EVER be there for me" with the question "Ever?" I then had him close his eyes, look at the image of Ted and to talk to Ted about how he had been so significant in his life. After this emotion filled experience, John was able to retain a memory of his connection with Ted. He later referred to his relationship with Ted, "At least someone was once there for me." John's life script was changing.

One day he came into session and said that he had had a new dream. He was in the woods near my office and this time he was with someone. They were talking and laughing together. He did not know who was in the dream yet he knew he liked the person. I asked him what the dream meant to him and he said that "Maybe this is what is in the future for me." He smiled slightly and then gave a big, relaxing sigh. I asked, "What do you experience with that sigh?" "I went through a lot," John answered. "Now I do not feel so crazy and so alone anymore. My body is not as tense as it used to be." He then went on to talk about his father and his wish that his father were still alive so that he could "now have a real relationship."

As John's therapy continued, he developed a new sense of self. After two years, he was able to articulate the narrative of his life script. His script beliefs were no longer active; he changed many of his behaviors and he was expressive of his feelings. He understood and appreciated the coping, self-protective functions that his script beliefs once served him. John took the quality of our interpersonal therapeutic relationship as a model in forming meaningful work and social relationships. He began meeting regularly with his mother and their new relationship became increasingly satisfying. He no longer felt driven to keep busy all the time to avoid his feelings. After a vacation, he reported that he thoroughly enjoyed relaxing and doing nothing. He said, "I no longer feel lonely."

The theory into practice

When under stress, or when current relational needs are either not responded to or satisfied in adult life, explicit and/or implicit memory, physiological reactions, or explicit decisions may be stimulated. A person is then likely to engage in compensating behaviors and/or fantasies that, in turn, distract from the internal emotion-laden experience by verifying script beliefs. These compensating behaviors and fantasies are referred to as the *script displays*. These script displays include any observable behaviors, such as choice of words, sentence patterns, tone of voice, displays of emotion, and/or gestures and body movements, that are the direct displays of the script beliefs and the repressed needs and feelings (an intrapsychic process).

People usually act in a way defined by their script beliefs, such as John never asking friends for help even in situations where it was needed, believing "I have to do everything myself." As a result, his friends neither knew what he needed nor offered to help. The absence once again of his friends offering or providing help reinforced the script beliefs "I have to do it myself" and "People are only interested in themselves."

Script beliefs may also be displayed through the absence of situationally appropriate behavior, such as the lack of eye contact or the socially typical expression of emotions in intimate interpersonal communications. John's lack of eye contact in his earlier sessions and the absence of natural emotional expressions are two examples of how an internal script belief will be externally displayed. Both of these types of behaviors emanated from the script beliefs "No one is ever there for me" and "My feelings don't matter." Each of these behaviors also serves to reinforce the script beliefs because they interrupted important interpersonal contact. Figure 2 is a diagram of the intrapsychic and behavioral dynamics of John's script system.

JONH'S SCRIPT SYSTEM

SCRIPT BELIEFS/FEELINGS	SCRIPT DISPLAY	REINFORCING EXPERIENCES
Beliefs About	**Observable Behaviours**	**Current Events**
Self No one is ever there for me. I have to do everything myself. My feelings don't matter.	Absence of emotional expression in interpersonal communication. Lack of eye contact. Observable body tension. Works hard. No complaints.	No emotinal conversation with wife. Wife divorcing. Father dying. Little emotional contact with mother.
Others People are only interested in themselves.	"Just keep on going." Therapists "not helpful". Struggles to be with therapist.	No help from friends.
Quality of Life Life is lonely.	**Reported Internal Experience** Muscle tension Erratic breathing	**Old Emotional Memories** Mother and father "don't get excited", "don't get angry". Protesting made matters worse. Mother: "You were a burden". Sadness identified by mother as tiredness.
(Intrapsychic process)		Mother remembered as silent and non-involved. Father critical of everyone.
Repressed Feelings Lonely Sad Angry		Loss of Ted. Awareness of muscle tenstion of "I have to do everything myself".
Repressed Needs To be validated and acknowledged. To rely on someone. To have companionship. To define one's self. To make an impact.	**Fantasies** As child: Being a "hero" Getting appreciation from others. (Dream) Holding hands and talking abruptly ends. As an adult: Being admired by others. Imagining wife being interested in only herself. Exaggerating father's criticisms. "I'm too active and emotional for mother".	**Result of Fantasies** No actual appreciation for being a hero. No actual holding of hands and talking. Waits for admiration. Many examples of wife's interest only in herself. Father: "a bunch of rhetoric" and "friends don't stay around".

Figure 2. John's script system.

As part of the manifestation of the script, individuals may have physiological reactions in addition to, or in place of, the overt behaviors. Often, these internal experiences are not readily observable; nevertheless, the person can give a self-report on bodily sensations such as fluttering in the stomach, muscle tension, headaches, colitis, or any of a myriad of somatic responses to the script beliefs. In John's situation, his body tension was easily observable and reflected all three of his script beliefs. Careful attention to John's body sensations, such as his erratic breathing and muscle tension, was essential in helping him experience the existence and depth of his affect.

The manifestation of the script also includes fantasies in which the individual imagines behaviors, either his own or someone else's. These fantasized interpersonal interactions and the quality of the outcome lends support to script beliefs. Fantasized behaviors function as effectively as overt behaviors (in some incidences even more effectively) in reinforcing the script beliefs and keeping the original needs and feelings out of awareness. At the beginning of his psychotherapy, John reported that he kept busy at work in order to avoid his "imaginations, bad thoughts and feelings." With consistent phenomenological inquiry about the full nature of his imaginations and "bad thoughts," it later became apparent that the content of his fantasy about his former wife and father actually functioned to confirm his beliefs of "No one is ever there for me," and "My feelings don't matter," and "People are only interested in themselves." His fantasies were an elaboration of what he already believed.

Fantasies act within the script system exactly as though they were events that had actually occurred. An understanding of how fantasy reinforces script beliefs is particularly useful to psychotherapists in organizing the psychotherapy for clients who engage in obsession, habitual worry, and fantasies of abandonment, persecution, or grandeur (Erskine, 2002). As we explored John's childhood fantasies of being a hero and his current fantasies of being admired, the content of these fantasies did not directly reinforce his script beliefs. But when he compared his wonderful fantasies with his actual reality in which no one cheered or listened to him, the contrast provided evidence that "No one is ever there for me."

Any script manifestation can result in a *reinforcing experience*— a subsequent event that "proves" that the script belief is valid and, thus, justifies the behavior. Reinforcing experiences are a collection of affect-laden memories, either implicit or explicit, either real or imagined, of other people's or one's own behavior, a recall of internal bodily experiences, or the retained remnants of fantasies or dreams. John clung to the memory of his mother's silence and his father's criticism of his school story as "a bunch of rhetoric." He often recalled that event both at work and during his therapy when he was about to say something important. Retaining that selected memory and repeating it many times served to reinforce his script belief, "My feelings don't matter." John's frequent memories of the loss of Ted and his father's pessimistic comment, "Friends don't stay around," were often in John's mind. These repeated memories served to continually reinforce his script belief, "No one is there for me."

Because of the homeostatic self-stabilizing function of life scripts, reinforcing experiences serve as a feedback mechanism to further strengthen script beliefs and to prevent cognitive dissonance (Festinger, 1958). Only those memories that support the script beliefs are readily accepted and retained. Memories that negate the script beliefs tend to be rejected or forgotten because they would challenge the beliefs and the whole self-regulating, homeostatic process.

The intrapsychic process of *repressed needs and feelings* are an unconscious accumulation of intense affects experienced over time when crucial physiological and relational needs were repeatedly not satisfied. These feelings and needs are usually not conscious because the memory is either implicit, traumatically dissociated, or reflects a repressed explicit experience. Also, the biological imperative of both physiological and relational needs is not conscious, particularly in infants and young children. Often clients in psychotherapy gain awareness of these needs and feelings in the secure, reliable, and respectful therapeutic relationship where there is sufficient affective and rhythmic attunement accompanied by a nonjudgemental phenomenological inquiry (Erskine, 1993).

John could speak of his loneliness early in therapy but it was a long while before he could express the depth of his sadness or even talk about being angry at his parents' refusal to talk about emotions as well as the absence of intimacy. He was eventually able to identify and articulate his needs in relationship with people. Five unrequited relational needs were evident in John's narrative: to be validated and acknowledged; to rely on someone; to have companionship; to define one's self; to make an impact on others. Awareness of these crucial needs and feelings was no longer repressed by his script beliefs or distracted by his behaviors or fantasies.

Script beliefs are a creative attempt to make sense of the experiential conclusions (usually nonconscious), explicit decisions, and coping reactions. Script beliefs serve to cognitively mediate against the awareness of the intense feelings that the person lived during script formation. This cognitive mediation distracts from an awareness of both current relational needs and the developmentally crucial physiological and relational needs. The intense affects and needs may remain as fixated, implicit memories until life altering experiences or an effective therapeutic relationship facilitate integration. Prior to psychotherapy, John was perpetually immersed in his loneliness. The dream wherein he was walking with a friend near his therapist's office demonstrates the life altering effectiveness of an involved therapeutic relationship. John's life script of loneliness was coming to an end.

Each person's set of script beliefs provides a subjective self-regulating mental framework for viewing self, others, and the quality of life. In order to engage in a manifestation of the script, individuals must discount other options; they frequently will maintain that their behavior is the "natural" or "only" way they can respond. When used socially, script manifestations are likely to produce interpersonal experiences that, in turn, are governed by and contribute to the reinforcement of script beliefs. This cybernetic closed system provides a homeostasis, thus each person's script system is self-regulating and self-reinforcing through the operation of its four interrelated and interdependent subsystems: script beliefs; behavioral, fantasy, and physiological manifestations; reinforcing experiences; and repressed needs and feelings.

The unconscious script system serves as a distraction against awareness of past experiences, relational needs, and related emotions while simultaneously being a repetition of the past. The script system represents the client's unconscious organization of experience and provides a useful blueprint to help the psychotherapist and client understand how the script is lived out in current life.

A cybernetic system such as the script system is made up of "a set of components or parts that interact to form an organized whole" (Piers, 2005, p. 230). Therefore, a change in one of the parts or subsystems will effect a dynamic change in the whole system. By therapeutically attending to physiological sensations and bodily experiences, behaviors and the functions of behaviors, fantasies and dreams, conscious and unconscious (implicit) memories, affects and relational needs, and the client's core beliefs about self, others, and the quality of life, the psychotherapist facilitates changes in the various subsystems that comprise the life script. Hence, the more areas attended to in the process of psychotherapy, the more likely we will facilitate a "script cure" (Erskine, 1980).

CHAPTER EIGHT

Psychological functions of life scripts

Affectively and physiologically charged survival reactions; pre-symbolic and implicit experiential conclusions of self, others, and the quality of life; and even explicit script decisions, all produce distinct relational attachment patterns that are maintained by several *psychological functions* (Erskine, Moursund, & Trautmann, 1999). Life scripts are a creative strategy to manage the psychological stress, or even the shock, of repetitive, problematic relationships whether they be in early childhood interaction with parents, reactions to teachers or caregivers, interactions with other children or adolescents, and sometimes within an adult partnership, marriage, work, or social situation. This creative strategy is not actually a defense against someone or something as much as it is a desperate attempt to create *self-regulation, compensation, self-protection, or orientation* and establish *insurance against further stress*, psychological shock, or disruptions in relationship. The life script also functions to maintain *a sense of integrity*—a continuity of the struggle to define and value one's self within a variety of relationships. These six examples of the psychological functions of life script reflect the person's attempt to generate and maintain a sense of psychological equilibrium following affectively overwhelming disruptions in significant relationships. They are homeostatic strategies that provide predictability, identity, consistency, and stability (see Chapter Ten).

The six dimensions of psychological function described in this chapter, and frequently evident in psychotherapy practice, in part account for why a life script is a desperate "creative adjustment" (Perls, Hefferline, & Goodman, 1951) to manage pain and fear. These psychological functions also account for how life script is maintained over time—often for a lifetime—unless important interpersonal relationships and significant life events intervene or the person willingly engages in a life altering in-depth psychotherapy relationship with a skilled psychotherapist.

The psychological function of *self-regulation* is a biologically determined, correcting process. The human brain's hypothalamic-pituitary-adrenal axis is involved in the emotional and physiological homeostatic process of self-stabilization, self-soothing, and internal regulation (Cozolino, 2006, p. 60). The capacity to soothe oneself and to self-regulate is present from early infancy (Beebe, 2005) and is greatly intensified and often rigidified in response to trauma, the absence of important interpersonal contact, the lack of need fulfillment, or disruption and loss in primary relationship.

Self-regulation involves the reduction of intense affect and the calming of overstimulating physiological reactions in the absence of need fulfilling contact with significant others. It involves restabilizing and calming the organism, often through physical gestures, withdrawal from external stimulus, repetitive behavioral patterns, gratifying fantasy, and through a process of cognitive mediation that leads to the establishment of script beliefs (Erskine, 1980; Erskine & Moursund, 1988). For example, the script belief that "something is wrong with me" reflects both an explanatory cognitive mediation in response to humiliation and a disavowal of affect and needs. This script belief is an example of an attempt to self-regulate the disruption in a relational connection and to calm and distract oneself from the anger at the person doing the humiliation. The script belief facilitates the disavowal of the hurt at not being accepted "as I am" and the fear of rejection for "who I am"—a form of self-regulation (Erskine, 1994).

Another psychological function of life script is the *compensation for relational needs that were consistently unsatisfied in significant primary relationships*. Relational needs can only be satisfied through contactful relationships. A life script is an attempt to compensate for the lack of interpersonal contact and the unfulfilled needs by either disregarding the need or, alternatively, attempting to fulfill a need by oneself. However, since relational needs are relational, they can never be adequately satisfied, over time, by oneself. Yet many experiential conclusions or script decisions result in the beliefs, "I don't need anything from anyone," or "I'm not important," as an attempt to compensate through cognitive mediation for significant disruptions in relationships. Often these beliefs are accompanied by fantasies, such as being self-sufficient or imagining other people receiving valuable recognition instead of oneself—a form of compensation.

A third psychological function is the establishment and maintenance of *self-protection against the memory of the pain and fear of relational failures and loss of interpersonal connection*. Script beliefs are cognitive attempts to distract and distance oneself from the pain and fear by creating a cognitive mediation that either anesthetizes intense affect or seemingly renders such intense affect as less significant (Erskine & Zalcman, 1979). Such disavowal of affect makes disappointing, emotionally painful, and fearful relationships more manageable by eliminating the fear, pain, and anger from conscious memory. "There is no use" or "Nothing matters" are but two examples of how such script beliefs are self-protective strategies that disavow affect, desensitize physically and deny cognitively the awareness of pain, fear, and physical tension of consistent relational failure, rejection, or even cruelty. Rather than remember and feel the pain and fear once again, while realizing the contrast between the current situation and the previously disruptive relationships, a person will seek to maintain and reinforce the script beliefs, hence have an illusion of protection against pain and fear.

These script beliefs are significant impediments to having current relational needs come to awareness and from having relational needs fulfilled through current relationships. Various affects, fantasies, body tensions or repetitive behaviors may also be used as self-protection. Because they reflect a previous experience wherein self-protection seemed necessary, they create an interruption to contact in the now and interfere with the satisfaction of current physical and/or relational needs. These self-protective affects, fantasies, body tensions, or repetitive behaviors either interrupt contact internally, externally, or both. Contact interruption is a significant element in a person maintaining a life script.

A fourth psychological function of life scripts commonly evident in clinical practice is the *orientation of one's self in relationship to others*. The script beliefs "No one is there for me" and/or "I have to do it all alone" are examples of how an individual may orient himself with all other people. They are the core beliefs that justify an avoidant attachment style and provide an orientation to both current and future relationships. How we are psychologically attached to others, where we belong, and how we fit in with others are each elements of the biological imperative to form relationship. Mirror and resonance systems within the neural networks of the brain's orbital medial prefrontal cortex and the amygdala provide people with the capacity to read the behavior, intentions, and inner emotions of others and to develop emotional bonding, pair attachment patterns, and a social orientation of self with others (Nelson & Panksepp, 1998).

When a child's biological imperative for physical or emotional relatedness and developmentally based relational needs is repeatedly not satisfied, the hunger for relationship may become overstructured and a rigid attitude and behavioral pattern may be formed in orientation to significant others' attitudes, behaviors, and relationship patterns (Erskine, 1997b).

A life script provides *insurance against the possible shock of potential disruptions and loss of relationships*. This fifth psychological function is the structuralization of anticipation and expectation as a cushion against future disappointment and the shock of the potential failure of significant relationships. "I'll always lose," "People can't be trusted," and "Life is full of suffering" are three examples of the predictive quality of script beliefs and the insurance that there will never be a shocking surprise again. Hindsight is creatively turned into foresight in order to never experience future pain in interpersonal relationships.

Maintaining *integrity* is another function of life scripts. Self-definition and the capacity to make an impact are significant and necessary relational needs from the beginning and throughout life. One's sense of integrity is a reflection of how others respond to those crucial needs. "I'm of no value" or "My needs won't be met" are two examples of an overly structured and rigidified self-definition. Because of the human being's biological imperative to create structure, people struggle to maintain a continuity of self-definition by maintaining, reinforcing, and even defending a self-definition formed in an earlier period of time—*an out-of-date or archaic integrity*. These out-of-date explanations or self-definitions were at one time effective cognitive mediations that distracted from the intense stress of the original relational disruptions. Because they were once highly effective in mediating awareness and disavowing affect, they are repeatedly used until they form the only self-definition.

It is often necessary in an effective psychotherapy that the psychotherapist account for the psychological functions of self-regulation, compensation, self-protection, orientation, insurance, and archaic integrity in understanding how life script is a creative strategy to accommodate to painful and fearful disruptions in significant relationships. It is important to address each of these psychological functions in the client's psychotherapy. Each psychological function may need to be separately investigated and its importance understood and even appreciated by both client and therapist as new thoughts and attitudes, new behaviors and physical movements are explored in the psychotherapy. Such investigation involves a great deal of phenomenological and historical inquiry, as well as inquiry into the details of the client's various systems of coping and self-management. To be effective in facilitating a script cure, such inquiry must occur within a quality of therapeutic relationship that affirms and validates the client's phenomenological experience; normalizes the process of creative adjustment, psychological functions, and script formation; and provides an attuned and understanding other who brings both professional skill as well as her whole self to the relationship.

CHAPTER NINE

Integrating expressive methods in a relational psychotherapy

Therapeutic involvement is an integral part of all effective psychotherapy. This chapter is written to illustrate the concept of therapeutic involvement in working within a therapeutic relationship—within the transference—and with active expressive and experiential methods to resolve traumatic experiences, relational disturbances, and life shaping decisions.

Recent discussions with colleagues have focused on two different perspectives of therapeutic involvement in psychotherapy. One perspective emphasizes the effectiveness of a psychotherapist working only in the "present moment" of the therapy relationship—of working solely within the transference/countertransference matrix. This first approach is referred to as a "two-person therapy" because of the emphasis on the centrality of the therapeutic dialogue between client and psychotherapist in facilitating change in clients' dysfunctional relational patterns. In this point of view the most important factor in the therapeutic process is the psychotherapist's sustained empathetic presence. Fixated archaic wounds, traumas, script conclusions, and relational disruptions are resolved through a fully involved, person-to-person therapeutic relationship.

The second perspective describes an approach wherein the psychotherapist makes use primarily of experiential and expressive methods that facilitate the client's resolution of intrapsychic conflict and archaic decisions. It has been labeled by some as a "one person therapy" because it is viewed as though the psychotherapist is "doing something" to the client. The psychotherapy sessions emphasize the use of expressive methods and emotionally evocative techniques, the active expression of intrapsychic dialogue, and/or experimentation in new behavior and physiological expression. Involvement is in the psychotherapist being fully present, actively inquiring about the client's phenomenological perspective, and engaging with the client in creating experiences that make unconscious material conscious. In this point of view the psychotherapist's active engagement with the client, while using the various expressive and experiential methods, is the most important factor leading to change both in clients' self-perception and in their relationships with others.

The two key questions in this discussion are: "Are we in a contactful, involved therapeutic relationship with a client when we use expressive, experiential, or intrapsychic methods that facilitate the awareness, expression, and change in the client's fixated archaic experiences?" and "Is relational psychotherapy in and of itself sufficient to heal the life-shaping effects of cumulative neglect, traumas, and relational failures?"

I believe that the answers depend on the quality of the therapeutic relationship, whether we use expressive methods or not. Healing occurs through a contactful therapeutic relationship. A healing relationship depends on the psychotherapist's willingness to be contactful and fully present with and for her client in such a way that they co-discover the function of the client's unconscious relational patterns as they emerge both within the therapeutic relationship and in the transferences of everyday life. Equally important is the psychotherapist's emotional presence and full involvement that offers a new and unique response to the client's archaic patterns of relationship, affect, developmental level of functioning, and cognitive style of making meaning. Such a healing relationship includes attunement to the client's unique rhythm and a responsiveness to both the client's current and archaic relational needs. Much of the healing power of a therapeutic relationship depends on the psychotherapist's authenticity, reliability, and willingness to take responsibility for therapeutic errors.

I have found that an involved psychotherapist is consistently invested in the client's welfare and spends considerable amounts of time building and maintaining a quality relationship with the client through phenomenological inquiry, acknowledgement, validation, and sustained empathy—not as a set of techniques but as a genuine interest in knowing the client while helping the client to know and express himself.

The annotated transcript in this chapter provides an example of the use of both perspectives: working within the transference/countertransference dyad—focusing on an authentic person-to-person relationship—and also making effective use of expressive, experiential, and intrapsychic methods to change life-shaping decisions. Rather than thinking in terms of a one- or two-person therapy, I find it more professionally useful to think about therapeutic involvement, that unique experience of client and psychotherapist working in harmony, co-creating a mutual transformative experience.

I invite you, the reader, to join in this interesting discussion, to read this transcript with a discerning eye, to reflect on your own clients, and to articulate your own perspectives. What would you have done differently? Why? What is your experience of therapeutic involvement as a client and as a psychotherapist? As we discuss these professional concerns together the result may well be that we will all learn how to be fully involved psychotherapists. Our clients will reap the benefits.

Paul is a forty-year-old psychotherapist who has attended a couple of previous training workshops with me. In this particular workshop I have just finished a long theoretical presentation when Paul asked to do some personal therapy. Usually he has a good understanding of himself yet, on this day, he is troubled by unresolved thoughts and feelings. The session begins with Paul and me sitting in chairs facing each other. Paul sits with his legs crossed; his body language is relaxed and comfortable.

RICHARD: Paul, what are you experiencing?

PAUL: You have just given me a smile. You have touched me and I got emotional.

RICHARD: What kind of emotion?

PAUL: Sadness. Better said, it is sadness and pain. My intention about working with you is precisely because I noticed that I easily enter into transference with you.

RICHARD: Please tell me your story about transference.

PAUL: I notice that in some moments I have difficulty in relating with you in a natural way. But that it is not your fault. I am conscious enough to realize that I am having fantasies. I notice that I have a big mistrust of you and that I want to withdraw. Then I say to myself, "Look for the contact."

RICHARD: In these fantasies what are the ways in which I might I hurt you … so the drawing back is absolutely necessary?

PAUL: Let me tell you my internal movie. The first day you made a comment to me about what I had said following Martin's therapy demonstration. I understood that what you wanted me to do was to reflect on why I had said it. But the following day I felt out of my center. I felt that I was in trouble with you.

RICHARD: So I must have shamed you.

This is the fifth transaction that I have made. It contains several elements of an involved therapeutic relationship: acknowledgement, vicarious empathy, responsibility for the therapist's errors, and my introducing the concept of shame that could possibly enhance Paul's understanding of his experience. It sets a stage for how the work may proceed; we could build on any and perhaps all of these elements. And it may be too soon; most likely Paul has much more to say before we focus on a particular element or two.

This transaction follows four transactions that are examples of phenomenological inquiry. They are not all questions but each phenomenological inquiry invites an internal search—a discovery and expression of what is internal—a revealing of one's subjective experience. Together these four inquiries form a unit of involvement that supports Paul in further describing his internal process.

PAUL: (pauses for several seconds) The fantasy I got was what I call a black fantasy. I imagine that you think or … even that you comment to other people that what I do is not right. You say, "Paul does not behave well."

RICHARD: You mean that at dinnertime or on a walk in the evening that I am gossiping about you?

PAUL: Not gossiping, but maybe having a commentary with somebody.

RICHARD: What's the difference? In either case I would be belittling you. In either case, I would be making a humiliating comment.

PAUL: Or at least a disapproving comment.

RICHARD: It seems that what makes your fantasy painful is that I would be doing it behind your back and not to your face.

In the three previous transactions I am clarifying and identifying the significance of Paul's distress. This transaction and the one to follow are examples of two types of empathy: vicarious and emotional. First I am making use of vicarious introspection—using my own experience to cognitively identify and explore Paul's possible subjective experience of belittlement or humiliation. This is coupled with the next transaction, a second aspect of empathy—an expression of my affect: "That would hurt". At this moment we are engaged in a shared affective experience: the essence of emotional empathy. The core of therapeutic involvement is in the capacity of the psychotherapist to express empathy accurately within a tone or facial expression that provides the reciprocal to the client's affect; in this situation affective attunement is in the compassionate tone that responds to Paul's sadness.

PAUL: Correct.

RICHARD: (said compassionately) That would hurt!

PAUL: Of course. If there is something between you and me, and you would come and tell me, that would give me a lot of security and trust.

RICHARD: So as a result of the fantasy that you are telling me about … you pull away … and you are not centered within yourself. (Richard pauses for a few seconds) Paul, those are all the symptoms of shame.

PAUL: (pauses for several seconds, looking sad and looks to the ground and shrugs his shoulders)

RICHARD: Can you tell me about those feelings of sadness?

PAUL: (pauses for ten seconds) I feel it inside of me as an old companion. I don't really know where it originated from, but it is familiar to me.

I have introduced the concept of "shame". Paul has not mentioned it, but his sense of hurt and sadness, long pauses, and lack of eye contact all hint that he may be experiencing shame. All the person may know is that he is sad, nervous, feels small, or cannot make contact. The origins of shame are often not immediately available as explicit memory—only as procedural memory—until there is safety-in-relationship. It is often necessary that the psychotherapist introduce a concept such as shame, envy, revenge, or betrayal so that the client can begin to think about his relational experiences.

> RICHARD: Well then, let's stay between you and me. Here you had trust in me and in your internal movie I betray you by talking about you behind your back.

Rather than take Paul to some unknown historical story, I keep the focus on the two of us in the present moment. I am building on the trust in our relationship that Paul previously experienced by suggesting to him that he maintain the sad feelings that have arisen as a result of my behavior and that we talk about those feelings and his self-regulating reactions, as if transference did not exist.

If there have been misattunements or therapeutic errors, or even humiliating comments that I have made, they are more likely to be evident, and resolved, if the therapeutic work is in the present, between us, rather than searching for an origin of Paul's feelings. We can always do the historical work later if it proves necessary. Keeping the dialogue about our current relationship seems most important at this point in the therapy. It is "between us" that Paul can form a new relational pattern; perhaps I too will learn and grow from this encounter.

> PAUL: That is it. When I lose contact with you and I enter into old stories, I lose my trust in you. (Paul starts to cry)
>
> RICHARD: Those tears are important. (Paul nods while he cries) Just close your eyes and go where that cry takes you. (Paul closes his eyes … a few seconds pass) It looks like you are stopping your body from weeping, as though your body knows a sense of betrayal … having trusted someone and they don't live up to your trust.
>
> PAUL: (takes some deep breaths and pauses for thirty seconds with his eyes closed. He opens his eyes and smiles at Richard) These words touch me. Your words describe that I trust somebody that betrays my trust. I'm sad and I feel like I

am shaking inside. (Paul wipes the tears from his face …
and after a pause is no longer crying)

In this last set of transactions I validated Paul's feelings and experiences while also bringing his attention to the connection between his crying, shaking body, and the betrayal of trust from a significant other. His shaking body is telling a significant story that he is not yet putting into language. He has been able to tell a bit about his emotional experience by using the metaphor of an internal movie—a movie in which he is humiliated.

Is his yet untold story solely about how my behavior has impacted him? Or is it about other significant relationships? Or both? It may be time to explore beyond our relationship (he did mention that this feeling is "familiar") and then perhaps return to articulating the quality of connection we have with each other: both his former trust and now his "big mistrust" of me.

An effective, relationally focused integrative psychotherapy continually weaves the client's and psychotherapist's experiences of their relationship in the present moment with an exploration of the emotional and self-stabilizing results of past relationships in the client's life. It is this dual focus that provides a double opportunity to resolve the troubling effects of relational disruptions with introjected others while also establishing new patterns of relationship with the psychotherapist. I then take the risk of expressing my intuition about why he may be crying. I phrase it as a tentative question rather than as an interpretation.

RICHARD: Paul, what was your relationship with your previous mentor? You mentioned at lunch that you no longer see him.

PAUL: I always kept a secure distance from him. I did not feel sufficiently protected and taken care of to open up for a closer relationship.

RICHARD: Did you want a closer relationship with him before you kept him distant … or even while you kept him distant?

PAUL: It is like a double movement. A wish to be nearer, while a part of me says "Stay away!"

RICHARD: Have you done that double movement with me these past two days … after I made that comment? Had your mentor also done something that kept you away, or did you sense something would go wrong and never got close?

Here I open two possible avenues of discovery: the nature of the relationship between Paul and me and the nature of the relationship between Paul and his previous mentor. This multifaceted question allows for discovering where Paul will go; he has referred to "old stories" but he also has a strong emotional reaction to me. If he talks about our relationship it will provide the opportunity to explore new possibilities between us. If he chooses to talk about his mentor, we can work on resolving that relational conflict first and then I will also use it as a metaphor about our relationship, eventually bringing our therapeutic dialogue back to what is both present and missing in the contact between us.

> PAUL: He did not do any negative or hurtful comments to me, but I saw his behavior with other people and so I said to myself, "I am not getting into this!"
>
> RICHARD: Previously you used the word "transference." Do you suppose with him that was transference or observation? (a few seconds' pause) Can you tell me about both?
>
> PAUL: Both are there. I think my observations were correct. But, also, when I can relate with somebody in a relaxed and a natural manner, that is one thing … But when I notice that I feel uncomfortable and I don't know how to be … That happened to me on the second day with you. That used to happen often with (he speaks the name of his former trainer and supervisor).
>
> RICHARD: Then I will assume that I hurt you the other day by either the content or the style in which I spoke to you … or at least in the context of doing it in front of your colleagues here. That was a break in our relationship!

"At this point I am bringing the focus back to my failure—to the error I made that ruptured Peter's trust. That rupture in trust resulted in his sadness and silence and perhaps stimulated memories of previous breaches in trust. But, for now, I want to keep the work between us; there is no rush to explore any possible unfinished business with his mentor or any other person. I have some reparation to do before we turn our attention to his disappointments in other significant relationships or to explore his sense of shame. If I take responsibility for how I have failed or betrayed him and make the necessary corrections, then it may not be necessary to explore his loss of trust with his previous mentor or any other significant person. The healing of his shame or sense of betrayal may occur in how I repair our relationship."

> PAUL: I think for me it was your tone of voice.
> RICHARD: Can you share with me the tone of voice that you heard? I don't remember it.
> PAUL: For me it was strict.
> RICHARD: So it is the tone that is shaming … the strictness of it? (Paul pauses and nods) Does the tone say, "You did it wrong"? (Richard says this shaking his finger at Peter to emphasize the "tone" with a body gesture)

My gesture is used to validate Paul's experience of the tone—a shaming gesture that describes the strict tone that Paul heard. At this point acknowledging and validating Paul's experience are the most important transactions—transactions that signal my involvement. Any explanation or description of what I felt or meant would be non-therapeutic and may create an even greater rupture in his sense of trust. It is therapeutically necessary that I de-center from my own experience and stay with Paul's. How Paul makes meaning of our transactions is most important in understanding how he organizes his experience and in eventually co-creating a new set of relational anticipations. My immediate therapeutic priority is in reestablishing a trusting relationship.

> PAUL: Yes, that gesture shows how I received it. The content was a question, but the tone got me in a different manner.
> RICHARD: What was the psychological message you heard? Not the social message … the psychological?
> PAUL: I felt that at that moment you did not approve my words that I addressed to Martin. It is like you said, "You did wrong by saying that at that moment."
> RICHARD: It is true that I did not approve of it. That is true. (small pause) What do you think?

Being straightforward and honest about my behavior is important in our relationship. I could imply that the disapproval Paul is experiencing is the result of his misunderstanding and/or transference, but the effect would be a loss of my authenticity and genuine involvement. Truth telling is essential if we are to have a healing relationship. In the next several transactions my honesty and authenticity, as well as making Paul's point of view central, are significant in establishing Paul's security-in-relationship.

> PAUL: (paused for five seconds) You linked this comment of mine with other comments, saying to me that after other pieces of work I also make diagnostic comments of this type.
>
> RICHARD: That's true. I did say something to that effect. I had seen a pattern in two other workshops.
>
> PAUL: For me, this comment was not correct.
>
> RICHARD: Do you think I made a mistake ... and that I was not correct?
>
> PAUL: I think you are not precise.
>
> RICHARD: Tell me about that. You know, I could be wrong.
>
> PAUL: (pauses and starts to talk, but hesitates and stops)
>
> RICHARD: You just interrupted yourself there. What did you interrupt inside?
>
> PAUL: (pauses for a couple of seconds, looks to the ground and sighs) A commentary about what I did in other workshops leaves me defenseless, because we can either reflect on what is happening at this moment ... such as my comment on the work that Martin did ... this for me is here and now. But when you connect it with other stories and you say "It is like this," I get lost.
>
> RICHARD: That makes sense. So, in the future, if I think you are misunderstanding someone, you want me to keep it only in the now. And you need me not to bring in other events ... only the current event.
>
> PAUL: Yes, that is it. In the present I can find myself and understand myself. And I can understand what you are saying.
>
> RICHARD: I can do that for you!

Graciousness is an important aspect of involvement. "I can do that for you!" is one of the most wonderful interpersonal transactions, provided there are no strings attached—no "you owe me". A freely given, "I can do that for you!" is a form of unconditional positive regard for the other, an intimate connection. It is beyond apology; it is a commitment to future action and therefore reparative.

PAUL: (Paul nods his head) While we are talking I noticed that my body is tense ... and for the last five minutes I have noticed that it has tensed a bit more.

RICHARD: Well, let's go back to your movie. Run it ahead at fast speed and see what the terrible ending could be from this conversation.

PAUL: This conversation or of my movie?

RICHARD: It could be mixed, so you choose.

PAUL: (closes his eyes and thinks for thirty seconds) In the ending of my movie I remain alone. And not only alone regarding you, but alone in a deeper sense of being really alone. (pause) What moved me, especially yesterday, was the theme of "belonging" that you were illustrating.

RICHARD: Earlier this week you seemed very relaxed and free ... when you made that comment about Martin. Perhaps it would have been much better for you if I just kept my mouth shut.

PAUL: (sighs) To exchange and also not to agree with ideas and opinions seems all right to me. I see how you work and I appreciate you a lot. I sometimes see a piece of work that I don't agree with, but that does not change my appreciation for you.

RICHARD: Oh, I did not know that you disagreed with it. I would like to know about that.

PAUL: (Laughs) Some I have told you.

RICHARD: Yes, but it's the ones you have not told me that I am curious about now. But you have also said it was my tone, not specifically the content, but the tone.

There are many potentially therapeutic directions to follow in these previous few sentences: what was occurring between us in the past five minutes that increased his body tension, his internal movie, his deep sense of aloneness, the theme of belonging, his different opinions, and my errors. Investigating each of these may well reveal useful therapeutic material; each will take Paul to different awarenesses, memories, and beliefs about self and others. I have only seconds to make a choice. Therapeutic involvement includes making use of all the personal and professional experience that the psychotherapist has accumulated: from our understanding of theory, from supervision, from working with similar clients, from cinemas and novels, from our own personal therapy, and from our unique sensitivities. We then selectively use these experiences to choose our areas of inquiry. Therapeutic involvement includes a sense of somatic resonance with our clients. As an outcome of my somatic resonance with Paul I steered the therapy to what I suspected was the source of Paul's body tension— that tension which may have been building up in the past several minutes. I thought it was important to bring Paul's attention back to the tone of my voice and how he sensed my "strict" tone. But I was not certain. I wondered if his body tension was a reaction to my tone, or something that has happened between us that we were not yet talking about, or if he was having a bodily reaction to some emotional memory?

PAUL: Yes, and the tone was badly done. That is how I received it. (Paul shakes his finger at Richard)

RICHARD: Please do that gesture again. (Richard shakes his finger at Paul in imitation of a gesture that Paul has just made … a gesture that Richard made earlier to emphasize the strict tone that Paul heard) You did this (shaking his finger).

PAUL: (shakes his head) No, I was not conscious that I did that.

RICHARD: So the tone is badly done. Can you translate those words into German and say it? "Badly done" … or something similar? (Paul no longer lives in Germany, but the language of his first twenty-five years was German)

PAUL: Das hast du falsch gemacht. You did it wrong (shaking his finger at Richard).

RICHARD: Now do that again with your hand.

PAUL: Das hast du falsch gemacht. You did it wrong (shakes his finger, then fist at Richard).

RICHARD: Now close your eyes and do it.

I have directed Paul to speak in his original language. At this moment I am relying on my previous experiences in doing psychotherapy with bilingual people. I am also assuming that his body tension is because of what he is not saying. Having him express himself in German may facilitate self-expression and new awarenesses. Closing his eyes may also be effective because it may take him out of the present context and activate memories that have not been conscious until now. Speaking in German with his eyes closed will likely intensify the "familiar feeling" that Paul has mentioned and may allow us to work with both his body tension and his old self-stabilizing reactions.

In the last four transactions I am using the method of therapeutic direction. In these transactions the therapeutic work is not directly in the transactions between us but, rather, it is in the client's discovery of his internal processes. Therapeutic direction is not in the moment directly "relational" but it does facilitate the client's self-exploration— a learning about his unconscious or intrapsychic processes. Therapeutic direction should only be used within the context of a securely established relationship—the relational dynamics bracket any intrapsychic work. In the next several transactions please observe how the therapeutic direction is based on the psychotherapist's full involvement with the client.

PAUL: (closes his eyes). Das hast du falsch gemacht. You did it wrong.
RICHARD: Now with the right tone and louder.
PAUL: Das hast du falsch gemacht. You did it wrong.
RICHARD: Keep going.
PAUL: Das hast du falsch gemacht! You did it wrong!
RICHARD: Now, keep going and finish the sentence.
PAUL: Das hast du falsch gemacht!! You did it wrong!!
RICHARD: Keep going ... keep talking.
PAUL: Das macht man nicht so. Das hast du falsch gemacht!—one does not do it like this. You did it wrong! (takes a heavy sigh and looks like he is close to crying).
RICHARD: You know that tone.

This transaction and my next are examples of validating what has been significant in Paul's life. My validating comment opens the possibility for Paul to express emotions that have remained unexpressed. Prior to these last few transactions I was not sure if he was expressing how he experienced my behavior, the meaning in my tone of voice, or whether he was quoting someone else. From the intensity of his emotional reaction I assumed that he was speaking from an archaic experience, hence my comment, "You know that tone."

PAUL: (nods his head then bows his head and cries for over a minute)

RICHARD: You know that tone very well (said very gently).

PAUL: (long pause; he sighs and nods his head) That is true (he wipes the tears from his face with a tissue and blows his nose). It takes me back directly to the two years I lived alone with my father after my parents' separation and my mother moved back to England, when I was fourteen to sixteen. I realize now that there was nobody else. I think that before then, when we lived together, his tone did not hurt me because there were five people. After their separation I was there with him alone.

RICHARD: (touches Peter's hand) Show me again (after a pause Richard shakes his finger at Peter) "Badly done, badly done."

At this point there are two primary nonverbal transactions that I am doing. I tenderly touch Paul's hand to make physical contact and provide a sense of security between us before he goes on with his story. He may need our physical contact as a safe reference point as he uncovers old memories. Secondarily, I repeat the gesture of a pointing finger while simultaneously repeating the words, "badly done." My finger pointing and critical words constitute an enactment that may stimulate his memories. An important aspect of a relationally focused integrative psychotherapy is in the psychotherapist's willingness to be actively involved by engaging the client in reexperiencing difficult or even traumatic events. Through a combination of a well established secure relationship and the judicious use of experiential methods, the psychotherapist creates a "safe emergency" in which the client can recover previously unconscious memories, feelings, and life script forming conclusions and decisions.

PAUL: I have one memory that stands out. For me it is so incoherent that I always kept it apart. For me it is not understandable and it only happened once.

RICHARD: What is that?

PAUL: That my father at a certain moment told me: "I wished you were dead."

RICHARD: What a betrayal. It may have lasted only a moment, but the memories lasted for years and years and years.

PAUL: Yes, It disturbed me completely. I could not understand, but I never forgot.

RICHARD: Say it again so it makes an impact on me.

PAUL: Ich wünschte, du wärest tot. I wished you were dead.

RICHARD: Now do it in his tone.

PAUL: (in a strict voice) Ich wünschte, du wärest tot! I wished you were dead!

RICHARD: And with the same gesture.

PAUL: No, I don't remember his gesture.

RICHARD: But you know the tone and you know the message.

PAUL: He said it with total disapproval.

RICHARD: Not only disapproval of your behavior.

PAUL: (points to himself with his finger to his chest) But of myself … that is what I felt with him (he places his hand on the side of his face, put his head down and cries). I feel tremendous loneliness.

RICHARD: "Tremendous loneliness."

Here I am using the technique of therapeutic highlighting, repeating the client's words, therefore acknowledging and validating what the client has just said as a way to underscore the significance of his words and affect. The previous enactment has stimulated Paul's memory of his father's words, "I wished you were dead!" Now Paul is aware of the context of his "tremendous loneliness" and his anticipation of disapproval.

PAUL: I remember this year as the most difficult year in my life; a black year.

RICHARD: Did he destroy something that day?

PAUL: Not only that day but with everything that happened. He never said these words again, but his message was that I was not valuable.

RICHARD: And I did a mini-version of the same thing when you heard my tone. The tone in my voice implied that you were of no value.

I am again bringing the focus back to the relationship between Paul and me. I am taking responsibility for implying that he is of no value. Even though I did not say those words, for Paul my tone implied that he was "not valuable." It would be easy to keep the focus only on his father's behavior but if this is going to be a healing relationship, my taking responsibility and making the necessary corrections will be extremely important. The work will now weave back and forth between a focus on us—our present relationship, as Paul experiences it—and a focus on his relationship with his father.

> PAUL: This was the trigger. Do you remember the first work we did together?
>
> RICHARD: At this moment, no, but if you keep going I will. You have to press the right buttons on my computer.
>
> PAUL: Four or five years ago in London.
>
> RICHARD: I remember meeting you there, but at the moment I don't remember, so keep going.
>
> PAUL: I worked there for the first time with respect to my father and I couldn't talk to him in an empty chair.
>
> RICHARD: Yes. I remember that you could only talk to me about him.
>
> PAUL: Because my experience of that period of my life was that he was this big (Peter opens his arms outward and wide) and I without power.
>
> RICHARD: Now I remember that session we had. So, is it accurate to assume that when you got the verbal message from your father—at age sixteen—that you were of "no value," that it had been happening all along, but much more subtly?

Rather than make a pronouncement or an interpretation about the psychological dynamics between Paul and his father, I ask Paul a question that solicits his understanding. This is based on an important principle of a relationally orientated psychotherapy: the absence of certainty on the part of the psychotherapist. The therapist's theory, interpretation, or wish for behavioral change is less important than the mutual experience of client and psychotherapist. There is no certainty in our theory, opinions, or even observations. If we are to be effective in building a new relationship with the client we need to co-create with the client a fresh understanding of his psychological dynamics. If I take the position that I know nothing about the client's internal experience, then I must engage in a continual phenomenological inquiry about what he is feeling, thinking, fantasizing, remembering, or sensing in the body. Involvement then includes holding the self-expressions and opinions of the client in high esteem. Both client and therapist learn and grow from this shared experience.

> PAUL: In some manner, yes. When my parents separated and my two sisters went to England with my mother, I chose to be with my father … to not leave him alone … the family broke and that was horrible for him. Two years later, when I was fifteen, his mother died and that for him was like the last blow. I think he was not there for me.
> RICHARD: So it was the last blow to you also (Peter nods his head intensely and says yes). A real knockout?
> PAUL: Enough that I left.
> RICHARD: So yesterday … were you leaving me?

Here I again bring Paul's attention to our relationship. I inquire about how he may be using his self-stabilizing strategies with me that he learned to use when his father was "not there." It is in our current therapeutic relationship that he can relax his old self-stabilizing patterns that interfere with both full internal and interpersonal contact.

> PAUL: The day before yesterday. Yesterday I reencountered myself and therefore I felt more comfortable with you.
> RICHARD: So how did you reencounter yourself? Can you teach me how you do that?
> PAUL: No (Paul laughs out loud).
> RICHARD: No? You don't know how?
> PAUL: It is a matter of time; it is like recovering the tranquility. There comes a moment when the movie stops.
> RICHARD: Why didn't you stay distant? Why give me a second chance?
> PAUL: I feel a need to be near to you.
> RICHARD: So what happens if I continue to make other mistakes like this one? Let's look at the future film. Let's say I make these mistakes again.

Now I am shifting the focus of our therapeutic work to the future. What have we each learned from this session? How will we be different with each other? I have already committed myself to speaking only about a current event and not bringing external events into any discussion.

The therapy that follows has a distinctive cognitive and behavioral focus—thinking together about how to do "it" differently in the future. This is still an integral part of a relational psychotherapy. If done with respect, it constitutes a shared experience: inquiring about how Paul envisions being different and me sharing my perspective of how he can change his reactions.

> PAUL: I think that with two or three occasions we will repeat ourselves and then I would withdraw in a definite manner.
> RICHARD: So to withdraw is a self-stabilizing solution for you?
> PAUL: That is one solution, to protect myself.
> RICHARD: Oh, … you call that protection?
> PAUL: (laughs) Yes. Not because you are so dangerous, but because when I connect with this disapproval and loneliness it leaves me knocked out.
> RICHARD: Yes, and then you probably stabilize yourself by withdrawing. (pause) Can I argue with you?
> PAUL: OK.
> RICHARD: The real protection … the most effective protection … is to do what you did here today.
> PAUL: (nods his head) Yes. I woke up this morning and I felt that I had to work for two reasons. Because our relationship matters to me.
> RICHARD: And for that I am very happy. I did not know that you were distancing; I could not tell. And the second reason?
> PAUL: Because I want to heal this wound.

This is a mini-contract from Paul that allows me to take the next therapeutic direction—a direction that takes Paul back to his original relationship difficulties with his father. As I emphasized earlier, the healing of relational disruptions can occur in two dimensions: between us by working within our relationship and intrapsychically by expressing his feelings and needs to his introjected father. As we do both in the therapy we strengthen the possibility that he can again find security-in-relationship rather than in his use of a self-stabilizing withdrawal.

RICHARD: Then just close your eyes and go back into that house where you lived alone with father. Go right into that situation … right into the room where he said that cruel comment that day. Look at his image, the way he looked then. And this time, Paul, don't go silent. This time when he tells you not to live, respond to him.

PAUL: (his eyes are closed and he pauses for several seconds)

RICHARD: Do the opposite.

PAUL: (pauses for another thirty seconds with his eyes still closed) I cannot believe what you are telling me!

Through this experiential method of talking to the representation of his father, Paul is undoing an old retroflection, the holding in of his feelings and self-expression. He is speaking out. He is telling his truth. He has broken his silence. Over the past twenty-five years, in the face of relational discord, Paul has re-stabilized himself through remaining silent and withdrawing rather than speaking about what he needs in a relationship. He could not rely on his father for a sense of stabilization and security so he relied on his own ability to remain quiet. Yet, in life today, this old pattern of managing relationships through silence and withdrawal is no longer working. Here he is experimenting with a new way of being in relationship with at least the internal image of his father—a new way that may carry over into other relationships. In a previous workshop Paul was reluctant to speak to the internal image of his father. Now he is speaking his mind.

RICHARD: Keep going.

PAUL: It is completely out of place.

RICHARD: (grabs Paul's hand and with each word he bangs Paul's hand on the pillow) I can't believe it!

Here, again, I am using therapeutic highlighting. I repeat Paul's words, "I can't believe it," to emphasize the emotional significance of what he has previously said. Helping Paul hit the pillow is a bodily active method of encouraging him to express his retroflected energy, feelings, and words. It is a means to express all that has been held inside in silence. It is also a gesture of making an impact. It is not about releasing a specific amount of feelings; it is about undoing the process of retroflecting so that he has a physical as well as a verbal sense of expressing himself.

> PAUL: (he starts to cry and his voice gets loud; he is banging his hands on the pillow while he yells the words) How can you say something like that?
>
> RICHARD: Paul, make it a statement. Make it a statement rather than a question.
>
> PAUL: (eyes still closed, crying and very emotional; as he yells he bangs his hands on the pillow) You cannot say something like this to your son! Fuck!
>
> RICHARD: Keep going, Paul.
>
> PAUL: (crying with his eyes closed, shaking his head and banging his hands on the pillow while he yells out the words) Do you have any idea how this hurts? It hurts me when you say that (sobbing for thirty seconds ... Paul pauses for another forty seconds, calmer now and his eyes open) I have a clear feeling that I need to have you near, Richard (pauses for ten seconds).
>
> RICHARD: (reaches out and takes Paul's hand) I will hold on to this hand and you talk to him with this one.
>
> PAUL: (looks at Richard and smiles, then looks again to the pillow that represents his father) My head says it cannot be. How can you say that?
>
> RICHARD: Now just turn that question into a statement.

Several times Paul has asked questions and most of the time I have urged him to turn his questions into statements. His questions to the image of a father will go without answers and will avoid his experience and feelings. Changing his questions into statements allows him to express his feelings and reactions—to speak his own mind. Statements express his need to make an impact; questions get into the endless loop of "why." Statements will empower him! His growth will be in telling his previously silent story to his father, by expressing his feeling and relational needs.

> PAUL: Papa, das kannst du einfach nicht sagen, dass geht nicht. Dad, you just cannot say something like this, no way.
>
> RICHARD: Yeah, say it louder.

PAUL: Du kannst frustriert sein, es kann dir schlecht gehen, was auch immer. Aber es gibt was, das geht nicht! Es geht einfach nicht. Du kannst mich nicht so behandeln! You can be frustrated, you can be down, whatsoever. But there are things you cannot do! No way. You cannot treat me like this!

RICHARD: Yeah.

PAUL: (cries and bangs his one hand again and again on the pillow while still holding onto Richard's hand and continuing to speak in German) Da gibt es eine Grenze, da kann man einfach nicht drüber! Du kannst da nicht drüber. Das geht bis dahin! Es gibt Sachen, die kannst du nicht sagen, es gibt Sachen, die kannst du nicht tun! Das ist einfach zu unmenschlich, das ist bestial! There is a limit that you cannot pass! Until there! There are things you just cannot say, there are things you just cannot do! That is just too inhuman, that is brutal!

RICHARD: Tell him what you decided that day.

PAUL: (pauses for twenty seconds and takes some deep breaths) Dazusein und nicht dazusein. Einerseits brauche ich dich, aber andererseits traue ich dir nicht. To be there and to not be there. On the one hand I need you and on the other hand I don't trust you.

Paul made an explicit decision as an adolescent—a decision that he has not forgotten, but one that has affected some of his relationships since then. When decisions are made in response to specific events they are often available as explicit memory and therefore an active redecision is possible. In this piece of work we do not yet know if this decision is the only source of Paul's self-limiting silence and withdrawal. It is possible that he has made a number of similar implicit conclusions that have built up over a long period of time. Such implicit conclusions are usually not conscious or thought about because they seem to the person to be a natural reaction to repeated relational failures. Implicit conclusions, as well as explicit decisions, form self-limiting script beliefs. When I am working with a client whose life script was composed primarily from implicit conclusions in response to cumulative neglect, the therapy must be relational. The healing process occurs through the psychotherapist's consistent attunement to the client's affect, rhythm, relational needs, and representation of self-in-relationship. It is often not useful to use the active methods that I am using here with Paul if the life script is formed primarily from implicit conclusions. Even with Paul I would not want the therapy to end with only a redecision. He said that "there was nobody" and implied that his father was too occupied with his own losses to be contactful. Paul may need the ongoing presence of a respectful, caring psychotherapist who offers an alternative way of being in relationship. But, for now, it seems as though an awareness of the profoundness of his original decision and a possible redecision will make a tremendous difference in his life.

RICHARD: (moves the hand he is holding) On one hand (points to Paul's other hand) … and, on the other hand.

PAUL: (looks at Richard) Yeah.

RICHARD: Paul, talk to your daddy. Stay with him. Tell him about being torn inside, "On one hand and on the other." Tell him how that decision affected all of your relationships.

PAUL: Ich traue dir nicht. Heute kann ich mit gewissen Dingen zählen, aber gefühlsmässig traue ich dir nicht. Ich brauche diesen Sicherheitsabstand, und nicht nur mit dir, sondern mit allen Menschen, wo ich mich in Gefahr fühle. Und es ist nicht einfach für mich. I don't trust you. Today I can count on certain things, but emotionally I don't trust you. I need this safe distance. And not only with you but with all the people where I feel in danger. And this is not easy for me.

RICHARD: (moves Paul's hand that he is holding) Now tell him what this hand needs.

PAUL: Papa, ich brauche dich, und ich hätte dich damals sehr gebraucht. Heute kann ich mich selber behaupten, aber ich hätte dich damals sehr gebraucht. Dad, I need you and I would have needed you then very much. Today I can take care of myself, but then I needed you very much. (pause of thirty seconds) Ich hätte gebraucht, dass du mich richtig findest; dass du mich bestärkt hättest in meinem Eigensein; dass ich dich um Rat hätte fragen können; dass du mir geholfen hättest, mich zu orientieren. Ich habe meinen ganzen Weg selbst gemacht. (switches from German into Spanish) Nadie me ha dicho como hacerlo. I would have needed you to have found me appropriate and valuable.

> That would have confirmed me in being as I am. That
> I could have asked you for advice. That you would have
> helped me to orient myself. I have done all of my way on
> my own. Nobody told me how to do it.

RICHARD: (holds up the hand he is holding, then points to Paul's other hand) That one pushes him away.

PAUL: Yes. (pause)

RICHARD: Now what just happened inside? The muscles in your face changed just slightly; something happened.

PAUL: (looks at Richard with a calm smile) It makes me feel so good to have you next to me, looking at me with an expression of love and appreciation. It relaxes me and it makes me feel happy.

RICHARD: Now tell that to father. "Father, what I need from you is ..."

This last therapeutic direction is called "priming the pump." It is an active method that encourages the person to say what he is holding back from saying. Yet the psychotherapist does not complete the sentence; we only prime the client to speak and the client finishes the sentence in his own manner. Most of the time it is essential that the therapist not finish the sentence so the client can have the experience of saying "it" in his own way and/or to avoid compliance with the psychotherapist. I have often been surprised by how a client ends the sentence when I have primed the pump and refrained from finishing the sentence. On rare occasions I may finish the sentence: if the client cannot get the words out because of inhibition or threat of punishment; or, if my cognitive attunement is such that I sense that I can provide the words that reflect the client's internal experience—words that the client has not yet thought about speaking.

PAUL: Was ich von dir brauche, ist, dass du einfach zu mir stehst. What I need from you is to simply be on my side and back me.

RICHARD: Let me add one more: "And believe in me, papa, believe in my way, not just backing me."

Here I am going beyond priming the pump. I am actually saying what I think the client is not saying. I take this risk of saying it for the client as a way to show my attunement with what the client needs to say and has not put into words. The attunement is the important ingredient; if I am misattuned and say something that is not in accord with the client's inner experience, then I will rupture our relationship. Paul's laughter and next response indicates that I made an appropriate expression of what he could not yet say. Sensing what to say at a moment like this is an expression of involvement.

PAUL: (laughs) For me they go together.

RICHARD: "Believe in me, trust me."

PAUL: Yeah. Vertraue mir, dass ich das Richtige mache. Trust me that I am doing the right thing. (pause for thirty seconds)

PAUL: (said angrily) Für mich warst du unendlich brutal. In deinen Worten, in deinem Ton, in deinem Verhalten. Du hast mich nicht geschlagen, aber warst unendlich brutal. For me you have been infinitely brutal, in your words, in your tone, in your acts. You did not beat me, but you have been infinitely brutal. (Pause for one minute. Paul sits with his eyes closed. Richard remains silent while keeping his gaze on Paul the whole time.)

PAUL: (loud with anger) Du hast mir sehr wehgetan. Es war wirklich das schlimmste Jahr in meinem Leben. Ich wünsche das keinem. You have hurt me a lot. It has really been the worst year in my life. I don't wish that for anybody else.

RICHARD: And tell him what you decided that year.

PAUL: Es gibt keinen, auf den ich zählen kann; zumindest keinen Mann. Im Grunde bin ich allein. There is nobody, I cannot count on anyone; at least not on any man. Basically I am alone. (pause for forty seconds; then Paul switches from German into English) There are some people where it is better to protect my fragility. And where I don't dare show myself; it is better to withdraw instead. (pause for forty seconds, then lovingly looks at Richard) It is a little bit complicated to deal with me in our relationship.

Paul has just spoken his script decision. He is now aware of the decision and how it has affected his life for the past twenty-five years. I do not push Paul to make a redecision out loud; I trust that a redecision is going on inside. His emotionally intense awareness is powerful enough that his life will change significantly. In the next few transactions Paul is already anticipating a different quality to our relationship.

RICHARD: What do you mean, Paul?

PAUL: Predicting the future, I assume that it will happen again with you.

RICHARD: Yes, a probability.

PAUL: Therefore it will be a bit complicated sometimes (laughs).

RICHARD: OK. So then the question is, "What do we do about it?"

PAUL: What I am going to do is to bring my difficulty with you to the relationship.

RICHARD: Well, thank you. That would be good for both of us because then I don't have to be guessing about what is going on inside of you.

PAUL: And I would like it that when I signal my distress you would take me seriously.

RICHARD: Taking you seriously would be no difficulty at all. In fact, it would probably be quite pleasing to do … just as it is to sit here and hold your hand at this moment.

With this transaction I am making a commitment to Paul—a commitment to respecting him and taking him seriously. This is therapeutic involvement! Another element of therapeutic involvement is in my question to Paul, "What do we do about it?" Notice the use of "we," a small but significant word that signals that he is not alone and that I will take his concerns seriously. "We," a word that means someone else is there to help him resolve potential conflicts. The "we" communicates our relationship and my commitment to a co-constructive process. The healing of relational disruptions and psychological distress occurs through a contactful therapeutic relationship. Observe the next few transactions: when I say that it would be pleasing to take him seriously, Paul becomes aware of both new possibilities and another script decision.

PAUL: Something interesting is happening in the meantime (slowly points his finger to himself then to Richard) I am realizing that … is it possible that a man can love me? It is like a question (moves his body back and laughs), which brings me to another decision of that time.

RICHARD: Can you put it in words?

PAUL: Back then I decided that there are no men that can love me. (Richard and Paul look caringly at each other while sitting with relaxed body language for twenty seconds, then they smile at each other)

PAUL: I feel that you love me. (Richard reaches out and again takes Paul's hand)

RICHARD: For children … and that is what you were when your father did that; you were still a child … love is not in the abstract words, "I love you." (Paul begins to cry … after a pause he wipes the tears from his eyes and nods yes.) Love is in action … through the action that the child needs. And your father's behavior that day was not loving.

PAUL: Not on that day … and neither on many other days.

RICHARD: I am so sorry to hear that.

PAUL: This is the wound in here (points to his heart).

RICHARD: So maybe now that we have cleaned the infection the wound can heal naturally. That wound has been infected for a long time by the decision you made.

PAUL: I understand. (pauses for several seconds then lets go of Richard`s hand) I would like to have a hug.

RICHARD: A standing up one?

PAUL: Yes! Richard and Paul stand up and have a long embrace.

Although Paul has not verbalized a redecision, the way in how he relates to me at the end, and after this session, is different; this is evident in his desire for affection from a man and saying "I feel loved by you." There may be more relational work to do. But, for today, we have accomplished much in this therapy. In this work I have focused the therapy on both the centrality of the therapeutic relationship and the use of experiential and expressive methods. Without a quality relationship the experiential methods would simply be "doing something" to the client. Within a caring therapeutic relationship the expressive and experiential methods are used in a co-creative process with and for the client. When the psychotherapist is fully contactful and completely involved in the relationship with the client, the client can then risk experimenting with active methods that create a reenactment of old relational failures and traumas.

I would like to conclude our discussion by articulating some of the important principles that are inherent in therapeutic involvement. My first awareness in establishing a therapeutic relationship with Paul was of being curious about his perspective, feelings, and how uniquely different he is from me. I became particularly curious about exploring Paul's description of my tone of voice and the meaning he ascribed to my words and tone. I am not suggesting that psychotherapists become confluent with the client, but rather that we temporarily get out of our own frame of reference and appreciate the client's way of organizing his experience. With Paul, as with all clients, I assume that I know nothing about his (or their) experience or inner life. All my observations and theories are mere impressions. These impressions do not tell me enough about what it is like to be in Paul's experience. It is therefore essential that I engage in an ongoing phenomenological inquiry to discover Paul's perspective, feelings, and what he needs in a therapeutic relationship.

When I am dependable, reliable, and consistent in how I establish an environment of emotional stability for my clients, I experience a sense of integrity. My honesty in telling Paul that I did not approve of what he said was significant and necessary in providing a dependable working relationship. Honesty and truth telling are important aspects of integrity. I find it essential to repeatedly ask myself the question, "What is the effect of my inner affect or behaviour on the client?" Taking responsibility for how I affect the other is part of maintaining my inner sense of integrity.

When I am less certain of the truth, or the right way, then I allow clients to influence me; as a result, they become more self-expressive. I want my clients to have the sense that in this therapeutic relationship they can make an impact on me. Paul went silent with his father; he withdrew and did not make an impact. In the work with Paul I listened and accepted his description of my "strict" tone rather than focusing on or explaining my experience.

I strive to provide my clients with an opportunity for choice whenever possible. My wish to provide choice is based on the assumption that the client's behavior seems to him to be the best possible option given his past experiences and motivation. Paul was without choice in his family. He had no voice in his parents' separation. He said that he chose to stay with his father but that choice was made out of his wanting to take care of his father; it was not a choice for his own welfare.

In my clinical experience, I have found that clients become less guarded and self-protective in an atmosphere of graciousness. When I am both respectful and gracious, it provides the client with a sense of security and the opening to express himself more fully. When I said to Paul, "I can do that for you," I said it with a sense of respect and an honoring of his "OKness." Shortly after making this statement of reparation, Paul was able to shift his focus to the necessary work with his father.

When I have made a commitment to the welfare of the client, I am touched by a sense of compassion. This sense of compassion includes both emotion and an attitude of being with and for the other person; it is the highest form of being interpersonally contactful. Compassion involves a commitment to understanding my client's feelings and motivations while valuing his uniqueness and differences. Throughout Paul's therapy I felt a strong sense of compassion for the man who was pained by my "strict" tone and the adolescent whose father said, "I wish you would be dead." Paul's years of loneliness touched my heart; I wanted to be fully present with him!

Curiosity, personal integrity, the absence of certainty, the opportunity for choice, and a sense of compassion are all aspects of contact-in-relationship. Each of these is an internal attitude and feeling about being in relationship; they are the characteristics of therapeutic involvement.

CHAPTER TEN

Bonding in relationship: a solution to violence?

An integrative psychotherapy theory of motivation emphasizes the dynamic interplay of biological imperatives for *stimulus, structure,* and *relationship* (Erskine, 1997b). Bonding, attachment, and connecting are all aspects of these biological imperatives for relationship. As such, relational needs are the components of bonding and relationship that are present throughout our lives. When these relational needs are sufficiently satisfied, the result is a sense of well-being in the relationship. When relational needs are not satisfied, the need becomes more intense and it is phenomenologically experienced as longing, emptiness, a nagging loneliness, or an intense urge often accompanied by nervousness. The absence of satisfaction of relational needs may be manifested as frustration, anger, or aggression (Erskine & Trautmann, 1996). When relational needs are repeatedly not satisfied over a long period of time, one of the results is violence. Another is depression.

Stanley was referred by another patient as "depressed and weird." Stanley arrived for his sessions slovenly dressed in all black clothing with his belly protruding and shoulders drooped. He looked quite depressed. He described himself as a twenty-five-year old photographer whose "photos don't sell." In the early sessions, it became clear that his script beliefs were "I am a failure" and "I don't belong." As I investigated his feelings about these beliefs, there were no emotions. He did, however, talk about various incidences of not belonging and of being a failure. To emphasize what a failure he was, he would bring to the session his black and white abstract photographs, all of which were depressing images of destruction and mayhem.

He talked about how no one was interested in his photography. He claimed to have no feelings associated with the photographs or people's lack of interest in his work. Eventually as we talked about the photographs, he made passing references to some of the photographs representing mass killing. On one occasion, he talked about his plan to buy another gun and his desire for revenge. However, the more I would inquire about his wish to destroy, revenge, killing, or guns, the more distant he would become in the therapy. It seemed as though he wanted me to only listen as he chose when and how to tell me his stories.

Over the next several months each of his stories ended with the script belief, "Something's wrong with me." As we investigated the significance of this belief, he had a number of childhood memories about how he was often used by and picked upon by his peers. Although he was a large boy, he always thought of himself as "the weakling" with "no friends." The other kids called him strange, ugly, and helpless. He was often hit by groups of even smaller boys who took delight in punching him because he was "so fat."

He found no solace or comfort in his relationship with his mother who he described as controlling, pushy, and over-parenting. She would often lie to her friends about Stanley and tell them about his great school and athletic accomplishments. In actuality, Stanley failed at all sports activities and barely passed school exams even with the extensive help of tutors. He always felt that he could not live up to his mother's expectations of greatness. Hence, by comparing his failures with his mother's expectations, he formed the script belief "Something's wrong with me" and "I am a failure." His script belief, "I don't belong" was continually supported by memories of both his father's ignoring him and the behavior of several other children, particularly during adolescence.

Except for the fact that he looked like his father he often thought that he wasn't his father's child. His father was successful, athletic, outgoing, accomplished, and on the surface had many acquaintances. Stanley remembers lying in bed waiting for Father to come home to acknowledge him, to reach out and touch him, to sit and talk with him. Father usually was preoccupied with his own interests. Stanley remembered that on some occasions, his father had actually told him that he looked or acted weird. These events were continually used by Stanley as a reinforcing memory that maintained the shame-based belief, "Something's wrong with me."

As we explored Stanley's profound sense of shame, he remembered how he would often escape to the woods when humiliated by the family or by the other kids. He would get relief by taking big sticks and smashing them against the trees. Following several sessions of a relationally focused integrative psychotherapy that emphasized empathetic inquiry, he was finally able to vividly remember a long-forgotten experience. At age thirteen, his mother had thrown a large swimming party for him and invited all his school and neighborhood acquaintances. Stanley described how "at the party all of the kids ganged up on me and teased me." "They laughed at me when I cried." Stanley fled his own party, went to the woods, and imagined smashing all the kids as he banged sticks against the trees. In this therapy session, Stanley wept for the first time in thirteen years.

As the therapy progressed into the second year, Stanley's distress became much more apparent. He told several stories about how people were unreliable, dishonest, or selfish. The script beliefs that he formed from these experiences were "All people have an angle" and "All people are hiding something." As we explored the memories related to these beliefs, he talked about his father's many sexual affairs and his parents' public pretense of a good marriage.

Throughout this period, he repeatedly accused me of hiding something or having a "false angle." He also talked about his own hiding "things" from me. I told him that I thought that his telling me that he was hiding something from me was an important confession, and that he needed to have his own timeframe and personal readiness before he could tell me the details. Following this, he asked for three sessions a week instead of his usual one. Because of my time schedule, I was able to give him only two sessions per week.

What emerged during our twice-weekly sessions was Stanley's combination of both distrusting and idealizing me. He was worried about the idealization and brought in many examples about how politicians, church leaders, and important people in the community were often hiding something and were dishonest. It became clear in listening to these stories that he needed someone who was consistent and dependable on whom he could rely for security while telling his secrets.

As the second year continued, he described his violent fantasies in more detail. Very slowly at first, he alluded to his images of mass killing, of taking powerful weapons and shooting large numbers of people. In the fantasies, he was strong, brave, powerful, and valued. In real life, he felt weak, foolish, powerless, and "a piece of trash." The fantasies provided a very different self-definition. We often worked with the contrast between his sense of shame and his sense of power and omnipotence in his fantasies. With this, he began to talk about how he was worried that he was like the kids who have done the killings at Columbine High School in Colorado. He began to reveal the extent of these murderous fantasies—their frequency and intensity.

My accepting attitude about Stanley's fantasies encouraged his detailed elaboration and allowed us to look at the psychological functions of the fantasies (Erskine, Moursund, & Trautmann, 1999). We examined his self-definitions and how his identity in fantasy was in such contrast to his identity in relationships with people. Each fantasy also provided predictability; he would encounter a group that had hurt someone or humiliated someone. He would have the group of followers behind him. He would kill those who had done the humiliation or harm. People would be proud of him and declare him a hero.

These fantasies expressed the power that he longed for and imagined as a child when he went into the woods to smash sticks against trees. By continually fantasizing, he didn't feel the humiliation and loss of relationship that he suffered in his childhood; he was powerful rather than shamefully powerless. In the process of telling me the fantasies and my reciprocal attunement to both his affect and level of development, the function of the fantasies began to shift. Our therapeutic relationship rather than the fantasies provided the arena for the expression of his psychological functions. With me, he could define himself. I provided both continuity and stability through my accepting attitude toward him. His identity began to change as he felt more and more OK in my presence and, because of the consistency of our meeting and sometime frequent phone calls, he would predict my responses when he would get worried about his violent fantasies. He found comfort in my attitudes toward him and in remembering my words.

Much of the therapeutic work in that year centered on the elaboration of his fantasies and his relational need to make an impact and to define himself. In his fantasies he was a hero with a group of followers. He would take guns and lead a group of men to attack those who created some injustice; after much killing people would know that he was powerful. He would avenge the oppressed and be a hero. In each fantasy he made an *impact*. Often I did not make comments on the content of the fantasy but rather focused on the relational needs expressed in the fantasies. Through these fantasies Stanley was trying to define himself and to make an impact on others. Gradually Stanley had fewer and fewer violent fantasies.

Following the long summer recess, the beginning of our third year of therapy was marked by Stanley having a return of violent fantasies particularly when on his way to therapy sessions or on the weekends when I was away. As we again talked about his unique relational needs imbedded in each of the violent fantasies, his anger with me kept emerging. He was furious with me because I saw him only twice a week, because I had gone away for the summer, because I had defined him and ignored him, and because I had not confiscated his guns. In his anger at me, he wanted to move me, to shake me up, to get me to feel what his father never felt: compassion, protection, responsibility, and companionship. Eventually, he said, "I want you to see the world through my eyes."

In this third year, by focusing the psychotherapy on the analysis of the transference, I was finally able to reach a much younger Child ego state in Stanley—a child who was humiliated by his peers, and who felt neglected and betrayed by the lack of protection from each of his parents. Stanley was a child who was defined as strange and different. I saw Stanley as a child and a man who needed security and validation for his internal process, to define himself, and make an impact in his relationships. The therapy provided the validation of the psychological function of the fantasies and a respect for Stanley's need to be in the presence of someone who is secure, dependable, consistent, and reliable (ibid.).

Stanley has now sold all his guns! He has gotten a new job working in the film industry in a very unique capacity. He is excited about his accomplishments. He reports having no violent fantasies but he is fantasizing and actualizing his desire for relationships and meaningful work. For the first time in his life he has a close woman friend. Through a contactful therapeutic relationship that focused on relational needs and the psychological function of fantasy Stanley has changed his life. Stanley has achieved an adult life complete with self-definition, impact, and intimacy. Has the therapeutic bonding, attachment, and relationship provided a solution to violence?

Author's postscript

After the speech on which this chapter is based, "Bonding in Relationship: A Solution to Violence?" both Bill Cornell and Robin Fryer raised some interesting questions about how I was affected by Stanley's fantasies of committing acts of mass murder. The following is my response to each of their five questions.

Were you ever worried Stanley would act out before the therapy could take effect?

Early in the therapy, I was focused on treating Stanley's depression and underlying cumulative trauma manifested in the script beliefs, "I'm a failure" and "I don't belong." I assumed that his depressing photographs of destruction and mayhem were only a visual metaphor to describe the "destruction" of his sense of self-worth and the "mayhem" of his family and peer relationships. I became alarmed when he talked about revenge and buying another gun for his already large collection. I tried in vain to get more information. I was worried about his potentially acting on the fantasies.

The only thing that eased my worrying about him between sessions was that he often arrived early for our therapy sessions and he seemed eager both to show me his photographs and to tell me how something was "wrong" with him. Periodically he would call me "just to talk." We were forming a relationship even though he would not let me ask about his fantasies of revenge and killing or about his guns.

The more he voluntarily told me about his childhood the more relaxed I became. He was at least talking out his frustrations and anger, even though he claimed to have no feelings. Once Stanley's profound sense of shame became central to the therapy and he was again able to cry, my worry about his violently acting out his childhood humiliation and rejection began to subside. He seemed committed to psychotherapy.

Did you ever consider whether to report Stanley to authorities as a potential threat to someone?

Yes, this was a major consideration in response to both state laws and professional ethics. My consultations with respected colleagues helped organize priorities and concerns about public safety, therapeutic effectiveness, and ethics. I often thought about how ineffective such a report to the police would be. I had no useful information except that he was buying another gun. In the first year and a half, I had no knowledge of the extent of his fantasies; all I had was my impressions of his photographs and his refusal to answer my questions.

Any police report I could have made would have either produced a routine and inconsequential police investigation or it would have been ignored by authorities because I had no useful information—I only had my intuition about the meaning in the photographs, his comment that he was "hiding things" from me, and the knowledge that he legally possessed several guns. Any inkling of a report or investigation would have prompted Stanley to abruptly terminate therapy. At no time were Stanley's fantasies about specific people who may have been in danger. By the time I knew the content, extent, and frequency of the fantasies Stanley was highly committed to the therapeutic relationship.

Did you ever fear for your own safety?

No, Stanley never displayed the exaggerated physical presence that many paranoids have nor did he try to induce fear in me as a psychopath may have tried. I grew up in an inner city neighborhood where physical violence and murder were prevalent. I also worked in a maximum-security prison for four years. I've lived and worked with many severe paranoids and psychopaths. I know their vibes. I had no inner sense in relating to Stanley that I was ever in danger. We were able to make real contact and that is an important antidote to violence.

At first he seemed depressed and later full of shame. By the time I discovered the content and intensity of Stanley's fantasies we had developed a strong interpersonal bond. By the second year I learned that one of my primary therapeutic functions was to provide protection—protection for Stanley against both the escalation of his own fantasies and his being overwhelmed by shame.

I provided a protective barrier to his continued sense of shame and script belief, "Something's wrong with me." Our therapy centered on helping him understand the relational disturbances that were the origin of the shame and to acknowledge his hurt at not being accepted, *as he was*, the fear of rejection for *who he was*, and his natural anger at the humiliation he received. I provided protection against the escalation of fantasies by listening and being interested in the details of his many fantasies and particularly by helping him identify the psychological functions imbedded in each fantasy, for example, predictability, identity, continuity, stability.

Did you work with Stanley in any way that was different than usual because of fears of violence or acting out on Stanley's part?

During the first year of therapy my fear of Stanley's acting out violence propelled me to question him about his guns, thoughts of revenge and killing, and photos of mayhem rather than maintain a phenomenological inquiry and a sustained attuned response. My use of interrogation almost ruined the therapy; he became distrustful, more distant, and told me even fewer details. Rather than inquire—a therapeutic method intended for the client to gain greater awareness of his own inner process of feelings, needs, memories, fantasies, and motivations—I asked factual questions, a form of interrogation, as a way to satisfy my curiosity and hopefully (although this was unconscious at the time) alleviate my anxiety about the potential of Stanley's acting out his inner violence. Stanley trained me to listen to him rather than question him. It was only when I attentively listened to what he chose to tell me that he became more elaborative and began to rely on our relationship.

When I returned to a phenomenological inquiry, he became more expressive; repressed memories and feelings emerged. Eventually through phenomenological inquiry and sustained attunement, Stanley was able to be conscious of the previously unconscious functions of his fantasies.

What kind of countertransference issues came up for you?

As I described in the previous question, my use of interrogation rather than phenomenological inquiry was for the relief of my own anxiety. I wanted to know all the details about Stanley's revengeful fantasies and plans and I wanted to know them quickly. This is one form of countertransference that almost destroyed the therapy.

Another form of countertransference was quite beneficial in advancing the therapy. I was repeatedly surprised at how Stanley's fantasies reawakened in me my own adolescent fantasies of revenge against humiliation. I remembered the powerful feelings of omnipotence and success that accompanied my fantasies of revenge. I could once again appreciate that the wish imbedded in each fantasy to be strong, brave, powerful, and valued. I too, wanted to be a hero rather than feel shame.

The awareness of my own developmental processes, psychological functions, and psychotherapeutic journey increased my sensitivity to Stanley's level of fixated development, the effects of cumulative trauma, and relational needs imbedded in the fantasies—the need for security in relationship, the need for self-definition, and the need to make an impact on significant others.

Through my own identification with Stanley, my internal use of free association (mindfulness), and subsequent increased awareness of my own psychological processes, my countertransference reactions helped to relax my anxiety, provided a sensitivity necessary for sustained affective attunement, and facilitated the establishment of a consistent healing relationship. It has been a personal and professional privilege to be a part of Stanley's network of relationships.

CHAPTER ELEVEN

A Gestalt therapy approach to shame and self-righteousness: theory and methods

Several years ago a colleague telephoned and began the conversation by criticizing my behavior and defining my motivation as pathological. Although I apologized, attempted to explain the situation, and tried to rectify the problem in writing, the previously warm and respectful relationship ended in a lack of communication.

In each subsequent attempt to talk to that person I tripped over my own words, experienced myself as inept, and I avoided talking about both my feelings and our relationship. The experience of having been humiliated by the colleague whom I respected left me feeling a debilitating shame. I longed for a reconnection with the colleague. I wished that the person would inquire about my feelings and our lack of interpersonal contact, recognize my distress, and respond empathetically and reciprocally to the humiliating experience I had in the original phone conversation.

The sense of shame and longing for a renewed relationship compelled me to examine my own internal reactions to the humiliation. In my own psychotherapy sessions I reexperienced being a little boy of seven and eight years, filled with hurt and fear and adapting to a highly critical teacher. The personal benefit of the psychotherapy was a reclaiming of sensitivities to others and to myself and a personal sense of contentment.

The professional benefit of resolving my own shame was an evolution in the therapeutic methods and interactions of my own clinical practice. I was faced with several questions: How and when do I define people? Do I ascribe motivation rather than facilitate the person's self-understanding of their behavior? What is the effect of my inner affect or behavior on the other person? Am I, in my attempt to be therapeutic, implying to the client, "Something is wrong with you"?

Shame and self-righteousness are protective dynamics to avoid the vulnerability to humiliation and the loss of contact-in-relationship with others. When a relationship with another person is tainted by criticism, ridicule, blaming, defining, ignoring, or other humiliating behaviors, the result is an increased vulnerability in the relationship. The contact or attachment is disrupted. Shame and self-righteousness result from humiliating disgrace or reproach and a loss of self-esteem.

Both shame and self-righteousness reflect the defenses used to avoid experiencing the intensity of how vulnerable and powerless the individual is to the loss of relationship. Simultaneously, shame is an expression of an unaware hope that the other person will take the responsibility to repair the rupture in relationship. Self-righteousness involves a denial of the need for relationship.

The theoretical ideas on shame and defensive self-righteousness and the clinical interventions presented in this article are the result of several years of my investigating my errors as a therapist, the ruptures I have created in the therapeutic relationship with clients, and the methods that may increase a client's sense of shame. A respectful inquiry into each client's phenomenological experience of our therapeutic dialogue has provided a transaction-by-transaction exploration of my empathetic failures, misperceptions of developmental levels of functioning, and affective misattunements—the interruptions to contact-in-relationship. When I *take responsibility for the ruptures* in the therapeutic relationship my therapy focuses on attuning to the client's affective experience and responding with a reciprocal affect. My therapeutic involvement is in my consistency, responsibility, and dependability. It is in the exploration and resolution of the ruptures in our relationship that I can be most effective in uncovering the core life script beliefs that determine the significant interpersonal experiences in my client's life (Erskine & Moursund, 1988).

Confrontation or an emphasis on intense, emotional expression, or an excessive value placed on aggression, or an emphasis only on the "here and now" all intensify the likelihood that a client may experience being humiliated in the psychotherapy. Fritz Perls described his confrontational therapy as teaching clients "to wipe their own ass" (Perls, 1967). Subsequently, Gestalt therapy has been characterized as defining clients' behaviors as "phony," "irresponsible," or "babyish."

To define or confront someone, even if accurately, may devalue and humiliate him. Genuinely to inquire about another's experience, motivation, self-definition, and meaning in his behavior avoids the potential of humiliation. To respond with empathy and attunement empowers the person to express fully feelings, thoughts, perceptions, and talents. Inquiry, attunement, and involvement—methods of a contactful, relationship-based Gestalt therapy—invite the client's self-discovery of his underlying meaning and unconscious motivation and enhance an interpersonal contact that values the client's integrity and sense of self (Erskine, 1995).

Gestalt therapy perspectives

In the Gestalt therapy literature the phenomenon of shame has received little attention, either as a theoretical topic or as an area of therapeutic concern. Yontef describes a Gestalt therapy perspective on shame and the use of a dialogical approach in psychotherapy (1993). Evans postulates the Gestalt therapy of shame as repairing disruptions in relationship (1994). Wheeler's (1991) description of a clinical case identifies the significance of shame. Lee and Wheeler's compilation of a collection of Gestalt therapy articles, *The Voice of Shame* (1996), provides a broad spectrum of understandings on the psychotherapy of shame. Lynne Jacobs (1996) describes the role of shame and righteousness as a defense against shame, in both client and therapist as it emerges in the therapeutic dialogue. The topic of self-righteousness has received no attention, either theoretically or methodologically.

Clinical practice and theoretical development push and pull each other in their process of evolution. Clinical interventions that make use of respect (Yontef, 1993), the therapeutic dialogue of an I-Thou relationship (Buber, 1958; Jacobs, 1996), inquiry, attunement, and involvement (Erskine, 1993; Erskine & Trautmann, 1993) have revealed that shame and self-protective fantasies are dominant in the lives of many clients. These phenomena have not been adequately placed within a Gestalt therapy theory. My clinical experience has helped to evolve a theoretical understanding that places shame and self-righteousness as the result of both introjected shame and as archaic, fixed gestalten that protect from reproach, humiliation, and the loss of contact-in-relationship. Both unresolved archaic shame and introjected shame potentiate the pain of any current criticism, adding a toxicity that floods current humiliation with debilitating shame or defensive self-righteousness.

Shame: a theoretical clarification

The formulation of a Gestalt therapy theory of shame and self-righteousness requires that the phenomenon be integrated within a theory of contact and of Gestalt formation and fixation. To arrive at an understanding of how the phenomena of shame and self-righteousness are manifested, it is necessary to utilize the concept of id-, ego-, and personality-function of the self and the concepts of interruptions to contact, specifically, introjection, retroflection, and confluence, although it is recognized that many other interruptions to both internal and external contact are activated in shame and self-righteousness (Perls, Hefferline, & Goodman, 1951).

In the service of establishing a Gestalt therapy theory that describes the phenomena of shame and self-righteousness, the terms humiliation and humiliating transactions are used to refer to interactions that occur between people where one person degrades, criticizes, defines, or ignores the other. The terms shame and self-righteousness are used to refer to the intrapsychic dynamics occurring within an individual that may be described as consisting of introjections, confluence, and/or archaic fixated systems of defense—retroflection, deflection, projection, etc. When the sense of shame has become fixated it represents an intrapsychic conflict between an influencing introjection of another person and a defended and confluent archaic fixation: a child who longed for relationship. Fixation refers to a relatively enduring pattern of organization of affect, behavior, or cognition from some earlier stage of development which persists into and may dominate later life. It is the fixated defenses that maintain a lack of full contact and interfere with archaic experiences being integrated into a here and now, fully contactful, sense of self (Erskine & Moursund, 1988).

Shame is a self-protective process used to avoid the affects that are the result of humiliation and the vulnerability to the loss of contact-in-relationship with another person. When children, and even adults, are criticized, devalued, or humiliated by significant others, the need for interpersonal contact and the vulnerability in maintaining the relationship may produce a self-protective defensive affect and confluence with the imposed diminishing definitions—a sense of shame. Shame is a complex process involving: 1) a diminished self-concept, 2) a lowering of one's self-worth in confluence with the external humiliation and/or previously introjected criticism; 3) a defensive transposition of sadness and fear; and 4) a disavowal and retroflection of anger.

Shame involves a disavowal and retroflection of anger in order to maintain a semblance of a connected relationship with the person who engaged in humiliating transactions. When anger is disavowed and retroflected a valuable aspect of the self is lost—the need to be taken seriously, respectfully, and to make an impact on the other person. One's self-worth is diminished because both id- and ego-functions of self are disrupted. Shame also involves a transposition of the affects of sadness and fear: the sadness at not being accepted as one is, with one's own urges, desires, needs, feelings, and behaviors, and the fear of abandonment in the relationship because of who one is. The fear and a loss of an aspect of self (disavowal and retroflection of anger) fuel the pull to compliance—a lowering of one's self-esteem to establish compliance with the criticism and/or humiliation.

The confluence with the humiliation, the transposition of fear and sadness, and the disavowal of anger produce the "sense of shame and doubt" described by Erikson (1950). Writing from a feminist perspective on relationship therapy, both Miller (1987) and Jordan (1989) validate this explanation by relating shame to the loss of human connection. Shame is most importantly a felt sense of unworthiness to be in connection, a deep sense of unloveability, with the ongoing awareness of how very much one wants to connect with others. While shame involves extreme selfconsciousness, it also signals powerful relationship longings (ibid., p. 6).

Kaufman similarly expresses that shame reflects the need for relationship. "In the midst of shame, there is an ambivalent longing for reunion with whomever shamed us" (1989, p. 19). Shame is an expression of an unaware hope that the other will take responsibility to repair the rupture in the relationship.

Tomkins (1963) said that shame is the affect present when there has been a loss of dignity, defeat, transgression, and alienation. He implied that shame is an affect different in nature and function from the other eight affects in his theoretical schema. The affect of shame, according to Tomkins (Nathanson, 1992), serves as an alternator or impediment to other affects—a defensive cover for interest and joy. Tomkins's (1962, 1963) ideas parallel Fraiberg's (1982) observations of the formation of psychological defenses in children. She described the process of "transformation of affect" (p. 71) where one affect is substituted or transposed for another when the original affect fails to get the necessary contact between the child and the caregiving adult, sometimes as early as nine months of age. When the child is humiliated, the fear of a loss of relationship and the sadness of not being accepted are transposed into the affect of shame. *Shame is composed of sadness and fear, the disavowal and retroflection of anger and a lowered self-concept—confluence with the humiliation.*

This confluence with the humiliation insures a semblance of a continuing relationship and, paradoxically, is a defense as well. This self-protective lowering of worth is observable among wild animals where one animal will crouch in the presence of another to avoid an attack and to guarantee acceptance. It is self-protective to lower one's status, to withhold aggression, where a fight for dominance might occur. The lowered self-concept or self-criticism that is a part of shame lessens the pain of the rupture in relationship while at the same time maintaining a semblance of relationship. The often quoted boxing coach's phrase, "Beat 'em to the punch" describes the function of a lowered self-esteem and self-criticism that is a defense against possible humiliation from others. However, the punch is delivered to one's self in the form of diminished self-worth.

A defensive fantasy

As a normal developmental process, young children often use fantasy as a way to provide controls, structure, nurturing, or whatever was experienced as missing or inadequate. The function of the fantasy may be to structure behavior as a protection from consequences or to provide love and nurturance when the real caregivers are cold, absent, or abusive. The fantasy serves as a buffer between the actual parental figures and the desires, needs, or feelings of the young child. In families or situations where it is necessary to repress an awareness of needs, feelings, and memories in order to survive or be accepted, the self-created fantasy may become fixated and not integrated with later developmental learning. Over time the fantasy functions as a "reversal" of aggression (ibid., p. 73): the criticism, devaluation, and humiliation that the child may have been subject to are amplified and turned against the self as in self-criticism or self-abjection (retroflection). Such shame-based fantasies serve to maintain an illusion of attachment to a caring relationship when the actual relationship may have been ruptured with humiliation (a disruption of ego-function of the self).

Many clients report a persistent sense of shame accompanied by degrading self-criticism. They repeatedly imagine humiliating failures of performance or relationship. In fantasy they amplify the confluence with introjected criticism and humiliation while defending against the memories of the original sadness at not being accepted as one is and the fear of abandonment because of who one is. When emotion-laden memories of early traumatic humiliations are defensively repressed, they may reemerge in consciousness as fantasies of future failure or degradation—such foresight may actually be hindsight! The self-criticism and fantasy of humiliating failure serve two additional functions: to maintain the disavowal of anger (a disruption of id-function of self) and to protect against the shock of possible forthcoming criticisms and degradation (an interruption to contact at the pre-contact stage).

Self-righteousness: a double defense

Self-righteousness serves an even more elaborate function than the defensive aspects of shame. Self-righteousness is a self-generated fantasy (occasionally manifested in overt transactions) that defends against the pain of the loss of relationship while providing a pseudo-triumph over the humiliation and an inflation in self-esteem. While shame and self-criticizing fantasies leave the person feeling devalued and longing for a repair in the relationship, self-righteous fantasies are a desperate attempt to escape humiliation and be free of shame by justifying oneself.

Self-righteousness is: 1) a defense against the sadness and fear of humiliation; 2) an expression of the need to make an impact and be taken seriously and respectfully (a partial release of disavowed and retroflected anger); and, 3) a defense against the awareness of the need for the other to repair the ruptured relationship. The person fantasizes value for himself often by finding fault with others and then loses awareness of the need for the other. The self is experienced as superior. As Alfred Adler described, a fantasy of superiority defends against the memories of humiliation (Ansbacher & Ansbacher, 1956) and projects the sense of shame outward. A clinical case example may illustrate this concept.

Robert, a thirty-nine-year-old married father of two had been in group therapy for two and a half years. Robert described that, while driving to work, he would frequently fantasize arguing with his co-workers or department supervisor. He often elaborated these fantasies with an imagined long, well-articulated oration before the board of directors. In these fantasized arguments he would point out the errors of others, how their criticisms of him were wrong, and most important, how they had made mistakes that he, Robert, would never have made. The board of directors in Robert's fantasy would be emotionally swayed by his eloquent and convincing arguments. He would be exonerated of all criticism while the others would be blamed both for criticizing him and also for their own failings. These obsessive fantasies were often initiated by some criticism at work that was not accompanied by an opportunity for Robert to explain his motivation. The lack of continued dialogue with people seemed to propel him to obsessive fantasy wherein he could debate with the other in front of an audience that in the end agreed that Robert was correct, even righteous.

These obsessive fantasies gradually diminished and finally ceased when we explored the humiliations he experienced repeatedly in early elementary school at a time when he had a speech impediment. Both teachers and other children made fun of his impediment. Although in psychotherapy he could not remember any of the specific instances of taunts or mockery, he knew that they had ridiculed him. He had a constant sense of their reaction to him as implying "Something's wrong with you."

Over the years he painstakingly worked on improving his speech, overcame the impediment, and eventually developed an impeccable diction. However, for four years of elementary school he had been subject to the humiliation by the other children and by teachers. In confluence with the humiliating behavior of teachers and classmates, he adopted the life script belief, "Something's wrong with me" as an explanation for his loss of close friendships with other children and his desire to be approved of by the teachers. He further defended against the awareness of the life script belief by perfecting his speech. No matter how perfect his speech became in adult life, whenever someone criticized him he would listen intently to their comments. The current criticisms would activate the emotional memories of earlier humiliations wherein the introjected criticisms would intrapsychically influence the fixated archaic shame, thereby potentiating the current criticisms. To comfort himself, on the way to work the next day he would obsessively defend himself from this colleagues' or supervisor's remarks, longing for someone (the board of directors) to say he was right.

In Robert's case the defensive process of disavowal and retroflection of anger, confluence with the original criticism, transposition of affect, and fantasy became fixated like any defensive process that is not responded to early in its inception with an empathetic and affectively attuned relationship (Erskine, 1993). It was through respect for Robert's style of relating to people and a gentle and genuine inquiry into Robert's experience that he began to reveal the presence of his obsessive fantasies. The self-righteous fantasies defended against the natural desire for contact-in-relationship and his need for the others to repair the ruptured relationship. Through affective attunement and empathetic transactions he was able to experience the original shame— the sadness, fear, anger, and confluence in response to the humiliations. When expressing the sadness and fear at the loss of contact in his relationships with teachers and other children, he rediscovered his longing to be connected with others (an id-function of self). The defensive fantasies stopped. Tender involvement on the part of the therapist and other group members made it possible for Robert to experience his need for close emotional contact as natural and desirable.

The life script

The central Gestalt therapy concepts of contact, interruptions to internal and external contact, and an "I-Thou" therapeutic dialogue provide the basis for a contact-in-relationship-oriented psychotherapy. In the psychotherapy of shame and self-righteousness, as with many other psychological disturbances rooted in disruptions of relationship, the therapy is enhanced if the psychotherapist has a consistent and cohesive relationship-oriented theoretical basis for determining treatment planning and subsequent clinical interventions.

In theoretical discussions and in writing, Frederick Perls used the concept of life script (1967, 1973). He focused on the structure and reorganization of the life script and how individuals use other people to reinforce the life script. Life script is an encompassing concept that describes fixed gestalten of an earlier age as they are lived out years later (Erskine, 1979). The life script is formed by introjections and defensive reactions made under the pressure of failures in contactful and supporting relationships. The need for contact and the related feeling of loss of relationship are denied and suppressed. The introjections and/or fixated defensive reactions, conclusions, and decisions that form the core of the life script (Erskine, 1980) are cognitively organized as "script beliefs" (Erskine & Moursund, 1988; Erskine & Zalcman, 1979).

In a child's attempt to make sense of the experience of a lack of contact-in-relationship he is faced with answering the question: "What does a person like me do in a world like this with people like you?" When the child is under the pressure of a lack of contact-in-relationship that acknowledges, validates, or fulfills needs, each of the three parts of this question may be answered with a defensive reaction and/or the unconscious defensive identification with the other that constitutes introjection. When the introjections and the defensive conclusions and decisions are not responded to by a contactful, empathetic other person they often become, in an attempt to gain self-support, fixated beliefs about self, others, and the quality of life—the core of the life script. These script beliefs function as a cognitive defense against the awareness of the feelings and needs for contact-in-relationship that were not adequately responded to at the time when the script beliefs were formed. The presence of script beliefs indicates a continuing defense against the awareness of needs for contact-in-relationship and the full memory of the disruptions in relationship—an archaic, fixated gestalt.

In Robert's case, during the elementary school years he adopted the script belief, "Something is wrong with me" as a confluence with the humiliation by the children and teachers and as a pseudo-satisfaction of his need to be accepted by them. The core of Robert's sense of shame consists of a child's self-protective transposition of sadness and fear, a disavowal and retroflection of anger at not being treated respectfully, and a fixated diminished self-concept in confluence with the introjected criticism. When the pain of not being accepted as one is becomes too great, as in Robert's situation, a defensive self-righteous fantasy may be used to deny the need for relationship while simultaneously expressing the previously disavowed and retroflected anger, the need to make an impact, and the desire to be treated respectfully.

From the perspective of life script theory the sense of shame is composed of the core script belief, "Something's wrong with me" that serves as a cognitive defense against the awareness of the needs for relationship and the feelings of sadness and fear present at the time of the humiliating experiences. When the script belief "Something's wrong with me" is operational the overt behaviors of the life script are often those that are described as inhibited or inadequate: shyness, lack of eye contact in conversation, lack of self-expression, diminished expression of natural wants or needs, or any inhibition of natural expression of oneself that may be subject to criticism.

Fantasies may include the anticipation of inadequacy, failures of performance, or criticism that conclude with a reinforcement of the script belief, "Something is wrong with me." Other fantasies may involve a rehashing of events that have occurred and reshaping memory in such a way as to reinforce the script beliefs. In some cases, the script belief is manifested in physiological restrictions such as headaches, stomach tensions, or other physical discomforts that inhibit the individual from behaving in such a way that might be subject to humiliating comments from others, while simultaneously providing internal evidence that "Something's wrong with me." Often old memories of humiliating experiences are repeatedly recalled to maintain a homeostasis (Perls, 1973) with the script beliefs and the denial of the original needs and feelings. Yet in inhibiting oneself or in self-criticizing fantasies, the need for contact-in-relationship remains as an unaware hope for the reestablishment of a contactful relationship and for full acceptance by the other. It is as if he were saying to those who did the ridiculing, "If I become what you define me to be, then will you love me?"

Robert, as an example of the dynamics of a double defense of self-righteousness, entered therapy unaware of any hope or need for relationship. His life script was manifested seemingly opposite to the script belief: he perfected his speech and behavior in such a way that there was no external evidence that "Something's wrong with me." His fantasies were self-righteous, focusing on what was wrong with the others. Yet he remained hypersensitive to criticism with an unaware longing for someone in authority to tell him he was OK.

"Something's wrong with me"

The compounded and continual reinforcement of the script belief, "Something is wrong with me" presents the therapist with complex challenges which are specific and unique to the psychotherapy of shame and self-righteousness. In many clinical cases this particular script belief is inflexible to the frequently used Gestalt therapy methods that involve hot seat work, confrontation, aggressive encounters, and an emphasis on self-support or self-responsibility. Each of these sets of methods provides only partial or temporary change in the frequency or the intensity of the complex script belief that is at the core of shame and self-righteousness. In fact, the very use of these methods frequently communicates "Something is wrong with you," which then can serve as a reinforcement of the script belief, increase the denial of the need for contact-in-relationship, and thereby increase the sense of shame or self-righteousness. Through the use of methods that emphasize respect (Erskine & Moursund, 1988), the therapeutic dialogue (Jacobs, 1996; Yontef, 1993), and gentle inquiry, affective attunement and involvement (Erskine, 1993, 1995; Erskine & Trautmann, 1993), the opportunity for reinforcement of the script belief during the therapy process is considerably lessened.

In order to facilitate treatment planning and refine psychotherapeutic interventions, it is essential to distinguish the *intrapsychic functions* as well as the historical origins of the script belief. Each of the ways in which the script belief was formed has unique intrapsychic functions that require specific emphasis in psychotherapy. The complex historical origin of an archaic, fixated gestalt "Something is wrong with me" can be understood from three perspectives: 1) messages with confluent decisions; 2) conclusions in response to an impossibility; and 3) defensive reactions of hope and control.

In the face of a potential loss of relationship, a child may be forced to make a defensive, confluent decision to accept as his identity the definition of those on whom he is dependent (a disruption of ego-function of self). This may be an adaptation to and confluence with overt or implicit messages of "Something's wrong with you." In many cases the message is delivered in the form of a criticizing question, "What's wrong with you?" The psychological message is, "You wouldn't be doing what you are doing if you were normal." Such criticism fails to value the child's natural and spontaneous behavior, understand the child's motivation, or investigate what may be missing in the relationship between the child and the person criticizing. A child who forms such a script belief in confluence with criticism may become hypersensitive to criticism, fantasize anticipated criticisms, and collect reinforcing memories of past criticisms (a disruption of personality function of the self). The intrapsychic function is to maintain a sense of attachment in the relationship at the expense of a loss in natural vitality and the excitement of spontaneity (a disruption of id-function of the self).

When children are faced with an impossible task, they often conclude, "Something's wrong with me." In such a conclusion they can defend against the discomfort of the missing contact needs and maintain a pseudo-semblance of relationship. Dysfunctional families often present impossible demands on children. It is impossible, for instance, for a young child to stop an alcoholic parent from getting drunk, or a baby to act as a marriage therapist, or an elementary school child to cure depression. It is impossible for a child to satisfy a parent's desire to have his or her dream fulfilled by attempting to change gender. Each of these examples represents a reversal of the caregiver's responsibility to the welfare of the child and a loss of contact-in-relationship. Further disruptions in relationship are experienced as "my fault" and deflect from the awareness of needs and feelings present when the welfare of the child is and was not being honored (disruptions of both id- and ego-functions of the self).

The script belief, "Something's wrong with me" may be formed in a third way, as a self-stabilizing reaction of control and hope—the hope for a continuing, interpersonally contactful relationship. When family relationships are dysfunctional, a child, needing contact-in-relationship, may imagine that the caregiver's problems are his own fault. "I made dad get drunk," or "I made mother get depressed," or "I caused the sexual abuse to happen ... so therefore, something must be wrong with me!"

By taking the blame, the child is not only the source of the problems, but can also imagine being in control of solving the family's problems: "I'll be very good"; "I'll hurry up and grow up"; "I can go to therapy to get fixed"; or "If things get very bad I can kill myself since it is all my fault." The psychological function of such reactions is to create a hopeful illusion of need-fulfilling caregivers that defends against the awareness of a lack of need fulfillment within the primary relationships. The caregivers are experienced as good and loving and any ignoring, criticizing, beating, or even rape is because "Something's wrong with me." Here the core script belief may function as a self-protective control over the vulnerability in relationship (a disruption of id-, ego-, and personality-functions of the self).

Each of these three origins of the core script belief has specific homeostatic functions of identity, stability, and continuity. With any particular person there may be only one way the script belief was formed. Frequently, however, the core script beliefs have more than one origin, multiple intrapsychic functions, and multiple disruptions of the function of self. Any combination of these three defensive reactions made under pressure increases the complexity of the functions. The core script belief, "Something's wrong with me" is often compounded by these multiple functions.

It is essential in an in-depth Gestalt therapy to assess the origins and intrapsychic functions of a script belief and to value the significance of how those multiple functions help the client maintain psychological homeostasis (Perls, 1973). The psychotherapy of shame and self-righteousness is complex because of the compounded and continually reinforcing multiple intrapsychic functions. Merely to identify or confront a script belief and attempt methods of empty chair work, emotional expression, or premature self-support, overlooks the psychological functions in forming and maintaining the script belief. Such efforts may increase the intensity of the intrapsychic function and may make the fixed core of the life script less flexible. A respectful and patient inquiry into the client's phenomenological experience is required to learn the unique combination of intrapsychic, homeostatic, and self functions. It is then the task of a relationship-oriented Gestalt therapist to establish an affective, developmental attunement and involvement that provides for the transferring of defensive intrapsychic functions to the relationship with the therapist. Through the therapist's consistency, dependability, and responsibility in contact-in-relationship the client can relax defensive contact-interrupting processes and integrate archaically fixated gestalten, introjections, and id-, ego-, and personality-functions of the self. The psychological functions of identity, stability, and continuity are once again provided through contact in an interpersonal relationship and are no longer a self-protective function.

Shame as an introjection

When the fixated core script belief is formed either as compliant decisions, conclusions in response to an impossibility, self-stabilizing reactions of hope and control, or any combination of the three, there is most likely an absence of a caring, understanding, and communicating relationship. When there is a lack of full psychological contact between a child and the adults responsible for his welfare, the defense of introjection is frequently used. Through the defensive, unaware identification that constitutes introjection, the beliefs, attitudes, feelings, motivations, behaviors, and defenses of the person on whom the child is dependent are made part of the child's ego as a fragmented, exteropsychic state (Erskine & Moursund, 1988). The function of introjection is to reduce the external conflict between the child and the person on whom the child depends for need fulfillment. The significant other is made part of the self, and the conflict resulting from the lack of need fulfillment is internalized, so the conflict can seemingly be managed more easily (L. Perls, 1977, 1978).

The introjected other may be active in transactions with others (a disruption in personality function of the self), intrapsychically influencing (a disruption in id-function of the self), or phenomenologically experienced as self (a disruption in ego-function of the self). An individual may transact with family members or colleagues as the introjected other once did, for example, communicating, "Something's wrong with you!" The psychological function of such a transaction is to provide temporary relief from the internal criticism of an introjection and, via projection of the criticism, to continue the denial of the original need for contact-in-relationship.

The internal criticism is a replay of the criticism introjected in the past. It perpetuates the cycle of confluence with the criticism and the archaic, fixated defense against sadness and fear. This defensive cycle of shame functions to maintain an illusion of attachment and loyalty to the person with whom the child was originally longing for an interpersonally contactful relationship.

Introjected shame may not only be active and/or influencing, but may also be experienced as self. The parent's sense of shame may have been introjected. With the cathexis or energizing of the introjection the shame is misidentified as one's own. The script belief—"Something's wrong with me"—may actually exist as an introjected other. The cycle of shame-confluence with the criticism, transposition of sadness and fear, the disavowal and retroflection of anger, and longing for relationship may be the mother's or father's. Defensive self-righteousness may also be the result of the cathexis of an introjection.

For years Susan had suffered with a debilitating shame related to her own sense of inadequacy, having a mother who was alternately depressed and angry, and fearing that she would someday be "crazy" too. The initial phase of therapy acknowledged her own needs for attention, validated the emotional neglect of her childhood, and normalized the defensive process of "Something's wrong with me." The psychotherapy then focused on the introjected shame that was originally the mother's (Erskine & Moursund, 1988). With a contact-oriented, in-depth Gestalt therapy that emphasized inquiry, attunement, and involvement, Susan experimented with a two-chair dialogue where, in one chair she was "mother" and in the other chair the "Susan of a much younger age." She was able to remember vividly wanting to bear the burden for her mother so her mother could be free of suffering. During the two-chair dialogue, she succinctly described the process of unconsciously introjecting: "I love you so much, Mom, I'll carry your shame for you!"

Psychotherapeutic interventions

The psychotherapy of shame and self-righteousness begins with the therapist newly discovering each client's unique psychodynamics. Each shame-based client will present a different cluster of behaviors, fantasies, psychological functions, interruptions to contact, disruptions of self, and self-protective defenses. The theoretical perspectives described in this chapter are generalizations from clinical practice and the integration of several theoretical concepts. The theory is not meant to represent a statement of what is, but rather to serve as a guide in the therapeutic process of inquiry, attunement, and involvement. Importantly, the phenomenon of shame and self-righteousness explained within the perspectives of Gestalt therapy theory may encourage Gestalt therapists to explore with each client his unique experience of shame and to adopt a relationally oriented psychotherapy approach.

A patient, respectful inquiry into the client's phenomenological experience will provide both the client and therapist with an ever increasing understanding of who the client is and the experiences to which he has been subjected. The process of inquiring must be sensitive to the client's subjective experience and unaware intrapsychic dynamics to be effective in discovering and revealing needs, feelings, fantasies, and defenses. A major focus of a gentle inquiry is the client's self discovering of longing for relationship, interruptions to contact (both internally and externally), and memories that have in the past necessarily been excluded from awareness. A less important focus is the psychotherapist's increased understanding of the client's phenomenological experience and intrapsychic functioning. In many cases it has been important to clients to discover that the therapist is genuinely interested in listening to them and in knowing who they are. Such discoveries about the relationship with the psychotherapist present a juxtaposition between the contact available in the here and now and the memory of what may have been absent in the past.

The juxtaposition of the therapist's inquiry, listening, and attunement with the memory of a lack of interpersonal contact in previous significant relationships produces intense, emotional memories of relational needs not being met. Rather than experience those feelings, the client may react defensively to the interpersonal contact offered by the therapist with fear, anger, or increased shame. The contrast between the interpersonal contact available with the therapist and the lack of contact-in-relationship in the past is often more than clients can bear, so they defend against the current contact to avoid the emotional memories (Erskine, 1993). The juxtaposition presents an opportunity to acknowledge what was needed and to validate that feelings and self-esteem may well be related to the quality of relationship with significant others.

Shame may be a significant dynamic in most relationship difficulties, including depression, anxiety, obesity, addictions, and characterological presentations. The therapist's attunement to the unexpressed sense of shame provides the opportunity for clients to reveal their inner processes of feelings, fantasies, desires, and defenses. Attunement involves a sense of being fully aware of the developmentally based needs, affect, and self-protective dynamics—a kinesthetic and emotional sensing of what it is like to live with their experiences. Attunement occurs in the therapist's honoring the client's developmental level of coping with shame and the absence of any defining or categorizing of the client's fantasies, motivations, or behavior. Attunement also involves sensitively communicating to the client that the therapist is aware of the inner struggles; that he is not all alone in the sadness at not having been accepted as one is, and in the fear of loss of relationship because of who one is. The therapeutic processes of attunement and involvement acknowledge the difficulty in revealing the inner confusion and struggles, value the desperate attempt at self-support and coping, and simultaneously provide a sense of the therapist's presence.

Some clients who are shame-based will not have the experience of talking about needs or have a sense of language that is related to affect and inner processes. In some families, to have needs or express emotion may result in the child being ignored or ridiculed. When there has been a lack of attunement, acknowledgement, or validation of needs or feelings within the family or school system, the client may have no language of relationship with which to communicate about his affect and needs (Basch, 1988; Tustin, 1986). There is often an absence in such family or school systems of the interpersonal affective contact (a nonverbal transaction) where the expression of affect by one person in relationship stimulates a corresponding affect of reciprocity in the other.

Affect is transactional-relational in its nature, requiring a corresponding affect in resonance:

- The expression of the affect sadness is to elicit compassion and possible acts of compassion
- Anger is to elicit affect related to attentiveness, seriousness, and responsibility and perhaps acts of correction
- Fear is to elicit affects and actions of security
- Joy is to elicit affects of vitality and expression of pleasure.

This concept of affect is embodied in a two-person psychology or field theory perspective that is a basis of Gestalt therapy (Perls, 1944), although sometimes not accounted for in therapeutic practice. When an individual's affect is received by another as a relational transaction, the affect can be fully expressed. Metaphorically, the yin of the affect is met by the yang of a reciprocal affect in response.

Attunement includes the therapist's sensing of the client's affect and in reciprocity is stimulated to express a corresponding affect and resonating behavior, a process similar to the one Daniel Stern (1985, 1995) described in healthy interactions between infant and his or her mother. The reciprocal affect in the therapist may be expressed by acknowledging the client's affect and leads to validation that affect has a function in their relationship. It is essential that the therapist be both knowledgeable of, and attuned to, the client's developmental level in the expression of emotions. The client may need to have his affect and needs acknowledged but lacks the social language to express the emotions in conversation. It may be necessary for the therapist to help the client name his feelings, needs, or experiences as an initial step in gaining a sense of making an impact in relationship.

Involvement begins with the therapist's commitment to the client's welfare and a respect for his phenomenological experiences. It evolves from the therapist's empathetic inquiry into the client's experience and is developed through the therapist's attunement with the client's affect and validation of needs. Involvement is the result of the therapist being fully contactful with and for the client in a way that corresponds to the client's developmental level of functioning.

Shame and self-righteousness are defensive processes wherein an individual's worth is discounted and the existence, significance, and/or solvability of a relationship disturbance is distorted or denied. A therapist's involvement that makes use of acknowledgment, validation, normalization, and presence diminishes the internal interruptions to contact that is part of the defensive denial accompanying shame.

Through sensitivity to the manifestation of shame and in understanding the psychological functions of shame and self-righteousness, a psychotherapist can facilitate a client's acknowledgement and expression of natural feelings and needs for relationship. Acknowledgement is the therapeutic counterpart to discounting the existence of a disturbance in relationship. Acknowledgement, when given by a receptive other who knows and communicates about relational needs and feelings, dissolves the client's internal interruption to contacting affect or needs.

Therapeutic validation occurs when the client's sense of shame, diminished self-worth, and defensive fantasies are experienced as the effect of significant relationship disturbances. Validation is the cognitive linking of cause and effect, the therapeutic response to discounting the significance of a disturbance in relationship. Validation provides a client with an enhanced value of phenomenological experience and therefore an increased sense of self-esteem.

Normalization depathologizes a client's emotional experience; it counters the discounting of the solvability of a relational disturbance. Many clients as children were told, "Something's wrong with you" or when faced with the impossibility of being responsible for their parents' welfare, concluded "Something's wrong with me." The burden of responsibility for the rupture of relationship was falsely placed on the child and not on a grown-up caregiver. The therapeutic counterpart to discounting the solvability of a problem is the assigning of responsibility for the relationship. It is imperative that the therapist communicates that a client's experience of shame, self-criticism, or anticipated ridicule is a normal defensive reaction to being humiliated or ignored, and is not pathological.

The assignment of responsibility may begin with a therapist actively taking responsibility for any breach in the therapeutic relationship. Most therapeutic breaks occur when a therapist fails to attune to the client's affective or nonverbal communication (Kohut, 1977). When a client bears the responsibility for the relationship the discounting of the solvability continues and the sense of shame is reinforced. It may be necessary for a therapist to take total responsibility for not understanding the client's phenomenological experience, not valuing his defensive process, or not being attuned to the client's affect and needs.

Presence is the therapeutic involvement that serves as a counterpoint to the discounting of an individual's self-worth. Therapeutic presence is provided through sustained empathetic inquiry (Stolorow, Brandschaft, & Atwood, 1987) and consistent attunement to the developmental level of affect and needs. Presence involves the therapist's attentiveness and patience. It communicates that the psychotherapist is responsible, dependable, and reliable. Presence occurs when the behavior and communication of the therapist at all times respects and enhances the worth of the client. Presence is enhanced by the therapist's willingness to be impacted by the client's affect and phenomenological experience—to take the client's experience seriously. It is more than communication, it is communion—full interpersonal contact.

The psychotherapist's involvement through transactions that acknowledge, validate, and normalize the client's phenomenological experience is the antidote to the toxicity of discounting the existence, significance, or responsibility for solving the disruptions of contact-in-relationship. The dependable, attuned presence of the therapist is the antidote to discounting the worth of the individual (Bergman, 1991; Jordan, 1989; Miller, 1987; Surrey, 1985).

The effective psychotherapy of shame and self-righteousness requires a therapist's commitment to contact-in-relationship, a commitment of patience, and an understanding that such therapy is complex and requires a considerable amount of time. Inquiry, attunement, and involvement are all a mental orientation, a way of being in relationship, as well as sets of therapeutic skills. When used in resonance with the developmental level of a client's functioning, they are methods of providing a caring, understanding relationship that allows a client to express a sense of self-value that may never have been expressed before. Inquiry, attunement, and involvement are descriptions of respectful interactions that foster contact-in-relationship. It is through a contact-oriented, relationship-focused psychotherapy that protective dynamics of shame and self-righteousness are revealed and dissolved. A Gestalt therapy focus on contact-in-relationship enhances an individual's capacity for full internal and external contact.

CHAPTER TWELVE

The schizoid process

The term "schizoid" is often not well understood. It comes from the Greek term for scissors and means to cut or split. I became interested in the psychotherapy of the schizoid process through case presentations, readings, and discussions in the professional development seminars at the Institute for Integrative Psychotherapy. This work was an outgrowth of our consideration of issues related to both dissociation and shame.

As we worked with individuals who use dissociation as an ongoing coping mechanism and also with people for whom shame was a primary way of organizing their emotional experience, we found that we needed to refine our methods of psychotherapy to emphasize inquiry into the client's subjective experience. Such clients require the psychotherapist's consistent attunement to their affective state, a sense of meeting their sadness with compassion, their fear with security, and their anger with a sense of being taken seriously in the expression of that anger (Erskine & Trautmann, 1996).

These clients have a particular need for responsiveness to the fear-laden affect state that is so dominant in the schizoid process, one often related to a nonverbal experience. They also need the therapist's attunement to their developmental level of functioning, especially to what

Daniel Stern (1995) described in his writings as the emerging self, the core self, and the intersubjective self—those levels of developmental functioning that are pre-language. In fact, many schizoid clients regress to pre-linguistic developmental functioning as a safety zone in the presence of threat (Guntrip, 1968).

Much of our therapeutic work and research has shown the importance of validating the client's subjective experience. When therapy emphasizes change, not as the primary goal but as a by-product of therapy, when the therapeutic focus is not on behavior but on the client's internal process, we wind up with a slower form of therapy but one that can fill the psychological void the schizoid individual experiences internally. What becomes evident in a phenomenologically focused psychotherapy is the sequestered, hidden, encapsulated affect of the client's self.

With schizoid individuals, the affects of terror and rage have often never found their way into verbal dialogue with another person. We know from treating trauma victims that trauma remains traumatic in the person's life because of the failure of a healing relationship. Many people have traumatic experiences but do not remain traumatized because someone was there in a healing, supportive, and clarifying way that allowed the trauma to be integrated within the individual's experience (Erskine, 1993).

The schizoid process is clearly defined in Eric Berne's (1961) description of the states of the ego—the ego fragmented by trauma—and how the fixation of Child ego states interferes with here-and-now neopsychic functioning. Berne defined ego fragmentation and boundary issues—such as loss of reality, estrangement, and depersonalization—as "schizoid in character" (p. 67). Each of these Child ego states, fragmented by trauma, requires a responsive, healing relationship. "The ego state can be treated like an actual child. It can be nurtured carefully, even tenderly, until it unfolds like a flower" (p. 226). Clients who engage in a schizoid process need the therapist to create a therapeutic relationship that allows each Child ego state to emerge and be met with a safe, attuned response.

Berne (1972) indicated that the psychoanalytic writer who provided one of the best heuristic bridges to transactional analysis was Ronald Fairbairn. He (Fairbairn, 1952) was the first psychoanalyst to describe thoroughly the relational dynamics of early childhood—of a child in relationship since the first moments of life—and the damage to the child when there is a failure in those primary relationships. Thus he articulated the antecedents of the schizoid process.

These relationship failures are not the acute traumas that we think of in, for example, our work with multiple personalities. Rather, they are what Masud Khan (1963) referred to as "cumulative trauma" (p. 286)—the little missed attunements, discounts, punishments, and rejections—like grains of sand that pile up until they form a dune. The accumulation of missed attunements and missed connections creates the conditions wherein the child hides more and more in his own sequestered world while adjusting his behavior to provide what the other demands (Lourie, 1996). For clients engaging in a schizoid process, intimacy and interpersonal connections are a threat to the sense of self. They experience a great fear of contact; for such individuals, a genuine relationship is dangerous.

Bob Goulding (1974) described the schizoid process as a third-degree impasse. It is the split in a child's ego that occurs when the individual's natural organismic functioning is repressed and denied—split off—and the child becomes the social façade required by the grown-ups around him. The adaptive, social façade becomes "me," and the natural, fundamentally human part becomes "not me." What is natural is lost and split off so intensely that the person experiences no other way of being in the world. Both my own clinical experience and the contemporary psychotherapy literature have led me to believe that a patient, consistent, respectful, and attuned therapeutic relationship allows those hidden aspects that were made "not me" to become "me" (Bollas, 1987; Erskine, Moursund, & Trautmann, 1999; Mitchell, 1993; Stolorow, Brandchaft, & Atwood, 1987).

Harry Guntrip (1961, 1968, 1971; Hazell, 1994) wrote extensively on the treatment of the schizoid process. He described how the person is driven into hiding by fear and then experiences a deep, sequestered loneliness that drives him out of hiding back into an adaptive interface with the world. Such a person is constantly caught in the struggle between hiding or connecting to others, but in an adaptive way. Guntrip (cited in Hazell, 1994) defined the psychotherapy of the schizoid process as the provision of a reliable and understanding human relationship of a kind that makes contact with the deeply repressed traumatized child in a way that enables one to become steadily more able to live, in the security of a new, real relationship, with the traumatic legacy of the earliest formative years, as it seeps through or erupts into consciousness ... It is a process of interaction, the function of two variables, the personalities of two people working together towards free spontaneous growth (p. 366).

Donald Winnicott also had extensive experience in treating the schizoid process (Hazell, 1994; Little, 1990). He (Winnicott, 1965) described the essential ingredients of an in-depth psychotherapy as providing a respectful, understanding, reliable environment, one that the client never had and needs if he is to redevelop out of inner conflicts and inhibitions. Such an environment allows the person to find out for himself what is natural for him. Both Guntrip and Winnicott encouraged a psychotherapy that focuses on the client's internal process and not specifically on behavioral outcome, a psychotherapy that provides a healing relationship to a traumatized Child ego state.

In closing, it may be fitting to again quote Guntrip's beliefs about the psychotherapy of the schizoid process—an attitude that one of his clients described as providing a "cherishing" of her.

> It is the psychotherapist's responsibility to discover what kind of parental relationship the patient needs in order to get better ... The child grows up to be a disturbed person because he is not loved for his own sake as a person in his own right, and as an ill adult he comes to the psychotherapist convinced beforehand that this 'professional man' has no real interest or concern for him. The kind of love the patient needs is the kind of love that he may well feel in due course that the psychotherapist is the first person ever to give him. It involves taking him seriously as a person in his difficulties, respecting him as an individual in his own right even in his anxieties, treating him as someone with the right to be understood and not merely blamed, put-off, pressed and molded to suit other people's convenience, regarding him as a valuable human being with a nature of his own that needs a good human environment to grow in, showing him genuine human contact, real sympathy, believing in him so that in the course of time he can become capable of believing in himself. All these are ingredients of true parental love (agape not eros), and if the psychiatrist cannot love his patients in that way, he had better give up psychotherapy. (cited in Hazell, 1994, pp. 401–402)

CHAPTER THIRTEEN

Early affect-confusion: the "borderline" between despair and rage

First impressions and uncertainties

The woman's voice on the phone was brusque. She launched into saying that she had been referred by a colleague because she was "depressed over relational difficulties" with her lover and she was searching for a new psychotherapist. Before I had an opportunity to ask her name, she told me that she had previously seen four psychotherapists; she shouted, "None of them were any good. They did not understand me." She proceeded to tell me why the therapy had not been beneficial to her. I tried to slow down the rush of information by asking her name and why she had chosen to call me. She was urgent to tell me more about the "cold" male psychoanalyst who she had worked with for "two long years" and two other female psychotherapists who were always criticizing her and wanting her to change her behavior. I wondered to myself if she was unconsciously communicating the relational qualities she needed in a psychotherapist.

In the first three minutes on the phone I could hear her anger and despair, her blame of others, and her sense of neediness. I asked more about her reasons for seeking psychotherapy. Instead, Theresa told me about a "good therapist" that she had worked with when she was in her mid-twenties. That therapist had been "kind and understanding" but the therapist abruptly ended their sessions after a year and a half. Theresa did not know why the therapist insisted that she terminate; she was confused and didn't know whether to blame herself or the therapist. Theresa said that she was telephoning me in the hopes of finding a new psychotherapist who would understand her, be "kind," and "help fix" her relationships. Someone at work had told her that she needed group therapy; she was calling about whether I had an opening in one of my groups.

In those first few minutes I sensed that Theresa was going to require a sensitive and firm therapeutic relationship—a relationship that would be attuned to her affect and reflect an understanding of her internal struggle while also setting some necessary therapeutic parameters. Such a relationship would take a considerable amount of time to develop if I was going to be therapeutically effective. I suspected that she required a much more careful attention to her needs than I could provide in a group therapy. I offered her three individual sessions as a period of mutual evaluation. I told her I needed to know much more about who she was before I could recommend group therapy or, perhaps more important, commit to the long-term therapy that I suspected she required. She had already mentioned several difficult relationships that I surmised were transferentially expressing previous, and perhaps early, childhood relational conflicts. Many questions rushed through my mind. If she became my client was I too going to be defined by her as criticizing or cold? Originally, who had been cold and criticizing? Could I build a therapeutic relationship with this yet unseen woman that may have a positive effect in resolving her relational difficulties?

For her first series of appointments Theresa arrived a few minutes early. She was well dressed and coquettish and articulate and factual when we discussed appointment times and payment. She commented on the beautiful early October weather and made several compliments to me about the office décor. Theresa was certainly much more charming than she had been on the telephone and was quite willing to answer factual questions about her life; inquiries about her affect and physical sensations or early life were repeatedly deflected. She wanted to tell me about all the problems she was encountering with her boyfriend and with some women at work. I wanted to hear how she organized her story and realized that any inquiries at this point distracted her from what she had planned to say.

She proudly announced that she was a highly paid legal assistant in a large law firm. She adored her boss whom she described in idealizing terms, adding that he had defended her "once or twice." Theresa again spoke in glowing terms of her first psychotherapist and remained consistent in her "hatred" of her three other therapists as well as two of the women at work. She was outraged that one of the psychologists had diagnosed her as "borderline psychotic" and that the psychiatrist told her that she had a "bipolar disorder" that required medication.

I suggested that we not go into the details of these "hated" relationships in this first session but that we would come back to discuss her feelings about these relationships in a future session. She seemed to respond well to my bracketing her intensely emotional stories. Theresa went on to say that she was now thirty-eight years old and divorced for ten years after having been married for eighteen months when she was in her late twenties. Since then she had had several boyfriends (lovers) for a few months or a year. She described how each relationship ended because of "incompatibility." At this point it was too early for me to ask about the details of "incompatibility" but, from the little she did say, I could decipher that she perceived the men in her life as not understanding her and/or not respecting her needs. I knew that more details of these stories would come if we continued to work together. It seemed that being understood was going to be a central issue in our psychotherapy together.

A summary of my notes from our initial sessions show the following five themes in Theresa's narrative: she is often feeling depressed and fearing abandonment; she is in emotional pain with believing that no one understands her; she is either self-critical or critical of others; she is destructive in most relationships; and her behavior oscillates between being extremely needy of others and hating them for failing her.

My tasks would be to use both her transference on other people and the emerging transferences with me to understand and resolve three important relational dynamics: 1) her hyper-vulnerability and early affective confusion; 2) her relational needs that had been thwarted in the process of growing-up; and 3) her style of compensation and self-regulation in response to previous relational failures.

Beginning the psychotherapy

We contracted for a series of psychotherapy sessions that would last for seven months, until June, with the psychotherapy goals of resolving her fear of abandonment and of finding constructive ways to be in relationship with her boyfriend. Her narrative over the next few months was often disorganized. It alternated between blaming others and self-criticism, justifications for her rage, and confusion about how others treated her. Any of my attempts at inquiry into the history of her emotional reactions seemed to add to her confusion; such inquiry was as if I were abandoning her in the midst of her stories. It was too early in our relationship to draw the links between her childhood experiences and her current affect and behavior. What I could do was to listen respectfully and keep checking if she experienced me as understanding her. My task at that time was to learn how to establish and maintain a healing therapeutic relationship by understanding the conflictual elements in the stories she was telling about her troublesome relationships with others. I carefully listened to her unfolding story, was mindful of the emerging themes, and waited for opportunities to inquire both phenomenologically and historically. My attunement to her affect, rhythm, and developmental level of psychological functioning was most important at this early phase of the therapy, even though she scoffed at my expressions of empathy.

Theresa tearfully complained that her current boyfriend was often "disrespectful"; she "fights" with him, he threatens to leave her, then she takes him to bed to "seduce him into staying." After, she repeatedly criticizes herself for being "seductive" and "just a slut." I knew that this repetitive drama captured some important childhood story. I waited for the opportunity to follow any possible leads to her original story—a story that I imagined may be even more filled with emotion and confusion than the ones she was telling about her current life. I was aware that she would need my sustained empathy if we were ever to get to the original story. Yet, at this point in the therapy, I did not have much empathy for the "devastating hurt" she was describing. Her cry did not move me to compassion. I was cautiously focused on her many examples of manipulation and self-criticism.

Theresa then spent several sessions telling me about Joan, an older lesbian who was "the only loving person I have ever had in my life." Theresa was extremely confused as to why Joan loved her so much since

Theresa was convinced that she was unlovable. She was also thoroughly bewildered as to why Joan did not want to continue a relationship with her. In several sessions she wept like a very young child whenever she talked of Joan's love for her. Theresa tearfully told me about Joan's care and affection. She had been amazed to find someone like Joan who was so different than her parents and she declared that, "Sometimes the contrast was so great it made me feel crazy."

Although she and Joan had had a "loving relationship," they also had some "violent fights." After one such fight Theresa had attempted suicide by cutting her wrists and Joan called the police to take her to the hospital. While Theresa was recovering in the hospital's psychiatric ward Joan shouted at her, "I never want to see or talk to you again in my whole life." During several sessions Theresa curled up in a fetal position and deeply sobbed, "No one is there for me." As she cried out the emotional turmoil of this lost love, my genuine empathy was absolutely essential for building our therapeutic relationship. This was real grief. There was none of the superficial emotionality that seemed to be present when she cried about feeling "rejected" by her boyfriend. And, no matter how much I sensed that it was also an enactment of a much earlier abandonment, she needed my compassion and understanding in response to the depth of her emotional pain(s).

The story of her relationship with Joan led Theresa into talking about other experiences of emotional abandonment. She went into detail about her relationships with five male lovers with whom she had fallen "madly in love" until the men became "aggressive." Each of these affairs ended in a "big fight" with Theresa feeling deeply hurt and confused. She compensated by blaming the men for not "understanding" her. Although she was still blaming others, her crying appeared more genuine. She expressed what seemed to me to be a more authentic vulnerability whenever I would identify what she may have needed in relationships with Joan, each of these men, or her current boyfriend.

We specifically identified the interpersonal needs that were often absent for her in significant relationships: for the other to be patient, calm, consistent, dependable, and validating; for the other to provide opportunities for Theresa's self-definition and agency without any humiliating comments or gestures. On several occasions we discussed how kindness, acceptance, or caring gestures stimulated her memories of painful, rejecting experiences. We returned to these themes again and again until she clearly grasped how kindness and loving gestures were an integral part of intimate connection and belonging.

It was the possibility of an intimate connection and belonging that stimulated a psychological "borderline" between terror and longing—terror of all the destabilizing feelings associated with an intimate relationship and, simultaneously, a physical "gnawing, hungry feeling," those longings for intimacy. She could not comprehend that the purpose in "fighting and pushing people away" was to avoid her emerging terror, pain, and grief. Theresa was more focused on the desperate emptiness in her relationships. She was suffering from affect-confusion.

I was curious about her words "being seductive" which she had used in a number of contexts. With a series of inquiries about her feelings and associations with the word "seductive," she remembered the several times when she was "trying to be close with my father and my mother accused me of being seductive." She went on to describe her reaction, "I thought I was doing something terribly wrong." Theresa cried about how she had wanted affection and protection from her father. We talked about the various ways she tried to get his attention and companionship. She was angry at him for being more interested in either defending her mother or withdrawing into watching television.

We spent a few months talking about her grief in "not having a father," what she had needed from a father, and her anger at his parental incompetence. I kept bringing her focus to the reactions, conclusions, and decisions she may have made as a way to compensate for the relational loss. She became acutely aware that during her school age years she concluded, "No one is there for me." She had a vivid memory of sitting in her bedroom, feeling lonely, and wanting to be with her father who was watching TV in another room and telling herself, "I'm unlovable." She remembered often rocking herself on her bed while repeating the words "I'm unlovable" over and over, like a mantra. I wondered where her mother fitted into this story but Theresa was preoccupied with telling me about her confusing relationship with her father.

I held an image of that lonely girl in my mind and referred to that story several times when Theresa seemed absorbed by current conflicts. I described my impression of her rocking and repetitive "I'm unlovable" as a way to manage the loneliness and to make some sense of what was missing in the relationship with her parents. In subsequent sessions I inquired about her associations to either my image of the lonely little girl or my hypothesis about how she compensated for neglect. At first she described that bedroom memory as "comforting" but, as we talked about it several times, she realized that the rocking and the mantra-like repetition of "I'm unlovable" was a desperate attempt to avoid the intensity of the loneliness by soothing herself with repetitive words. As Theresa became increasingly aware of the intense loneliness, she also began to feel a seething anger at her father that she had disavowed for years.

I asked Theresa to look me in the eye and tell me about the intensity of her anger. It was important that she look me in the eye so that she could see that I was taking her anger seriously. Theresa still lacked an internal sense of relational security so I avoided having her express her anger at a fantasized father in an empty chair. She needed to see that she could make an impact on a man, an impact on me. It seemed important that she see my eyes and face as she clearly expressed what she did not like. In the following sessions we talked about this new experience with a contactful anger and how it was different from her habit of raging at people. We also focused on Theresa's bodily reactions to holding in her fury with her father's neglect of her.

One night, about a month later, Theresa telephoned, terrified and crying uncontrollably. She did not know why she was so scared. I remained calm on the phone while she shook with fear. I talked gently to her, agreed to see her early the next day, and assured her that we would resolve her terror. With my commitment, Theresa was then able to stop shaking with terror. The next morning, as we reviewed our previous night's conversation, she began to fearfully shake once again. I suggested that the shaking was probably a body memory and that I would remain right with her and watch over her. She curled up on the couch and trembled with fear while I encouraged her to stay with her body sensations and emerging affect. Within a few minutes she had a vivid memory of her father coming to her room. She was thirteen years old and had been on her bed rocking and comforting herself after an intense argument with her mother. She expected her father to comfort her. Instead he yanked her off the bed and slapped her face. He shouted, "Don't you ever argue with your mother again," and then walked out of the room and slammed the door. Theresa was left in shock.

As Theresa described this memory she cried out in anguish, "No one is there for me." Those words reflected a life-shaping decision she made that day, at age thirteen—a childhood decision that was still determining her perception of relationships decades later. That decision solidified a series of similar conclusions made over several years of realizing that neither parent had ever been sensitive to her feelings or needs.

On this occasion, I asked Theresa to imagine her father right in front of her while I sat next to her with my hand supporting her back. I encouraged Theresa to tell her father what she had never said aloud to him. As she told him about how he had hurt and neglected her, I also encouraged Theresa to express her anger and to protest his hitting her. She punched the sofa pillows and shouted, "Father, that is no way to treat me. Mother was at fault and you know that! You never protect me (still hitting the pillows). You are never there for me (hitting pillows). I need you to be like Richard, or even Robert; they are there for me. Richard believes me" (she hugged the pillow to her chest and sobbed for several minutes).

One of Theresa's core beliefs, "No one is there for me" was consciously being expressed. It had been her reality in her original family but that belief no longer had to determine how she was experiencing life today. She could make a new decision—a decision that meant that some people, Richard, and her boyfriend Robert, were there for her. She was now open to feel some of the interpersonal contact and emotional support that others could provide. Theresa was no longer completely alone and fighting against everyone.

Theresa's psychological growth was not a straight trajectory to health; there were many incidents of recycling to her old aggressive behavior, crying spells, internal criticism, and stoic self-sufficiency. But her fights with her boyfriend gradually decreased and she was "trying to get along with the women at work." In many sessions we went over what we had talked about previously; sometimes it seemed as though we had never talked about a situation before. Other times she had profound insight and used the insight to, at least temporarily, change her behavior. She seemed more trusting of me and frequently wanted to hear what I had to say. She was changing at her own rhythm, in manageable increments.

Resolving confusion between behavior, feelings, and needs

For many sessions during these first several months Theresa's behavior toward me alternated between being coquettish and aggressive, dependent and distrusting, self-sufficient and helpless. She would complain about being lonely, empty, and depressed and then would become elated about the future, only to follow this with rage as she anticipated being disrespected. She continually asked what she should do with her current boyfriend when he disappointed her; she wanted explanations. She alternated between seeing me as the person who could tell her how to solve all her problems and teach her how to manage the "difficult people" in her life and the "stupid ass" who was provoking her to "feel worse than when I began." Theresa frequently anticipated or perceived me as being critical of her when we talked about how she could modulate her accusations and anger with her boyfriend and the women at work. I requested that we think together about the reasons underlying her own behaviors when she expressed despair, flirtatiousness, criticism, or aggression with me or other people. I repeatedly suggested that perhaps she was reliving many previous relational experiences in all the stories she was telling me about her adult life.

One day I discovered that she had not talked to her mother for several years and she only talked to her father on the phone for a few minutes about three times a year. She said that she "hates" her mother and finds her father "spineless" because he will not stop her mother's criticism and ridicule. She shouted:

> My father never told my mother to shut-up and he seldom comforted me. When he did hold me a few times my mother went into a jealous rage. She told me I was "seductive" and would grow up to be a "slut". My mother is the one who can seduce anyone. None of my teachers ever knew how much she despised me.

I made a mental note that there were at least three areas that required further inquiry: more on her relationship with her father and the lack of protection represented in the word "spineless"; the psychological impact of her mother's "jealous rage"; and the cumulative effects of living with a sense of being despised by her mother. It seemed too soon to investigate her internal experiences and coping systems in response to each of these developmental crises. Now it was important to provide stability in our relationship and to eliminate Theresa's aggressiveness and fighting with other people.

In some sessions, rather than talking about her relationship with her mother, Theresa wanted to talk about the women at work who "hate me even though I have never given them any reason at all." In one of the sessions she said, "I just give them the evil eye and they stay away." I responded that she has a high degree of responsibility in how others treated her. Even though she objected to my premise, I continued over the next few months to describe just how she was "largely responsible" for the interpersonal conflicts in her life. She had survived by blaming others for her difficulties but such blaming was only making her life worse. We spent a considerable amount of time talking about the distinction between feelings, needs, and behavior. In one such session I emphasized that she had a normal need to be accepted and respected for who she was and I also pointed out that in most of her stories the significant people were described as not responding to her needs. There was a quiet moment in which her eyes moistened and then she quickly added, "By the way, you have lousy toilet paper in your bathroom. Why don't you spend some of your piles of money on good toilet paper?" It was evident that she feared vulnerability.

I could see a behavioral pattern emerging: following an expression of vulnerability, Theresa would find some reason to criticize me, such as our appointment time, my travel schedule, or my billing practice. In some sessions she would quote my articles that she had found on the internet. She announced that I was "not doing the therapy right." In one session she shouted, "You are un-attuned, you know nothing about relational needs, and you are a failure at validation." I responded by calmly asking three important questions designed to disentangle accusing transactions: "How do you expect me to respond when you shout at me?"; "What were you feeling just before you shouted at me?"; "How do you need me to respond to you?"

Exploring Theresa's answers to these three questions took the rest of the session and the entire next session. When her criticisms came late in a session or if they were tinged with rage, I would wait until her anger cooled down and would address it in the next or even a later session. On other days when her criticism of me was early in the session, or was rather mild, I would deal with it in the current session. This series of inquiries almost always led to some vague memory of her relationship with her mother but often she could not sustain either the memory or the associated feeling. I paid careful attention to deciphering what emotionally laden experience was unconsciously encoded in the stories she was telling me, what was unconsciously embedded in the way she interrupted our interpersonal contact, and what she was engendering in others when they were "aggressive" with her.

Her verbal assaults toward me were frequent. It was essential that I did not respond defensively, that I remain fully present and sensitive to what she unconsciously needed. If I were defensive, or even explained my position, I would be replaying the childhood drama she acted out with her boyfriends. Our therapeutic relationship required that I maintain the safety net as she walked that emotional "borderline" between acknowledging her unmet needs and angrily attacking people. This required a two-part treatment approach: first, teaching her how to engage in a relationally contactful anger and, second, validation and normalization of her relational needs. This process of teaching, validation, and normalization was repeated in many of our sessions. Relinquishing old self-regulating habits and learning a new way of being in relationship requires many repetitions. My consistency and respect were central to Theresa's learning to both value her needs and remain in relationship when she disliked what the other person did.

During this early phase of the therapy, Theresa was often angry at me. She was angry when I would not talk to her on the phone at night when she was "so upset." Her anger alternated with helpless crying and begging for "someone to understand me and care for me." When I was silent for a few moments in the therapy she would scream, "You don't care a damn about what I am feeling." If I said something comforting she would snidely call it "just therapy words." These were the sessions when I experienced her as a pain in the ass. I wanted to tell her that she deserved her miserable life. Other times I was feeling provoked to justify my behavior. Prudently, I kept these reactions to myself.

Theresa was engendering in me an aggressive and rejecting response similar to what her lovers and the women at work must have experienced. Perhaps I was being provoked to react as her mother did. My assortment of feelings and internal reactions served, later in the therapy, as a useful guide in my inquiry about her relationship with her mother. These transference/countertransference dynamics were an unconscious demonstration of Theresa's past, her developmental needs that had been thwarted, and her management in compensating and regulating herself. I was discovering how she had learned to manage relationships. It was important that I too walk on a tightrope, the "borderline," between my keeping the transference just active enough so her unconscious story could unfold within the healing responsiveness of our therapeutic relationship and, at the same time, take the responsibility to protect her from my becoming defensive or self-explanatory, a reactive countertransference, that would reinforce her original self-regulating script beliefs and archaic ways of coping.

Theresa was continually anticipating criticism from me, her boyfriend, co-workers, or anyone. She would then be either hurt or enraged at the perceived criticism. That was her old well-established pattern of psychological compensation. Rather than validating her current feelings about the perceived criticism (which is what she wanted me to do), I talked about how her feelings reflected what she had previously experienced. On several occasions I explained that her feelings and reactions were valid but only in another time and context. This led us to spend many sessions exploring her anticipated criticisms and relating them to the criticism she had actually received from her mother. I was patient; this work of disengaging from the many incidences of transference onto her boyfriend, co-workers, and me required many discussions.

I inquired repeatedly about Theresa's internal experiences and the meanings she made from all the criticism that she had actually received. Some of her ways of making meaning of her mother's criticism and her father's failure to protect her were: "I'm a piece of shit"; "I'm unlovable"; "I'm seductive"; "Something's wrong with me"; "No one is there for me"; "No one understands me." I kept these core beliefs in mind so I could understand how she organized her experiences. Many times I encouraged her to think about how significant these beliefs were in determining her emotional reactions.

Each of these beliefs was Theresa's childhood way of making sense of how she was treated. She needed validation, not that each belief was true, but that in such an untenable situation any child would form such conclusions and then go through life assuming that they were true. I explained to Theresa that, while being a competent, professional woman, she was also internally influenced by a confused, neglected, and angry little girl—a child that had accommodated and compensated herself so that she could live with all the criticism and neglect. I now knew that it was that little girl in Theresa who needed a consistent, dependable, and reliable therapeutic presence in order to relax her old styles of accommodation and to find new ways for affect-regulation and psychological stabilization.

I explained to Theresa that she could bring her troubled inner child to the therapy sessions rather than having her "helpless crying spells" or getting into fights with her boyfriend. But, to accomplish that, she needed to remain in psychotherapy and she needed to come more frequently than just once a week. It was now the end of May and our contract was soon coming to an end. I invited her to resume our work together in September and emphasized that too much emotional turmoil was happening in her day-to-day life to come to therapy only once a week; if she were to return in September it would be essential that she have more than one session per week.

She voiced her fear of becoming dependent on me. I explained that she was currently dependent on her old childhood coping patterns of feeling totally helpless, engaging in conflicts at work, and raging at her boyfriend. As a child she had no one on whom to depend and often felt as if no one was there for her. I acknowledged that she was not currently living in the intense series of crises that had prompted her to begin our therapy together, but I thought that it was important she continue in psychotherapy to both insure the gains she had made and to resolve the underlying early affect-confusion that motivated her relationally disruptive behaviors. It took some effort on my part to convince her to return to therapy in September. I was not concerned that she was suicidal but I was aware that there was a tremendous amount of psychotherapy ahead of us if Theresa was going to get off the "borderline" of affect-confusion and have meaningful and satisfying relationships in her life. We ended for the summer with my not knowing if Theresa would return in the autumn.

CHAPTER FOURTEEN

Balancing on the "borderline" of early affect-confusion

Our second and third year together

The following September, after a long summer recess, Theresa telephoned and expressed a strong interest in continuing the psychotherapy. I was pleasantly surprised since, during the summer, I wondered if there had been any lasting gain from the previous seven months of therapy and if she would return for more in-depth work.

The therapy that I provided Theresa over the past many months had consisted primarily of a combination of my consistent empathy, attunement to her relational needs, and a sustained non-criticizing presence. However, I also focused on the behavioral management of both her internal turmoil and her relationships at home and at work—a focus that, at the time, she did not appreciate. In our first session, in early September, Theresa reported that during the summer she did not feel "so lost inside" and that she had used my "advice" several times to avoid "fights" with her boyfriend. She missed our work together and wanted to continue.

We made a new contract for an ongoing in-depth psychotherapy to resolve her early affective confusion, to understand how she relived childhood conflicts in the present, and to find alternative ways of

213

stabilizing herself other than raging or demanding attention for her helplessness. Our plan included twice a week sessions with the opportunity for additional sessions when she needed them. In this way we eliminated many of the late night phone calls that had occurred when she was either enraged at her boyfriend or feeling totally helpless. Our new contract included the provision that we could talk on the phone "if necessary" for only five minutes and no longer. I defined "if necessary" as calling to extricate herself from an argument or "crying spell" and primarily to make an additional appointment for the following day. This strategy almost eliminated the late night phone calls and provided a relational stability that had been missing in her life.

For many sessions she was reluctant (and at times unable) to talk about her childhood. "My childhood was cursed," she cried. "I don't have any memories. It is my adult life that is full of problems." As she told me of each current relational crisis, I helped Theresa trace her feelings to previous experiences in her life. Theresa was beginning to tolerate my phenomenological inquiry. Historical inquiry about her early life stimulated a lot of anxiety but she was now able to talk about her teenage years—years that had been full of disappointments with friends and difficulties with teachers who "never understood" her. Many times she predicted that the rest of her adult life would be "a waste of time" just as her teen years had been. But, now, more and more of our time was spent on the difficulties of her adolescence rather than her conflicts with her boyfriend and co-workers.

Theresa related a painful story about her first year at university. Some girls disliked Theresa and did not want her living in the dormitory. She described how they "gossiped" about her and "criticized everything I was." On many occasions I reused this story as an opening to explore other criticisms and rejections in her adolescent life. With each exploration she began to remember humiliating school situations and eventually her mother's constant barrage of criticisms and ridiculing comments. "Even when my mother did not speak to me for days at a time, her scornful look always told me that I was just a piece of shit. When she did talk it was often to tell me I was useless and that something was seriously wrong with me." Theresa went on to describe how, as a little girl, she believed her mother. She added with great sobs, "Most days I still believe her. I'm afraid that I am really just a piece of shit."

As Theresa repeated this story in several sessions, I reiterated that she did not deserve a "scornful look" or being told that she was "just a piece of shit." I explained that it was normal for a young child to believe his mother and that Theresa had been an ordinary child who needed to be treated with caring respect. With each of these normalizing comments she would sob with a cry that shuddered throughout her entire body.

Theresa's previous statements of "I have no memories of my childhood" began to merge into an increasing awareness of the criticisms and verbal abuse she experienced as child. In response to my phenomenological inquiry she was having explicit memories in each session. She was able to describe her childhood as "incredibly lonely." She was increasingly reporting feeling "empty," "depressed," and having a "gnawing, hungry feeling in my stomach all the time." She was worried about getting fat because she was always trying to satisfy her hungry sensations. With each worry I inquired about how her mother would have treated her if she were "hungry" for natural attention, affirmation, or affection. This combination of both historical and phenomenological inquiry into the quality of her maternal relationship opened many new memories that had not been previously conscious. Our therapeutic work shifted from last spring's focus on her father to her vivid and painful memories about her mother. Theresa told story after story of her mother's criticisms. By validating and normalizing her anger at her mother's criticisms and continually inquiring about her internal sensations, I provided a forum for Theresa to express her anger directly to me about her mother's ridiculing behavior. I was concerned that Theresa still did not have sufficient internal security to engage in any imaginative anger work such as talking to the image of her mother in an empty chair.

Deconfusing both the child and adult

As she expressed her anger about her mother to me, I regularly inquired about her body sensations and what she had been feeling just a second before the anger. With these phenomenological inquiries, Theresa began to describe "penetrating body pains"—pains that we eventually identified as both sadness and shame in relationship to her mother. Since both her sadness and shame were experienced as body pains, I chose to focus on Theresa's shame before attending fully to her sadness. I suspected that her sadness represented a much earlier, and perhaps more profound, grief.

Prolonged and careful attention to her physiological sensations led us to spend many sessions identifying that her overwhelming sense of shame was the result of her mother's constant criticism and ridicule. The implied (and often direct) message from Theresa's mother was, "Something is wrong with you." Theresa lacked the capacity to express any protest; the result was that she constricted and immobilized many muscles while internally believing and complying with her mother's criticism.

Her mother repeatedly ignored or ridiculed Theresa's behaviors, emotional expressions, and relational needs. The combination of being frightened and physically immobilized by the criticism and ridicule, her inability to effectively protest, and a helpless sense of compliance resulted in Theresa's debilitating shame—a profound shame that was frequently masked by her self-righteous, aggressive behavior. An effective psychotherapy of shame required that I systematically and sensitively inquire about each element of shame: her self-righteous façade, her immobilized self-expression, her fear of ridicule and abandonment, her compliance with Mother's definition of her, and her unrequited needs for validation, self-definition, and making an impact.

Theresa and I often talked about how her developmental needs were ignored or ridiculed. On some occasions she was physically punished for defining herself differently from how her mother defined her or required her to behave. Our therapeutic discussions led to many sessions of identifying the normal needs of children and the effects of those needs repeatedly not being met. These talks provided an opportunity for me to inquire as to how she experienced my transactions with her.

Inquiring about how she perceived the intricacies of our relationship was a practice that I continued to do at those potentially transforming points in almost every session. She found my normalizing comments "unbelievable," but wished they were true. On some occasions she would ask me to repeat what I had said about the natural needs of a child and the qualities of an attentive parent; she wanted to listen again. One day she asked me tell her what I had said two weeks before so she could tape it and take it home. She had a hard time remembering that I had said, "You were a precious child who needed to be loved for who she was, never to be ridiculed, but instead to be treasured and cherished." She wept. I made an unspoken commitment to Theresa to make sure my transactions with her were respectful and cherishing.

Some days were marked by her disgruntlement with our relationship or her perception of being criticized by me. Yes, there were times when I made errors of attunement, misunderstood her, urged her to change her behavior, or operated from my own assumptions without inquiring about her point of view. When possible, I identified these relational errors prior to Theresa realizing my mis-connection with her. On other occasions she would be angry at me for misunderstanding her. In both types of situations it was important in our relationship that I acknowledged my errors and took responsibility for how my behavior affected her.

My recognition, responsibility, and corrections for how I had misconnected with her were uniquely different from her childhood, or even adult life, experience. Almost two years later, she told me how important it was the first few times I took responsibility for failing to be sensitive to her or misunderstanding her. Theresa had not forgotten those important transactions. She added, "My mother has never acknowledged or taken responsibility for how miserably she has treated me. At first I did not understand why you apologized. But now I do. That is normal. I even do it with my boyfriend now."

Our discussions would inevitably return to her memories of her mother's caustic comments and rejection. During this second year I also inquired about her internal experience when I complimented her. Early in our sessions she had said that she could not trust me when I said "something kind" to her. She added that I was probably "being seductive." She could trust me more if I was criticizing her.

Together, over time, we explored how these attempts to create a distance in our relationship, what we called juxtaposition reactions, reflected an attempt to maintain both a sense of continuity and predictability in her life. Theresa described being "very familiar with bracing myself for mother's criticisms." She exclaimed, "I don't know how to brace myself when you say something kind to me." One day, when she was confused by my empathy, she screamed, "I can't take kindness. I don't know what to do with it."

During the first two years of our work together many juxtaposition reactions occurred. I would say something in a caring way that both validated and normalized her needs-in-relationship and, in response, she would belittle my comment. For example, I arranged for her to have an extra session on a Sunday morning. As she arrived she thanked me for the "emergency session." I responded with a sincere, "It's my pleasure to be here for you." She scoffed, with a disgusted look on her face, and said, "You do it for the money."

Each juxtaposition reaction became an opportunity to explore together her previously unthought emotional memories. There were many relationally disruptive events in her childhood that her family never talked about or even acknowledged; now, together, we were talking about those events, her feelings, and what she had needed from her parents. Kindness, consideration, compliments, compassion, and affection were not part of Theresa's childhood experience. I talked to her about how these relational components are important elements in every child's formation of a secure attachment with a caregiver. When I expressed any of these qualities in our therapeutic relationship she would test me by saying such things as, "Do you really mean that?"

Theresa often asked such explicit personal questions. In some sessions I chose to give her a direct answer such as, "Yes, I mean what I just said." Such an authentic answer would periodically bring tears to her eyes; at other times she would rebuff my answer. In some sessions when Theresa would ask a direct question I would answer by asking her two questions. For example, she told me about the welts that formed when she had a severe spanking from her mother; then she suddenly turned and asked me if I believed her story. I answered with a bifurcated question, "What does it mean if I don't believe your story about your mother hitting you, and what does it mean if I do believe you?"

Such a bifurcated question usually produced answers such as: "If you don't believe me then you're not here for me and I'm just a shit for having tried to tell you." After prompting her to address the other half of the question a typical answer was, "If you believe me, that means I have just seduced you with my sob stories; I feel like shit; and you will never understand me anyway." I would take a moment in time to allow the significance of what Theresa just said to be central to both of us. After a thoughtful moment I would give a summarizing response similar to: "It seems that in either situation, if I do believe you or if I don't, in the end, you experience that you are 'shit' and that you will neither be understood nor will anyone really be there for you. That must hurt."

With such a summary of her complex answers, she would become pensive and on some occasions cry. I would then proceed with, "So, let's talk more about what is central to both of your answers; tell me more about the pain of your father and mother never understanding you and how they failed to be there for you," or, "Say more about how it feels to be defined by your mother as 'shit.'" The bifurcated questions and her answers led us to many memories of neglect, ridicule, punishment, and emotional abandonment.

We ended for the summer recess in June of the third year. As far as I could tell, Theresa was no longer manipulative in her relationships nor was she picking arguments to escape the inner loneliness. She no longer believed that no one was on her side. Instead of feeling constantly hurt and angry in the relationship with her boyfriend she was "sometimes feeling close to him." She had no thoughts or threats of suicide; much of her manipulation had stopped. She was clearly aware that as a child she had defined her life as "Something is wrong with me, I'm unlovable, no one understands me, and no one is there for me." She was also beginning to realize, at least some days, that she was the master of her own behavior and that she could choose to change both her behavior and her fantasies in order to not collect reinforcing experiences that helped prove her core beliefs.

We were now able to talk together about Theresa's "borderline" between neediness and rage, despair and self-reliance, impulsivity and manipulation. Yet I knew that her psychotherapy was still not complete. The relationship with her mother was still marked by Theresa's sense of "hate" and disavowal of a profound painful abandonment. She was distraught about the "gnawing, hungry feeling" she physically experienced every time we talked about what she had needed from a mother. There was so much in the life of that little girl that she had not yet remembered and resolved. As we parted in June she agreed to continue in September with our in-depth psychotherapy.

CHAPTER FIFTEEN

Relational healing of early affect-confusion

Our therapeutic relationship in years four and five

When our psychotherapy sessions began again in September, I often had in mind an impressionistic, developmental image of Theresa as a kindergarten and school age child who lived in fear of expressing her own ideas, needs, and what she liked or disliked. I felt an intense concern for the psychological safety of such a frightened and helpless child. I focused on staying attuned to her loneliness and felt a constant sense of compassion for her as a sad little girl. I often spoke in a calm way to engage that frightened and despairing child that she once was, to help her identify and talk about her feelings, needs, and how she made sense of her relational experiences.

When Theresa would lead a session into complaints about her boyfriend or concerns about work, I would return to that neglected and emotionally abused little girl by inquiring about Theresa's physiological and affective reactions in living with an angry and confrontational mother. My frequent focus on the lonely or hurt or frightened child stimulated many new memories of her mother's disdain. Now the memories were of the interactions with her mother at a younger age. Session after session was filled with deep crying and a number of painful memories of how "my mother squashed my desires" and "always told me that something was wrong with me." We were now getting to her childhood experiences of feeling helpless and worthless.

One day, when she was describing her mother's typical over-controlling behavior, Theresa suddenly screamed out, "She treated me like I was a piece of shit. But I was only a little girl with needs. I needed her help. I was too little to do everything like a grown-up. I am NOT a piece of shit. You, Mother, missed seeing the precious child that I was."

This emotional outburst marked a major step forward in Theresa's psychotherapy. We talked at length about the difference in acting help-less in life today (her crying spells and demands on her boyfriend) and actually needing to depend on her parents when she was a child. Together we imagined how her life could have been if she had been treated as "precious" and contrasted it with her experience of life as "a piece of shit." The psychotherapy had a whole different tone than in the previous three years. We were no longer talking about crises or Theresa's self-destructive behaviors; we were talking about her needs as a child and her self-worth today.

It was mid-morning when Theresa called me from her office. "I'm just so crazy! I do not know what to do. I'm in a rage inside. But this time I did what you told me to do; I did not scream at anyone. I cannot stand it when anyone is disrespectful. I need to talk to you." This was again a major step forward in her psychological growth. She contained her explosive rage, used my counsel about how to manage disagree-ments, and called me for support. I complimented her on not raging in the office and made a lunch hour appointment that was only two hours later.

When she first arrived she ranted about the disrespect from a woman at work and her boss's lack of support. Once she had aired her anger and had told me some of the details of what had occurred that morning, I asked her about what "disrespect" meant to her. After several inquir-ies it became clear that she defined disrespect as any disagreement with her point of view. She went on to describe how she often perceives disa-greement as confrontational. As I asked her to tell me more about what she associated with the word "confrontational," she had a sudden reali-zation that this was how her mother reacted in most situations. "I am being just like my mother," she shrieked; "I hate her for how she is so aggressive and makes even the slightest difference into a fight". She went on to say, "I have lived with her anger all my life and now I'm shocked to think that I am being just like her." She then began to cry and express her despair and utter hopelessness in trying to express her own ideas, likes or dislikes, wishes, and needs as a child.

I now had two clear focal points for our continuing psychotherapy: first, it seemed important to address the relational needs and survival reactions of a neglected and verbally abused child; and, second, it would eventually be beneficial to therapeutically engage with the internalized mother who was influencing Theresa's current life. In working with other clients suffering from early affect-confusion it has been extremely useful to decommission the influence of the introjected other, but only after a secure therapeutic relationship with the distraught "child" is well established.

I continued to address the previously untold experiences of that little girl while also acknowledging and normalizing her aspirations. As our psychotherapy continued, her unfolding narrative ebbed and flowed with my phenomenological and historical inquiry. My consistent inquiry stimulated her to remember numerous painful and humiliating experiences that she had never talked about. And each inquiry was also a form of acknowledging what she had just said and in turn stimulating the next memory, feeling, or insight. Our therapeutic dialogue included my frequent inquiry into how she coped and regulated herself when her mother was critical, aggressive, or rejecting. I periodically acknowledged her intelligence and creativity in managing the deficits in the relationship with her parents and verbally applauded how she managed to get a semblance of psychological needs met outside the family.

I continued to remember that she had said, "I am being just like my mother." I started to impose myself between Theresa and her internalized mother by telling Theresa what I would have said to her mother if I had been visiting in their home when her mother was being so criticizing and rejecting of Theresa. Examples of these therapeutic interpositions included: "I would have told your mother to stop yelling at you and to sit down and listen to your feelings"; "I want to tell your mother that 'your little girl needs your care and compassion NOT YOUR CRITICISM!'"; "You need to go to therapy, Mother, and not take out your anger on your daughter." She would sometimes cry when I would make such statements. On other days she would angrily say, "That is the protection I needed from my father."

It was too soon to provide actual therapy for the introjection of her mother's personality. My therapeutic interpositions would suffice for now since they were effective in stimulating Theresa's awareness of what she needed as a younger child and how she was creative in adjusting and coping with her mother's critical and controlling behaviors. Before I attempted any therapy with her parental introjects, more time was needed to support Theresa's self-definition, her need to make an impact, and her need for security and validation. Acknowledging and normalizing these relational needs seemed to be essential to her psychological growth. She was now depending on our therapeutic relationship for her internal support. Theresa described the qualities of that support as having someone in her life whom she could "rely on and receive guidance ... even protection when I am overwhelmed with feelings."

Verbalizing implicit memory

Many of Theresa's early childhood relational experiences—experiences in which she had been deprived of an opportunity to be put into language—were now coming to consciousness because we had co-created a safe place to talk about her childhood feelings, desires, needs, and bodily sensations. Her parents had not provided the necessary validating conversations that could have given words, concepts, and meanings to Theresa's experiences; her experiences had remained without linguistic symbolization until we talked about them in our psychotherapy. My phenomenological inquiry, curiosity, concerns, and personal presence stimulated Theresa's awareness of memories that she was unable to recall on her own. She had an increasing realization that much of her current life's conflicts were motivated by her emotional reactions to many unresolved relational conflicts with her parents.

I asked Theresa to describe the quality of conversations she had with her parents over breakfast or before going to school in the morning. All she could recall was her father's absence and her mother's insistence that she be on time, be dressed neatly, and that she stay clean. She could not remember any discussion about her excitement or fears, who she liked and who liked her, or her joys or stresses that could possibly be occurring during the school day. I asked about her returning from school and the quality of conversations with her parents at that hour. She could remember being criticized for getting dirty or being late but she was unable to recall any dialogue that acknowledged her experiences, feelings, or wishes. "My mother was only interested in my doing all my homework before I could play," she said angrily.

In several sessions I continued this type of historical inquiry with the focus of my inquiry shifting to the qualities of her maternal relationship at an ever-younger age. I spent three sessions inquiring about her bedtime routine and the quality of possible conversations with her parents at that relationally crucial hour. She said that during her school years she had to be in bed by nine each night and that she could read alone for fifteen minutes. Her father always watched TV and she would sometimes give him a kiss on the cheek before going to her room alone. Her mother demanded that the lights be off at 9:15; she never read to Theresa or sat on the bed to discuss the day's events or prepare for the next day. Often her mother never said, "Good night"; it was expected that Theresa would obey the rules. There was no one to help Theresa understand and manage her own world. As I focused my inquiry on bedtime for the preschool child, Theresa had no memory of being cuddled, read to, or having any pre-sleep conversations with either parent. Now I fully understood the cumulative neglect, over many years, that led to Theresa's conclusion: "No one is there for me."

Theresa's answers to my initial inquiries about her day-to-day life with her parents were often short and factual but each of these historical inquiries was followed by many phenomenological inquiries about her sensations, feelings, associations, thought processes, and desires. This often led to an inquiry into how she survived, accommodated, and stabilized herself when no one was emotionally or conversationally there for her. My questions were not aimed at merely gathering the facts of her history; my inquiry was always focused on her inner experiences and subjective processes in response to those historical experiences. My inquiry, attunement, acknowledgement, and normalization facilitated her to put her previously non-conscious body, her affective and relational experiences into words. It was slow work, yet Theresa and I were now co-constructing a narrative of her young life. Through our therapeutic dialogue we were acknowledging, giving meaning to, and validating what she called her "unthought about" experience.

I continued to focus my inquiries on a younger and then even younger child. Our work often involved long silences as Theresa struggled to put her physiological sensations and feelings into words. I proceeded by inquiring about her preschool experiences and eventually asked what she knew about her infancy and toddler years. I raised questions about her play activities when she was three or four years old. During this phase of our therapy together her first answer to many of my questions was, "I don't know."

In response to Theresa's "I don't know" I would ask her to close her eyes and imagine herself as a preschool child. In addition to many implicit images of "rules" and "nothingness," she did have three explicit memories: she could remember being about three years old and climbing on her father's lap and his laughing with her; she could remember her mother "being harsh" with her when she "could not use scissors properly when I was four"; she remembered playing alone with her stuffed animals when she was between three and four years and having an overwhelming sense of deep loneliness. As we talked at length about her loneliness Theresa said that all of her life, until now, she could not understand why all her "stuffed animals were lonely and scared." Much of this period of time was spent attending to Theresa's profound sense of loneliness—an early childhood loneliness that previously had no means of interpersonal expression except for her to imagine it in her stuffed animals or to deflect it into conflicts with people. She needed a consistent therapeutic presence and compassionate attunement to her loneliness and fear even though she sometimes angrily complained, "My loneliness and fears did not exist before this therapy."

Were Theresa's descriptions of her preschool years an accurate recall of actual interactions with her parents or were they her impressions? I'm not sure. However, I assumed that such impressions were created from many sub-symbolic and implicit memories and therefore were an avenue for inquiring further about Theresa's subjective world. As I listened to Theresa's phenomenological experience of her early childhood, I attended to my own sensations and impressions, my own affective pull to comfort and protect her, and my knowledge of child development and what any child needs in a parental relationship in order to form a secure attachment. All of this, and all that I had learned about her in the previous four years, became the data in forming many inferences about her affective/relational life.

Therapeutic inference was my most important tool when I was striving to understand and help Theresa express her pre-symbolic and non-linguistic memories. Her memories of early childhood and infancy were not available to consciousness through language because her experiences were either preverbal or did not have a relational opportunity to be put into language. Although Theresa lacked a coherent narrative of her life's experiences, her sub-symbolic memories were expressed in body sensations, emotional reactions, and self-regulating patterns. Her unconscious attachment patterns were disorganized, often on an oscillating borderline between avoidant and anxious. Theresa lived on a "borderline" of intense neediness and rage, despair and self-reliance, impulsivity and manipulation.

In observing her oscillations between avoidant, anxious, and disorganized attachment patterns, I assumed (even though I had no explicit data) that the first few years of her life were as psychologically tumultuous as her school and teenage years had been. My attunement to her affect, rhythm, and developmental levels, as well as my physiological resonance, were essential in forming an involved connection that facilitated a communication of her sub-symbolic experiences and implicit memories. I attended to how her preverbal story was expressed in nonverbal enactments, encoded in her stories and metaphors, embedded in her relational conflicts, and engendered in my emotional reactions to her. It was up to me to make use of all of this information to create a healing relationship for this distressed infant and toddler.

I asked Theresa to imagine being a child about sixteen or eighteen months of age, who was sitting in a high chair and being fed by her mother. I inquired about the look she imagined would have been on her mother's face, how her mother would have reacted if she disliked the food, her mother's tempo in feeding her, her mother's joy or disapproval, and all the body sensations that went with each inquiry. I also asked similar questions about her emotional and physiological experience of nursing, diaper changing, bath time, toilet training, and mutual play.

This whole series of inquiries lasted several months and provided both of us with a plethora of information about Theresa's early affect-confusion: her physiological sense of feeling both repulsion toward her mother and simultaneously a painful longing for an intimate connection. She remembered being frightened by the harsh looks on her mother's face, squirming as her body sensed her mother's rough touch, disgusted with how she was forced to eat, and the muscle contractions in her body in reaction to her mother's rhythm. In many sessions Theresa wept over what she had missed in a mothering relationship and she raged at her mother's callous behavior. She also cried in terror as she sensed her mother's harsh treatment of her. In our therapeutic work together Theresa reexperienced the trembling body sensations of emptiness and emotional abandonment when her mother would not look at or talk to her for "hours or even days." She now identified her "gnawing, hungry feeling" as a need for nurturing. At the same time she realized that "Even as a baby I must have avoided her rough touch and mean face." Theresa had many reasons to be profoundly confused as an infant and to have formed a relationally avoidant life pattern.

I was reminded how loving and forgiving young children can be; in several sessions Theresa wept and pleaded: "Momma, please love me"; "Momma, don't leave me … I'll be good"; and, "Please, please, please, Momma." Sometimes she would curl up on the couch and just moan the word "Momma." She feared the deep sensations of loneliness that would come when Mother ignored her. She described how, as a preschool child, she would do anything to get her mother to talk kindly to her. In another session, while experiencing herself as an older child, she screamed in anguish, "I have adapted, adjusted, accommodated and conformed my entire life just to get my mother to stop hating me." Theresa became increasingly able to relate her infant and early childhood loneliness to the clinging demands she made on her boyfriend. She realized that she was demanding that Robert be a "good mother" to her.

Dispelling early affect-confusion

Following these and other realizations Theresa's age regressions began to lose their thrust of urgency. In our ongoing therapeutic dialogue we reviewed these childhood experiences many times to understand their significance in her life and we also returned to these expressive early childhood emotion-filled sessions when a supportive regression seemed to be an important form of communicating and resolving her previously non-conscious story. But Theresa now had less and less of an urge to regress to earlier periods of relational neglect. Theresa was now able to make many associations and connections to her adult life behaviors and emotional reactions. She had a good understanding of her habit of pushing people away, her fear of intimacy, her rage (particularly at women), and her "tremendous longing for someone to be there for me."

As the spring of our fifth year together approached and we would again be taking a summer recess, I began to turn my attention to finding opportunities to inquire about Theresa's aspirations. What were her future plans? What did she always want to do and had never got around to doing? She said that she was tired of the subservient position of being a legal assistant and had always hoped to become an attorney. She added that she wanted to "have a loving relationship … with Robert." This was how we ended in May of our fifth year. Theresa was enthusiastic about returning in September "in order to better understand myself."

In these previous two years, while I attended almost exclusively to Theresa's experience as an infant and very young child, I kept in mind her words, "I'm just like my mother." Since I would be traveling most of the summer this was not the time to approach this issue. Previously I had postponed doing any psychotherapy with her introjected mother; I would postpone it again until autumn. The therapeutic interpositions that I periodically made between the criticizing comments of an introjected mother and the natural expressions of a little girl had been effective in quieting much of Theresa's internal criticism and distress. But the psychotherapy was not complete. I considered the resolution of Theresa's introjection of her mother's personality to be essential to our doing a comprehensive and in-depth psychotherapy.

During this time my first two priorities had been to establish a greater sense of relational security for Theresa and to facilitate her expression of her own relational desires, what she liked and disliked, and her private aspirations. I was primarily focused on the child's unrequited need for self-definition and the need to make an impact-in-relationship while always keeping in mind Theresa's needs for security and validation. As a child, Theresa was never effective in making an impact on her angry mother. Her attempts at self-definition were met with confrontation and ridicule, an absence of validation, and a lack of security-in-relationship. To avoid the unending conflicts with her mother, Theresa reactively sacrificed her natural forms of self-expression.

As this year came to an end, I reviewed what I had learned in my work with Theresa; I had a renewed appreciation of Theresa's aggressive behavior toward people being a non-conscious expression of her unmet relational needs for validation, self-definition, and her need to make an impact. By picking fights at home and at work she was expressing these unrequited developmental needs, never achieving satisfaction because her angry expressions were out of their original context. Our psychotherapy co-created a therapeutic space that simulated memories of her original family context—a therapeutic space in which her vital needs could be expressed, validated, and normalized. It was also clear to me as to why I intuitively had never used confrontation as part of my therapeutic dialogue with Theresa; confrontation would have been non-therapeutic, perhaps even reinforcing of the psychological damage that she had already experienced. She seemed to thrive on my sustained affective and developmental attunement, my gentle phenomenological inquiry, and my firm and respectful involvement.

When I returned from vacation in August there was an urgent phone message from Theresa requesting "a special session as soon as possible." Two days later I discovered that she had been waiting a month to give me her "good news." Her boyfriend had been offered a job promotion; he had to move to a distant city. Theresa had decided that since they had been having a "great relationship" for the past couple of years that she would "take the risk of moving with Robert." She talked at length about how much she had changed and how she and Robert were now capable of intimate discussions instead of fighting. They had discussed their future: with her savings and his increased income, she could afford to go to law school and become an attorney. She was full of joy and excitement. She added that she had a secret: "I've been thinking of getting married. I am planning a big surprise for Robert when he comes home this Saturday night. I am going to propose that we have a wedding just before we move."

I had tears of joy in my eyes as I reflected on our five-year therapeutic relationship. I was personally enriched by what we had shared together. Theresa had taught, or at least re-taught, me about the importance of patience, respect, kindness, uncertainty, priorities, parameters, and the need to attend to sub-symbolic and implicit memory in its many forms of nonverbal expression.

In the first couple of years it had been a difficult journey for both of us but she had grown in many ways. For the past couple of years Theresa was no longer acting helpless at home by having "crying spells" or making demands on her boyfriend; she was no longer getting into conflicts at home or work; she self-regulated her affect-confusion and understood how her early relational life had influenced both her helplessness and ragging conflicts; and she now had a satisfying sense of self-worth and aspirations. Theresa had changed in significant ways. My only concern was with Theresa's lingering internal criticism and the lack of opportunity to provide therapy for her introjected mother. But now it was time to say "goodbye"; Theresa was no longer living on a psychological "borderline" of early affect-confusion.

CHAPTER SIXTEEN

Introjection, psychic presence, and Parent ego states: considerations for psychotherapy

In a memorial tribute to Eric Berne, Franklin Ernst (1971) declared that Berne's most significant contribution to the profession of psychotherapy was in identifying Parent ego states and differentiating them from Adult or Child ego states. This significant differentiation provides a theoretical framework for clinical transactional analysis which suggests a psychotherapeutic focus that may relieve many manifestations of anxiety, depression, and low self-esteem stemming from intrapsychic conflict. Yet, most of the clinical transactional analysis literature has either focused on freeing the Child ego states from a compulsion to adapt, strengthening Adult ego state control, replacing a harmful introjected message with a benevolent introjected message or making behavioral changes that facilitate Adult to Adult "ego state" transactions.

A few articles or books have emphasized an in-depth psychotherapy of Child ego states. Very little has been written on the treatment of Parent ego states and the resolution of intrapsychic conflict. The purpose of this chapter is to clarify and elucidate the intrapsychic functions of Parent ego states and to outline methods of an in-depth, integrative transactional analysis psychotherapy of introjected Parent ego states. The chapter that follows, Chapter Seventeen: "Resolving intrapsychic conflict: psychotherapy of Parent ego states," is co-authored with Rebecca Trautmann; it includes a verbatim transcript of an actual psychotherapy session along with my annotated comments about the process of the psychotherapy.

Prior to Berne's writings on ego states (1957a, 1957b, 1961) previous psychoanalytic writers had identified the distinction between adult-like and childlike "personalities," "conditions," or "states" and had developed the analytic methods of free association, non-gratification, and interpretation as a means of both providing understanding and alleviating internal distress. Much has been written on the psychological effects of "parental influence" or superego; however, the psychoanalytic literature is lacking in an adequate description of the treatment of the superego whether it is called internalized object, parental influence, anti-libidinal ego, introjected other, or unconscious fantasy.

In 1895, Josef Breuer and Sigmund Freud wrote in *Studies on Hysteria* about Anna O's "two entirely separate states of consciousness," which alternated frequently and spontaneously—one relatively normal and a keen observer, the other was childlike and naughty. In the case they presented about Emmy von N., Breuer and Freud described how she alternated "states of consciousness" between describing her primal experiences and making comments to Freud about how he was conducting the analysis (Breuer & Freud, 1950d).

In *Ego Psychology and the Psychosis*, Paul Federn (1953) observed that his patients exhibited a current ego that both identifies with internal sensations and at the same time, identifies with or discriminates from environmental stimuli. In addition, this ego manifests a feeling of identity and a response to the environment which is like that of a young child. He described these different manifestations as subdivisions or *states* of the ego, i.e., different identities. He went on to refer to the internalization of parental figures in his patients as "acquired ego attitudes" and related this constant psychic presence to the psychoanalytic concept of the superego. Federn's views on the ego and states of the ego significantly differed from those of other ego psychologists within the psychoanalytic movement, such as Hartmann (1939, 1964), Kris (1951, 1979), and Rapaport (1967). Although using somewhat different terminology, Federn influenced the theories of Berne (1957, 1961), Guntrip (1961), Jacobson (1964), Kernberg (1976), Kohut (1977), Watkins (1978), and Winnicott (1965).

John Watkins, like Eric Berne, also studied with Federn but developed his ideas of ego states without an awareness that Berne was developing similar concepts. John and Helen Watkins's book, *Ego States: Theory and Therapy* (1997) defines an ego state as "an organized system of behavior and experience whose elements are bound together by some common principle, and which is separated from other such states by a boundary that is more or less permeable" (p. 25). They describe both a "core ego" as that which the person and others perceive as "self" and "other ego states" as "segments of self" that are "differentiated for adoptive purposes." These consist of either "introjects of significant others" or ego states "split off from the core ego because of trauma" (p. 26).

In *An Outline of Psychoanalysis*, Freud described the development of the superego as occurring in the long period of childhood, during which the growing human being lives in dependence upon his parents. This dependency forms within the child's ego a special agency in which this parental influence is prolonged. The parents' influence includes not merely the personalities of the parents themselves but also the racial, national, and family traditions handed on through them (1940a). In essence, because of the child's dependency, internalized elements of the parents' personality influence the ego (the person's sense of "me") and cause the person to psychologically function differently and under stress.

In the development of psychoanalytic object relations theory Fairbairn (1954) and Guntrip (1961, 1968) dispensed with Freud's concept of superego. Instead they theorized that in the presence of fear a child may split off parts of himself and form an ego state that is a combination of an internalized parental control and a child's fearful compliance with that control. They termed this state the "anti-libidinal ego" to emphasize how it suppresses and controls the "libidinal ego"—an ego state that has the remnants of what would have been the natural nature of the person. They describe this conflict as occurring intrapsychically for the purpose of maintaining a semblance of relationship by keeping the natural nature of the person suppressed. Their "central ego" is the state which functions in the external world and may serve as a cover for intrapsychic conflict.

Edoardo Weiss prefers the term internalization since to him it refers to an "inclusion within the ego" of an identification with aspects of the other's personality (1950, p. 76). "Internalization is complete when it *substitutes*, within one's own ego, the bodily and mental aspects of a person. This substitution may be an autoplastic egotized duplication or only the egotized imagination of the physical and mental features of another personality" (ibid., p. 95). In 1912, "Ferenczi introduced the term *introjection*, as a synonym for 'incorporation' to indicate the ego-tization of the autoplastic duplication of the object" (ibid., p. 76). Weiss does not like the term "introjection" because in his way of thinking it does not adequately describe how the person is both changed by the other and how the internalization is also not exactly the same as the other.

In Gestalt therapy the concept of psychological introjection—the internalization of elements of another person—is central to understanding the core theory of the need for internal and exter-nal contact. Introjection is defined as an unconscious defensive identification with another. The maintenance of an introjection prohibits full contact with both self and others (Perls, Hefferline, & Goodman, 1951).

The concept of the Parent ego state may indeed be Berne's great inno-vative gift to our profession. In 1957 Berne quoted Freud's description of superego and added that both superego and Parent ego state imply that a portion of the external world has become an integral part of the internal world, hence both are in origin exteropsychic. Berne often uses the term exteropsyche interchangeably with Parent ego states. Berne states that the idea of an exteropsyche has interesting neurological con-notations but he does not say what they are (Berne, 1957a). Forthcom-ing research in neurobiology may map the basic circuits and identify the brain's defensive identifications with others, or their psychic pres-ence, and perhaps even identify second and third levels of exteropsy-chic material.

Berne (1961, Chapter Sixteen) described theoretically the second and third order of the Child and Parent ego states. He referred to the second and third order Parent ego states as containing "genealogical material." It is my opinion that this influencing material can be brought to the client's awareness through a respectful and attuned therapeutic rela-tionship and a phenomenological inquiry that facilitates the client's dis-covering his experiences, fantasies, ideas, and meaning making about his present life. This is accomplished through an analysis of the trans-ference and is often the prerequisite to an in-depth theory of a Parent ego state. Berne's "particular interest" in working with characterologi-cal problems was in "the persistent stringency" of a Parent ego state, specifically "the Child segments of the Parent and the Adult parts of the Child" (1961, pp. 196–197).

The Latin origins imply that the word introjection means "thrown inside." However, neither the Latin nor the Greek "exteropsyche"— outside the sole or mind—explain *how* it happens. In integrative psychotherapy (Erskine & Moursund, 1988; Erskine, Moursund, & Trautmann, 1999) the following definition is used as an operational definition based on child development literature and clinical observations: *Introjection occurs in the absence of relational needs being met; it is a defensive unaware identification with elements of the personality of the other as compensation for unmet relational needs.* All introjections, because of their defensive nature, are dysfunctional in meeting today's relational needs, even though the content may sometimes be nurturing or effective. When external behavior or intrapsychic influence is the result of introjection, it is the manifestation of a defensive internalization of a foreign object and is an impediment to full internal and external contact (Gobes & Erskine, 1995).

Eric Berne (1961) extended psychoanalytic thought with his elaboration and application of Paul Federn's (1953) concept of states of the ego. Berne's contribution to the theory of ego states produced the possibility for a dramatic change in the practice of psychotherapy and predated by several years the more recent changes in psychoanalytic theory and practice (Bollas, 1979; Greenberg & Mitchell, 1983; Guntrip, 1968; Kernberg, 1976; Kohut, 1971, 1977; Masterson, 1976, 1981; Miller, 1981; Stolorow, Brandchaft, & Atwood, 1987).

In the popularization of transactional analysis that has occurred since Berne's death in 1970, many of his original theoretical concepts have been presented simplistically. Often, Berne's examples and explanations have been used as definitions of ego states and the therapeutic richness and depth of his original concept of ego states has been overlooked. In this chapter, we will begin by returning to Berne's original conceptualization of ego states as the theoretical base for the psychotherapy of the contact-interrupting, defensive process of introjection and the resolution of the resulting intrapsychic distress.

The ego and states of the ego

In *Ego Psychology and the Psychoses*, Paul Federn (1953) described the ego as a real, experienced state of feeling and not simply a theoretical construct. The Latin word "*ego*," as used in the English translation of early psychoanalytic writings, replaced Freud's "das Ich"—"the I." The ego is the identifying and alienating aspect of the self; it is our sense of "This is me" and "That is not me." The ego discriminates and segregates internal sensations from those originating outside the organism. The ego is our identity—the "I am hungry," "I am a psychotherapist," or "I am not a bus driver, although I can drive a bus."

Berne assumed throughout his early writing (pre-1966) that the reader was familiar with a working definition of ego; he described a state of the ego "phenomenologically as a coherent system of feelings related to a given subject, and operationally as a set of coherent behavior patterns" (1961, p. 17).

Berne further used a colloquial description of ego states (Parent, Adult, and Child) to refer to phenomenological *manifestations* of the psychic organs (exteropsyche, neopsyche, and archaeopsyche), whose function it is to organize internal and external stimuli. Exteropsyche, archaeopsyche, and neopsyche refer to the aspect of the mind taken from an external source, the early mind from a previous developmental period, and the current mind. Throughout *Transactional Analysis in Psychotherapy* (1961) Berne used the psychic organ terms interchangeably with the term "ego state" to "denote states of mind and their related patterns of behavior" (p. 30).

Berne stated, "The Adult ego state is characterized by an autonomous set of feelings, attitudes and behavior patterns which are adapted to the current reality" (p. 76). In this description Berne's use of the term "autonomous" refers to the neopsychic ego functioning without intrapsychic control by an introjected or archaic ego state. When in the Adult ego a person is in full contact with what is occurring in a manner appropriate to that developmental age.

This neopsychic (current mind) function of the ego accounts for and integrates: 1) what is occurring moment-by-moment internally and externally, 2) past experiences and their resulting effects, and 3) the psychological influences and identifications with other significant people in one's life. This Adult ego consists of current age-related motor behavior; emotional, cognitive, and moral development; the ability to be creative, and the capacity for full contactful engagement in meaningful relationships. Berne (ibid., p. 195) emphasized these aspects through the use of the Greek terms *ethos* and *pathos*—to which I add *logos*, the ability to use logic and abstract reasoning, and *technos*, the ability to create—to describe the full neopsychic capacity of the Adult ego to integrate values, process information, respond to emotions and sensations, and be creative and contactful (Erskine, 1988).

The term "Adult ego" is used in integrative transactional analysis theory rather than the more popular "Adult ego state" to denote that it is not a state of the ego but symbolizes the full neopsychic capacities of an individual without the intrapsychic control of introjected parent or archaic Child ego states. Parent and Child ego states are non-integrated fixations of unresolved previous experiences that drain psychic energy and distract an individual from spontaneity and flexibility in problem solving, health maintenance, or intimate relationships with people. Through corrective life experiences or an effective healing psychotherapy Child and Parent ego states can be fully integrated into the adult's ego. With integration the past experiences of childhood and the introjected experiences of significant others are now in one's awareness, are de-energized as separate entities, and no longer serve their defensive functions. They can now function like a valuable resource library rather than as separate states of the ego that influence, control, and produce intrapsychic conflict.

The neopsychic ego was contrasted by Berne with archaic ego states which consist of fixations at earlier developmental stages. In Berne's (1961) words, "The Child ego state is a set of feelings, attitudes, and behavior patterns which are relics of the individual's own childhood" (p. 77). When in a Child ego state the person perceives the external world and internal needs and sensations as he did in an earlier developmental stage. Although the person may appear to be relating to current reality, he is actually experiencing what is happening with the intellectual, social, and emotional capacities of a child at the developmental age of unresolved neglect, trauma, or confusion, i.e., a psychological fixation.

It should be noted that using the term Child ego state in the singular form is somewhat misleading. A child develops through a number of phases and stages (Erikson, 1950; Mahler, 1968; Mahler, Pine, & Bergman, 1975; Piaget, 1936; Stern, 1985), and repression and fixation may occur at any of them. Under the influence of one set of stressors, we may think, feel, and act much as we did when we were six years old; under another we may perceive ourselves or the world around us as we did as infants.

The archaeopsychic state of the ego is much more complex than implied by various writers who use simple examples of spontaneity, intuition, compliance, or emotive capacity to describe the Child ego states. The Child or archaic states of the ego are the *entire personality* of a person *as he was in a previous developmental period of time*. This includes the needs, desires, urges, and sensations; the defense mechanisms; and the thought processes, perceptions, feelings, and behaviors of the developmental phase where fixation occurred.

The archaic state of the ego is the result of developmental arrest which occurred when critical early childhood needs for contact were not met. The child's defenses against the discomfort of the unmet needs became egotized—fixated; the experience cannot be fully integrated into the Adult ego until these defense mechanisms are dissolved.

Berne (1961) also explored Federn's observations that in many of his clients there was a constant psychic presence of parental figures influencing their behavior. This parental influence is from real people who years before interacted with and had responsibility for this particular individual when he was a child. This parental presence is more tangible than the Freudian construct of "superego" (*"Uber-Ich"*). Through historical investigation it is possible to trace what was actually said or done, by whom, and at what time during the person's childhood. Through introjection (an unaware defensive identification and internalization) the child made the parental person part of the self, i.e., ego.

Berne concluded that the introjected parents also became a state of the ego which he defined as "a set of feelings, attitudes, and behavior patterns which resemble those of a parental figure" (p. 75). However, the phrase "resemble those of a parental figure" is somewhat misleading. From Berne's examples and descriptions in *Transactional Analysis in Psychotherapy* and from my own clinical observations it is apparent that Parent ego states are an actual historical internalization of the personality of one's own parents or other significant parental figures as *perceived* by the child at the time of introjection. Berne emphasized this point:

> The patient whose (mother) parent habitually or at a given moment is not acting *as though* her mother "observes, orders, corrects, and threatens," but instead is acting *just like* how mother did, perhaps even with the same gestures and intonations. She is not acting with one eye on her mother, so to speak [which is likely to be Child ego state]; she is reproducing her mother's total behavior, including her inhibitions, her reasoning, and (this is a crucial factor) her impulses. (1957a, p. 300)

Parent ego state contents are taken in, i.e., introjected, from parenting figures in early childhood—and, to a lesser degree, throughout life—and, if not reexamined in the process of later development, remain unassimilated or not integrated into the neo-functioning ego of an adult. Since the child's perceptions of the caregiver's reactions, emotions, and thought processes will differ at various stages of development, so also will the actual content and intrapsychic function of the Parent ego state vary in relation to the developmental age when the introjection occurred.

Introjection is an unconscious defense mechanism (involving disavowal, denial, and repression) frequently used when there is a lack of full psychological contact between the child and the caregivers responsible for his or her psychological needs. The significant other is made part of the self (ego), and the conflict resulting from the lack of need fulfillment is internalized so the conflict can seemingly be managed more easily (Perls, 1978).

In addition to the various physical needs of childhood (Maslow, 1970), a child's relational needs require the attuned involvement of parents or significant others (Erskine, 1998a; Erskine, Moursund, & Trautmann, 1999). These relational needs include:

1. security within a relationship—a physical closeness and the freedom from humiliation and physical violence
2. validation of the child's feelings, thoughts, fantasies, and various needs
3. being in the presence of someone on whom the child can rely for protection, support, and guidance
4. having a shared experience such as playing and learning together
5. self-definition within the relationship
6. making an impact—influencing the other, at least some of the time to respond in accordance with the child's wishes or desires
7. having the other initiate contact, and
8. the expression of gratitude and love to the caregiver—the manifestation of bonding and loyalty.

When these relational needs are not acknowledged, validated, and normalized by significant others there is a rupture in interpersonal contact—the bond between child and caregiver is disrupted and a conflict ensues between the caregiver's mis-attunement, invalidation, emotional neglect, or physical abuse and the child's desperate attempts to have his relational needs satisfied.

As a biological imperative children require both a physical and psychological attachment to maintain psychological health (Bowlby, 1969, 1973, 1980). When needs are not met the resulting anxiety stimulates an unconscious defensive identification with the other. The external conflict is solved by internalizing the other and disavowing one's own needs, thereby the child can stay attached, bonded, and loyal. This is often accompanied by a sense of resignation and the formation of a compensating script belief such as "If I can't get my needs met then I don't need." The external conflict of relational needs not met becomes internal where it is handled within the individual rather than continue the external relational conflict. Metaphorically, the conflict of needs-not-met is as though there was a psychological vacuum in the relationship. That psychological vacuum—the absence of interpersonal contact—is filled by unconsciously identifying with the significant other.

Brown says, "Introjection allows a person to avoid her painful feelings associated with the loss of a person, place, or event by creating within herself an image of the lost object. Her unconscious fantasies maintain her association with the lost object and prevent her from working through the painful emotions connected to the loss" (1977, p. 5). Introjected elements may remain as a kind of foreign body within the personality, often unaffected by later learning or development but continuing to influence behavior and perceptions. They constitute an alien chunk of personality, embedded within the ego and experienced phenomenologically as if they were one's own, but, in reality, they form a borrowed personality (Erskine, 1988, 1991).

Ego state determinants

Berne said, "Transactional Analysis consists of determining which ego state is active at a given moment in the exhibition of a transactional stimulus by the agent, and which ego state is active in the response given by the respondent" (1966, p. 223). Verification of which ego state is cathected is only possible with a four-part correlation of the behavioral, social, historical, and phenomenological determinants of ego states. *"The complete diagnosis of an ego state requires that all four of these aspects be available for consideration, and the final validity of such a diagnosis is not established until all four have been correlated"* (Berne, 1961, p. 75; my italics).

Berne (ibid., pp. 74–76) described the four diagnostic determinants of ego states in the order he saw them in psychotherapy: behavioral, social, historical, and phenomenological. From a perspective of facilitating an integration of the fragmentation of the ego, I have supplementally defined the identifying criteria and listed them in the following order of clinical significance (Erskine & Moursund, 1988):

1. The identifying criterion of the phenomenological determinant is the subjective experience of the person. It includes the sensations, desires, and needs, feelings, and beliefs that shape the person's perspectives—the *how* and *what* it is like to live in his experience. Included in the phenomenological criteria are the physiological, emotional, and cognitive associations of significant life events and the times when elements of the personality of another were introjected. Also included is the subjective experience of the internal defense mechanisms fixated at times of neglect, traumatic experience, or cumulative devaluation.
2. The historical determinant is gleaned primarily from memories of the dynamic events between oneself and others, or the relationship between mother and father or other important family members. These can provide essential information regarding early conflicts. The *who* and *when* of early life may reveal memories of similar feelings and behavior in childhood or memories of the parental person who offered the prototype behavior. Included is an inquiry into the distinction between the person's own fixated childhood defenses and the defense mechanisms possibly introjected from significant others.
3. The behavioral determinant involves a *developmental* focus (Berne, 1961, p. 154) on gestures, posture, vocabulary, tone of voice, or other mannerisms, and the content of what is communicated. The assessment of the person's current observable behavior is compared with information about human development regarding early mother–child interaction; motor and language development; emotional, cognitive, and social development; defense mechanisms; moral development, and adult life transitions. All of this comparative information provides a background of data to assist in determining the stage of development at which emotions, behaviors, or

interactions have become fixated. Behavior that is not congruent with the current context may have been normal and appropriate for a child at a specific developmental age or may be an indication of how the patient defended himself in a traumatic situation. Childlike behavior may be an indication of the person's own active Child ego state, or just as likely, an indication of the Child ego state of an introjected parent. Interweaving the developmental assessment with the historical or phenomenological may be necessary to determine if a specific defensive reaction, behavioral pattern, or emotion is the manifestation of an exteropsychic ego state or of an archaeopsychic fixation.

4. The fourth determinant in verifying ego state cathexis is the social or *transactional*. The analysis of transactions provides data to indicate which ego state is active, the nature of the intrapsychic dynamics, and what stimulus from the psychotherapist served to trigger the cathexis. The intrapsychic dynamics include the influence of the introjected Parent ego state and Child ego state's need for a contactful relationship. Transactions between the person and psychotherapist, or, in group or family psychotherapy, between any two people, may reflect a transference either from an exteropsychic or archaeopsychic ego state. These transferences may take the form of "roles" such as childlike "compliance," "impertinence," or "rebelliousness"; adult-like roles of "problem solver" or information exchange, or parental roles of "comforting" or "controlling" (ibid., pp. 93–96). It is essential in diagnosing ego state cathexis and intrapsychic conflict to evaluate these transactional roles or social entities within the context of a correlated phenomenological, historical, and developmental (behavioral) assessment.

It is only through the careful and systematic use of the *four-part correlated diagnosis* that it is possible to verify which ego states are influencing and which are cathected and proceed with the appropriate psychotherapeutic interventions (Erskine, 1991).

The functions of influencing and active Parent ego states

An introjected Parent ego state may be either *active* or *intrapsychically influencing*. An active Parent ego state communicates with the outside world while an influencing Parent ego state operates internally. Berne (ibid.) described the *active* Parent ego state as reproducing the feelings, attitudes, and behavior of the introjected parent or other significant persons in actual transactions with people. The psychological function of an active Parent ego state is that the person diminishes anxiety and experiences some intrapsychic relief from the internal influence of the introjection. For example, a mother may scream at and criticize her children in the same way her father screamed at and criticized her when she was young. She is able to feel some temporary relief from the pressure and anxiety of father's psychic presence and internal criticism by externalizing the verbal abuse. Others in her life, such as her children, may suffer the effects of the rage and criticism that is an expression of an active Parent ego state. She most likely remains unaware that the quality of her contact both with self and others is under the dominance and control of a Parent ego state. Clients seldom describe this externalization as a problem except to report their discomfort regarding what others say about their behavior. Family members may complain how "Mother acts just like or even worse than grandfather."

In psychotherapy, it is much more typical that the client will describe the phenomenological experience of self-doubt, a constant sense of being controlled, the loss of knowing what one desires, and/or chronic anxiety, and/or depression. The phenomenological experience of some clients is as if they were criticizing themselves or under an internal control. Other clients may be aware of the presence of an influencing introjection or psychic presence of another person; they hear another voice that is criticizing, warning, or rule-making. Berne referred to the influencing Parent ego state as "the voice of an actual person" that the client may misidentify as a hallucination (ibid., p. 32).

"The Parental *influence* can be inferred when the individual manifests an attitude of child-like compliance" (ibid., p. 76) and/or may make use of childhood defenses such as avoidance, freezing, or fighting (Fraiberg, 1982); ego splitting (Fairbairn, 1954); transformation of affect and reversal of aggression (Fraiberg, 1982), and archaic fantasy (Erskine, 1988/1997; Erskine & Moursund, 1988). The "child-like compliance" resulting from parental influence may be evidenced in the reactions of shame:

- a sadness at not being accepted *as one is* with one's own urges, desires, needs, feelings, and behaviors
- the fear of abandonment because of *who one is*

- a diminished self-concept, a lowering of one's self-worth in *compliance* with introjected criticism, and
- a sense of "something's wrong with me."

Shame is often an internal expression of an intrapsychic conflict between a reactive Child ego state and an influencing Parent ego state (Erskine, 1994). *When a Child ego state is either active or internally cathected* (either behaviorally observable or subjectively reportable), *by theoretical inference a Parent ego state is cathected and intrapsychically influencing.* Various Child ego states are always in a relational unit with Parent ego states. Berne (1961) described the intrapsychic dynamics of ego states as representing "the relics of the infant who once actually existed, in a struggle with the relics of the parents who once actually existed" for it "reduplicates the actual childhood fights for survival between real people, or at least that is the way the patient experiences it" (p. 66).

The intrapsychic conflict emerges from a child's need for relationship (Fairbairn, 1954), attachment (Bowlby, 1969), or contact (Erskine, 1989). When those needs are repeatedly not satisfied, a child may defend against full awareness of contact, attachment, and relationship needs and the resulting psychological discomfort. These needs are evident in a Child ego state's *psychological loyalty* to an intrapsychically influencing Parent ego state (Erskine, 1988, 1991). The loyalty is in the defensive avoidance of the realization that "My psychological needs were unmet" or in the unconscious fantasy of "If I'm good enough, I'll be accepted and loved" (Stolorow & Atwood, 1989). The intrapsychic functions of forming Parent ego states is to lessen the external conflict and have a semblance of relationship—at least an illusion of being accepted and loved, but the price of the internalization of the conflict is a loss of valuable aspects of self—a loss of spontaneity, flexibility, and intimacy. The psychic presence or Parent ego state is maintained over the years because, like script beliefs and obsessions, the intrapsychic conflict functions to provide a sense of predictability, identity, continuity, and emotional stability (Erskine, 2001b).

Theory into practice

Berne stated that "the ultimate aim of transactional analysis is structural readjustment and reorganization ... Reorganization generally features reclamation of the Child, with emendation or replacement of the Parent. Following this dynamic phase of reorganization, there is a secondary analytic phase which is an attempt to deconfuse the Child" (1961, p. 224). Most of Berne's descriptions of psychotherapy emphasize his first phase, the decontamination of the Adult ego from Child or Parent ego states. Berne (1966) defined eight therapeutic operations; six are interventions used to facilitate decontamination and strengthen ego boundaries—the structural readjustment of phase one. Only one therapeutic operation, psychoanalytic interpretation, is used to "decode and detoxify" the Child ego states' past experiences, "rectify distortions, and help the patient regroup the experiences" (pp. 242–243).

It is primarily through his clinical examples that one can infer Berne's use of a second analytic phase, a therapeutic deconfusion of the Child ego states. In the chapter on "Regression Analysis" Berne rather poetically says, "When a previously buried archaic ego state is revived in its full vividness in the waking state, it is then permanently at the disposal of the patient and therapist for detailed examination. Not only do 'abreaction' and 'working through' take place, but the ego state can be treated like an actual child. It can be nurtured carefully, even tenderly, until it unfolds like a flower, revealing all the complexities of its internal structure" (1961, p. 226). The reader is left to assume that Berne is applying psychoanalytic methods in this "secondary analytic phase." Yet he also experimented with and encouraged an active psychotherapy: "The optimal situation for the readjustment and reintegration of the total personality requires an emotional statement from the Child in the presence of the Adult and Parent" (ibid., p. 224). Other transactional analysis writers have developed or described active treatment methods effective in deconfusing Child ego states (Clark, 1991; Clarkson & Fish, 1988; Cornell & Olio, 1992; Erskine, 1974, 1993; Erskine & Moursund, 1988; Erskine, Moursund, & Trautmann, 1999; Goulding & Goulding, 1979; Hargaden & Sills, 2002).

In all of Berne's writing he says surprisingly little about therapeutic methods. He does not adequately describe a course of treatment for the Parent ego states. He writes about an "emendation"—an alteration designed to correct or improve—"or replacement of the Parent" (1961, p. 224). But no guidelines for an in-depth and integrating treatment are suggested. It is as if Berne, like many in both the psychoanalytic and Gestalt therapy traditions, did not know what to do with the pain, fear, anger, and defensive strategies of an influencing Parent ego state and the intrapsychic pressure and distress it causes in the client.

He primarily follows the psychoanalytic tradition of identifying the intrapsychic influence and then goes a bit further with therapeutic operations such as confrontation and explanation aimed at decontaminating the Adult ego. He also suggests the use of a therapeutic interposition such as illustration or confrontation, "an attempt by the therapist to interpose something between the patient's Adult and his other ego states in order to stabilize his Adult and make it more difficult for him to slide into Parent or Child activity" (1966, p. 237). In Berne's writings the theory of Parent ego states is not sufficiently related to or correlated with therapeutic methods that decommission the influence of an introjection.

For transactional analysis to be a comprehensive theory of personality and methods, it is essential to integrate the theories of personality with a theory of methods: The development of an in-depth therapy of Parent ego states would be one example of the further refinement in the congruence of methods and theory in transactional analysis. To this end I would like to propose an addition to the quotation from Berne used earlier about "the ultimate aim of transactional analysis": *Following, or in some cases concurrent with, a deconfusion of the Child ego states there may be an additional psychotherapeutic phase which decommissions a Parent ego state for the purpose of eliminating its toxic influencing effect on Child ego states and eventually integrating it into the Adult ego as a memory and historical resource.*

The decommissioning of a Parent ego state may be described by paraphrasing Berne's (1961, p. 226) poetic comment on the treatment of Child ego states: When a previously introjected exteropsychic ego state is revived in its full vividness and made conscious, it is then available to the client's full awareness and to the therapist for either an in-depth therapy of the Parent ego state or at least an effective interposition. The Parent ego state can be treated like an actual client—even a client in regression. It can be nurtured carefully, or confronted or guided in how to adequately parent in accordance with his or her actual child's needs. This is one aspect of a comprehensive theory of methods (Erskine, 1997c) for an active, in-depth psychotherapy "for the readjustment and reintegration of the total personality" (Berne, 1961, p. 224).

I think that the "replacement of the Parent", as Berne (ibid.) phrased it, with another introjection is *not therapeutic*. This would be akin to replacing one toxic introjection with another somewhat more benign introjection—but it is still a contact interrupting introjection. Rather,

I would like to augment Berne's previous statement about an in-depth psychotherapy of Child ego states: "The optimal situation for readjustment and reintegration of the total personality requires" in addition to "the emotional statement from the Child in the presence of the Adult and Parent," *an emotional statement from a Parent ego state that either apologizes to or deconfuses Child ego states*. This allows egotized and fixed identifications—introjections—to be externalized, decommissioned, and integrated into an Adult ego. An in-depth psychotherapy for "reintegration" of the total personality includes relaxing the Child ego states' defenses, allowing the natural inclination of the client to be expressed, decommissioning the introjections, resolving the intrapsychic conflicts, and facilitating an awareness and integration in the client of his other need-fulfilling experience with parents.

I have been using parents in this text, but the reader is to be aware that parents may not be the only ones introjected; teachers, clergy, aunts, uncles, grandparents, older siblings, any one in authority, even other teenagers, may be introjected in the absence of need-fulfilling contact. The chapter, "Robert: Challenging a Cultural Script" in *Integrative Psychotherapy in Action* (Erskine & Moursund, 1988) is a detailed example of a psychotherapy for an introjection of a culturally imposed value.

Experiential and written background

In 1974, I was conducting a weekend therapy marathon with another therapist. He informed me that one of the women in the group was severely depressed and she was convinced that she was possessed by the devil. Halfway through the evening the woman began to snarl and growl at me and then in a harsh low voice threatened to kill "her". At first both group members and I were shocked! I then remembered hearing a similar voice before at a Pentecostal religious-healing service I attended as a child on the Southside of Chicago. One of the evangelists was well known for "casting out devils." I had watched with childlike awe as a person was brought in restraints, snarling, growling, threatening. The evangelist "called out the devil" and proceeded to "pray over him."

The memory of the healing-evangelist's active encounter with the "devil" person was swirling in my mind. At the same time, I was also thinking about how to make sense of the client's bizarre behavior. I wondered if this "devil" person was a manifestation of the Gestalt therapy concept of introjection and Berne's concept of Parent ego states as representing the personality of another. I began to talk to the "devil" voice. He continued to curse at me, repeatedly threatened to kill me or "her," hissed, growled, and raged. He refused to talk to a "crazy therapist." I continued to talk to "him," inquiring about his message and purpose.

During the next half hour, the voice gradually became that of an angry, drunken man—a man with a secret. He had threatened to kill his daughter if she ever revealed the incestuous rape and choking he had inflicted on her. After about two hours of a combination of both empathetic and confrontational therapy the "father" began to apologize to his "daughter". Subsequently, that confession and apology stimulated in the woman client, over the next few months, several memories that had previously been repressed. The active therapy directly with a Parent ego state opened the door for the client to do some intense regressive therapy both in individual sessions and subsequent weekend marathons. The Child ego state regressions were accompanied by the slower, ongoing work at resolving her experiences of distrust and a lack of protection as it emerged both in the transferential transactions and the absence of interpersonally contactful transactions.

This serendipitous therapy experience with the "devil" who was a manifestation of the psychic presence of her father opened a whole new perspective for me in doing psychotherapy. I no longer saw a Parent ego state only as a depository of injunctions. Nor could I any longer see the resolution of serious intrapsychic conflict as occurring in a twenty or thirty minute two-chair dialogue alternating between the client's Child and Parent ego states. Rather, I became increasingly aware of the possible complexity of psychic presence or introjections to include not only the attitudes and thoughts of significant others, but also their emotions, defensive processes, physiological reactions, age regression, and relational needs. This can all be internalized by a child through an unconscious defensive identification when there is an absence of need-fulfilling contact, and the child's dependency is such that the other is introjected as a way to have a semblance of relationship.

The transactional analysis literature provides a few theoretical articles on Parent ego state problems, but there is not much written about an in-depth therapy. Bill Holloway described theoretically the "crazy child in the Parent" and related the harshness, frequency, and consistency of the parent's "craziness" to the formation of tragic life scripts (1972,

p. 128). In 1976, John McNeel published "The Parent Interview" which described a two-chair therapy with a Parent ego state wherein the therapist elicits feelings and experiences of a Parent ego state in response to requests made by a son or daughter. "In this way, the therapist demonstrates to the client how his wants or behavior were once threatening to the parental figure. This investigation is based on the belief that the original parent did not act with malice" (p. 66). McNeel designed the parent interview to be part of the final stage of psychotherapy, where the individual becomes aware of the internal conflicts of the internalized parent and, through understanding him or her, achieves some level of forgiveness and acceptance of that person. McNeel warned that if the client's introjected other was "crazy" then the therapist should not engage in a parent interview.

Dashiell (1978) also described therapy with a Parent ego state. She wrote about "minimal resolution" wherein the therapist provides permission or reparenting to a Parent ego state that allows for an introjection to be disconnected. Such interventions free Child ego states for further therapy. "Maximum resolution" included working with a Parent ego state to resolve archaic events in the parent's life, the release of stored feelings in the Parent ego state, or challenging the crazy or hostile Parent ego states while not abandoning the client's Child ego states. Concurrently, (1978) I wrote a theoretical synopsis about the necessity of doing Parent ego states therapy in which I describe the "Fourth Degree Impasse" as representing the confusion within the client between the feeling introjected and forming a Parent ego state and the person's own feelings in a Child ego state.

Mellor and Andrewartha (1980) expanded on working with the emotions in a Parent ego state and gave several short examples. Their focus, like Dashiell's, was also on reparenting—providing a new program for a Parent ego state. They also advocated making direct interventions with the internalized parent: confronting, supporting, and giving permission as necessary, to facilitate a redecision being made by the client. This was seen by Mellor and Andrewartha as especially important when a Parent ego state was experienced as having the power to sabotage or exert a harmful influence on the individual who was about to change his life decisions, usually decisions which maintained the family system or protected the parent. Unlike McNeel who warns against working with a "crazy" Parent ego state they suggest that the technique works well when the Parent ego state is "disoriented, confused, and/or 'crazy' …

the 'craziness' goes when the needs, feelings and wants stimulating apparently incoherent or bizarre responses are identified and are accounted, when the 'craziness' is affirmed as the person's best effort to deal with these feelings, needs and wants, and when new methods, experienced as effective, are provided and tried" (ibid., p. 201).

Bruce Loria in his careful review of Berne's writings made a plea for clinicians to remain consistent with Berne's original "core concepts" (1988, p. 39) and to be mindful of the intrapsychic complexity of both Child and Parent ego states. Loria summarizes: "Berne is stating that a person takes into their Parent ego state the complete personalities of significant parental figures, *including their level of pathology (contamination)*. Therapists working to decontaminate the Adult ego state are likely to succeed only after they have assessed fully the extent of the introjected parental figures. Concomitantly, specific treatment strategies are needed for resolving the contaminations *of the introjected Parent and archaic Child in the Parent ego state* in the offspring" (p. 41).

In writing about the therapy of relationship problems, Landy Gobes identified that the treatment of abandonment or engulfment issues involves an evaluation of "the form and the degree of pathology in the Parent ego state" and then possibly "therapy with the Parent ego states of the client" (1985, p. 217). In describing how she does Parent ego state therapy Gobes says, "The therapist can proceed as though the entire personality of mother or father were in the person's body and can ask the person to sit in another chair and be mother or father ... A client who is her mother seems to experience greater depths of mother's thoughts and feelings than one who role-plays her mother" (1990, p. 164).

In *Beyond Empathy: A Therapy of Contact-in-Relationship*, the methods of an in-depth psychotherapy of both Child and Parent ego states are provided in detail (Erskine, Moursund, & Trautmann, 1999). The client's gaining an awareness and appreciation of the psychological function of introjection is essential to the process of an in-depth psychotherapy of Parent ego states. Fred Clark identified an intrapsychic function of introjection: "What is internalized is the thinking, feeling and behaviors of significant others (Parent ego state) as a defense against the loss of relationship with those persons" (1990, p. 42). This concept, common to object relations theory, differs from psychoanalytic theory where defenses are used in service of protecting against Id drives. In relationship therapy, defenses are understood to be used in service of avoiding the pain or loss of contact (neglect) or painful contact (abuse), both being disturbances in relationship (1990, p. 42).

The fantasy parent

In *Integrative Psychotherapy in Action* (Erskine & Moursund, 1988), we described Berne's original theoretical model of ego states and how to use his four-part diagnostic system to identify Parent ego state influence in clients' lives. Four chapters are devoted to both an explanation of the Parent ego state psychotherapy and verbatim examples from actual clients; the other chapters emphasize psychotherapy with Child ego states. The concept of a "self-generated parent"—the fantasy of a young child that functions like a controlling or punitive Parent ego state, was also described (pp. 21–23).

As a normal developmental process in early childhood, children will often create an *imago*, a fantasy figure, as a way to provide controls, structure, nurturing, or whatever that young person experienced as missing or inadequate. Some children create their own personal "boogeyman," a frightening creature who threatens them with dire consequences for minor misdeeds. Investing the "fantasy parent" with all the bad and scary aspects of being parented allows them to keep Mom and Dad as perfectly good and loving. Throughout his elementary and junior high school years, Richard was haunted by the boogeyman. As he developed into a teenager, the boogeyman ceased to be a concern; however, there was always the possibility of a stern teacher or policeman who could punish him if he got out of line. In his late twenties, Richard's grandmother died and he helped the family clean out her house. As he cleaned her bedroom and in her closet, he felt extremely anxious. He anticipated some terrible punishment and, although he told himself that his thoughts were not rational, he kept expecting to find the remains of the boogeyman.

Working with his therapist, Richard began to remember that as a young child he thought the boogeyman "lived" in grandmother's bedroom, and that he also had the capacity to follow Richard to school or at play. If Richard misbehaved, the boogeyman was sure to punish him. In the process of therapy, Richard began to remember a spanking at age four, which was administered by his mother, in grandmother's bedroom, during a family party. Shortly after the spanking, Richard developed his fear of the boogeyman and could then turn to his mother for comfort, protection, and reassurance. The fantasy of the boogeyman helped the four-year-old Richard remain adapted to external parental controls and at the same time experience his mother as all loving and fully tolerant of his behavior.

Others may create a fairy godmother sort of fantasy parent who loves and nurtures them even when the real parents are cold or absent or abusive. This created image serves as a buffer between the actual parental figures and the desires, needs, and feelings of the young child. The inevitable discomforts of growing up in an imperfect world are more tolerable because the fantasy figure provides what was missing with the real parents.

Anne-Marie, for example, had periods of depression in which she would eat a large amount of food. During this time, she would long for her dead grandmother, whom she described during her therapy as affectionate, understanding, consoling, and who she said used to bring her wonderful food to eat. The therapist, out of curiosity, asked how old Anne-Marie had been when her grandmother died and she replied, "Fourteen months." A fourteen-month-old infant was not likely to have the experiences with a grandmother that Anne-Marie reported. As the therapist began to explore the discrepancy between Anne-Marie's longing for her grandmother and the fact that the grandmother had been dead since infancy, the client began to remember experiences from childhood that had been lost from memory for many years. Anne-Marie had repeatedly been abused by both mother and father and had often been locked in the wine cellar for days at a time without food. Anne-Marie related how the grandmother would "appear" to her after the beatings or in the dark wine cellar to comfort her, to encourage her, and to promise her wonderful meals. By creating these images of grandmother, Anne-Marie was able to satisfy in fantasy some of the needs for appropriate nurturing that were drastically lacking in her parents' behavior toward her.

As they mature to later developmental phases, children often let go of their self-generated images. But when the child represses his awareness of needs, feelings, and memories in order to survive in the family, the self-created image is fixated and does not become integrated with later developmental learning. Whatever the characteristics of the fixated self-created parent, over the years it comes to operate similarly to the Parent ego state described by Berne. It functions like an introjected personality; however, it is often more demanding and illogical and unreasonable than the actual parent was (after all, it had its origin in a small child's fantasy). The self-created parent made from fantasized images provides and encapsulates a non-integrated package of thoughts and feelings and behaviors to which the person responds as if they were truly internalizations from the big people of early childhood.

Treatment planning

Psychotherapy of an introjected ego state or a self-generated parental fantasy may become part of the psychotherapist's treatment plan after much therapeutic work has been done on the various Child ego states. Such Child ego state therapy may include the use of a wide variety of methods to facilitate the client's:

- relaxing of habitual defenses
- increased awareness and perhaps expression of feelings and needs that were repressed, and
- resolution of both specific or cumulative traumatic experiences.

Although some of this Child ego state therapy may include active methods, such as redecision work or the dramatic expression of sadness or anger, much of the therapy occurs by working within the client-therapist relationship. By working with the unconscious process of the client's transferences, the developmentally aware and affectively attuned psychotherapist can help the client identify the archaic interruptions to either internal or interpersonal contact. These minute interruptions to contact and their related images and fantasies constitute the subtle dynamics of transference.

Transference is a constant attempt by the client to reparatively enact fixated childhood experiences by simultaneously repeating both archaic defenses and developmental needs in a current relationship. These subtle unconscious enactments are an expression of an intrapsychic conflict between elements of an influencing Parent ego state and the developmental needs thwarted and fixated in Child ego states (Erskine, 1991).

The intrapsychic conflict between Parent and Child ego states continues years later because of a child's biologically driven needs for relationship and the resulting, though often unconscious, loyalty to his parents or significant others. Therefore, it is essential to establish a solid therapeutic relationship with any client prior to therapeutically engaging Parent ego states: the psychotherapist must be fully protective of the Child ego states' vulnerabilities. The effectiveness of a therapeutic relationship is built upon the therapist's:

- attunement to the client's affect and psychological rhythms
- sensitivity and responsiveness to both Child and Adult ego state needs
- a constant inquiry into the client's phenomenological experience
- facilitating the client's appreciation of his style of coping, as well as
- honoring of the vulnerabilities of both childhood and adulthood.

Much of this is accomplished by working within the transference and by the therapist not personalizing the client's defensive reactions.

Just as effective psychotherapy of Child ego states produces major reorganization of psychological processes, experiences, and meaning making, so also psychotherapy of a Parent ego state produces major psychological reorganization. The client's Child ego states have been loyal to the intrapsychic influence of Parent ego states because of children's natural need for contact, attachment, and relationship.

This biological imperative for relationship must be accounted for and respected by the therapist and, in most situations, a sufficient therapy relationship established prior to the treatment of Parent ego states or a self-generated fantasy. It is generally advised to only engage in decommissioning a Parent ego state when the client has an ongoing experience of "This therapist is there for my welfare." If therapists engage in an in-depth psychotherapy that decommissions Parent ego states without such an involved relationship, then the Child ego states may be without a significant other to whom they feel a sense of protection and attachment. Metaphorically, it is akin to creating an orphan and may result in increased anxiety or depression.

In some clients, the intrapsychic relationship disrupted by a premature intervention may result in increased clinging to the intrapsychically influencing Parent ego state or self-generated fantasy out of a desperate need for attachment. The quality of the therapeutic relationship, as experienced by the client, is a central factor in determining when to proceed with treatment of either a self-generated fantasy or a Parent ego state. The therapist's phenomenological inquiry throughout the duration of the therapy and the constant investigation and repair of breaches in the therapeutic relationship are two of the best monitors for both identifying the subtle transferences and determining the degree to which the client can rely on and draw emotional support from the therapist.

In the "devil" example at the beginning of the previous section I actively intervened with a Parent ego state prior to developing a consistent and reliable therapeutic relationship. This is a rare situation where neither my colleague nor I, during the early hours of the therapy-marathon, could establish a therapeutic alliance with her Child ego states. Her Parent ego state was interfering with the psychotherapy, primarily through intrapsychic influence and then in the marathon group, by externalization—the active cathexis of the "devil voice." The client had been in therapy with my colleague for the treatment of her depression and she had gained a trust in him and, by association, a degree of trust in me. This was coupled with an idealized hope for "therapy magic"; such idealization is often an expression of the relational need to be in the presence of someone who is both protective of the Child ego states' vulnerabilities and potent enough to stop intrapsychic abuse.

The therapy of her depressed Child ego states had reached an impasse. In the process of witnessing other people's therapy in the marathon the psychic presence or influencing Parent ego state became externalized. It was an opportune moment to actively engage the Parent ego state: To keep it externalized rather than allow it to retreat to a position of intrapsychic abuse, and to provide psychotherapy to that psychic presence just as I would with an actual client. This instant intervention with an active Parent ego state is particularly helpful when the influencing Parent ego state is interfering with the psychotherapy, psychologically beating up on a Child ego state, or is so controlling that the Child ego states cannot express or even sense feelings or needs. In most clinical situations, psychotherapy with a Parent ego state is initiated only after a protective therapeutic alliance is established with various Child ego states.

In some situations, a Parent ego state may become threatened by or envious of the blossoming relationship between the client's Child ego states and the psychotherapist's reliable, consistent, and dependable involvement. This may result in an increase in anxiety, the activation of internal voices, or self-criticism that interferes with Child ego state therapy. It may then be effective to identify the internal criticism through the interweaving of a phenomenological, transferential, and historical inquiry. Such a detailed inquiry is to determine if the internal voice or criticism is either that of a specific other person, a self-generated Parent-like ego state based on a child's fantasy, or a self-criticism that preempts another's criticism. Such identification and differentiation of these possibilities along with a well-timed explanation may provide the client with cognitive awareness of the source of the internal conflict and anxiety and thereby some temporary respite. A description of the treatment of self-generated Parent-like ego states or self-criticism that preempts another's criticism is beyond the scope of this chapter. However, a differential diagnosis may be useful before proceeding with Parent ego state therapy. Sometimes the self-generated fantasy is clearly evident after the Parent ego state therapy is successfully completed. The Child ego states hold on to a fantasy as an expression of attachment. Preemptive self-criticisms are related to shame and self-righteousness (Erskine, 1994).

Sometimes a Parent ego state is continually or even increasingly influencing, particularly following regressive therapy, a redecision, or the resolution of a transferential expression of conflict and needs. I have found it more effective to address the criticizing voice on behalf of a Child ego state by speaking as though the actual parent were sitting next to the client. An example of what I have said with one woman's father is: "Stop talking to her like that; I will not let you berate her. Don't punish her for having normal child needs; let her be natural. I know life is hard for you, but you cannot solve your problems by taking it out on her. Be quiet now; later you and I can talk." This is but one of many examples of an *interposition* wherein the therapist protectively interposes herself between the client's Parent and Child ego states. This often provides a large measure of relief from the intrapsychic influence, particularly if the therapeutic relationship is well developed. The client's sense is often one of the therapist being fully protective.

It is essential that the therapist make such a confrontation caringly and with respect. After all, this influencing voice represents the client's parents or significant others and any disrespectful comment or arrogant tone may threaten the client's loyalty and thereby reinforce the Child ego state's attachment to a Parent ego state. When making an interposition I often silently paraphrase for myself an old cliché: "Blood is thicker than therapy." With this cliché in mind I remain respectful of the Parent ego state even when I may feel disgusted by or ferociously angry at his or her behavior. For the sake of the child I'm often both firm and empathetic with the Parent ego state.

The interposition has two purposes: to temporarily stop the intrapsychic conflict until such time when an in-depth psychotherapy of the Parent ego state is both possible and therapeutically prudent; and, primarily, to create an opportunity to further establish the therapeutic relationship so that the client's experience is: "This therapist is thoroughly invested in my welfare."

Once deconfusion of Child ego states is accomplished, survival reactions relaxed, and script beliefs relinquished then it may be essential to engage in treating the Parent ego states. There are also times when the client experiences not being able to change; he is still depressed, anxious, or oppressed in response to the intransigent and destructive nature of a Parent ego state. In either of these situations, it may become necessary to actively treat the Parent ego state and later engage in further treatment of Child ego states.

In conducting Parent ego state therapy the client is invited to cathect the relevant Parent ego state, in essence to "be" mother or father and to engage in conversation with the therapist as mother or father might. This involves the client in taking on the body posture, the facial expression, the attitude, the feelings, and the style of relating of that particular parent. In essence, the internalized parent becomes externalized. The therapist first establishes a safe and accepting emotional climate that allows the internalized other to begin to open up and become more revealing. This is often accomplished by realistic, straight talk in the Parent ego state's frame of reference. The quality of the interaction gradually begins to shift to a more therapeutic focus. Because the therapist already has a previous knowledge about the actual parent and some of the family dynamics, she is able to make very personal and pointed interventions which reveal areas of conflict or emotional difficulty in the introjected parent. The Parent ego state is then invited to work through those issues with the therapist.

John McNeel's (1976) "Parent Interview" was designed as the last stage of a short-term redecisional therapy. The goal of the recent interview was forgiveness and acceptance of the parent through understanding his or her internal conflicts. McNeel's therapeutic caveats included a warning against working with a "crazy" Parent ego state. Sharon Dashiell (1978) as well as Mellor and Andrewartha (1980) encourage therapy with the "crazy" Parent ego state. However, their approach is one of reparenting the Parent ego state; this involves replacing a harmful introjection with a more benign introjection. As stated earlier in this chapter the replacement of a Parent ego state with another introjection is *not therapeutic*. Rather, this chapter describes both the theoretical necessity and the practical considerations of an in-depth psychotherapy of introjections for the purpose of relieving intrapsychic conflict in our clients. In my clinical experience, I have found that an empathetic, relationally oriented psychotherapy aimed at dissolving defenses, honest expression of attitudes and feelings, and therapeutic respect for the individual's desires, frustrations, and conflicts provides for the decommissioning of Parent ego states, the end of intrapsychic conflict, and the opportunity for the person to engage life with awareness, spontaneity, and intimacy.

The same methods of inquiry, attunement, and involvement that are used with many clients may be used to treat a Parent ego state, including regression therapy and even, sometimes, treatment of the parent's Parent ego states. Examples of in-depth therapy of a Parent ego states include: 1) psychotherapy for a frustrated and angry thirty-five-year-old mother dealing with an alcoholic husband and blaming her kids for her plight, 2) facilitating a regression to a father's childhood experiences, and working through memories of early physical abuse, 3) using the variety of methods suitable for deconfusion or redecision, and 4) psychotherapy for the Grandparent or Great-grandparent ego states—third and fourth generational therapy. If the Parent ego state is unwilling to engage in this process and continues to be destructive, the therapist may then continue to relate with that ego state in order to advocate for the client's Child ego state. This is often experienced by the Child ego states, especially in situations of child abuse, as a kind of protection the child never had and can be a very powerful experience that brings about change.

The historical accuracy of the portrayal is not particularly relevant. What is important is the parent-as-experienced by the client. A person introjects not so much what his parents "actually" thought and felt and did, as what he experienced them thinking and feeling and believing about the child, about themselves, and about the world. As the Parent ego state begins to respond to the therapeutic challenges to his life script, the introject loses its compulsive, entrenched position and the client begins to experience that it doesn't have to be this way. "The thinking process, attitudes, emotional responses, defense mechanisms, and behavioral patterns that were introjected from significant others no longer remain as an unassimilated or exteropsychic (Parent) state of the ego but are decommissioned as a separate ego state and become integrated into an aware neopsychic (Adult) ego" (Erskine & Moursund, 1988).

Conclusion

The experience of treating a Parent ego state feels very real: to the therapist, to observers, and most especially to the client. It is not an "as if" experience once the person gets fully involved. Therefore certain precautions are suggested:

1. It is essential that the client experience a therapeutic alliance with the therapist first. As a client's Child ego states, though not active, observe the understanding, sometimes empathetic interaction between therapist and Parent ego state, he may experience that the therapist is taking the parent's "side" and has effectively abandoned the child. For this reason it is also imperative that the therapist come back to both Child ego states and the Adult ego of the client before the work is completed in order to reestablish the relationship. It also reaffirms that the purpose of the procedure is only for the client's benefit (although benefits to the actual physical parents have been reported as a consequence of this experience).
2. After the therapeutic work with Parent ego states, make sure that the client, whether in Adult ego or Child ego states, has an opportunity to respond to the Parent ego state. This strengthens the sense of self as separate from the parent and allows for meaningful interpersonal contact that may have been interrupted or perhaps never present. Failure to do so sometimes results in headaches or a sense of confusion and disorientation.
3. Keep in mind the loyalty of a child toward its parent, no matter how abusive that parent may be or have been. Even if a client is angry at or ambivalent about a parent, if the therapist confronts too strongly or is in any way disrespectful to the parent the client is likely to feel a pull to protect the parent.

Treating a Parent ego state can take place in one session, an extended session, or over a number of sessions. After a successful process, the client generally feels a combination of feelings: relief and freedom, yet often a deep sadness as a result of knowing the parent's experience so closely and having it responded to empathetically by the therapist. Often anger is stimulated and is best dealt with immediately by having the client address a Parent ego state, as in Gestalt two-chair work. People usually need plenty of time to process the experience, express any residual feelings, and talk about the meaning they have derived from it.

In the process of treating a Parent ego state, the conflict with that significant person is claimed, experienced, and dealt with (albeit in fantasy, since the real parent is not actually present). The result is that the client regains the self that was lost in the process of avoiding the external conflict by internalizing it instead. He is less likely to act out his Parent ego states toward others and, without the internal influence, will also be in a Child ego state less. In addition, as the content of the Parent ego state becomes integrated with the Adult ego the client now has the possibility of dealing with the real person of the parent differently. Therapists may also find that previously unresolved transference issues with the therapist are now more easily resolved. In-depth, reintegrating psychotherapy of Parent ego states is transactional analysis's most significant contribution to the profession of psychotherapy.

CHAPTER SEVENTEEN

Resolving intrapsychic conflict: psychotherapy of Parent ego states

Anna was a competent, attractive fifty-year-old insurance company executive. She was divorced for twenty years, with two adult children who had recently moved to their own homes. Her presenting problem was that she was becoming depressed, was becoming increasingly withdrawn from social contacts, afraid she would never find a man who would love her, and was considering dropping out of the university where she was studying part-time for a master's degree in business administration. Anna identified her depression as caused, in part, by her children no longer living in her home where she could "shower them with all the love I never got."

Much of the first year and a half of therapy was spent establishing Anna's sense of trust and developing a working therapeutic relationship with both her Adult ego and various Child ego states. By working with the here-and-now interruptions to interpersonal contact between Anna and me, we were able to identify how childhood fears, expectations, and script beliefs were transferred into our therapy relationship. The major script beliefs that shaped Anna's life were: "I'm a nothing"; "I won't get what I want"; "I'm all alone"; "It's all my fault"; "People can't be trusted"; and "It (life) doesn't matter."

In analyzing the transferential transactions we were able to uncover many childhood memories that she had often cried over alone but had never told anyone. She repeatedly talked about how she felt oppressed by both her mother's and father's criticisms and how she learned to be quiet, without needs, helpful with household chores, and to withdraw into her own private and safe world. My therapeutic attunement to Anna's affect and psychological rhythms, to child developmental levels of functioning, and to relational needs (both current and archaic) created the security for Anna to recall early childhood experiences and to regress to early Child ego states. The regressions provided the opportunity for me to assist Anna in her archaic expression of feelings and needs. The result of those therapeutic regressions was a deconfusion of her Child ego states. In the weekend therapy marathons, body therapy helped her to kick, scratch, and scream out much of the anger at her parents for her childhood needs having been neglected by them. Such disconnecting of the childhood rubber bands and resulting redecisions resulted in lessening the effect of the script beliefs in shaping Anna's behaviors, fantasies, and catastrophic expectations.

The following example of therapy took place in a weekend therapy marathon. At the time of this example, Anna had been in weekly therapy for two and a half years and had attended three other weekend therapy marathons. During the summer recess in our therapy sessions, many of the script beliefs started to be active in her life again. Prior to the summer these script beliefs had ceased to be operative because of the transferential work, deconfusion therapy, and redecisions that resulted in a reorganization of her psychological processes.

I explored the possibility of a rupture in our therapy relationship caused by the summer break in our weekly schedule. This led to revisiting her memories of her childhood experiences where she again got clarity on her original script conclusions. She was increasingly able to differentiate her childhood construction of meaning from that of her adult perspective. Yet the script beliefs were periodically active, particularly when she was home alone. She identified that she was lonely and we explored how the script beliefs might function to either distract her from feelings and/or to keep her psychologically attached to another person—specifically to her mother and/or father who were the important people when the script beliefs were originally formed.

In the few weeks prior to the therapy marathon I increasingly wondered if the return of the script beliefs was the result of psychological homeostasis, or due to her childhood dependence on her family, or if the beliefs were also those of one of her parents. From what I had already learned from her memories of her parents' frequent fights, I hypothesized that her mother may have some of the same script beliefs. I know from clinical experience that frequently parents do not inform children of optional meanings or confront beliefs if the child's beliefs are similar to the parent's own script beliefs. I began the therapy marathon with these hypotheses in mind. Rebecca Trautmann was co-therapist at the marathon.

RICHARD: Anna, ready to work?

ANNA: I feel like you forgot about me. (her shoulders are slumped)

RICHARD: No, I was waiting for Rebecca to come back; she said she wanted to be with you when you work.

ANNA: I know that, but it feels like I'm nothing. Like I didn't matter. (cries) I won't get what I want. (cries)

RICHARD: (pause) So are you saying that you're not going to get what you want or what you need. (short pause) So how are you going to deal with it?

ANNA: I'll just take care of myself. (she curls up)

RICHARD: Take care of yourself. And deep inside?

ANNA: Can't give up hope.

RICHARD: Tell me about the hope.

ANNA: (sobs) I keep hoping that something will change before I give up.

RICHARD: (pause) "Something" or is it somebody will change? Perhaps somebody will have to change so you don't give up.

ANNA: I'm closing down … (pause)

RICHARD: Was I off-target saying somebody will have to change?

ANNA: That's too hard to feel.

RICHARD: "Too hard to feel." (pause) Feel what, Anna?

ANNA: You're a nothing. Then I say "nothing matters."

Prior this sequence of transactions, Rebecca, my co-therapist in the marathon, had left the room temporarily. Anna was disappointed and relied on archaic script beliefs "I'm a nothing," "I don't matter," and "I won't get what I want" to make sense of her disappointment. Anna's physiological reaction, voice tone, and crying are all an expression of her unconscious attempt to convey the disappointments of her childhood and her developmental needs via her transferential reaction to

Rebecca's leaving. Her enactments are an out-of-awareness attempt to express an intrapsychic conflict and to seek a reparative relationship. Much of the individual therapy time over the previous two months had been spent in unraveling similar transferential enactments. I wondered if the increase in transferential transactions and the reactivation of her script beliefs were an expression of an intrapsychic conflict between Child and Parent ego states.

RICHARD: Rebecca, I'm wondering if this is one of those situations where the mother in her head is so controlling of her that we're not going to get anywhere with the child in her until we take care of the mother.

REBECCA: Since you see her regularly, and I don't, I have to say that I was more following your lead. And trying to match where she is here in the moment.

RICHARD: An argument against doing Parent ego state work is that I think Anna's been reaching out to you for the last two days. But I think her mother keeps getting in the way between me and her.

RICHARD: (to Anna) What do you think?

ANNA: Makes sense. And scares the hell out of me.

RICHARD: I'd love to get all that "hell" out of you. Any way to get the "hell" out of you would just be fine with me.

ANNA: I was glad that Rebecca was here, but I was afraid if I connected with her then I would lose you.

RICHARD: Lose me …?

ANNA: I was my father's favorite, but my mother really hated me for it. So I had to distance from him to have a relationship with her.

REBECCA: So is it your sense that we need to work with your mother first? That she's the one who's controlling this whole show?

ANNA: Yeah.

REBECCA: Would you like us to talk to her?

RICHARD: But only if you get some guarantees along the way.

ANNA: What?

RICHARD: Oh, like Rebecca would let you be close to me. Not only let, but that she might take pleasure in your being close to me. Would you like that kind of guarantee?

ANNA: You mean, she won't get mad at me?

RICHARD: Yes. And that you could also go and be with her, and there'd be no fighting from me.

REBECCA: That'd be good.

ANNA: I might even help you fold the laundry. (Rebecca had been absent earlier because she had to take towels out of the dryer.)

REBECCA: (laugh) (pause) I enjoy your being close to Richard. It's no problem.

RICHARD: Why, in that case ... (Richard moves closer to Anna)

REBECCA: So do you think we should leave you with Richard, while I talk to your mother, or does he need to talk to your mother while you stay with me?

RICHARD: Or, who would your mother be most affected by? A man or a woman talking with her?

ANNA: I don't know; she'd just crumble.

RICHARD: I doubt it. I know that's really scary for you ...

REBECCA: We're good with mothers ...

RICHARD: This is not a fragile woman we're talking about. She has her ways of getting what she wants. So I'm not so concerned about her crumbling. I hear you: she may present that way ... we'll take care of her. This is not about beating up your mom.

ANNA: I wanted to take care of her.

RICHARD: That's the other side of it. You were always taking care of her.

ANNA: (cries)

RICHARD: (pause) So one thing is you're scared of mama crumbling. The other is, it's your job to take care of her. Yet she made your life hell for being you're dad's favorite.

ANNA: Um-hm.

RICHARD: Were you supposed to repair their marriage as well?

ANNA: (nods a yes)

RICHARD: That's an impossible job.

ANNA: (nods a yes)

REBECCA: Do you want one of us to talk to your mother?

ANNA: Yes, that might be good.

REBECCA: Do you want a voice in choosing who will talk to your mother?

ANNA: You decide.

These previous few transactions contain the development of a therapeutic contact. This is not a contract for a behavioral outcome—none of us can predict what will emerge in Parent ego state therapy—but rather the beginning of an ongoing negotiation to engage in a therapeutic process. When repressed or unconscious material is involved a person cannot contract for a predetermined outcome. The process of the therapy is often a discovery of something new to each person involved. The possibility of working with two therapists has rekindled the emotional fires of childhood—Anna is reliving her desire for being with both parents and her fear of the possible conflict between them. One of her childhood tasks was to take care of mother. Now one of the therapists will assume this responsibility while the other will be available for Anna's Child ego states.

RICHARD: Rebecca, will you talk to her mom? I like being there for her kid.

REBECCA: OK ... Richard's right here for you; let's find a chair for your mom. (A straight armchair is brought up for Anna to sit on; Rebecca stays on the mat. After things are rearranged, the work resumes ...)

REBECCA: Sit the same way your mom would sit ... just close your eyes. Let your body get right into her posture. See if you can put the same expression on your face that reflects what mom feels. (pause) What is your name, Mom?

The experiencing of physiological cues such as body posture and facial expression help to facilitate an externalization of Parent ego state feelings, attitudes, and experience. This is being mom, not merely playing a role, and what may emerge is often a surprise to the client. It is important to help the client stay in the Parent ego state. This is accomplished in part by the therapist's repeated use of the name associated with that particular ego state. In the next several transactions Rebecca uses the name Debra several times to facilitate Anna staying in the Debra ego state—to feel and externalize that psychic presence that is internally causing conflict. Often in the first few transactions or when emotional material in-and-of itself is confrontational, the person will switch out of a Parent ego state. The therapist directs the person to "be" the other—to get into his or her skin, affect, and experience. The therapist then talks to the "other" as though he or she were an actual client.

ANNA: Debra.

REBECCA: Debra. You can call me Rebecca ... (pause) What do you think about being here, Debra?

ANNA
(AS DEBRA): I don't like it.

REBECCA: You don't like it? Why, Debra?

DEBRA: Why do I need to be here?

REBECCA: Well mostly so that I can get to know you Debra ... Ultimately, it's to help Anna. And for Anna to understand how important you are in her life.

DEBRA: Important to her? (emphatically)

REBECCA: Debra, are you saying that you don't know that you're important in her life? Hmm. How would *you* describe yourself in her life, Debra?

DEBRA: She doesn't need me.

REBECCA: Hmm. How long have you thought that?

DEBRA: Always.

REBECCA: You always felt that, Debra? That she didn't need you? Debra, help me to understand how you came to believe that ... Even from when Anna was tiny?

Rebecca's series of questions is designed to get Debra, the client's Parent ego state, to tell the story from the beginning of Anna's life. Perhaps there is much earlier material in Debra's life going back to her own childhood, but starting with Anna's infancy will make a good beginning. Perhaps later in the therapy it will be evident that Debra is in a Child ego state and that regressive therapy with Debra would be most effective. For now the focus is on the adult Debra.

In the following sequence of transactions watch how Rebecca is using a therapeutic inquiry, both historical and phenomenological, to heighten Debra's awareness of her experience and emotions.

DEBRA: She always cried.

REBECCA: And what did you think when she always cried?

DEBRA: She wanted something.

REBECCA: And then?

DEBRA: And then what I did wouldn't help.

REBECCA: Hmm. How did you feel then?

DEBRA: That I couldn't help her. Couldn't do anything.

REBECCA: "Couldn't do anything."
DEBRA: I had my other children too. I had my son.
REBECCA: Uh-huh. So how did you start responding to Anna then? If you thought there was nothing you could do.
DEBRA: I didn't know what to do. So I ignored her.
REBECCA: But somehow there was the opinion that she didn't need you. How did that happen?
DEBRA: She had her father.
REBECCA: Was he able to make her stop crying?
DEBRA: Yeah.
REBECCA: Oooh. Did it make you wonder about being a good mother?
DEBRA: Mmm.
REBECCA: Do you want to tell me about that?
DEBRA: I couldn't do it all. (Spoken softly, her head is looking down).
REBECCA: "Couldn't do it all." Is that what you said, Debra?
DEBRA: I had two others.
REBECCA: Debra, did you feel like you were a good mother to them?
DEBRA: I tried.
REBECCA: Did they seem to prefer him too?
DEBRA: No.
REBECCA: So you could make them feel good.
DEBRA: Um-hmm.
REBECCA: But something about this little girl, you couldn't be a good mother to her?
DEBRA: No.
REBECCA: What was that like Debra? To feel that?
DEBRA: (pause) It made me feel like I was a bad mother— a nothing.
REBECCA: You look as if you're feeling really sad now. Do you want to tell me about those feelings?

"Do you want to tell me about those feelings" is an example of both a phenomenological inquiry and a process contract. It is an opportunity for Anna as Debra to have a choice both in continuing with the therapy and in expressing what has until now been unexpressed. Each of Rebecca's sentences is an inquiry into Debra's subjective experience, even when her words are not questions but merely a repeat of what Debra has just said: "Couldn't do anything." Each inquiry is to deepen the client's experiences, for her to discover aspects of herself as Debra-in-Anna, not necessarily to gather information. Each inquiry is accompanied by the therapist's genuine interest in hearing her feelings, acknowledgement of what was said and a validation that Debra's emotions and psychological process are significant.

DEBRA: It was hard to get everything right all the time. It was never enough.

REBECCA: Yeah …

DEBRA: And having two other children …

REBECCA: Three. All little?

DEBRA: Yeah. And he was always working. So I was alone with the kids. There was nobody around.

REBECCA: Um-hmm. "Nobody around" … That's a lot of stress. (silence) Keep going, Debra. I'm really interested in what this was like for you.

DEBRA: (breathing heavily; long pause) But I had to do it all, alone.

REBECCA: So Debra, you tried to be strong, even though you were feeling so sad and alone?

DEBRA: Yeah. I tried to make the kids behave, so he wouldn't be upset. So he wouldn't yell.

REBECCA: Mmm. What happens when he starts yelling?

DEBRA: He hollers and screams. And he hits.

REBECCA: Hits?

DEBRA: My son.

REBECCA: How do you feel about that, Debra?

DEBRA: Like I can't do anything. I can't stop him …

REBECCA: Why not?

DEBRA: Cause he'll hit me.

REBECCA: Did he ever hit you, Debra?

DEBRA: He just threatened.

REBECCA: But you were scared that he would hit you.

DEBRA: Yeah.

REBECCA: So you let him hit your son …

DEBRA: (begins to cry; nods a yes)

REBECCA: Keep going, Debra, I'm listening. What do you need to say about that?

DEBRA: (crying) I felt bad that I couldn't do anything (sobs loudly).

REBECCA: That phrase is really important; "I couldn't do anything." There's a lot behind that, isn't there, Debra? (pause) What couldn't you do?

DEBRA: I couldn't be a wife, and I couldn't be a mom.

REBECCA: Was he mad at you for not being a good enough wife?

DEBRA: Always. He'd make fun of me, too.

REBECCA: About what, Debra?

DEBRA: (sigh) How I'd have to get undressed in the dark, in another room. I was shy. I was embarrassed. (Hangs her head down).

REBECCA: So Debra, you wanted to undress in the other room?

DEBRA: I didn't like sex. (sigh)

REBECCA: Do you want to say more about that? (silence) Did you like sex before you had children?

DEBRA: No. Never! Never.

REBECCA: Do you know what you didn't like about it?

DEBRA: (shakes her head in a no gesture).

REBECCA: But you knew you didn't like sex … and is that what became an issue between you and your husband? And is that what made you feel like you couldn't be a wife?

DEBRA: Um-hmm. He said so.

REBECCA: So no matter how much you did and what a good job you did with the children, and keeping the house, and all of that, basically in your mind you were a failure and "couldn't do anything?" Is that about right?

DEBRA: Oh, he always made me feel like I was a failure. Whatever I did was wrong, no matter what. (her words are now clipped and her face muscles tight)

REBECCA: Debra, I have to ask you—were you angry at him?

DEBRA: (pause) Yeah. (pause) Yeah—all the time.

REBECCA: Can you tell me about that anger, Debra?

Rebecca introduces an idea in the therapy: "Were you angry at him?" Usually it is not the best choice for the psychotherapist to introduce an idea into the therapy, lest she lead the client in an erroneous direction or, even more problematic, prematurely introduce an experience. Rebecca's quotation of Debra's helpless statement "I couldn't do anything" is designed to inquire about Debra's resignation and possible anger—a rather natural human reaction to such ridicule. Is it possible that Debra's feelings are not acknowledged or expressed and therefore the affect finds a sublimated form of release, as in anger at the father being directed to a child? Further phenomenological inquiry will reveal if the therapist's idea about the anger is significant or if another area of investigation is more appropriate. When the therapist does introduce an idea or chart a direction it is essential that the client's sense of agency—the human needs for self-definition and to make an impact—be supported through the therapist creating an opportunity for, and even encouraging the client's saying, "No, that's not right for me." This is often done by the therapist raising a genuine question about the introduced idea or direction: "Were you angry at him?"

DEBRA: I couldn't really get mad. I could maybe slam a pot.

REBECCA: Right. There's always the threat he's going to hit you. So tell me about the feelings of anger that you did have. Even though you couldn't really get angry.

DEBRA: (sigh) I'd get angry at her.

REBECCA: You'd get angry at Anna? Oh, you mean instead of being angry at him?

DEBRA: Yeah, he would talk to her all the time.

REBECCA: And what did that feel like to you?

DEBRA: Like I didn't matter. I was just to have babies and clean and cook.

REBECCA: Mmm. Ouch. So you believe that you don't matter. You didn't matter to him.

DEBRA: Yeah, I'm a nothing to him. He was interested in Anna.

REBECCA: So did you feel jealous of Anna? Or were you just angry at him, for giving to her what you needed from him?

DEBRA: I'd get jealous. Then I'd get angry if he did things for her. (sigh) And he would take it out on my son.

REBECCA: Well, was there something Anna did that made it like this? (silence) What are you thinking, Debra?

DEBRA: She wouldn't listen to me. She wouldn't help me enough. And he'd be nice to her but then he wouldn't be so angry.

REBECCA: What I imagine is that it must have been pretty tough on Anna to try to be taking care of both parents at the same time. Keep her father happy and also help her mom out.

DEBRA: She did all of it.

REBECCA: She probably tried her best. But we've got to get something straight here. Debra, was it Anna's fault? Or is the person you're angry with really your husband?

DEBRA: (long pause) I think it's both.

REBECCA: Tell me? (pause) How is it both?

DEBRA: 'Cause she really enjoyed being with him, that's her fault.

REBECCA: Um-hmm.

DEBRA: She wanted to be with him.

REBECCA: Sure. Especially if he was nice to her. Why not?

DEBRA: He wasn't always nice to her.

REBECCA: He wasn't? Oh, I thought you said he was nice to her.

DEBRA: Sometimes. But later as a teen, he criticized her a lot. And she stayed away from him.

REBECCA: How come you weren't nice to her?

DEBRA: I didn't like her.

REBECCA: Why, Debra?

DEBRA: (sigh) I just didn't like her. She made me feel inadequate.

Through Rebecca's therapeutic inquiry, Debra is revealing her disappointments in her relationship with her husband and her jealousy with her daughter. It seems that from infancy onward, Anna did not satisfy some important relational need of Debra's as implied in the comments, "I didn't like her"; "She wouldn't listen to me"; "She made me feel inadequate." Three factors seem to emerge: Debra's anger at her husband is directed to Anna; Debra is jealous of the relationship between her husband and daughter; and Debra does not experience Anna as providing important interpersonal psychological functions such as making an impact, experiencing security through the relationship, or receiving validation of her uniqueness, vulnerabilities, and experiences. Debra's "I don't matter" and "I'm a nothing" sound very similar to some of Anna's script beliefs. Are Anna's beliefs an expression of Debra's, are they the result of Anna's childhood conclusions and decisions, or both? When the same script beliefs are present in both a Parent ego state and a Child ego state the synergy between them creates an even stronger resistance to dissolving, reorganizing, and updating one's perspective. As this transcript continues Rebecca's involvement and later Richard's is aimed at dissolving script beliefs in both Parent and Child ego states.

REBECCA: Because she made you feel inadequate? (silence) Go ahead, Debra, let me know what's going on inside. (Her face has become increasingly tense.) Something's really moving inside. Will you let me know?

DEBRA: (breathing hard) I *was* inadequate.

REBECCA: You were?

DEBRA: Yeah.

REBECCA: What do you mean by that? (silence; Anna breathes heavily) Let it come Debra. Don't hold that all inside ... In some ways you sound like you're ready to explode in there. It's OK if you want to explode out here; I'm going to make sure no one hurts you.

DEBRA: (long pause) Not supposed to say anything.

REBECCA: (whispering) I want to hear!

DEBRA: Not supposed to say anything. Just be quiet, nice ...

REBECCA: Yeah, I know. But I want to hear. I want to hear those unsaid things. Those feelings, those thoughts. What do you mean, you were inadequate?

DEBRA: I didn't know how to love my kids. How to show them (begins to sob). I'd just get mad at them all the time. They wouldn't listen. I'd just tell them it was their fault (crying continues)

REBECCA: Because inside you were feeling ...

DEBRA: I couldn't do it; I was bad—a nothing.

REBECCA: You were bad?

DEBRA: Um-hmm.

REBECCA: Debra, did you feel loved by your parents?

DEBRA: (pause) I don't think so. (pause) My mother worked hard.

REBECCA: Yeah ... Did she tell you you were inadequate, too? (pause)

DEBRA: Yeah.

Now there is an opening of a new theme—Debra's lack of feeling loved. The therapist has an opportunity to work with both Debra's experience of her early relationship with her parents and how Debra made sense out of her mother's message that she was inadequate. The therapist can either cognitively explore Debra's early childhood or support a therapeutic regression that leads to a corrective experience, redecision, and the dissolving of script beliefs. The therapist decides instead to explore how the experience of being unloved is relived and reinforced in Debra's marriage; this timeframe and marital relationship may be most pertinent to Anna's therapy. Perhaps later regressive therapy with Debra may be necessary, but for now the work has already been about Debra's anger at her husband and the displacement of that anger onto Anna. By focusing on the difficulties in Debra's marriage, the source of Debra's jealousy may emerge. If focusing on Debra's experience of feeling unloved by her husband is not useful then the therapist can return to early childhood experiences in Debra's life that may be the source of her jealousy and that have shaped her script beliefs.

REBECCA: Did you hope to get some of that loving in your marriage?
DEBRA: Yeah. (with a mournful sound)
REBECCA: Oh boy, I heard that. What was the disappointment there?
DEBRA: Didn't get it. No, just cook and clean and sex. Take care of the kids.
REBECCA: "Cook and clean and sex." (pause) "Take care of the kids."
DEBRA: And he'd flirt with other women.
REBECCA: Ooh. Did he tell you how inadequate you were?
DEBRA: Mmm. That I was cold.
REBECCA: Even in bed?
DEBRA: Yeah, he said I was cold ... that I wasn't sexual.
REBECCA: Um-hmm. What do you feel when he says that?
DEBRA: Garbage.
REBECCA: And yet you don't say anything, just keep going along. But you were—you were angry, weren't you? And the only way you could let that loose just a little bit was at Anna. Am I right?
DEBRA: (nods a yes)
REBECCA: (pause) I'm going to ask you to do something that's probably never been possible for you before. I want you to imagine that your husband is here in this chair right in front of you, and say to him the things that you're angry about. And I'll make sure he doesn't hit you. Would you do that? (pause)
DEBRA: (nods a yes).
REBECCA: Just imagine him right here ... what's his name?
DEBRA: Jason.

Rebecca establishes the possibility for two-chair work where Debra will talk to her husband. Such therapeutic experiments allow an opportunity for the contact that may have been interrupted or never made, to be finally made, at least in fantasy. The person can say what has been inhibited and in imagining the other person present, affect, attitudes, hopes, and disappointments can finally be expressed. Debra nods agreement, part of the ongoing nature of a process contract, that signals her willingness to experiment with expressing what has been pent-up inside her.

Anna has, most likely, introjected Debra's anger, resentment, hurts, and fears along with her script beliefs and psychological defenses. An opportunity for Debra to express what has been inhibited, yet unconsciously introjected by Anna, may provide a great relief of the intrapsychic conflict that Anna experiences day-to-day.

REBECCA: Just imagine Jason is right here. He's sitting in a chair across from you. What would you say to him if you knew you could say anything that was in your heart?

DEBRA: Hmm. (sigh; long pause) Nothing was ever right. Couldn't you ever just be pleased, or appreciate anything? Why was it always wrong?

REBECCA: Now a little louder, Debra. Make your questions into your own statements. A little more forcefully. I'm angry that …

DEBRA: It was never enough. Never right. Never right what I did.

REBECCA: Keep going Debra.

DEBRA: And it was always my fault. Always, everything. Everything everybody did was my fault.

REBECCA: You're doing great, Debra. Just raise your voice a little bit more so you can let that energy out. "My fault!"

DEBRA: (sigh) My fault. (sigh)

REBECCA: "And what I want to say to you, Jason, is …"

DEBRA: It's not my fault!

REBECCA: Hey, good! Let me hear more!

DEBRA: It was your fault.

REBECCA: Tell him how it was his fault.

DEBRA: Because he was always angry, always yelling, and he wanted more.

REBECCA: Say it to him: "*You* wanted more! *You* yelled. *You* were the angry one." Keep going Debra!

DEBRA: Everybody was afraid of you. Nobody wanted to be near you. Everybody ran away from you (sigh).

REBECCA: Keep going. Tell him all you've held inside.

DEBRA: You were rotten. You were cruel!

REBECCA: Keep going. Feel that anger in those fists. (hands were clenched)

DEBRA: You were miserable. You made everybody around you miserable. (sigh)

REBECCA: "And I feel …"

DEBRA: Like nothing. Like you didn't care. (sigh)

REBECCA: Keep going, Debra. Tell him how you feel about his making you feel like a nothing.

DEBRA: Mmm, I get tired.

REBECCA: Right, but that may be in order not to feel angry. Keep going, Debra. You've got lots of energy inside you.

DEBRA: (sigh) I showed you when I got my driver's license!

REBECCA: Ah, some spunk too. Good.

DEBRA: He tried to teach me.

REBECCA: Keep talking to him. "You …"

DEBRA: You tried to teach me to drive; all you did was yell at me and make me cry. I feel like showing you. I went and I got lessons and passed the driving examination myself. (She is pushing on the arm of the chair with both hands.)

REBECCA: Yeah. Feel the power in that, Debra. I bet you'd like to use those hands. Right? Those hands … they've got energy in them.

DEBRA: He'd smash me back.

REBECCA: We're not going to let him do that. Would you like to smash him?

DEBRA: I'd like to pound on him.

REBECCA: Tell that to him. "I'd like to …"

DEBRA: Pound on you. I'd like to smack you. Like you smacked my son. You smacked David!

REBECCA: Yeah, tell him.

DEBRA: You smacked David. You crushed him. Over and over again until he gave up (crying). And you blamed me! Over and over again, you hit your son. He's your son!

REBECCA: Now tell him all that you feel, Debra.

DEBRA: He's your son, too; and you did it.

REBECCA: And tell him how enraged you are at what he did to your son. Your mutual son.

DEBRA: I hate you for it.

REBECCA: Again—louder, Debra.

DEBRA: I hate you for it.

REBECCA: Again! Louder!

DEBRA: I hate you.

REBECCA: Again! Keep going!

DEBRA: I hate you for what you did. What you had to do was just love him. That's all he wanted from you (crying). You made everybody hate him, and everybody leave him.

REBECCA: Say the whole thing, Debra. All those feelings, to Jason … Don't shut down. What you're saying is really important.

DEBRA: Why didn't you love us? Why didn't you show us that you loved us? Not by buying things …

REBECCA: "What I needed was …"

DEBRA: For you to be kind, and gentle, and loving, and caring (sigh). Not to be hateful.

Rebecca has been directing the process in several distinct ways while attempting not to direct the content. Debra has retroflected her feelings, complaints, and physical reactions and now needs a cheerleader, someone to encourage the free expression of what has been inhibited. Rebecca begins by directing Debra to turn her go-nowhere questions such as "Couldn't you ever just be pleased?" into direct statements: "It was always my fault." She then encourages Debra to be louder. There is no magic in volume but there is often a greater expression of pent-up emotions and thoughts as the person gets louder. As a result of expressing what has been retroflected the client gains increased awareness of his own defenses, inhibited reactions, unfulfilled desires, and script conclusions. Rebecca then "primes the pump," a further encouragement for Debra to express what may be held back. Priming the pump refers to the therapist's open-ended prompts that allow room for the client to finish the sentence with his own self-expression: "And what I want to say to you, Jason, is …"; "What I needed was …"; or "I'd like to …". Debra attempted to talk to Rebecca about Jason; Rebecca directed her back to communicating with the image of Jason with, "*You* wanted more! *You* yelled. *You* were the angry one." Another type of prompt is used when Rebecca encourages Debra to address Jason with, "Keep talking to him." This is often used when the person is either becoming quiet and retroflecting what needs to be said or is attempting to address the therapist instead of talking to the significant other.

REBECCA: I'm going to ask you to go one step more now. Debra, talk to Jason about him and Anna.

DEBRA: (sigh)

REBECCA: Look at Jason (silence) It's hard, isn't it? Because it's all mixed up.

DEBRA: Um-hmm.

REBECCA: Start with what you can. "What I feel toward you, Jason ... about you and Anna, is ..."

DEBRA: (pause, very softly) You're too close. It's not right.

REBECCA: Keep going, Debra. Say the whole thing ... It's important, Debra, to say what you need to say to Jason. (pause) Debra, you need to say it. This is definitely not one of those times you should be quiet and keep it inside.

DEBRA: (sigh) It's not right the way you look at her.

REBECCA: Tell him what you mean.

DEBRA: I can see it in his eyes—sexual.

REBECCA: Tell him what you see, Debra. Be very specific ... I know this is hard. You're doing great. But you've got to say it all.

DEBRA: Mmm. (sigh) You shouldn't be looking at her that way; it's not right. You're confusing her.

Rebecca's prompt, "Tell him what you see ... be very specific" may have provided effective support for Debra to express what she has inhibited. Debra has finally made a corrective comment to her husband, "You shouldn't be looking at her that way; it's not right. You're confusing her." Such a statement from mother to father is part of setting psychologically healthy boundaries within this family and providing protection for the daughter, Anna. This is a mere beginning of the Parent (Debra) ego state's task of deconfusing Anna's Child ego states. One of the possible therapeutic benefits of an in-depth Parent ego state therapy is in the internalized other's truth telling, and the resulting deconfusing of the Child ego states that are listening.

REBECCA: That's good, Debra. Keep going ... say what you mean, Debra. "You're confusing her ... you shouldn't be looking at her that way …" … Hang in there, Debra. You've made a really good start. There's much more to say.

DEBRA: I can't say more.

REBECCA: You need to, Debra.

DEBRA: (quietly) It's not my place.

REBECCA: It is absolutely your place. You are her mother! Now talk to Jason about what he's doing!

DEBRA: He won't listen to me. (head and eyes down)

REBECCA: He will now! Now come on. I'll back you up! (pause) (Rebecca puts her hand on Anna's-cum-Debra's back) "You shouldn't be looking at her that way! You're confusing her!" (pause) What does that mean, Debra? Tell him the whole thing. Tell him what he's doing to her.

DEBRA: He knows. He has ideas.

REBECCA: You say it.

DEBRA: He knows they're his fantasies.

REBECCA: Debra, he can be lying to himself, even if he knows. You need to say it, Debra. Say it for your sake as well as Anna's. (pause) Do you want me to try to say it first?

DEBRA: I don't know how to say it.

REBECCA: Will you tell me if I'm saying it right or not?

DEBRA: (nods a yes)

REBECCA: (pause) "Don't look at her as a sexual object? Don't look at her like you're having fantasies of what sex with her would be like?" (pause) Is that close, Debra?

DEBRA: Um-hmm. (pause) Yes.

REBECCA: You keep going, Debra. Say it your own way.

DEBRA: (breathing hard, shaking).

Following Debra's, "You shouldn't be looking at her that way," Rebecca's prompt of "Keep going … there's much more to say," came too soon to have a lasting supportive effect. At that moment, attunement to Debra's difficulty in telling her truth may have been far more supportive than encouraging her to express what has been retroflected. Debra gives up: "It's not my place." Attunement and empathetic understanding of Debra's reticence to talk freely to Jason may have taken the therapy in a different direction—perhaps in the direction of Debra's need for security and validation. Instead Rebecca confronts her with, "It is absolutely your place. You are her mother!" Such confrontation has three purposes: first, the therapist takes the stance of a child advocate confronting for the sake of the child; second, it is aimed at correcting the distortions and possible script beliefs in the Parent ego state; and third, it begins the process of deconfusing the Child ego states.

Even if such a confrontation does not impact Debra, Anna's Child ego states are listening to Rebecca's message and perhaps this will be empathetic for Anna and an opening to new possibilities for her. Debra becomes confused. She is both afraid of Jason and is in a conflict between denial, "I don't know," and maternal protection for her daughter. As a result she shuts down rather than correct her husband. Rebecca models for Debra how to correct Jason and protect Anna: "Don't look at her as a sexual object?" Yet, Rebecca does so with a questioning attitude, "Will you tell me if I'm saying it right or not?" and "Is that close?" This is another example of the process of ongoing contracting between client and therapist; frequent use of such questions provides a constant guide to ensure that the therapist is congruent with the client's experience—an important element is insuring that the therapist is following the client and not programming or even suggesting the client's experience.

REBECCA: (whispering) Debra, you need to do this ... You know something about this so well—There's something in this story that's very important. And there's something that's happening between Jason and Anna that really confuses you. I imagine that you don't know what to do about it. Is that right?

DEBRA: I hate her ... (long pause—she seems to shut down).

REBECCA: Anna is not the problem! She is only a child. The real problem has got to be talked about straightforward, Debra. What is the story here?

DEBRA: I don't know the story.

REBECCA: Will you tell Jason what is happening in your relationship? Will you tell Jason about him and Anna?

DEBRA: It's wrong—the way he is with her.

REBECCA: (long pause; whispering) Debra ... What's happening? What are you doing inside?

DEBRA: Just going blank.

REBECCA: Will you talk directly to me, Debra? What got scary just now? Why do you need to go away?

When Rebecca states one possible hypothesis about what Debra is not saying, "Don't look at her as a sexual object" and then continues with "... there's something happening between Jason and Anna that really confuses you." Debra is back to: "I hate her"; she shuts down emotionally and physically. Rebecca urges Debra to tell her story and Debra answers "I don't know the story." Is Debra denying what happened? Is she so afraid of Jason that she cannot express what she knows? Or is the therapist's hypothesis taking the story in a direction that is not consistent with Debra's experience? These are all questions that the therapist must rapidly assess before making the next intervention. Rebecca's answers to each of those questions about Debra's behavior and internal process will determine how Rebecca will respond. When Debra continues to avoid facing Jason, Rebecca establishes the communication between Debra and herself with "Will you talk directly to me?" Transactions with Rebecca may be easier for Debra to manage than talking to Jason and may clarify the direction of this therapy. But even this communication is too difficult for Debra so she returns to blaming Anna.

DEBRA: (pause) I don't know. (pause) I just can't say anything. (pause) But I know.

REBECCA: You know what?

DEBRA: It's familiar, but I can't think. It's just that the feeling is very familiar when I see him with her.

REBECCA: (pause) OK, then let's you and I talk about what may actually be more important. What happened between you and Anna? (pause) You said, "I hate her." Can you tell me about that? (long pause) Are you with me, Debra?

DEBRA: Trying to get to it.

REBECCA: OK, I'll be patient. (silence) But you're feeling something, Debra. (her head and shoulder are slumped) Is that right? Can you tell me?

DEBRA: It's her; she's doing it. That's what is familiar.

REBECCA: "It's her?" "She's doing it?" She's doing what, Debra? (silence) Are you talking about Anna?

DEBRA: Yes, Anna.

REBECCA: What is Anna doing?

DEBRA: It's her fault.

REBECCA: What is her fault?

DEBRA: Everything is her fault. She's bad.

REBECCA: What makes Anna "bad"? What is it she does that's "bad"?

DEBRA: She's a girl.

REBECCA: Because she's a girl. It's her fault because she's a girl?

DEBRA: She's bad—because she's female.

REBECCA: Are you bad because you're female?

DEBRA: Um-hmm.

REBECCA: Am I?

DEBRA: (pause) I don't know.

REBECCA: Say more about how you and Anna are both bad or at fault for being female. (silence) Are you thinking about that? (silence) Debra, is that what you end up believing when you dare not think about how Jason treated you and Anna?—that it's your fault and Anna's fault just because you were born girls? I wonder if it blocks out something else.

Earlier Rebecca provided an opening to explore the hypothesis that Debra's emotional reaction to Anna was related to the possibility of Jason having sexual fantasies about Anna. This exploration is met by Debra "going blank." Is this resistance? Is the hypothesis wrong or even worse, premature? Or, is the relationship between Debra and Anna more significant to Anna's welfare at this time? Here again Rebecca is making a therapeutic assessment regarding the direction of her next interventions. Experienced therapists are constantly observing the client's behavior and selecting from a variety of hypotheses. It is not so important that the therapist always have the correct hypothesis but it is essential that the client be active in confirming or disconfirming what the therapist imagines to be going on inside the client.

Since this therapy is ultimately for Anna's sake and the primary contract for this therapy is for the resolution of intrapsychic conflict between Anna's Child ego states and her Parent (Debra) ego state, Rebecca then shifts the focus: "Let's you and I talk about what may actually be more important. What happened between you and Anna?"

The therapist then asks Debra to explore the psychological function of her beliefs that females are bad or at fault: "… is that what you end up believing when you dare not think about how Jason treated you and Anna?" Such beliefs may function as a distraction from feeling and knowing about traumatic experiences. It is essential to an in-depth Parent ego state therapy to facilitate the internalized other in unraveling his or her own story—the story of how the parent's script beliefs were formed, how they were maintained and reinforced during the client's childhood, and, what is important, how they may have been introjected by and/or adopted by a child.

Debra's script beliefs and defensive process have become part of Anna's life script. For Anna to have maximum benefits from this work the therapist will focus on helping Debra to acknowledge her defenses and her underlying feelings and needs. A few transactions later Rebecca crystallizes the therapeutic session by summarizing the effect of Debra's script beliefs on both her and, more important, on Anna. Yet this is not enough; another confrontation ensues—a confrontation that is both respectful and valuing of Debra's and Anna's human worth, and also challenges the script beliefs that have been passed from mother to daughter.

DEBRA: My mind is … it's real dizzy, and it hurts.

REBECCA: You've been working really hard here, I know that … you can blame her and you can blame yourself. Maybe instead of …

DEBRA: Blaming somebody else?

REBECCA: That sounds possible?

DEBRA: It's possible.

REBECCA: Well, I would like to tell you something.

DEBRA: (nods yes)

REBECCA: The effect of it on you and on her is exactly the sort of thing you were telling me at the very beginning. Which are things like: There's nothing you can do; there's nothing you can do right; you're at fault because you're female; you're not worthwhile; you don't matter. (pause) Am I right, am I on track so far?

DEBRA: She wants something from me and I don't want to give it to her.

REBECCA: Why, Debra? What does she want and why don't you want to give it to her? (silence) What does she want?

DEBRA: She wanted me to take care of her, and I don't want to.

REBECCA: Umm. (silence) Debra, what does Anna need from you?

DEBRA: (sigh) She wants me to love her. I don't know how.

REBECCA: I believe you. I really believe you. If you think so badly about yourself, and especially if it's just because you're a woman, how can you love a child who's the same, a female?

	And in essence, to tell her she's special to you. (pause) Am I right?
DEBRA:	I didn't get the last part.
REBECCA:	Tell her she's good and special to you.
DEBRA:	Because I know she's a nothing.
REBECCA:	Well, I disagree with you. I don't think she's a nothing. And I don't think you are either. But I think you got some very mixed up ideas about being female, and what that means about your own self-worth, what that means about your relationship with men, and what that means about your role in life. You didn't know what to do with a girl child, except to put on her all those feelings that you have about yourself.
DEBRA:	I didn't know what to do with anybody.
REBECCA:	Yeah. (pause) In your heart of hearts, do you think she's a nothing?
DEBRA:	(reluctantly shakes head "no") All mixed up. (pause) She got big and she helped me.
REBECCA:	Yeah. Then you got some of what you needed.
DEBRA:	Um-hmm. Yeah.
REBECCA:	What you waited so long for.
DEBRA:	Um-hmm. (crying, pause)
REBECCA:	Yeah.
DEBRA:	She helped me.
REBECCA:	Um-hmm. That was really nice of her. (pause) I'll tell you, it's left some real big holes in her. She really needed to be special to you and loved by you from the day she was born. Instead, you passed on your story of the low worth of women and your beliefs "I won't get what I want," "I'm a nothing," and your sense of being all alone.

Rebecca has made a confrontation to Debra about her statement, "She's a nothing" and then continues with a therapeutic opinion, "I don't think you are either!" This is followed by an interpretation based on what Debra had previously declared—that she gave Anna the same message as her own script beliefs. Then a therapeutic challenge: "Do you think she is a nothing?" The confrontation is followed by crystallizing statements from the therapist that are a short analysis of both Debra's and Anna's life script: "I won't get what I want," "I'm a nothing," and the sense of being all alone. Rebecca says to Debra, "You were angry at your husband … and instead you hated her and that damaged her." These therapeutic operations are aimed at both Parent and Child ego states—deconfusing for both Anna's Child ego states and her introjected mother, and therefore part of resolving intrapsychic conflict.

DEBRA: I didn't mean to. (crying)

REBECCA: I know. You were really quite mixed up. And stressed. And angry with your husband. And alone. All those things? And instead you hated her and that damaged her.

DEBRA: Yeah. I didn't mean to. (crying again)

REBECCA: Anna needs a chance to talk about what it was like, living with you. Even though we understand that you didn't mean to, and we understand that you were mixed up, and we understand that in your heart of hearts you don't think she's a nothing; still she's left with a lot of the garbage of you blaming her, she is mixed-up. And she needs to be able to talk about that without feeling that she's hurting you, or that you're going to get angry at her, or hate her. Do you think we can allow her to do that? Is that OK with you?

DEBRA: (sobs)

REBECCA: Tell me about those tears?

DEBRA: It's nice to talk to you.

REBECCA: You know, I wish I had been in your life many years ago listening to you. It all could have been so different, perhaps getting what you wanted instead of deciding you were a nothing and at fault.

DEBRA: Then I would have known how.

REBECCA: Yeah. Yeah. (pause) Well, Debra, I really appreciate your coming and talking. And being as honest as you were able to be. Now we need to listen to Anna. OK? Let her talk, and not get in the way, OK? (pause) When you're ready you can come back another time (long pause). Anna, Richard is right next to you, ready to support you. Do you want to turn to him?

Even at the end of the piece of therapy with Debra, Rebecca continues to engage her in a process contract—the little agreements between client and therapist that both provide the client with a sense of being in charge and making an impact and also provide a continual feedback to the therapist about the client's willingness to proceed with the therapy. Rebecca has been doing the therapy with Anna's Parent ego state while Richard has been on reserve for Anna's Child ego states. Now it is time for Richard to provide the support to Anna for her to express her own feelings, thoughts, and needs. It is essential in most situations of Parent ego state therapy to provide a supportive relationship for the Child ego states.

When the client has an opportunity to respond to the Parent ego state a cycle of interpersonal agency and efficacy is established that may have been ruptured or perhaps never existed. This allows for the Child ego state to define himself and to make an impact—self-expressions that may have been inhibited or prohibited in the original relationship with the parent. To make an impact within a relationship and to define oneself within a relationship are two essential relational needs.

ANNA: Dizzy … (as she gets out of the chair and sits on the therapy mat).

RICHARD: Yeah, but you've been listening to your mom. All those angry words. Now it's time to address mom. Try saying to mom, "I'm dizzy listening to you, Mom."

ANNA: I am dizzy. I'm tired.

RICHARD: Tell her what you're reacting to. What you heard.

ANNA: (pause) It was hard for her.

RICHARD: She made it hard on you as well. That's what I heard. Life with him must have been hell.

ANNA: Yeah. (sighs) Life with him was hell. For her and me!

RICHARD: Talk to Mom. Just talk directly to her as though she's right there in that chair.

ANNA: (turns to empty chair) I didn't want to listen to him; that was your job.

RICHARD: Keep going, Anna. Say it again. "I didn't want to listen to him …"

ANNA: I didn't want to have to be there.

RICHARD: "It was your job to …"

ANNA: I didn't want you hating me. Because I was doing your job! (angrily)

RICHARD: "I was doing your job, and you were hating me!"

ANNA: Sucked!

RICHARD: Keep going!

ANNA: He could get angry at me, too.

RICHARD: "And you didn't ..."

ANNA: You didn't protect me; you didn't love me. You even told me if I did something wrong, it was all my fault so he would get angry at me.

RICHARD: "And I don't like ..."

ANNA: I don't like your dirty looks.

RICHARD: "And I don't like ..."

ANNA: I don't like you hiding inside.

RICHARD: "And I don't like ..."

Richard is intentionally slow in directing Anna to talk to Debra a second time. She appears to need contact with Richard first. Then a few sentences later he again directs her to make verbal contact with the internalized mother who has been externalized by Anna's imagining her in the empty chair. The therapist is "priming the pump"—giving the client an open-ended phrase that if completed by the client may be an expression of what has been inhibited and needs to be said. It is important that the therapist carefully follow the client's body clues, emotional charge, and the contextual material so as not to program the client's words. The therapist's "priming the pump" may help the client to overcome his inertia of self-expression, for example, when Richard says to Anna, "And you didn't ..."; "And I don't like ..."; "I need ..."

The expression of Anna's, "I don't like ..." is a form of contact-making anger, rather than the contact-disrupting rage or withdrawal that she learned in her family. This is a new form of expression, a making of contact with the internalized mother that was both prohibited in childhood and then inhibited for more than forty years. Anna is reexperiencing the feelings of childhood, but instead of reliving them, which is reinforcing of inhibition and repression, she is doing something new—an undoing of retroflections—and the old pattern of script related behavior is altered.

ANNA: I don't like you not loving me. And making me feel it was all my fault.

RICHARD: "Because I need ..."

ANNA: I need your love. I need you to be there.

RICHARD: Tell her about her being worried about you being a sexual object to him.

ANNA: Us.

RICHARD: Say that to her.

ANNA: Us.

RICHARD: Tell her what the word "us" means.

ANNA: Me and him. He paid attention to me. But then I got nervous … (pause)

RICHARD: Yeah, tell Mom about your nervousness.

ANNA: Yeah, but she knew. She knew something was wrong. She knew.

RICHARD: Tell it to Mom.

ANNA: You didn't say anything, you'd just sit there.

RICHARD: "And I needed …"

ANNA: (crying) I needed you to do something …

RICHARD: Keep talking. "Mom, I needed …" (pause) You needed her to "do something." Try saying: "Mom, I needed …"

ANNA: (pause) I needed you to take care of me, and I needed you to protect me. (angrily)

RICHARD: That movement of your arm is saying something. (silence) Anna, Mom's right there. She told you some important things, and now it's your turn. Tell her what your arm is saying. (long pause)

Anna has been responding to the therapist's encouragement for her to express her pent-up emotions and words. Anna's right arm is cocked as though she were preparing to hit, grab, or push. Richard directs her to express what her arm is saying. This is too much, Anna shuts down. Rebecca, suspecting that Anna's Parent ego state is again internally influencing addresses Debra. Rebecca's following remarks are an interposition—imposing herself between the influencing Parent ego state and the Child ego states who are subject to the influence: "Just because you couldn't talk about it doesn't mean that Anna can't either. Debra, let Anna do what you need to do—to say what she thinks and to be angry. You also needed to make an impact." This is permission giving to both Debra and Anna and protective of Anna.

REBECCA: Debra, just because you couldn't talk about it doesn't mean Anna can't either.

RICHARD: Tell her, Anna, what you mean when you say "I needed you to protect me."

REBECCA: Debra, let Anna do what you needed to do—to say what she thinks and to be angry. You also needed to make an impact.

ANNA: I couldn't talk to you, Mom. (sigh) You weren't even around; you didn't want to listen.

RICHARD: Talk to her now, Anna.

ANNA: (pause) She'll get angry at me.

REBECCA: Debra, you said you were going to let Anna do what she needed to do.

ANNA: She'll blame me, she'll get mad at me, and she'll only hate me more.

REBECCA: Not anymore, Anna. I'm keeping her out of the way. You're not going to get any more from her by holding back. You know that not speaking up is a dead end. Go ahead and do what *you* need to do.

ANNA: (pause) I needed you to protect me.

RICHARD: From?

ANNA: How he looked at me. The way he made me feel.

RICHARD: Name it.

ANNA: Dirty.

RICHARD: Keep going. "He made me feel dirty …" (pause) So tell the whole thing: "I needed you to …"

ANNA: To protect me.

RICHARD: From feeling …

ANNA: Dirty. That it was my fault. It was not my fault! You fix it (she again slams her fist on the mat). You fix your marriage or get the fuck out of it! (said very loudly)

RICHARD: Hmm. Tell her why you chose those words. "Get the fuck out of it."

ANNA: (to Richard) I didn't want to be in the middle of it! You fix it (she again slams her fist on the mat).

RICHARD: Tell her what you've been holding back from saying.

ANNA: I didn't want to be in the middle, Mom. It's your marriage. I don't want to hear it. What you are doing and not doing. It's not my business! Your marriage is not my business, your sex life is not my business, your problems are not my business, your kids are not my business. Your whole fucking world is yours, not mine.

Anna has made a powerful statement about her needs within the family system: "I don't want to be in the middle." Rebecca makes another interposition and confrontation of Debra on behalf of Anna. Such an interposition and confrontation often deconfuses a Child ego state. Anna no longer slumps, she continues with, "Your marriage is not my business," etc.

RICHARD: Is there anything else you want to say to her?

ANNA: Yeah. I don't want to fix it—the fucking craziness in your marriage is your business not mine.

RICHARD: Then resign from the job, Anna. (pause) You could send your mother to ongoing therapy with Rebecca.

ANNA: Permanently? She needs it.

RICHARD: Do you like that?

ANNA: Um-hmm. Definitely. (pause) I was kind of waiting for my father to die so she could live. She needed therapy to get out of her marriage just like I did. But, she died first.

RICHARD: Did she ever get what she needed?

ANNA: (crying) No … (pause while crying) But, I will from now on. I'm going to have the life I want.

RICHARD: Anna, let's not let the same thing happen to you. Your time is *now*—your future has lots of possibilities.

ANNA: Yeah … (pause) (big sighs and eye contact with both Richard and Rebecca)

This therapy session ends with Anna's declaration of emancipation, "I'm going to have the life I want." This following Anna's expression of her anger at her mother for failure to protect her from the conflicts of the parents' marriage. The dynamics of a discordant family system and Anna's early childhood relationship with her mother influenced the formation of Anna's life script—a script that is both the result of many of Anna's childhood conclusions and the introjection of mother's script beliefs: "I'm a nothing"; "I won't get what I want"; "I'm all alone"; It's all my fault"; "People can't be trusted"; and "It (life) doesn't matter."

Anna's reaction to the dynamics of her parents' marriage and the accompanying anger had been retroflected for years. The therapist's protection, encouragement, and prompting opened an opportunity for Anna to begin to express what had been pent-up for so long. The undoing of retroflections is an essential part of script cure. It is through physiological constriction that vital aspects of self-expression are contained and reinforced. Retroflections maintain lifelong script patterns of beliefs, behaviors, and physiological restrictions learned or decided upon in the original family. Although Anna's mother had been dead for several years, Anna's Child ego states remained loyal to the intrapsychically influencing Parent (Debra) ego state. The loyalty of children cannot be overemphasized—children naturally bond to parents and may remain attached to the memories (often unconscious) of the parents' psychological dynamics—their feelings, attitudes, psychological and interpersonal defenses, behavioral patterns, and messages of attribution and injunction. Psychotherapy includes making the unconscious memories conscious—that includes the memories of one's own childhood experience, affect, decisions, and defenses that are fixated in Child ego states, as well as the script beliefs, feelings, and defenses introjected from parents.

Many of Anna's script beliefs were both in Parent and Child ego states. Mother's influence and Anna's loyalty were both so strong that Anna's childhood experiences and conclusions were similar to her mother's. The defensive fixations of Anna's Child ego states clustered around the formation of script beliefs, the loss of awareness of her needs, and the retroflection of her natural expressions.

In the absence of need-satisfying contact with her mother, Anna used a common defense. She disavowed her own needs and feelings and instead identified with the feelings, thoughts, beliefs, and coping style of Mother. Mother's script beliefs also become Anna's via introjection. It is through the unconscious defensive identification with a significant other, in the absence of relational needs being satisfied, that Parent ego states are formed.

Introjections are maintained years later because they provide a pseudo sense of attachment to significant others and an archaic sense of identity and familiarity. Introjections are analogous to the invasion of foreign bacteria in the human body; they produce disease. The dis-ease of intrapsychic conflict between Parent and Child ego states is manifested as a loss of knowing what one desires, chronic anxiety, depression, a sense of constant self-doubt, or internal criticism. An in-depth psychotherapy includes identifying and externalizing what has been internalized. The methods are similar to those used with a variety of clients to allow the opportunity for the defensive processes to be relaxed: phenomenological and historical inquiry, affective attunement, validation of relational needs, and caring confrontation. Then regressive therapy, redecisions, corrective explanations or therapeutic interpretations may be used to deconfuse the Child ego states in an introjected Parent ego state. The therapist's caring involvement with a Parent ego state is like an antibiotic to the diseased body; it lessens the internal distress and facilitates a natural healing process. The goal of Parent ego state therapy is the alleviation of intrapsychic conflict.

In the first two and a half years of therapy Anna had made a number of significant changes that included no longer being depressed, the relinquishing of childhood script beliefs, increased job satisfaction, and a beginning interest in wanting a permanent love relationship. Anna's loneliness was triggered by a combination of the summer recess in our therapeutic relationship, the end of her busy schedule pursuing a master's degree, and a loss of hope in having a significant relationship. In reaction to the loneliness, Anna intrapsychically activated the introjected script beliefs of her mother—now she was not alone. Mother's psychic presence was always available. Mother's script beliefs provided a primitive sense of attachment and meaning.

Following this piece of Parent ego state therapy Anna remained in individual therapy another year and a half and attended three other weekend marathons. We continued to address her emotional reaction to her mother, her profound sadness about her family dynamics, and her sense of a lack of love throughout her life. Later a significant aspect of her therapy was the resolution of her confused relationship with her father.

Her self-esteem continued to grow; she was in script less and less. There were some occasions, often accompanying disappointments in relationships, that the script beliefs would be active for a couple of hours. With continued therapeutic focus on both the Child and Parent ego states origin of those beliefs, the exploration of new meanings for life's events, and the discovery of current options, her life script has ceased to be operative. She is now free to live her own life without intrapsychic conflict. Recently she has fallen in love with a partner who cherishes her.

CHAPTER EIGHTEEN

What do you say before you say goodbye? Psychotherapy of grief

"Give sorrow words. The grief that does not speak."

—W. *Shakespeare*, Macbeth, Act IV, Scene iii, line 208

Introduction

Eric Berne asked the question "What do you say after you say hello?" In his book by that name, Berne (1972) focused on the influence of early relational protocols, parental programming, fantasy and fairy tales, explicit decisions, and existential dilemmas in the formation of life scripts. Berne described how self-protective behavioral patterns, implicit conclusions, and explicit script decisions inhibit an individual's spontaneity and flexibility in problem solving and in relationships with people. However, he did not raise another essential question, "What do you say before you say goodbye?"

Neither the psychoanalytic nor the general psychotherapy literature has adequately addressed the nature of psychotherapy for clients who face major losses in their lives through death, divorce, ailing health, or lost jobs. A search of the *Gestalt Journal* and the *Transactional Analysis Journal* archives showed that there were no articles that directly addressed the topics of grief, grieving, sorrow, mourning, or melancholia. Fred Clark (2001) comes closest to addressing this topic when he uses Kübler-Ross's (1969) description of five stages of mourning as a template to describe the processes of psychotherapy. However, he did not relate the five stages to the resolution of the client's grief.

During the 1990s Elaine Childs-Gowell conducted a series of workshops on the psychotherapy of grief at the annual conference of the International Transactional Analysis Association. She focused on how therapists could create what she called "good grief rituals" to help grieving clients say a final goodbye to loved ones (2003). Bob and Mary Goulding briefly address the psychotherapy of grief in their book *Changing Lives through Redecision Therapy* (1979). They identify grief as the failure to say "goodbye" and present a "formula for goodbyes: 1) Facts, 2) Unfinished business, 3) Goodbye ceremony, 4) Mourning, and 5) Hello to today" (p. 175).

The literature on the psychotherapy of grief, mourning, and bereavement is replete with articles that address: various stages of grieving (Axelrod, 2006; R. Friedman, 2009; Kübler-Ross, 1969); complications in the natural process of grieving (Bowlby, 1980; Wetherell, 2012); the treatment of despair and anger (Greenwald, 2013); grieving as an attachment disruption (Parkes, 1972); how grieving may potentiate other mental health issues (Greenwald, 2013); various treatment models (A. Clark, 2004; Hensley, 2006); and attention to the need for supportive relationships in the family, in therapy, and in the community (Olders, 1989). In general, these authors tend to focus the treatment of grief on accepting the loss, understanding the necessity for supportive and caring relationships, providing a suitable amount of time for healing from the loss, and developing new interests and activities (Wetherell, 2012). However, these articles seem to emphasise a soothing of loss, grief, and melancholia rather than an in-depth resolution of grief.

In his essay, "Mourning and Melancholia", Sigmund Freud writes about grief and clarifies the difference between mourning and melancholia. He describes mourning as a normal and regular "reaction to the loss of a loved person" (1917e, p. 243). Freud goes on to describe mourning as a conscious response to a specific death. He considers mourning non-pathological because it is a normal reaction to events and generally is overcome with time. During the mourning period the person realizes that the loved person is truly gone. As a result, he suffers from a loss of interest and an inhibition in activities, a sense of dejection, and an inability to love. Similar symptoms are present in melancholia; however, in mourning an acceptance of the loss eventually occurs and slowly the person returns to his normal state.

Melancholia is pervasive, unconscious, and continuous. It is marked by an ambivalent relationship where there is a love and hate reaction to the other person that is often accompanied by anguish and a diminished sense of self-esteem. Freud says, "In mourning it is the world which has become poor and empty; in melancholia it is the ego itself" (ibid., p. 246). Although the term "melancholia" is not in common usage today, Freud is describing some of the dynamics of protracted grief.

John Bowlby (1961, 1980) was one of the early psychologists to study the process of mourning and described grief as resulting from the loss of attachment. Parkes (1972), and later Parkes and Weiss (1983), made use of Bowlby's ideas about attachment and loss and proposed a theory of grief that included four stages: shock-numbness, yearning-searching, disorganization-despair, and reorganization. Kübler-Ross (1969) popularized the idea that grief occurs in distinct stages and outlined five stages: denial, anger, bargaining, depression, and acceptance.

Axelrod (2006) makes the point that not everyone will experience all five stages of grief, and that it is not necessary (or expected) that one will go through the stages in a particular order. The Yale Bereavement Study (Maciejewski, Zhang, Block, & Prigerson, 2007) examined the concept of stages of grief and found that many people seemed to progress through various stages and that "yearning was the dominant negative grief indicator" (p. 716). Recently Friedman (2009) challenged the notion of stages of grief as a simplistic taxonomy that does not allow for individual variances in the process of grieving. He suggested that each person grieves in his or her own unique way.

Protracted grief and *compounded grief* are each terms that describe a persistent grief that is emotionally paralyzing and interferes with current relationships. Some of the symptoms of protracted or compounded grief may include emotional distance in relationships, fear of losing control, frequent irritability or anger, the absence of emotions, overwhelming confusion, obsessive thoughts, or a nagging sense that "life will never be the same." It can appear as depression or indifference and may be compounded by substance abuse.

In this chapter compounded grief refers to grief that is burdened by many other unresolved problems: economic and legal, relocation and family disruptions, mental health difficulties, suicide or natural disasters, etc. These unsolved problems compound and interfere with the resolution of grief. Protracted grief refers to grief that is "unfinished"; where there is an absence of meaningful communication in an interpersonal relationship, where the person cannot say "goodbye" because there is an incomplete "hello" (Perls, 1973), as described by Freud in his discussion of melancholia (1917e). People suffering from either protracted or compounded grief need to have a way to verbalize and physically express their grief to an interested and involved listener or the untold personal stories of loss may be enacted in physiological reactions, dreams, fears, and obsessions.

Considerations of theory and practice

The death of a parent, child, or friend, the separation from a spouse or loved one, the loss of a job or an important role often results in a deprivation of interpersonal contact. In an attempt to manage these deficits in interpersonal contact, people will often interrupt internal contact (Erskine & Moursund, 1988), they disavow affects and deny their needs and personal experiences while they tighten muscles to desensitize their body, but a sense of loss persists. As a result of these internal interruptions to contact, individuals are less able to be present in the moment, to be in full contact with others, to say a complete "hello" or "goodbye" (Perls, Hefferline, & Goodman, 1951).

Incomplete goodbyes leave a person with a feeling of despondency, never-ending privation, or a nagging sense that something is missing. Often the missing component is the absence of interpersonal contact and the opportunity for full expression of one's inner experience. Telling one's own "truth"—one's personal narrative—is an essential factor in "making meaning," completing significant unfinished experiences, and providing an end to protracted grieving (Neimeyer & Wogrin, 2008). The resolution of protracted grief involves restoring the individual's capacity for full internal and interpersonal contact—the capacity to say an authentic "hello" before a genuine "goodbye."

I learned about the psychotherapy of protracted grief while watching Fritz Perls use his Gestalt therapy "empty chair" technique to help people complete what he called "unfinished business." In his teaching he made a distinction between genuine grief and pseudo-grief. He defined pseudo-grief as "feeling sorry for oneself." He confronted workshop participants' self-pity and insisted that people develop self-support and take responsibility for living in the "now." When trainees expressed genuine grief he responded empathetically and considered it a natural process of mourning the loss of someone. However, if the grief persisted over time, if it was pervasive, he defined the grief as "holding on to unexpressed resentments" (F. S. Perls, personal communication, September, 1969).

Perls would ask the grieving person to use the "empty chair" and fantasize that the significant other was sitting in front of him or her (1969). He would then encourage the client to speak to the image of the other, just as though the other were actually sitting in the chair, and to express his resentments and anger. He encouraged him to be fully vocal and to use body gestures that conveyed his anger and resentments.

When teaching about the psychotherapy of grief, Perls accentuated how grief was maintained by holding on (retroflection) to old resentments and he highlighted the importance of unexpressed appreciations. He taught that the resolution of grief is in the expression of both resentments and appreciations. However, in practice, Perls often gave more consideration to the grieving client's expression of anger and resentments than he did to the expression of appreciations (Perls, 1973). The Gouldings (1979) follow Fritz Perls's template on the treatment of grief. Their brief therapy vignettes show that they emphasize resentments and anger and give only cursory attention to appreciations.

For several years I followed Perls's example and placed the therapeutic focus on the client's unexpressed resentments and anger. I would include the expression of appreciations, often as a closing to the work, but my focal point was on undoing retroflections and expressing resentments. Yet, in my psychotherapy practice some clients would talk about their love for the dead person. In reviewing the grief work several clients talked about how expressing their love, gratitude, and even indebtedness was far more meaningful in their resolution of protracted grief than expressing resentments.

I was stimulated by my clients' stories—painful and angry, grateful and loving—to give more therapeutic prominence to the expression of what they loved, what they treasured, and what they considered precious about the other person. This often led us to stories of delightful moments, cherished memories, and how they would like to memorialize the other person. Unexpressed love, gratitude, admiration, and appreciations, like unexpressed anger and resentments, also create the "unfinished business" of an incomplete "hello" or "goodbye"—the basis of protracted grief.

I found that it was necessary to create a therapeutic balance between emotional polarities such as: unacknowledged anger, resentment, and bitterness on one side of the scale and unrealized dreams, precious experiences, unexpressed affection, and loving memories on the other side. Therapeutic focus on anger and resentments alone was insufficient for the resolution of protracted grief. It became evident that clients needed to express all dimensions of their feelings and that these feelings all interact with each other—relationships involve a myriad of emotions. I began to organize my therapeutic interventions to interweave each of these many emotions. Sometimes the work focused on one emotion until it was well expressed; then, when appropriate, I drew the client's attention to the other end of the emotional spectrum, then back again, always searching for and interweaving the unexpressed emotions, striving for a healing balance.

The therapeutic balance is not always an equal one. With some clients, depending on the history of their relationship with the other person, the emphasis may be more on appreciations. With other clients the emphasis may be more on resentments. If clients are focused on expressing only their love and appreciation, I may encourage them to also express what they did not like about the other. If they are intent on remaining angry and resentful, I encourage them to remember the good experiences, any possible loving moments, and anything that they may have learned from the other. We may spend a considerable amount of time articulating the person's resentments and then later in the work move to an expression of his appreciations and love. With other clients I weave back and forth between their love, anger, what they hold dear, what they resent, and what they will treasure. No matter where the emphasis is placed in any particular therapy, it is often beneficial to integrate both appreciations and resentments into any grief work.

> When you are sorrowful look again in your heart, and you shall see
> that in truth you are weeping for that which has been your delight.
> (Kahlil Gibran, 1923, p. 29)

When working with unexpressed experiences it is important that the person gives voice fully to the many internal feelings, needs, thoughts, and interpretations that have never been expressed. This is what my clients call "truth telling"—it is the verbal (and sometimes physical) expression of the unsaid, and often unacknowledged feelings, thoughts, attitudes, associations, and reactions that the person has kept internal. "Truth telling" is not about the expression of facts, of verifiable information that can be confirmed by others. It is a "narrative truth," the expression of one's own internal experience and the endeavor to make meaning (Allen, 2009; Burgess & Burgess, 2011).

"Truth telling" involves translating affect and physiological reactions into language and honestly expressing what has never been expressed in a relationship. When we psychotherapists emphasize "truth telling" we are inviting the client to attend to and express the interrupted expression of feelings, attitudes, and physical gestures (Erskine, Moursund, & Trautmann, 1999). It is these interrupted gestures, words, and affect that interfere with the capacity to say "hello" and "goodbye." Many clients are not accustomed to sharing their private thoughts. We encourage the client to speak with candor. Such "truth telling" is the opposite of the inconsequential conversations that many people have throughout their lives. Inconsequential conversations begin as self-protective measures to maintain a relationship but, over time, they erode intimacy and interpersonal contact.

The psychotherapy of grief and loss is most effective when done within a relational context whether it is face-to-face with an interested other or through an imagined conversation with the internal representation of the other. That context may be in the interpersonal contact between client and therapist, or in the empathetic communication between client and group members, or in the honest communication between the client and the internal image of the significant other. For some clients a combination of these approaches is best.

I often make use of the empty chair method by inviting the client to visualize the significant other, to energize an interrupted physical gesture, to express the unexpressed feelings, to create words that convey his subjective experiences to the other. By working with the internal image of the other person we create the possibility for clients to use their imagination to express what needs to be said to the other person. I use an old concept from child therapy: *create in fantasy what is not possible in reality*.

For most clients it is essential that they express what they feel to the internal image of the other person, that they make the necessary contact in fantasy—to finally do what was missing in the original situation. For other clients the interpersonal contact between client and therapist is more therapeutically effective than using the "empty chair" method. If the client cannot visualize the other because he lacks internal support or fears the rejection or ridicule of the visualized other, I then have the person look me in the eyes and tell me his experience of the other. I bring his "unfinished business" into the relationship with me: "Please tell *me* what you would say to your father if he were sober enough to listen to you," or "Since you are certain that your mother will again say you are 'silly' and will deny what really happened to you, please tell *me. I'll listen.*" I want him to see the emotions in my face, to hear my expressions of sympathy, and to experience my full presence.

It is often necessary to do the grief therapy in a relational context, face-to-face, when:

- the therapy session is soon after the loss
- there is a lack of supporting and caring people in the person's life
- there are not enough internal resources to make effective use of visualizing the other in the "empty chair," or
- the grief is complicated by other interfering problems.

The aim of either method, talking to the visualized other or talking directly to the psychotherapist or group members is the same: the creation of a verbal narrative (and sometimes physical expression) of the unexpressed and unarticulated affects, fantasies, and subjective meanings. It is through the skillful help of the psychotherapist that the client's physical sensations, feelings and needs, explicit and implicit memories, reactions and attitudes can come to awareness and finally be articulated as a personal narrative.

Before working with a grieving client I ask myself a series of ethical questions: "Is this a normal grief reaction that will be resolved in its own natural course of time?" "Is the client's grief protracted and inhibiting the person from living life fully?" "Is this grief complicated by other problems that require additional help?" "Will the client's welfare be enhanced if I therapeutically intervene in this client's grieving process?" "If I intervene is it more effective to: work relationally, face-to-face; use the "empty chair"; use the interactions within a group; or combine approaches?

> All sorrows can be borne if you put them into a story or tell a story about them. (Karen Dinesen, 1957)

Compounded grief: interpersonal contact

Ruth was a mother of a nineteen-year-old boy who died in a car accident. She had come to the city to settle legal issues, to close her son's apartment at the university, and to meet the family of another dead boy. A former therapist in her home town gave her my name and suggested that she talk to me. Ruth was agitated with grief and several unresolved problems. Her initial conversation on the phone was a mixture of despair, irritation, confusion, and loneliness. I knew that I would have one, or perhaps at the most two, sessions to help Ruth express and process her grief. We scheduled an initial two hour session.

Ruth's grief was compounded by many worries: not only had she lost her son but she had to face the families of the other boys in the car; several legal responsibilities were pending, and her former husband was blaming her for their son's behavior. I did not have sufficient time to help her sort out the myriad legal and interpersonal issues that were overwhelming her. After the first thirty minutes I formed a therapeutic priority: I chose to have her focus on the death and loss of her son and the qualities of their relationship—to make contact, to say "Hello," and then to perhaps say "Goodbye." Other unresolved problems would have to wait until she had some relief from her intense grief.

Ruth was disturbed and irritated by all the external demands being put on her. She was so confused and alone in her grief that it seemed premature for her to talk to a fantasized image of her son in an "empty chair." I was not certain that she possessed the internal resources to say "hello" through imagination; I sensed that it was too soon after her son's death. Instead of an empty chair approach I had Ruth look me in the eye. I asked her to tell me all about her son. I wanted Ruth to experience my full emotional resonance with her feelings and experiences of being a mother of a child who had just died. Our interpersonal contact, our relationship, took precedence. First I would focus our work together on an authentic "hello," a full interpersonal connection between Ruth and me.

I began by asking Ruth how her son had died. I asked about the factual details. She told me that he had been driving the car. He and three other boys had been drunk and they crashed into a store front. As I inquired about her feelings she expressed her anger at his frequent drinking of alcohol and his reckless driving. It was important that she see that I was taking her anger seriously. I asked about other instances when she was angry at him. She told me about previous times when he had been irresponsible, his drinking alcohol throughout adolescence, his taking her car without permission, and their frequent arguments. I listened with interest and expressed how disturbing it is for a parent when children act irresponsibly. My intention was to acknowledge her anger, to attend carefully to her resentments, and to provide attunement and validation for her emotions.

I then inquired about what else she was feeling. She talked about the sadness in never seeing him graduate from university, his never getting married, and her never having grandchildren. She wept at the losses. I encouraged her to tell me about earlier experiences with her son. She continued to cry as she described some important events from his preschool years. Throughout these stories I hoped that she could see the compassion in my eyes.

I then inquired about some of her precious memories. She told me about his brilliant school accomplishments, about the delightful things they did together in his early teenage years, and how loving he had been to her during her divorce. I rejoiced with her as she told me about these important memories. I again asked if there was anything she resented. She further expressed how she detested his drinking alcohol and his not paying attention to his safety. During all these stories I kept eye contact with her. Although I did not say much, I expressed my involvement with my facial and body expression.

I then asked Ruth to tell me more about their relationship in his early childhood. She wept as she talked about his birth, several precious times during his early childhood, and the many instances of loving contact that they shared together. She told me how she admired her son for his many sport and academic accomplishments. Along with her I felt an appreciation of his many qualities. She could see the tears in my eyes as she recalled many special experiences that she and her son had together.

The therapy of Ruth's grief was in our interpersonal contact. I was compassionate when Ruth was sad; I took her anger seriously; I expressed my joy when she was remembering the precious moments with her son; I felt protective when she expressed fears about the unresolved legal issues. Her emotions oscillated from despair and confusion, to anger, to sadness, to resentment, and then to more anger, to further sadness, and finally to joy and appreciation.

The intersubjective contact—Ruth's expression of each affect and my attuned responses—was essential in Ruth's finding some relief from her grief (Stolorow, Brandschaft, & Atwood, 1987). This process of resolution of grief was done face-to-face, person-to-person. Yet it included all the elements that I may use in an "empty chair" technique with another client who had more internal resources and relational support or whose grief was not so recent. For Ruth the healing was in the quality of the relationship.

Protracted grief: the "empty chair"

Zia was a forty-seven-year-old woman who had grieved over the loss of a child for several years. Although she and her husband had talked about the loss of their child years ago, Zia had not spoken of her grief in several years. She mourned in silence. Another client in a therapy group had talked about his grief over the death of his five-year-old daughter. This was the impetus for Zia to speak to the group.

ZIA: My heart is racing. Fourteen years ago, I got pregnant. After four or five months, my baby was diagnosed with an incomplete brain and a spinal deformity. On the doctor's advice and for the sake of the child we decided to terminate the pregnancy. I went to the doctor and after two days of cramps I gave birth to a dead boy. But I have always felt that there is still a baby inside me. (She begins to weep. Long pause.) I think I need to say goodbye to my baby.

In the next few minutes I made a contract with Zia about how she can say goodbye within our group. I explained the usefulness of using an "empty chair" and gave her a choice between talking to me, the group, or the fantasized image of her son. She agreed to talk to the image she has often fantasized over the years.

RICHARD: Close your eyes and hold this baby. (I hand her a small, soft cushion.) I am not in a hurry, take your time. Let us assume that your baby is born alive and that you have all the time you need to talk to that baby. (She weeps deeper. This is the beginning of her "hello" to her dead baby.)

RICHARD: (after a half minute pause, in a gentle voice) Let yourself imagine how it will be to feed your baby the first time. Feel those sensations in your body. Tell your baby about it. (Here I am providing "therapeutic direction" and inviting the client to be aware of her fantasies of holding a live baby.)

(After a few minutes Zia stops crying. In the next several minutes Zia describes her imagination of the first nursing experience. She talks to her baby that is represented by the cushion she is holding in her arms. She describes in detail her body sensations, her love of feeding the child, and her son's delight in her feeding him. She is actively caressing the cushion.)

RICHARD: Keep stroking your baby. (This therapeutic direction is to intensify her physiological sense of being in contact with an internal image of the baby). Tell your son what it is like for you to change his diapers. Feel how soft your baby is. (pause) Just experience how special this moment is for both of you. (Zia, in talking to her son describes her delight in changing him and his joy in their being together. She is smiling as she talks to the baby; there is a bit of a giggle in her voice.)

RICHARD: Listen to how he says "mommy" for the first time. Tell him how you hear it, how you feel his voice. (For the next five minutes Zia speaks to the baby and talks about how much she loves him and all the things she will do with him as he gets older.)

RICHARD: Tell him what it is like for you when he is ready to walk. (Zia bursts into tears. She tells the baby that he will never walk and that he may never be able to talk. Her body is shaking with grief as she cries deeply.)

RICHARD: (After three minutes of silence) Tell your son the dreams you had when you thought that he would be normal. (Zia describes a number of important images such as bathing him, playing on the floor together, and reading to him. She continues to tell her son several dreams that she had of being the mother of a normal child.)

RICHARD: Now tell him what it will be like to grow up with his physical deformities. (Zia continues to tell him of his mental and physical deformities. She describes the extensive and costly medical attention that he may need and the lack of a suitable care facility. She tells him about her love for her other children and how she would not be available to the other children if she had to take care of his many physical needs. She is no longer crying; she is sounding factual.)

RICHARD: (after a short pause) Tell him about your family ... And tell him the important lessons that you'd like to teach him. (Zia talks about the love in her family and the value system she would like to teach her son. She describes his brother and sister and how they will also love him. She again describes her fear of neglecting her other children because of the constant care her baby will need. The therapist encourages her to keep talking to her baby. She talks about society's disregard for the handicapped, and the many medical complications he will have as he get older, if he lives.)

RICHARD: Now tell your son what you want to do for him. (Zia describes how she wants to send him to heaven. She tells him that there are not enough medical services to help him and that he may be in constant pain if he were to live. She goes on to say that she has to protect her other two children. She continues to weep as she tells him that she is protecting him by sending him to live with God. She ends with describing the peace she has in knowing that he is in heaven. She has stopped crying.)

After three minutes Zia opens her eyes and looks at the group. Several of the group members are crying. The therapist motions them to gather around Zia and asks them to talk to her about their feelings. Everybody gathers in tears and they share their own stories while supporting the client. After about fifteen minutes I suggest that the group create a goodbye ritual. Several group members hold Zia while someone in the group sings a song. Another group member takes the baby and dramatizes a burial. Another person then gives a short speech about Zia being a good mother. Zia is smiling, her body is relaxed. After a few minutes she inquires about other group members' feelings.

In the next session Zia reported that she is "feeling greatly relieved." "I had the best night's sleep I have had in fourteen years. It is a big load out of my belly. My husband and I had a wonderful talk. I did not realize that I carried such grief."

Further reflections

Zia and Ruth are both mature women dealing with adult issues of profound heartache and despair—a mother's pain over the death of a child and her corresponding bewilderment about intimate feelings and dreams. Central in Zia's protracted grief was her untold ethical dilemma and her continuing love for both the aborted child and her other children. Ruth, like Zia, was also in great emotional pain but her suffering was compounded by her anger at her son's irresponsible behavior, pending legal issues, and the lack of support from her former husband. For both women the healing of grief required that they articulate their personal narrative to an interested and involved listener.

These are two examples of grief therapy involving the client's Adult ego state. With other clients the psychotherapy of grief may focus on the articulation of Child ego state feelings, physiological and behavioral reactions, and self-stabilizing beliefs. Child ego state therapy is most likely to occur when a client is dealing with the death of a parent (either after the parent has died or in anticipation and preparation for saying a final goodbye). When the clients have "unfinished business" with their parents or other important people from their childhood (grandmother, uncle, sibling, teacher), it may be necessary for the psychotherapist to facilitate the emotional expressions and deconfusion of one or more Child ego states, the decontamination of the Adult ego (Berne, 1961), or bringing meaning to the manifestations of life script (Erskine, 2010a).

As described in these two cases the psychotherapy of grief will be unique with each client. To illustrate some of the possible variations I have included a few brief examples. When protracted grief is in response to a divorce or the breakup of a romance, it may be important to start with the client's anger, bitterness, or sense of betrayal because that is often what is evident as uppermost for the person. However, some clients can become mired in their hate or anger. It may be equally important to facilitate the client's awareness of his sadness about the tarnished dreams and to remember the special or loving experience that the couple once shared.

To achieve a balance it may be necessary to shift the client's focus away from the resentments and bitterness to pleasant memories. I use questions such as: "What was it like when you first met each other?" "What were some of the wonderful things you did together?" "What attracted you?"

When the client's long-term partner has dementia, the therapy may begin with reviewing the memories of the good times that they had together. The therapy may then focus on the client's disgruntlements and anger at the partner's loss of interest in life and his or her diminished physical ability, and then back to the precious memories. A significant aspect of the psychotherapy is in the balanced expression of all affect.

Anthony's brother had committed suicide and for almost two years Anthony would wake up each day feeling depressed. As part of a more comprehensive therapy we used the "empty chair" so that he could express his sadness directly to an image of his brother. He finally allowed himself to cry. He repeated several versions of "I love you," "I miss you," and told his brother about several of the good times they had together throughout childhood. However, he continued to suffer a great sadness at the loss of his brother.

A few sessions later I asked him to continue talking to his brother. This time I encouraged him to attend to the muscle tension in his body and to describe his sensations. Slowly he began to express his anger and resentment with statements such as, "How dare you kill yourself," "I am furious that you have hurt our mother and father," "You are a shit for doing that to your children." He became enraged with the image of his brother and kicked the "empty chair" across the room. In Anthony's therapy the balance between appreciations and resentments was less important than a thorough expression of his anger. He no longer woke each day feeling depressed; his depression was caused by disavowing his anger at his brother for committing suicide.

Suzanne, a client in individual therapy, had not attended her father's funeral when he died twenty years before. After two sessions of "empty chair" work and "truth telling" I asked her to make a painting of her father. In the following session we went to the park, built a fire, and had a "goodbye" cremation. Later in therapy she talked about how important it was for her that we went out of the office and made a special cremation ceremony. She said, "In the park, I made a final goodbye."

If I use the "empty chair" method in a group I will often have the client repeat the story to the group members so that he can experience emotional resonance with the group, similar to what may happen at a funeral. We periodically create a funeral ritual or psychodrama that addresses both the person's grief and/or the grief that may be stimulated in other group members. With some clients it may be beneficial if the grief therapy is done entirely within a relational group process where the therapeutic emphasis is on the healing power of relationships between group members. In such a relational group psychotherapy the leader's tasks include stimulating the flow of contactful dialogue, modeling the importance of phenomenological inquiry, and creating an atmosphere of responsiveness to each individual's relational needs (Erskine, 2013). The respectful involvement between group members fosters the resolution of grief and enables everyone in the group to become aware of and express their own experiences. The healing of grief becomes possible through the group members' contactful, caring relationships.

Grief is not always about losing a person. Malisse, age fifty-two, came to individual therapy, five years after having a mastectomy, with a contract to resolve "relational problems" and her "withdrawal from people." Several months into the therapy, after she had formed a secure relationship with me, I asked her to close her eyes and talk to her breast. She sat with her hand over the surgical wound in her chest and cried for several minutes. She then talked to the breast just as though she was talking to her best friend. She told her breast that it was beautiful and that she loved it. She described the pleasure she had always had with her body. Then she wept. Her whole body shook with grief.

In our next session, after reviewing the previous week's grief work, I suggested that she put the cancer in the "empty chair" and talk to it. She became angry at the cancer, cursed its existence, and shouted "I ban you from my body." She shouted, cried, and shouted her anger again at the cancer, both for herself and on behalf of all women. Eventually she expressed thankfulness that the surgeon had removed all the cancer. She lamented that she no longer felt attractive to men and then suddenly made a decision to have a breast implant. Following these two grief sessions we continued our relational therapy as she recovered from her reconstructive surgery and explored new social relationships.

Anticipatory grief

Before the death of a loved one some clients suffer from a variety of symptoms related to grief. These grief related symptoms may include denial, bouts of intense sadness often alternating with periods of emotional numbness, confusion, avoidance of or anger at the dying person, repetitive arguments, a general sense of helplessness, or feeling overwhelmed and stressed. Many people experience intense anticipatory grief before a loved one dies. However, the psychotherapy literature does not address the treatment of grief that may occur in anticipation of the death of a loved one.

When clients experience anticipatory grief they may exhibit some of the same psychological dynamics described by stage theorists but their emotional reactions do not seem to pass through distinct stages. In my clinical experience clients experiencing anticipatory grief often display a mix of emotional reactions. With some clients there is an orderly progression from one emotion to another. With other clients their emotional reactions seem to oscillate from one extreme to another in a matter of minutes. They may be resentful, appreciative, despairing, openly angry, nostalgic, compliant with family traditions, and/or yearning for some words of acknowledgement or love. Frequently, grieving clients will focus on one specific emotion and disavow other feelings and thoughts. Whether we organize our psychotherapy to attend to each "stage" of grief or instead focus primarily on our clients' emerging experience of emotions, our clients often need us to attend to their "unfinished business" with the dying person.

Intimate and meaningful conversations are essential in the resolution of grief, whether the grief is protracted, complicated, or anticipated. Ideally such intimate conversation can occur before the death of a loved one. After the death of a loved one, grief is often potentiated by "unfinished business"—the emotional pain of what had happened and/or the regret of what never happened—and thoughts of "I wish I had said more," "If only we had had a real conversation," "I never told him (or her) how much he (or she) meant to me," or "I never told the truth." When intimate and honest conversations happen before the death of a loved one, the after-death grief is much easier for the remaining individual to assimilate and resolve. When such meaningful conversations do not happen before the death of the loved one, the after-death experience of grief is often intensified and prolonged.

The psychotherapy described in this section is about creating an opportunity for the expression of feelings, making interpersonal contact, and "truth telling" before the other person dies. Ideally, I prefer that the psychotherapy pave the way for sincere face-to-face conversations between my client and the dying person while he or she is still lucid. Many clients need encouragement and therapeutic support in order to engage in a meaningful dialogue with the other person. For some clients our psychotherapy provides an emotionally filled rehearsal that makes intimate and honest communication possible before the loved one dies.

In some situations the actual expression of true emotions, full interpersonal contact, and expressing one's own "truth" to the other person is not a viable option. The other person may be in a coma, suffering from dementia, or be emotionally unable to have a meaningful conversation. Because of script beliefs such as, "I have no right to say what I feel" or "Others are more important than me," many clients are extremely reluctant to initiate intimate and meaningful conversations (O'Reilly-Knapp & Erskine, 2010).

Clients may be inhibited in communicating meaningful experience because they believe that being honest with the other person will hurt or even kill him or her. Many families have forged a system that does not allow for intimate conversation. At the time of impending death the loyalty to such a family system may be intensified. In each of these situations it may be therapeutically necessary for the psychotherapist to facilitate a meaningful conversation in fantasy by using the "empty chair" method. In working with the client's fantasy, through the client imagining the other person sitting directly in front of him, we create the possibility for plausible interpersonal contact—contact that may not be possible in reality—an imaginative contact that can conceivably heal relational wounds.

A case example

Jason's brother, Andrew, had a brain tumor. He had been in a slow process of mental and physical deterioration for over two years. As his only living relative Jason had, for the past two years, assumed responsibility for his older brother's living arrangements, medical care, and financial needs. A year before the doctors predicted that Andrew would die within a month or two. Instead of dying, Andrew continued to live but his physical capacities worsened.

Jason is a member of a psychotherapy group that meets for one six hour day each month. He has attended the past thirteen such sessions. In the sixth and seventh sessions he talked to the group members about his brother's illness and about his frustration and exhaustion in continually caring for his brother. Jason reported to the group that through the relational group process he had felt understood, supported, and encouraged to continue his responsibility for his brother. I encouraged him to have several "truthful conversations" with Andrew. In the eleventh session Jason reported that he found it "impossible" to say anything meaningful to his brother. He again expressed to the group his despair and his annoyance at Andrew and told the group that he wished his brother would "get it over with and die." He then wept and said that he yearned for his brother to say "some kind words to me" or to "just show that he loved me."

In his thirteenth session Jason began by saying that his brother could no longer speak or feed himself. Jason had lost hope that Andrew would acknowledge him in some loving way. Jason was despondent; his body was rigid. I asked Jason if he was willing to use the "empty chair" method to have a "heart-to-heart" talk with Andrew. At first he was reluctant to imagine his brother sitting in front of him or to express what he was feeling. I assured him that I and the group members were there to support him and help him express all the feelings that he rigidly held inside. His tight fists revealed some of his unexpressed emotions. I pointed out that in previous sessions he had made some angry and caustic comments about his brother that I thought represented unresolved resentment. After some group discussion about his body tension he agreed to experiment with visualizing his brother and to honestly tell him about their relationship.

We began with my using a quasi-hypnotic introduction. "Jason, close your eyes and imagine your brother is in his hospital bed with only thirty minutes to live. He can hear you fully but he cannot talk. This is your last opportunity to say all the important things that you have never said to him. The important part is that you be truthful and not leave anything out. I will be right here to back you up. Just look at his image and tell him the truth about your relationship."

Jason hesitantly told his brother how much he had always admired and loved him. I encouraged him to keep talking to the image of Andrew and to tell him everything. He told Andrew how he had looked up to a brother who was five years older and very athletic. As he started to talk about Andrew in the third person I encouraged him to keep visualizing his brother and to "talk to him." He went on to tell Andrew how he had longed for "good times" with him. I prompted him to talk about some of the "good times" or important things that they had done together. Jason had great difficulty recalling pleasant moments. He described some of the games that they had played together and the one time when his brother had defended him from a bully on the playground.

Jason was struggling to recall shared experiences that were pleasurable or intimate. I suggested that he tell Andrew what was missing in their relationship. Jason expressed his yearning for a "kind and loving" brother. He spoke about how he, as a boy, waited for Andrew to come home and play with him. He expressed how disheartened he was that Andrew either ignored him or hit him. Jason bitterly described how, as a boy, he had longed to share a bedroom with Andrew but how Andrew had "tortured" him. He went on to tell his brother how, as an adult, he had misused him by borrowing money and not repaying it; how he expected Jason to take care of his "financial mess" but never said "thank you."

Jason's face had turned bright red, the veins in his neck were bulging, his fists were pushing against the chair. It was clear that he was physiologically containing his anger. I put a large cushion on the chair and suggested that Jason begin each sentence with the words "I don't like." Jason began to shout out several things that he detested. He hit the cushion and screamed at his brother, "I don't like the way you have always treated me," and reiterated several painful events in their relationship. He then added, "I have always loved you. I always wanted you to like me. I hate the way you used me and treated me. I have always kept quiet and waited for you to be good to me. Now I know you will never change."

He continued to shout and pound the cushion for a few minutes and then he began to weep. He said many of the same things again but this time he was full of sorrow. He lamented, "I longed for you to be my brother but most of my life you hated me. I have been so good to you but you never acknowledged it. It is time for me to say goodbye to all my hopes. I will never have the brother I wanted. You have been a real shit to me. Now I want you to die and get all this torment over with. Go now! Find the peace you never had in life. It is my time to be free of you. I want to be with people who like me." Jason's body relaxed and his face returned to a normal color as he quietly cried for several minutes. Later in the day he looked much livelier. The next day he telephoned to say that he had had the best night's sleep in two years.

Conclusion

The case of Jason illustrates the transformative power of "truth telling" and the importance of actively expressing emotions that have been inhibited and contained through physical tension. As we can see from each of the examples, the therapeutic use of imagination, the "empty chair" method, and the psychotherapist's caring involvement all provide the client with an opportunity to have a quality of interpersonal communication in fantasy that was not possible in reality.

Early in this chapter I outlined several models for the treatment of grief that are described in the professional literature. The case example used in this chapter illustrates the integration of a number of these therapeutic approaches, most notably:

- the acknowledgement of disavowed feelings
- the use of expressive methods in the healing of emotional pain and anger
- providing the time and space for the person to tell his story and to finish the "unfinished business"
- providing a supportive relationship by way of the group members' and psychotherapist's involvement, and
- assisting the client's movement through various emotional responses such as denial, despair, yearning, anger, and the reorganization of a sense of self.

In my years of treating clients suffering from either protracted or anticipatory grief I have found that it is necessary for the client to establish a balance between emotional polarities of anger, resentment, and bitterness with memories of precious experiences, unexpressed affection, and love. As described in this chapter, "truth telling" to the "empty chair" is an effective method for the resolution of protracted and anticipated grief. It is essential that the psychotherapist encourage and support the client's "truth telling" whether it be only in fantasy to a mental image in an "empty chair" or eventually face-to-face with a real person. The purpose of this type of psychotherapy is to restore the individual's capacity to have an honest and meaningful "hello" before engaging in a genuine "goodbye."

> I cannot know the pain you feel.
> I cannot share your memories or your loss.
> My words of sympathy are beneath measure, yet
> know that my heart reaches out with love to your heart.
>
> —Jonathan Lockwood Huie, 2014

CHAPTER NINETEEN

Nonverbal stories: the body in psychotherapy

S ome of my earliest memories are the sensations in my body, my
physical movements, and being cuddled in another person's body.
I must have been about three years old when my mother woke me
each morning by rubbing my back. Her touch provided a warm secure
feeling—an emotional memory that I periodically recall today when I
am in need of nurturance. There is a particular spot on my back that I
relate to being unconditionally loved, a spot that my mother always
touched with firm tenderness.

This physiological memory of nurturing is in strong contrast to
another early childhood experience of my parents having a loud argument in the kitchen. I tried to escape the emotional turmoil by going to
the next room and pounding on the keys of the piano. Yet I also kept
watching to see if my father would hit my mother again. My shoulders
and neck were tense. I must have been scared. I cannot recall a sense of
fear but I know that making noise on the piano was a distraction from
the emotional havoc caused by their screaming.

The tension in my neck and shoulders remained within my body
for years. The tension was intense whenever I faced conflict until I
attended a music therapy workshop conducted by two colleagues.
When I arrived the room was full of people so I sat on the floor next to

the piano. Although the general atmosphere felt safe there was some discussion among the presenters and the audience that made me feel uncomfortable. I spontaneously reached up and began to tinker the base notes on the piano. Before I could stop myself one of the music therapists encouraged me to continue, to close my eyes, and let myself hear and feel the sounds I was making. I pounded the piano harder and then even harder. I began to shake with fear. I was nauseous. A deep cry burst out of me as I screamed for my parents to stop fighting. This cry expressed the natural protest that I had inhibited as a fear-based reaction to my parents fighting. For more than forty years my tight neck and shoulder muscles had inhibited my need to make an impact; my need to protest had become *retroflected*, immobilized, and transformed by distraction (Perls, Hefflerline, & Goodman, 1951).

"The Body Keeps the Score" is the title of Bessel van der Kolk's 1994 article about trauma and memory. My body kept an unconscious "score" with emotional and physiological memories of the trauma of witnessing my parents fighting. Until that day of music therapy I had no conscious memory of those early events in my life. So it is with many of our clients. They say they have no memories of being younger than ten or twelve years of age yet they describe having anxiety attacks, bouts of depression or loneliness, digestive problems, backaches, or like me, the tensions in their shoulders and neck. All of these emotional and physical symptoms are the memories—often the only memories—of despairing loss, neglect, or traumatic events. These significant memories are expressed in our affect and through our bodily movements and gestures. Such body memories are without form or thought, what we often refer to as unconscious: a nonverbal, nonsymbolized pattern of self-in-relationship.

My body yearned for an opportunity to release the tension, to scream, to make an impact, to be protected and comforted. In not having parental affect regulation and psychological protection I had retroflected my fear and inhibited my protest; I held in my scream and distracted myself. The retroflection of my need to protest and the physical tension in my neck served the psychological function of affect *self-stabilization* in a situation where I needed my parents to provide the stabilization of my overwhelming fear.

My therapy experience was an expression of visceral, physiological, and emotional memories—memories that were pre-symbolic, implicit, and relational—coming to awareness as I sat beneath the piano and began to tinker the keys. This was an emotionally laden story waiting to be told. In my ongoing therapy I had talked about inhibiting my protest, being afraid of conflicts, and the tension in my neck. But my therapy had been completely verbal and my examples were of current life. The stimulus and safety of the music therapy demonstration made it possible for me to have a supported and therapeutic reenactment of my early trauma.

Our bodies hold our pre-symbolic, implicit, and procedural memories within the nervous system, muscles, and connective tissues. These emotional and physiological memories may be expressed as gestures, inhibitions, compulsions, physical tensions, and unique mannerisms. Eric Berne referred to such tensions and gestures as the "script signal". He said, "For each patient there is a characteristic posture, gesture, mannerism, tic, or symptom which signifies that he is living 'in his script.'" (1972, p. 315).

Gestalt therapy defines such habitual mannerisms and interrupted gestures as a "retroflection," a holding in what is needed to be expressed in order to avoid awareness of psychological discomfort (Perls, Hefferline, & Goodman, 1951). People tense the muscles of their body as a distraction in order to self-stabilize after being flooded with overwhelming affect. Often the retroflection becomes habitual and interferes with internal contact, the awareness of sensations, affect, and needs.

Unconscious or in the body?

Most of what we colloquially refer to as "unconscious" may best be described as pre-symbolic, sub-symbolic, implicit, or procedural expressions of early childhood experiences that are significant forms of memory (Bucci, 2001; Kihlstrom, 1984; Lyons-Ruth, 2000; Schacter & Buckner, 1998). These forms of memory are not conscious in that they are not transposed to thought, concept, language, or narrative. Such sub-symbolic or implicit memories are phenomenologically communicated through physiological tensions, body movements, undifferentiated affects, longings and repulsions, tone of voice, and relational patterns.

Freud postulated that "the unconscious" was the result of "repression" where uncomfortable affect-laded or traumatic experience were defensively prevented from coming to awareness (1912b, 1915e).

In working with many clients in psychotherapy it has become clear to me that particular memories, fantasies, feelings, and physical reactions may be repressed because they may bring to awareness relational experiences in which physical and relational needs were repeatedly unmet and related affect cannot be integrated because there was (is) a failure in the significant other person's attuned responsiveness (Erskine, 1993; Erskine, Moursund, & Trautmann, 1999; Lourie, 1996; Stolorow & Atwood, 1989; Wallin, 2007).

I have had clients who were extremely afraid of remembering their own childhood experiences. They knew that their memories were emotionally painful, even overwhelming, and they did not want me to do anything that disturbed their self-protective equilibrium. They actively repressed awareness of what they "sensed" had occurred in their past. These clients often found clever and sometimes destructive ways to distract themselves from remembering. I found that it was essential that I build a solid therapeutic relationship with these clients before doing any historical inquiry or body focused therapy—a therapeutic relationship based on patience, respect for their fear of remembering, and a sensitive responsiveness to their affect and relational needs.

Experience that is unconscious is not only the result of psychological repression and distraction. Research has shown that trauma and cumulative neglect produce intense overstimulation of the amygdala and the limbic system of the brain such that the physiological centers of the brain are activated in the direction of flight, freeze, or fight. There is little activation of the frontal cortex or integration with the corpus callosum so that time sequencing, language, concepts, narrative, and the capacity to calculate cause and effect are not formed (Cozolino, 2006; Damasio, 1999; Howell, 2005). The brain is then unable to symbolize experience (Bucci, 2001), but the experience is stored in the neurological interplay of affect and body.

This neuropsychology research provides a basis for the psychotherapist to work directly with the clients' visceral sensations, muscular reactions, movements and interrupted gestures, imagery, and affect. Along with body centered methods I often used phenomenological inquiry and therapeutic inference to help the client construct a symbolized mosaic composed of visceral sensations and emotions, body reactions and physical tensions, images and family stories. This co-constructed mosaic allows the person to form an integrated physiological, affective, and linguistic story of their life's experiences.

Some developmental experiences may be unconscious because the child's emotions, behaviors, or relational needs were never acknowledged within the family. When there is no conversation that gives meaning to the child's experience, the experience may remain as physiological and affective sensations but without social language (Cozolino, 2006). A lack of memory may also appear unconscious because significant relational contact did not occur. When important relational experiences never occurred, it is impossible to be conscious of them. If kindness, respect, or gentleness were lacking, the client will have no memory; there will be a vacuum of experience but the body may carry a sense of emptiness, loneliness, and longings. This is often the situation with childhood neglect. Lourie (1996) described the absence of memory in clients with cumulative trauma that reflects the absence of vital care and an ignoring of relational needs. Psychotherapy that integrates a focus on body sensations and affect with a sensitive phenomenological and historical inquiry provides the opportunity to address that which has never been acknowledged and to create a verbal narrative that reflects the body's story.

A consideration of methods

In the previous story about my music therapy experience the safety and nonverbal aspect of the music therapy made it possible for me to reexperience a trauma that had previously not been available to my consciousness. Music therapy is but one form of working with pre-symbolic and procedural memories. Art therapy is another. Movement and dance therapy may also be evocative of early memories. As a psychotherapist I use a number of body oriented methods such as these to facilitate my clients' psychotherapy. However, I am not a body therapist who relies on either evocative or provocative techniques alone: I am a psychotherapist who focuses on the body and the unconscious stories requiring resolution.

I often engage in doing body oriented therapy that involves clients becoming aware of their breathing. I facilitate their experimenting with various forms of breathing to find their own natural rhythm. Sometimes this alone is enough to stimulate an awareness of memories or where they are holding muscular tension in their body. Or, the therapeutic work may focus on grounding, that is, helping the client to feel a solid and dependable base under his or her feet or buttocks. I watch for the inhibited or interrupted gesture. These are often the "script signals" that reflect a much larger emotion filled story embedded in the body. I carefully watch for interruptions in internal contact, that is, a loss of physiological awareness: smell, taste, sound, sight, skin sensations, and digestion. I periodically inquire about or devise awareness enhancing exercises that stimulate a consciousness of various body sensations that may either be blocked or that may serve as a way into sub-symbolic and procedural memories which are physiologically retroflected and therefore not-conscious.

With other clients I may either encourage them to exaggerate the inhibited gesture, to tighten their jaw or fist even harder. I may ask them to complete the interrupted gesture and explore what sensations, affects, fantasies, or associations come to mind. This may revamp into work with larger muscles where the clients explore moving in space. Movement, movement awareness, and awareness of body tensions are often evocative of unspoken childhood experiences. I may have the clients focus on where they feel sensations in their body, where there is little or no sensation, and the mental imagery that this type of inquiry brings.

It is essential that I remain aware of my own body process when doing any physiological work with clients. In my attempt to have a physiological resonance I often vicariously experience their body tensions. Through attending to my own breathing and body sensations I seek an awareness of the difference between my sensations and the clients' sensations, even though I am simultaneously identifying with their bodily experience.

For some clients body awareness work can be done through fantasy. I ask them to imagine using their body in a different way, such as running away, hitting back, standing up for themselves, or embracing and cuddling. Some of the time the body focused therapy involves working with imagination, such as having them visualize reaching upwards and then imagining someone picking them up. In some groups what begins as one person's body awareness and movement work may morph in a psychodrama involving the whole group. Psychodrama is a powerful method of facilitating clients' resolution of traumatic or neglectful experiences.

Communicative sounds such as "Oh," "Uh," "Thisst," or a sigh all have a physical and affective component. I often respond to these communicative moments by asking questions similar to "What is happening in your body right at this moment?" or "What do you experience internally when you say, 'Uh'"? If the client seems open to such an inquiry, I may say something that reflects my observations of his body tensions: "Pay attention to your left shoulder," or "Feel what just happened to your throat," or "You made a sigh just now. Your body may be expressing something important."

Each of these body centered techniques and methods can be highly beneficial as an adjunct to a relationally focused, in-depth psychotherapy. When using body oriented approaches I am focused on the necessity of titrating the technique or method to the affect tolerance of the client. I am watchful that the awareness exercise, art expression, body movement, hitting or kicking a cushion, or psycho-drama experience is at a level where the client can affectively process the experience without becoming emotionally overwhelmed, triggering a reinforcement of the strategies of archaic self-stabilization. Titrating of the clients' level of affect requires constant phenomenological inquiry and observation of the clients' body movements before, during, and after using body centered methods.

I strive to attend to the subtle physiological shifts that occur when clients are talking, such as the changes in volume, inflection, rhythm, and tone. These utterances may reflect the sub-symbolic, implicit, and procedural memories embedded in the client's affect and body. I am also watching for the little physical gestures such as pupil dilation or enlargement, the tensing of the neck or jaw, changes in breathing, tightening the pelvis or legs, and looking away that may indicate that the client is becoming overwhelmed with unexpressed affect.

My therapeutic goal is to stimulate and enhance the client's sense of visceral arousal and awareness so that he has a new physiological-affective-relational experience. I want to activate the client's inhibited gestures and relax the retroflections while being attentive to the possibility of overstimulation and retraumatization. If the physical gestures that reflect possible affect overstimulation and potential retraumatization do appear it is my responsibility to shift the focus of our body work or the content of our conversation, to ease up or stop any touch, to change the physical activity, and to cognitively process the emotional experience with the client. Returning to phenomeno-logical inquiry and an interpersonal dialogue is often the best way to provide the client with the needed physiological stabilization and affect regulation so that he can integrate the therapeutic experience physiologically, affectively, and cognitively (Erskine, Moursund, & Trautmann, 1999).

Body oriented therapy without touch

Before I talk about body therapy that includes touch I would like to describe a therapy situation that was primarily body focused and did not involve touch during the early phase of the psychotherapy. Jim came to group therapy because he could not maintain friendships or find a life partner. In the first few sessions it was obvious he tended to invade people's space. When he entered the office he piled his coat on top of other people's coats rather than using his own hanger. He left his shoes where others tripped on them. He often plopped down on the sofa almost on top on others. He put his feet on someone's lap. People in the group began to find him a nuisance. When the group members first confronted him about his behavior and how they felt invaded he seemed to have no awareness of what they meant. After a few sessions of such discussions he gained some awareness of his own behavior but he seemed to have little self management.

I observed that he was lacking in exteroceptive sensitivity and was limited in knowing the boundaries of interaction between his own and other people's bodies. In the following session I had him close his eyes and feel the chair, to touch his legs, to then feel his feet solidly on the floor, to then spread his arms and feel the dimensions of his external space. He slid off the sofa onto his knees. I suggested that he keep his eyes closed and to feel his knees and hands grounded into the carpet.

He began to crawl like a toddler. I encouraged him to pay attention to each sensation in his body. As he crawled along the floor he seemed tight and restricted in his legs and shoulders. He was tense. I assumed that he was afraid. After several minutes of crawling he began to cry, at first softly, and then with deep sobs. He remained on his knees, eyes closed, with his arms stretched in the air crying to be picked up. In a later session he reported that he had a reoccurring dream in which he is crying for someone to take his hand, to help him walk, and to hold him on their lap.

In several subsequent sessions he surmised about the parental neglect that he may have received between the ages of one and two years. Through our group therapy sessions he created a mental mosaic composed of some explicit memories, physical sensations, observations of his mother's dismissive behavior toward his brother's children when they were toddlers, and family stories of mother's abuse of alcohol when he was under two years. He was forming a narrative of his sense of his own body in space and in relationship: lost, lonely, and longing for body contact with someone. He also became aware that he had a deep fear of rejection if he did reach out to touch someone. We spent several months in group therapy with Jim taking a portion of time each week to become aware of his body-based emotions, to explore space and the touch of others, to address his anticipation of rejection, and to receive encouragement from the group members for experimenting with new ways of being in relationship.

Therapy through healing touch

I touch some of my clients, yet I have had many clients that I have never touched. The decision to touch or not to touch depends on the therapeutic needs of the client, the quality of our psychotherapeutic relationship, and the level of body awareness and accompanying affect that the client can integrate. The decision to touch should not be based solely on the therapist's theoretical or technique preferences. Each client, at various times in the ongoing process of psychotherapy, may therapeutically benefit from touch—touch from the psychotherapist that may range from a gentle holding of the hand to deep massage of the back or shoulders to help the client vigorously move the large muscles to release previously retroflected emotions such as sorrow, disgust, terror, or anger.

Some clients benefit from a warm soft touch that to them feels supportive and protective. With one seventy-year-old woman I initiated holding her hand during a session as she talked about her despair and panic in having cancer. As I held her hand she had a pleasant memory of feeling secure when she was touched as a child. She experienced our hand holding as saying, "You can manage this crisis. I am with you." That triggered a memory of her father sitting at her bedside holding her hand when she had a high fever at age nine. For more than sixty years she had forgotten the warmth and security that this memory provided and she contrasted it with living alone as an older woman. This hand holding session opened the door for us to do an in-depth psychotherapy that focused on her body sensations, emerging associations and memories, the intersubjectivity of our therapeutic relationship, and the construction of a personal narrative that repaired the relational disruptions which had occurred before and during the time her mother was hospitalized with depression. The hand holding and goodbye hug were the only touching that we did but my initiating the hand holding remained meaningful to her.

I used therapeutic touch in a very different way with another person. Jennifer was an experienced psychotherapist. She had attended a series of training workshops where she was actively engaged in learning and supervision. On a couple of occasions she talked in the training group about her feelings of despair, the lack of energy she often felt at home, her growing resentment in providing therapy to others, and her desire to "withdraw and just give up." She was disappointed in her personal therapy.

She said, "I just talk and talk. My therapist is very supportive but I seem to go around and around on the same old subjects. I either need a different kind of therapy or I should just quit." Her posture reminded me of previous clients whose bodies were encumbered with a sense of hopelessness.

On the strength of our already established supervisory relationship (and with the support and permission of her therapist) she came to a five-day therapy marathon where I was doing personal therapy with a group of psychotherapists. I did not yet have a therapy plan but I sensed that something significant would emerge once we were more closely engaged in a therapy relationship and both coheasion and intrnal security had developed in the group. I did consider the likelihood that she was already slipping into an enactment of some significant childhood memory and the possibility that she may benefit from some form of body therapy but I needed more observations of her breathing patterns, physiological movements, and how she related to both me and others in the group before I formed a sense of direction.

My intention in the first couple of days was to create a secure and cooperative group environment where it was safe for clients to have a supportive therapeutic regression to resolve fixated fear, trauma, or neglect. Importantly, I want clients to feel protected so that they can relax their physiological retroflections, to finally put into movement what was previously inhibited, and to have a chance to make the therapeutically necessary physiological and affective expressions—expressions where the neurological system is transformed and healed.

On the afternoon of the third day I was working with another woman who was crying and talking about the neglect and physical abuse she suffered at the hands of her mother when she was young. I noticed that Jennifer was curling up, rocking herself, and whimpering like a very young child. As the work with the other women ended I went over to Jennifer and quietly sat with her. After several minutes she opened her eyes and acknowledged that I was with her. She said, "I am terrified. My body is so stiff. This is what happens to me when I am home. I just want to disappear." I talked to her about the possibility of our doing some touch therapy. I described both the advantages and possible adverse effects of such emotion inducing work. We talked about how she could stop my touch at any time by either pulling on my shirt or saying the words "Richard, stop." I knew intuitively that it would be essential for her to have a sense of choice and control. She agreed to the contract that gave me permission to do some therapeutic touch on her tight muscles.

I invited her to go back to the physical and emotional experience of curling up and rocking. As she tightened into a fetal position, with eyes closed, she wiggled away from me and tried to hide under one of the many mattresses. I put my hand on her back, over her heart. She was extremely tense as though her back was an iron barrel. I began to massage the tight muscle of her upper back, at first lightly, and then with more strength. During the massage she squirmed and wanted to escape being touched. I encouraged her to make sounds, any sounds that reflected what she felt inside. As I did a deeper massage in the thoracic area of her back she clawed at the mattress, cried like a young child, and struggled to move away. For the next few minutes she repeatedly howled, "Go away," "Don't touch me," "Don't feed me," "I don't want you," while alternately squeezing and scratching a cushion.

I could hear her sounds of helplessness and see that her full expressions of natural protest were still inhibited. If she was going to have a therapeutic closure that could alter the neurobiology of the original neglect and/or trauma she needed to move her body in a more expressive way and to feel the sense of anger that she was still retroflecting. I had her roll onto her back. I sat behind her head and began to massage her tight trapezius muscles. In this supine position she was able to move her legs and slowly began to push with them. I asked the group members to surround her with mattresses and pillows. As I continued with a deeper massage she began to kick. I encouraged her to kick harder and faster and to say out loud anything that came to her. She kicked wildly, with such a great force that it took six people to hold the mattress. During the intense kicking she screamed in a strong and determined voice: "I don't want your touch, mother." "You have always hated me." "You squashed me, but now I know the truth." "It was never my fault." "You are the hateful one … not me." "I was a good child and you never saw who I was." "All my life I have blamed myself and kept myself hidden—no longer, mother. I am now free." "I don't want to carry your depression." "I am not going to hide who I am."

Although Jennifer's words sound as though she made a cognitive redecision, the significance of the therapy was not in the words she screamed or what she was thinking or saying. The principal and predominant change was physiological and affective—a neurological reorganization facilitated by the working directly with the retroflections in her body. She changed some brain–body-affect neurological circuits by allowing herself to feel the deep touch on her back, the related emotions that had been disavowed, and the sub-symbolic and procedural memories that were housed in her tight muscles. She kicked, screamed, released her retroflected anger at her mother's disdainful and neglectful behavior. Then she relaxed into the caring touch of several group members who gathered around to hold her and express their support.

Conclusion

There are many other case examples of body centered psychotherapy that I could use to illustrate the great variety of therapeutic methods available when working with protracted affect, retroflected movement, and sub-symbolic memory. Most of the methods involve a combination of focused awareness on breathing and body sensations, experimentation with movement and body tension, fantasy, grounding, and self-expression. These methods my include touch that is warm and protective or deep and evocative of body memories. Of particular concern is the ethical practice of the client having the choice over the nature of the interventions and the control to stop any form of body oriented psychotherapy.

All experience, particularly if it occurs early in life or if it is affectively overwhelming, is stored within the amygdala and the limbic system of the brain as affective, visceral, and physiological sensation without symbolization and language. Instead of memory being conscious through thought and internal symbolizations our experiences are expressed in the interplay of affect and body as visceral and somatic sensations. To again quote the title of van der Kolk's article, "The Body Keeps the Score".

It is our task as psychotherapist to work sensitively and respectfully with our clients' bodily gestures, movements, internal images, and emotional expressions to stimulate and enhance our client's sense of visceral arousal and awareness so that he has a new physiological-affective-relational experience. Such sensitivity and respectfulness requires us to be attentive to the possibility of overstimulation and re-traumatization and to take ameliorative action. The narrative of the body is a special language with form, structure, and meaning. Through a body centered relational psychotherapy we are able to decode the stories entrenched in our clients' affect and embodied in their physiology.

CHAPTER TWENTY

Narcissism or the therapist's error?

Phillip was in his mid fifties with a full head of perfectly coiffured grey hair. He arrived for his first appointment on time, dressed in a suit and tie that portrayed a stylish, expensive, and immaculate appearance. He rose from the chair in the waiting room with a beaming smile and vigorously shook my hand. As we chatted about the day's news, I observed that he was soft-spoken and highly articulate with a mild Southern accent. His appearance and social demeanor immediately impressed me. Within seconds I formed one of those intuitive first impression questions: Was he genuinely contactful or was his greeting a well-rehearsed, superficial ritual?

As I invited Phillip into the inner office I suggested that he make himself comfortable by removing his tie and shoes. He abruptly refused and appeared to be offended by my suggestion. With words and tone that reflected more of a critical comment than a question, he expressed amazement that I would make such a suggestion. I wondered if I had violated some Southern social norm that was important for him or if he was revealing some aspect of his personality via these first few transactions. I decided to not explain the reasons behind my suggestion but to wait and see if this type of disconnecting encounter would occur again.

A week before this first session an attorney for a large advertising firm had called my office to make an initial appointment for one of the firm's partners. On the phone the attorney told me that Phillip was required to come for psychotherapy as part of the settlement in a harassment and safety-violation lawsuit that had been filed against the firm. The attorney said that Phillip was an important member of the firm who headed a major department and that he was embroiled in two lawsuits for harassing employees. Retaining a partnership in the firm was dependent on his engaging in at least two years of psychotherapy and in making some major behavioral changes. I agreed to do a three-session evaluation and then decide if a constructive working relationship was possible.

Phillip began our initial session by describing himself as a successful executive art director who had won many awards for his firm. His creativity and the department he headed were essential in his firm's success but his position was in jeopardy as a result of two harassment suits. Both of the suits had been resolved out of court but the financial settlements had cost the firm a large amount of money. Some members of the board of directors had demanded that he resign.

We had a brief discussion about my potential report to the attorney and the inherent confidentiality necessary for an effective psychotherapy. He appeared to be comfortable with our arrangements. As I asked particulars about his job, he lamented that his work was "only commercial" and "subject to the whims of advertising fashion and the short-sightedness of the clients." Continuing in a critical tone he told me that some of the artists and production people working for him had "no creativity—their only talent is to follow what I design." I suspected that he was using his employees' lack of creativity to justify his behaviors that led to the harassment suits. I wondered if his comments about his clients were also justifying internal conflicts or relational difficulties.

I asked more about his relationship with his employees. "I only yell once in a while when they screw up. The rest of the time I treat them very well. I've paid them well. I give them good bonuses. They owe me a lot." His words and tone conveyed entitlement—an entitlement to "yell" because he "paid them well." I felt heavy-hearted as I listened to his lack of empathy and his tenacious self-centered perspective.

Hesitantly, he went on to describe himself as a painter; then he added that he was not painting very often. He expressed how he never showed his paintings because they were "not excellent—not imaginative and innovative" in the view of the New York art reviewers. I wondered if his criticism and hesitancy were an expression of resentment and/or shame. If my wondering actually reflected his experience we would have to come back to both the resentment and shame later, once we agreed to an ongoing psychotherapy.

In this first session it seemed necessary to focus on the job situation that forced him into psychotherapy. He added that in order to retain his partnership in the firm he had suggested a compromise: he would commit to an intensive ongoing psychotherapy that would last at least two years; he would make dramatic changes in his behavior toward his employees, particularly women; and he would accept that a female partner in the firm would regularly monitor his relationships with his employees and write periodic reports to the board of directors. He said that he was not coming to psychotherapy under duress but that it was he who had suggested the compromises. He knew that he had to change but did not know why he acted the way he did to the women in his department. He intimated that there were other more personal reasons for being in therapy but that he did not want to discuss them during these early sessions.

Phillip went on to describe how he had a habit of screaming at his employees. Three years before a woman in his department also sued his firm for harassment after she was unable to return to work following humiliating sexist comments Phillip had made in the presence of many of her co-workers. I contemplated the significance of his description of the "humiliating sexist comments" and wondered how these comments reflected larger relational conflicts, particularly with women. I also made a mental note of a slight contradiction: earlier he said "I only yell once in a while" and now he described himself as having a "habit of screaming." If we were going to proceed with a relationally focused psychotherapy, rather than behavior therapy, it was too soon to explore this contradiction.

He went on to describe that in the most recent incident he screamed personal insults and hurled a bottle of orange juice at one of his artists. The bottle hit another person. The incident frightened several other people and collectively they filed a lawsuit claiming a violation of workers' safety rights. Even though Phillip was a partner, he was about to lose his high-paying position in the firm unless he engaged in a successful behavior-changing psychotherapy. This was his ostensible motivation for coming to psychotherapy. As we ran out of time in this first session I was left with two questions: What other motivations were at play in his request for psychotherapy? How did all this information fit into an unconscious life pattern?

It was too soon to have any idea on how to proceed. I knew that it was essential to keep an open heart and mind. It was necessary to focus on what Phillip needed in our relationship in order to develop an effective therapeutic alliance. I also knew that if I were to do an effective psychotherapy I could not focus only on solving the behavioral problem of his raging at employees; my task would be to facilitate his psychological growth in several domains.

Second evaluation session

In our second session, when I again talked about confidentiality, Phillip revealed that he was involved with Cocaine Anonymous (CA) and was actively working the twelve-step program. He said that he was going to two or three meetings a week. He described joining CA two years ago, after the second harassment suit, when he realized that his raging behavior was in part provoked by cocaine. He was currently cocaine-free for two years but he was disappointed in the program. In two years he had two sponsors; both "did not understand me," they were "not psychologically minded," and "I feel all alone in the program."

He went on to describe how he was still "periodically screaming at work" while trying to assure me that his outbursts of rage were far fewer than before and that they were justified by the way people acted. I wanted to engage in several phenomenological inquiries to discover what he was thinking and feeling just moments before his rage, what he meant by "not psychologically minded," and his experience of not being understood. It was still too soon for such an intimate relational interaction. In this session I listened to what he wanted to tell me and only asked a few questions that elicited specific information.

Most of this session was spent talking about his previous use of cocaine and the benefits of being in a twelve-step program. Near the end I asked why, in making the settlement in the harassment suit, he chose to come to psychotherapy as part of the compromise. He said that there were three reasons he choose psychotherapy: first, he needed to keep his previous cocaine habit under control and confidential; second, he knew he needed "professional help"; and third, he had "some other relationship issues to solve." He was not ready to identify or discuss these issues.

I was left feeling intrigued by what he had not revealed and also by his commitment to Cocaine Anonymous's twelve-step program. I was not certain if we could establish an intimate therapeutic relationship. What was genuine? What was superficial? Could I create the quality of relationship that would soften his air of aloofness, arrogance, and entitlement? Did I have the psychotherapeutic skills to connect with the vulnerable man and boy that lived under his self-protective façade? I was not sure.

I sensed that Phillip would provide a challenge for my therapeutic skills to remain interpersonally contactful and psychologically helpful. I was comforted when I remembered Heinz Kohut's (1971, 1977) writings about the treatment of narcissistic patients. Kohut had emphasized the importance of sustained empathy and the fostering of vicarious introspection rather than the use of interpretations, confrontation, or a focus on behavior change. From my previous experience I knew that it would be absolutely essential that I stay empathetic with his emotional experience and that I maintain a contactful *presence*. The Zen philosophy of "less is more" repeatedly came to my mind as I imagined the potential future of our psychotherapy together.

Evaluation session three

I entered the third and final session of our evaluation period still not certain if Phillip and I would be able to create the quality of therapeutic relationship that would reveal and heal what I imagined to be his psychological wounds. The morning of his third session I contemplated whether he was serious or not about pursuing an in-depth psychotherapy. Was he motivated to really know himself, his personality-forming history, and his motivations? Or did he merely want to change a problem-making behavior to retain his employment? I was surprised when early in the session he expressed his willingness to pursue an ongoing psychotherapy.

I explained that the changing of his behavior would be an important part of our work together but that often it may seem that our focus was elsewhere. I went on to say that if we were to do an effective psychotherapy together, we would have to focus on his whole life experience and particularly the early influences that shaped his personality.

I challenged him with the question, "Are you ready to deal with the discomfort of knowing yourself, your motivations, and the potential alterations in your personality?" He hesitated and then surprised me with a tentative "Yes," adding the proviso that he wanted to be able to both paint again and to display his art at gallery exhibitions. I had surmised from his comments in our first session that his sense of creativity was stymied and that there was a strong reluctance to show his paintings to anyone. I made a mental note to explore this further.

I also noted that he did not mention the "relationship issues" to which he had alluded in the previous session. I asked about his current life: he reluctantly said that he was never married but had a "significant relationship for four years" that "ended drastically" because of their mutual use of cocaine.

It was apparent that if we were to engage in a comprehensive psychotherapy we would have to explore several dynamics in his life:

- the nature of his intimate relationships
- what appeared to be his style of aloof attachment and entitlement
- his experience that others did not understand him
- his use of cocaine as a self-regulator
- the functions of both his arrogant and his raging behaviors.

I wondered if he experienced the loneliness that I sensed coming from his body tension and nonverbal expressions—a loneliness that reminded me of previous clients who used a narcissistic façade to cover deep despair. A series of treatment directions were now taking shape. I realized that we were facing the potential of a psychotherapy that would last for more than the two years.

I offered the possibility of our working together three, or at least two, sessions per week. He was willing to come for only one fifty-minute appointment once a week. He announced that he could no longer come during the workday because of the "pressures at work." We struggled with our schedules to find a time that did not disrupt his work and going to the gym or interfere with his attending CA meetings. Suddenly, just as things seemed to be going smoothly between us, we could not find an agreeable meeting time. I wanted him to stay active in Cocaine Anonymous. I knew from experience with alcoholic clients that the specifically defined twelve-step program and the shared experience with other CA members would serve as an important co-therapist and a necessary therapeutic support when we were not having sessions.

We ended our three evaluation sessions by his adamantly saying that he would not cancel any of his evening sessions with his trainer at the gym. He left abruptly without making any future appointment. My first thought was that we ran directly into the classical psychoanalytic concept of resistance—the refusal to engage in the intimate relationship of psychotherapy.

As I considered the concept of resistance and the psychodynamic theory underlying the concept, I was aware that it did not fit my developmental and relational perspective. Interpersonal contact is always a co-creative progression. Conceivably, something other than resistance could be motivating his refusal to adjust his schedule in order to come to psychotherapy. Maybe he was not resisting the emotional vulnerabilities that can emerge in the psychotherapy or the potentially intimate contact with me. These ideas stimulated me to think about how relationships are developed in early childhood and the human needs for emotional contact, self-definition, and to make an impact.

I wondered if he was struggling to maintain some form of self-support and personal integrity or attempting to enhance his self-esteem. Had I been too forceful in defining our therapy contract? Had I failed to be sufficiently empathetic or again violated some personal norm? What had I missed? Was his behavior an expression of narcissism or had I erred in some profound way? To answer these questions without knowing his phenomenological experiences would be mere speculation. I was at a loss.

It was now my responsibility to write a letter of evaluation to the attorney and provide referrals to other psychotherapists. I was left considering who among my colleagues might have the heart and skills to create a caring and healing relationship with Phillip ... "I have decided to recommend your name as his potential psychotherapist" ... If you become his psychotherapist what will you do with and for him?

REFERENCES

Ainsworth, M., Behar, M., Waters, E., & Wall, S. (1978). *Patterns of Attachment: A Psychological Study of the Strange Situation*. Hillsdale, NJ: Lawrence Erlbaum Associates.

Allen, J. R. (2009). Constructivist and neuroconstructivist Transactional Analysis. *Transactional Analysis Journal, 39*: 181–192.

Allen, J. R., & Allen, B. A. (1972). Scripts: The role of permission. *Transactional Analysis Journal, 2*: 72–74.

Andrews, J. (1988). Self-confirmation theory: A paradigm for psychotherapy integration. Part I. Content analysis of therapeutic styles. *Journal of Integrative and Eclectic Psychotherapy, 7*: 359–384.

Andrews, J. (1989). Self-confirmation theory: A paradigm for psychotherapy integration. Part II. Integrative scripting of therapy transcripts. *Journal of Integrative and Eclectic Psychotherapy, 8*: 23–40.

Ansbacher, H. L., & Ansbacher, R. R. (1956). *The Individual Psychology of Alfred Adler*. New York: Atheneum.

Arlow, J. (1969a). Unconscious fantasy and disturbances of conscious experience. *Psychoanalytic Quarterly, 38*: 1–27.

Arlow, J. (1969b). Fantasy, memory, and reality testing. *Psychoanalytic Quarterly, 38*: 28–51.

Axelrod, J. (2006). The 5 stages of loss and grief. *Psych Central*. Retrieved April 9, 2013 from: http://psychcentral.com/lib/the-5-stages-of-loss-and-grief/000617.

Bach, S. (1985). *Narcissistic States and the Therapeutic Process*. New York: Basic Books.

Bartholomew, K., & Horowitz, L. (1991). Attachment styles among young adults: A test of a four-category model. *Journal of Personality and Social Psychology, 61*: 226–244.

Bary, B., & Hufford, F. (1990). Understanding the six advantages to games and their use in treatment planning. *Transactional Analysis Journal, 20*: 214–220.

Basch, M. (1988). *Understanding Psychotherapy: The Science Behind the Art*. New York: Basic Books.

Beebe, B. (2005). Mother–infant research informs mother–infant treatment. *Psychoanalytic Study of the Child, 60*: 7–46.

Beitman, B. D. (1992). Integration through fundamental similarities and useful differences among the schools. In: J. C. Norcroff & M. R. Goldfried (Eds.), *Handbook of Psychotherapy Integration* (pp. 202–230). New York: Basic Books.

Bergman, S. J. (1991). Men's psychological development: A relationship perspective. *Work in Progress, No. 48*. Wellesley, MA: Stone Center for Developmental Services and Studies, Wellesley College.

Berne, E. (1947). What is intuition? In: E. Berne (Ed.), *Beyond Games and Scripts: Selections from His Major Writings* (pp. 29–36). New York: Grove Press, 1976. (Original work published 1947 as part of *The Mind in Action*. New York: Simon & Schuster. Later republished in 1957 as *A Layman's Guide to Psychiatry and Psychoanalysis*. New York: Simon & Schuster.)

Berne, E. (1955). Primal images and primal judgment. In: E. Berne, *Intuition and Ego States: The Origins of Transactional Analysis* (pp. 67–97). San Francisco, CA: TA Press, 1977.

Berne, E. (1957a). Ego states in psychotherapy. *American Journal of Psychotherapy, 11*: 293–309.

Berne, E. (1957b). The ego image. In: E. Berne, *Intuition and Ego States: The Origins of Transactional Analysis* (pp. 99–119). San Francisco, CA: TA Press, 1977.

Berne, E. (1958). Transactional analysis: A new and effective method of group therapy. *American Journal of Psychotherapy, 12*: 735–743. Republished 1976 in E. Berne (Ed.), *Beyond Games and Scripts* (pp. 44–53). New York: Grove Press.

Berne, E. (1961). *Transactional Analysis in Psychotherapy: A Systematic Individual and Social Psychiatry*. New York: Grove Press.

Berne, E. (1964). *Games People Play: The Psychology of Human Relationships*. New York: Grove Press.

Berne, E. (1966). *Principles of Group Treatment*. New York: Grove Press.

Berne, E. (1972). *What Do You Say after You Say Hello? The Psychology of Human Destiny*. New York: Grove Press.

Blizard, R. A. (2003). Disorganized attachment, development of dissociated self-states and a relational approach to treatment. *Journal of Trauma & Dissociation, 4*: 21–50.

Block, J. (1982). Assimilation, accommodation, and the dynamics of personality development. *Child Development, 53*: 281–295.

Bloom, S. L. (1997). *Creating Sanctuary: Towards the Evolution of Sane Societies*. New York: Routledge.

Bollas, C. (1979). The transformational object. *International Journal of Psychoanalysis, 60*: 97–107.

Bollas, C. (1987). *The Shadow of the Object: Psychoanalysis of the Unthought Known*. New York: Columbia Universities Press.

Bowlby, J. (1961). Processes of mourning. *International Journal of Psychoanalysis, 42*: 317–339.

Bowlby, J. (1969). *Attachment. Volume I of Attachment and Loss*. New York. Basic Books.

Bowlby, J. (1973). *Separation: Anxiety and Anger. Volume II of Attachment and Loss*. New York. Basic Books.

Bowlby, J. (1980). *Loss: Sadness and Depression. Volume III of Attachment and Loss*. New York: Basic Books.

Bowlby, J. (1988a). Developmental psychology comes of age. *American Journal of Psychiatry, 145*: 1–10.

Bowlby, J. (1988b). *A Secure Base*. New York: Basic Books.

Brenner, C. (1979). Working alliance, therapeutic alliance, and transference. *Journal of the American Psychoanalytic Association, 27*: 137–158.

Breuer, J., & Freud, S. (1950d). *Studies on Hysteria*. A. A. Brill (Trans.). New York: Nervous and Mental Disease Publishing.

Brown, M. (1977). *Psychodiagnosis in Brief*. Ann Arbor, MI: Huron Valley Institute.

Buber, M. (1958). *I and Thou*. R. G. Smith (Trans.). New York: Charles Scribner's Sons.

Bucci, W. (1997). *Psychoanalysis and Cognitive Science: A Multiple Code Theory*. New York: Guilford.

Bucci, W. (2001). Pathways to emotional communication. *Psychoanalytic Inquiry, 21*: 40–70.

Burgess, A. G., & Burgess, J. P. (2011). *Truth*. Princeton, NJ: Princeton University Press.

Childs-Gowell, E. (2003). *Good Grief Rituals: Tools for Healing*. Barrytown, NY: Station Hill Press.

Clark, A. (2004). Working with grieving adults. *Advances in Psychiatric Treatment, 10*: 164–170.

Clark, B. D. (1991). Empathetic transactions in the deconfusing of Child ego states. *Transactional Analysis Journal, 21*: 92–98.

Clark, F. (1990). The intrapsychic function of introjects. In: B. Loria (Ed.), *Couples: Theory, Treatment and Enrichment*: Conference Proceedings of the Eastern Regional Transactional Analysis Conference, April 18–21, 1990. Madison, WI: Omni Press.

Clark, F. (2001). Psychotherapy as a mourning process. *Transactional Analysis Journal, 31*: 156–160.

Clarkson, P., & Fish, S. (1988). Rechilding: Creating a new past in the present as a support for the future. *Transactional Analysis Journal, 18*: 51–59.

Cornell, W. F. (1988). Life script theory: A critical review from a developmental perspective. *Transactional Analysis Journal, 18*: 270–282.

Cornell, W. F., & Landaiche, N. M., III (2006). Impasse and intimacy: Applying Berne's concept of script protocol. *Transactional Analysis Journal, 36*: 196–213.

Cornell, W. F., & Olio, K. A. (1992). Consequences of childhood bodily abuse: A clinical model for affective interventions. *Transactional Analysis Journal, 22*: 131–143.

Cozolino, L. (2006). *The Neuroscience of Human Relationships: Attachment and the Developing Social Brain*. New York: W. W. Norton.

Damasio, A. (1999). *The Feeling of What Happens: Body and Emotion in the Making of Consciousness*. New York: Harcourt Brace.

Dashiell, S. R. (1978). The parent resolution process: Reprogramming psychic incorporations in the parent. *Transactional Analysis Journal, 8*: 289–294.

Dinesen, K. C. (1957, November 3). Interview with Bent Mohn. *The New York Times Book Review*.

Doctors, S. R. (2007). On utilizing attachment theory and research in self psychological/intersubjective clinical work. In: P. Buirski & A. Kottler (Eds.), *New Developments in Self Psychology Practice* (pp. 23–48). New York: Jason Aronson.

Efran, J. S., Lukens, M. D., & Lukens, R. J. (1990). *Language, Structure, and Change: Frameworks of Meaning in Psychotherapy*. New York: W. W. Norton.

Ellis, A. (1997). *The Practice of Rational Emotive Behavior Therapy (2nd ed.)*. New York: Springer.

English, F. (1972). Sleepy, spunky and spooky. *Transactional Analysis Journal, 2*: 64–73.

Erikson, E. (1950). *Childhood and Society*. New York: W. W. Norton.

Ernst, F. (1971). The diagrammed parent: Eric Berne's most significant contribution. *Transactional Analysis Journal, 1*: 49–58.

Erskine, R. G. (1974). Therapeutic intervention: Disconnecting rubberbands. *Transactional Analysis Journal, 4*: 7–8. (Republished in: R. G. Erskine, *Theories and Methods of an Integrative Transactional Analysis: A volume of Selected Articles* (pp. 172–173). San Francisco, CA: TA Press.)

Erskine, R. G. (1975). The ABC's of effective psychotherapy. *Transactional Analysis Journal, 5*: 163–165. (Republished 1997 in: R. G. Erskine (Ed.), *Theories and Methods of an Integrative Transactional Analysis: A Volume of Selected Articles* (pp. 227–228). San Francisco, CA: TA Press.)

Erskine, R. G. (1978). Fourth-degree impasse. In: C. Mosio (Ed.), *Transactional Analysis in Europe* (pp. 147–148). Geneva, Switzerland: European Association for Transactional Analysis.

Erskine, R. G. (1979). Life script: The fixed gestalt years later. Workshop presented at the First Annual Gestalt Therapy Conference, New York.

Erskine, R. G. (1980). Script cure: Behavioral, intrapsychic and physiological. *Transactional Analysis Journal, 10*: 102–106. (Republished 1997 in R. G. Erskine (Ed.), *Theories and Methods of an Integrative Transactional Analysis: A Volume of Selected Articles* (pp. 151–155). San Francisco, CA: TA Press.)

Erskine, R. G. (1981). Six reasons people stay in script. Lecture. Professional Training Program, Institute for Integrative Psychotherapy, April 4, 1981. New York.

Erskine, R. G. (1982a). Transactional Analysis and family therapy. In: A. M. Horne & M. M. Ohlsen (Eds.), *Family Counseling and Therapy* (pp. 245–275). Itasca, IL: F. E. Peacock Publishers. (Republished 1997 in R. G. Erskine (Ed.), *Theories and Methods of an Integrative Transactional Analysis: A Volume of Selected Articles* (pp. 174–207). San Francisco, CA: TA Press.)

Erskine, R. G. (1982b). Supervision of psychotherapy: Models of professional development. *Transactional Analysis Journal, 12*: 314–321. (Republished 1997 in R. G. Erskine (Ed.), *Theories and Methods of an Integrative Transactional Analysis: A Volume of Selected Articles* (pp. 217–226). San Francisco, CA: TA Press.)

Erskine, R. G. (1987). A structural analysis of ego: Eric Berne's contribution to the theory of psychotherapy. In: *Keynote Speeches: Delivered at the EATA Conference, July, 1986, Noordwikerhout, The Netherlands*. Geneva, Switzerland: European Association for Transactional Analysis.

Erskine, R. G. (1988). Ego structure, intrapsychic function, and defense mechanisms: A commentary on Eric Berne's original theoretical concepts. *Transactional Analysis Journal, 18*: 15–19. (Republished 1997 in R. G. Erskine (Ed.), *Theories and Methods of an Integrative Transactional*

Analysis: A Volume of Selected Articles (pp. 109–115). San Francisco, CA: TA Press.)

Erskine, R. G. (1989). A relationship therapy: Developmental perspectives. In: B. R. Loria (Ed.), *Developmental Theories and the Clinical Process: Conference Proceedings of the Eastern Regional Transactional Analysis Conference.* Stamford, CT: Eastern Regional Transactional Analysis Association.

Erskine, R. G. (1991). Transference and transactions: Critique from an intrapsychic and integrative perspective. *Transactional Analysis Journal, 21:* 63–76. (Republished 1997 in R. G. Erskine (Ed.), *Theories and Methods of an Integrative Transactional Analysis: A Volume of Selected Articles* (pp. 129–146). San Francisco, CA: TA Press.)

Erskine, R. G. (1993). Inquiry, attunement, and involvement in the psychotherapy of dissociation. *Transactional Analysis Journal, 23:* 184–190. (Republished 1997 in R. G. Erskine (Ed.), *Theories and Methods of an Integrative Transactional Analysis: A Volume of Selected Articles* (pp. 37–45). San Francisco, CA: TA Press.)

Erskine, R. G. (1994). Shame and self-righteousness: Transactional analysis perspectives and clinical interventions. *Transactional Analysis Journal, 24:* 86–102. (Republished 1997 in R. G. Erskine (Ed.), *Theories and Methods of an Integrative Transactional Analysis: A Volume of Selected Articles* (pp. 46–67). San Francisco, CA: TA Press.)

Erskine, R. G. (1995). Inquiry, attunement, and involvement: Methods of Gestalt Therapy. Workshop presented at the First Annual Conference of the Association for the Advancement of Gestalt Therapy, New Orleans. (Available on audiotape, Goodkind of Sound, (#SU8 A&B), Sylva, NC.)

Erskine, R. G. (1997a). Trauma, dissociation and a reparative relationship. *Australian Gestalt Journal, 1:* 38–47.

Erskine, R. G. (1997b). The therapeutic relationship: Integrating motivation and personality theories. In: R. G. Erskine (Ed.), *Theories and Methods of an Integrative Transactional Analysis: A Volume of Selected Articles* (pp. 7–19). San Francisco, CA: TA Press.

Erskine, R. G. (Ed.) (1997c). *Theories and Methods of an Integrative Transactional Analysis: A Volume of Selected Articles.* San Francisco, CA: TA Press.

Erskine, R. G. (1998a). Attunement and involvement: Therapeutic responses to relational needs. *International Journal of Psychotherapy, 3:* 235–244.

Erskine, R. G. (1998b). Psychotherapy in the USA: A manual of standardized techniques or a therapeutic relationship? *International Journal of Psychotherapy, 3:* 231–234.

Erskine, R. G. (2001a). The schizoid process. *Transactional Analysis Journal, 31:* 4–6.

Erskine, R. G. (2001b). Psychological function, relational needs and transferential resolution: The psychotherapy of an obsession. *Transactional Analysis Journal, 31:* 220–226.

Erskine, R. G. (2002). Bonding in relationship: A solution to violence. *Transactional Analysis Journal, 32:* 256–260.

Erskine, R. G. (2003). Introjection, psychic presence and Parent ego states: Considerations for psychotherapy. In: C. Sills & H. Hargaden (Eds.), *Ego States: Key Concepts in Transactional Analysis: Contemporary Views* (pp. 83–108). London: Worth.

Erskine, R. G. (2008). Psychotherapy of unconscious experience. *Transactional Analysis Journal, 38:* 31–35, 128–138.

Erskine, R. G. (Ed.) (2010a). *Life Scripts: A Transactional Analysis of Unconscious Relational Patterns.* London: Karnac.

Erskine, R. G. (2010b). Life scripts: Unconscious relational patterns and psychotherapeutic involvement. In R. G. Erskine (Ed.), *Life Scripts: A Transactional Analysis of Unconscious Relational Patterns* (pp. 1–28). London: Karnac.

Erskine, R. G. (2013). Relational group process: Developments in a Transactional Analysis model of group psychotherapy. *Transactional Analysis Journal, 43:* 262–275.

Erskine, R. G., & Moursund, J. P. (1988). *Integrative Psychotherapy in Action.* London: Karnac, 2011.

Erskine, R. G., Moursund, J. P., & Trautmann, R. L. (1999). *Beyond Empathy: A Therapy of Contact-in-Relationship.* Philadelphia, PA: Brunner/Mazel.

Erskine, R. G., & Trautmann, R. L. (1993). The process of integrative psychotherapy. In: B. R. Loria (Ed.), The Boardwalk Papers: Selections from the 1993 Eastern Regional Transactional Analysis Conference (pp. 1–26). Madison, WI: Omnipress. (Republished 1997 in R. G. Erskine (Ed.), *Theories and Methods of an Integrative Transactional Analysis: A Volume of Selected Articles* (pp. 79–95). San Francisco, CA: TA Press.)

Erskine, R. G., & Trautmann, R. L. (1996). Methods of an integrative psychotherapy. *Transactional Analysis Journal, 26:* 316–328. (Republished 1997 in R. G. Erskine (Ed.), *Theories and Methods of an Integrative Transactional Analysis: A Volume of Selected Articles* (pp. 20–36). San Francisco, CA: TA Press.)

Erskine, R. G., & Trautmann, R. L. (2003). Resolving intrapsychic conflict: Psychotherapy of Parent ego states. In: C. Sills & H. Hargaden (Eds.), *Ego States: Key Concepts in Transactional Analysis, Contemporary Views* (pp. 109–134). London: Worth.

Erskine, R. G., & Zalcman, M. J. (1979). The racket system: A model for racket analysis. *Transactional Analysis Journal, 9:* 51–59. (Republished 1997 in R. G. Erskine (Ed.), *Theories and Methods of an Integrative Transactional*

Analysis: A Volume of Selected Articles (pp. 156–165). San Francisco, CA: TA Press.)

Evans, K. (1994). Healing shame: A Gestalt perspective. *Transactional Analysis Journal, 24*: 103–108.

Fairbairn, W. R. D. (1952). *An Object-Relations Theory of the Personality.* New York: Basic Books.

Fairbairn, W. R. D. (1954). *Psychoanalytic Studies of the Personality.* New York: Basic Books.

Federn, P. (1953). *Ego Psychology and the Psychoses.* London: Imago.

Festinger, L. (1958). The motivating effect of cognitive dissonance. In: G. Lindzey (Ed.), *Assessment of Human Motives.* New York: Rinehart.

Field, T., Diego, M., Hernandez-Reif, M., Schanberg, S., Kuhn, C., & Yando, R. (2003). Pregnancy anxiety and comorbid depression and anger: Effects on the fetus and neonate. *Depression and Anxiety, 17*: 150–151.

Fonagy, P., Leigh, T., Steele, M., Steele, H., Kennedy, R., Mattoon, G., Target, M., & Gerber, A. (1996). The relation of attachment status, psychiatric classification, and responses to psychotherapy. *Journal of Consulting and Clinical Psychology, 64*: 22–31.

Fosshage, J. L. (1992). Self psychology: The self and its vicissitudes within a relational matrix. In: N. Skolnik & S. Warshaw (Eds.), *Relational Perspectives in Psychoanalysis* (pp. 21–42). Hillsdale, NJ: The Analytic Press.

Fosshage, J. L. (2005). The explicit and implicit domains in psychoanalytic change. *Psychoanalytic Inquiry, 25*: 516–539.

Fraiberg, S. H. (1959). *The Magic Years: Understanding and Handling the Problems of Early Childhood.* New York: Charles Scribner's Sons.

Fraiberg, S. H. (1982). Pathological defenses in infancy. *Psychoanalytic Quarterly, 51*: 612–635. (Also published in 1983 (Fall) in *Dialogue: A Journal of Psychoanalytic Perspectives*: 65–75.)

Freud, S. (1900a). *The Interpretation of Dreams. S. E., 4 & 5.* London: Hogarth.

Freud, S. (1912b). The dynamics of transference. *S. E., 12*: 97–108. London: Hogarth.

Freud, S. (1915e). The unconscious. *S. E., 14*: 159–215. London: Hogarth.

Freud, S. (1917e). Mourning and melancholia. *S. E., 14.* London: Hogarth.

Freud, S. (1920g). *Beyond the Pleasure Principle. S. E., 18*: 3–64. London: Hogarth.

Freud, S. (1940a). *An Outline of Psychoanalysis.* New York: W. W. Norton, 1949.

Friedman, L. (1969). The therapeutic alliance. *International Journal of Psychoanalysis, 50*: 139–159.

Friedman, R. (2009). Broken hearts: Exploring myths and truths about grief, loss and recovery. *Psychology Today.* Retrieved May 2, 2013 from: www.psychologytoday.com/blog/broken-hearts/200909/no-stages-grief.

Gibran, K. (1923). *The Prophet*. New York: Alfred A. Knopf.

Gobes, L. (1985). Abandonment and engulfment: Issues in relationship therapy. *Transactional Analysis Journal, 15*: 216–219.

Gobes, L. (1990). Ego states—Metaphor or reality? *Transactional Analysis Journal, 20*: 163–165.

Gobes, L., & Erskine, R. G. (1995). Letters to the editor. *Transactional Analysis Journal, 25*: 192–194.

Goulding, M. M., & Goulding, R. L. (1979). *Changing Lives through Redecision Therapy*. New York: Bruner/Mazel.

Goulding, R. L. (1974). Thinking and feeling in transactional analysis: Three impasses. *Voices, 10*: 11–13.

Goulding, R. L., & Goulding, M. M. (1978). *The Power Is in the Patient*. San Francisco, CA: TA Press.

Greenberg, J. R., & Mitchell, S. A. (1983). *Object Relations in Psychoanalytic Theory*. Cambridge, MA: Harvard University Press.

Greenberg, L., & Paivio, S. C. (1997). *Working with Emotions in Psychotherapy*. New York: Guilford.

Greenson, R. (1967). *The Techniques and Practice of Psychoanalysis*. New York: International Universities Press.

Greenwald, B. (2013). Grief issues in the psychotherapeutic process. Retrieved May 2, 2013 from: www.uic.edu/orgs/convening/grief.htm.

Guistolese, P. (1997). Failures in the therapeutic relationship: Inevitable and necessary? *Transactional Analysis Journal, 4*: 284–288.

Guntrip, H. J. S. (1961). *Personality Structure and Human Interaction*. London: Hogarth.

Guntrip, H. J. S. (1968). *Schizoid Phenomena, Object-relations and the Self*. Madison, CT: International Universities Press.

Guntrip, H. J. S. (1971). *Psychoanalytic Theory, Therapy and the Self*. New York: Basic Books.

Hargaden, H., & Sills, C. (2002). *Transactional Analysis: A Relational Perspective*. Hove, UK: Brunner-Routledge.

Hartmann, H. (1939). *Ego Psychology and the Problems of Adaptation*. New York: International Universities Press.

Hartmann, H. (1964). *Essays on Ego Psychology: Selected Problems in Psychoanalytic Theory*. New York: International Universities Press.

Hazell, J. (Ed). (1994). *Personal Relations Therapy: The Collected Papers of H. J. S. Guntrip*. Northvale, NJ: Jason Aronson.

Heimann, P. (1950). On countertransference. *International Journal of Psychoanalysis, 31*: 81–84.

Hensley, P. L. (2006). Treatment of bereavement-related depression and traumatic grief. *Journal of Affect Disorders, 92*: 117–124.

Hesse, E. (1999). The adult attachment interview: Historical and current perspectives. In: J. Cassidy & P. Shaveer (Eds.), *Handbook of Attachment:*

Theory, Research, and Clinical Applications (pp. 395–433). New York: Guilford.

Holloway, W. H. (1972). The crazy child in the parent. *Transactional Analysis Journal, 2*: 128–130.

Horowitz, L. M., Rosenberg, S. E., & Bartholomew, K. (1993). Interpersonal problems, attachment styles and outcome in brief dynamic psychotherapy. *Journal of Consulting and Clinical Psychology, 61*: 549–560.

Howell, E. F. (2005). *The Dissociative Mind*. Hillsdale, NJ: Analytic Press.

Huie, J. L. (2014). Pain you quotes and sayings. In: J. L. Huie, *Joyful Living through Conscious Choice*. Retrieved from http://www.jonathanlockwoodhuie.com/quotes/pain_you/

Jacobs, L. (1996). Shame in the therapeutic dialogue. In: R. Lee & G. Wheeler (Eds.), *The Voice of Shame: Silence and Connection in Psychotherapy*. San Francisco, CA: Jossey-Bass.

Jacobson, E. (1964). *The Self and the Object World*. New York: International Universities Press.

James, M., & Goulding, M. M. (1998). Self-reparenting and redecision. *Transactional Analysis Journal, 28*: 16–19.

Jordan, J. V. (1989). Relational development: Therapeutic implications of empathy and shame. *Work in Progress, No. 39*. Wellesley, MA: Stone Center for Developmental Services and Studies, Wellesley College.

Kaufman, G. (1989). *The Psychology of Shame*. New York: Springer.

Kelly, G. A. (1955). *The Psychology of Personal Constructs. Vol. 1: A Theory of Personality*. New York: W. W. Norton.

Kernberg, O. F. (1976). *Object Relations Theory and Clinical Psychoanalysis*. New York: Jason Aronson.

Khan, M. M. R. (1963). The concept of cumulative trauma. *Psychoanalytic Study of the Child, 18*: 286–301.

Kihlstrom, J. F. (1984). Conscious, subconscious, unconscious: A cognitive perspective. In: K. S. Bowers & D. Meichenbaum (Eds.), *The Unconscious Reconsidered* (pp. 149–210). New York: Wiley.

Kline, M. (1964). *Contributions to Psychoanalysis 1921–1945*. New York: McGraw Hill.

Kobak, R. R., & Sceery, A. (1988). Attachment in late adolescence: Working models, affect regulation, and representation of self and others. *Child Development, 59*: 135–146.

Kohut, H. (1971). *The Analysis of the Self*. New York: International Universities Press.

Kohut, H. (1977). *The Restoration of the Self: A Systematic Approach to the Psychoanalytic Treatment of Narcissistic Personality Disorder*. New York: International Universities Press.

Kris, E. (1951). Ego psychology and interpretation in psychoanalytic therapy. *Psychoanalytic Quarterly, 20*: 15–31.

Kris, E. (1979). *The Selected Papers of Ernest Kris*. New Haven, CT: Yale University Press.

Kübler-Ross, E. (1969). *On Death and Dying*. New York: Macmillan.

Langs, R. (1976). *The Therapeutic Intervention: Vol. II. A Critical Overview and Synthesis*. New York: Jason Aronson.

LeDoux, J. E. (1994). Emotion, memory and the brain. *Scientific American, 270*: 50–57.

Lee, R. G., & Wheeler, G. (1996). *The Voice of Shame: Silence and Connection in Psychotherapy*. San Francisco, CA: Jossey-Bass.

Lee, R. R. (1998). Empathy and affects: Towards an intersubjective view. *Australian Journal of Psychotherapy, 17*: 126–149.

Lewin, K. (1951). *Field Theory in Social Science*. New York: Harper & Brothers.

Liotti, G. (1999). Understanding dissociative processes: The contribution of attachment theory. *Psychoanalytic Inquiry, 19*: 757–783.

Lipton, S. (1977). The advantages of Freud's technique as shown in his analysis of the Rat Man. *International Journal of Psychoanalysis, 58*: 255–273.

Little, M. I. (1990). *Psychotic Anxieties and Containment: A Personal Record of an Analysis with Winnicott*. Northvale, NJ: Jason Aronson.

Loria, B. R. (1988). The Parent ego state: Theoretical foundations and alterations. *Transactional Analysis Journal, 18*: 39–46.

Loria, B. R. (1991). Integrative family therapy. In: A. Horne & L. Passmore (Eds.), *Family Counseling and Therapy. 2nd Edition*. Itasca, IL: Peacock.

Lourie, J. (1996). Cumulative trauma: the nonproblem problem. *Transactional Analysis Journal, 26*: 276–283.

Lyons-Ruth, K. (1999). The two-person unconscious: Intersubjective dialogue, enactive relational representation, and the emergence of new forms of relational organization. *Psychoanalytic Inquiry, 19*: 576–617.

Lyons-Ruth, K. (2000). "I sense that you sense that I sense …": Sander's recognition process and the specificity of relational moves in the psychotherapeutic setting. *Infant Mental Health Journal, 21*: 85–98.

Lyons-Ruth, K., Dutra, L., Schuder, M., & Bianchi, I. (2006). From infant attachment disorganization to adult dissociation: Relational adaptations or traumatic experiences? *Psychiatric Clinics of North America, 29*: 63–86.

Lyons-Ruth, K., Zoll, D., Connell, D., & Grunebaum, H. U. (1986). The depressed mother and her one-year-old infant: Environment, interaction, attachment, and infant development. In: E. Z. Tronick & T. Field (Eds.), *Maternal Depression and Infant Disturbance: New Directions for Child Development* (pp. 61–81). San Francisco, CA: Jossey-Bass.

Maciejewski, P. K., Zhang, B., Block, S. D., & Prigerson, H. G. (2007). An empirical study of the stage theory of grief. *Journal of the American Medical Association, 297*: 716–723.

Mahler, M. S. (1968). *On Human Symbiosis and the Vicissitudes of Individuation*. New York: International Universities Press.

Mahler, M. S., Pine, F., & Bergman, A. (1975). *The Psychological Birth of the Human Infant: Symbiosis and Individuation*. New York: Basic Books.

Main, M. (1990). Cross-cultural studies of attachment organization: Recent studies, changing methodologies, and the concept of conditional strategies. *Human Development, 33*: 48–61.

Main, M. (1995). Recent studies in attachment: Overview with selected implications for clinical work. In: S. Goldberg, R. Muir, & J. Kerr (Eds.), *Attachment Theory: Social, Developmental and Clinical Perspectives* (pp. 407–474). Hillsdale, NJ: Analytic Press.

Main, M., Kaplan, N., & Cassidy, J. (1985). Security in infancy, childhood, and adulthood: A move to the level of representation. *Monographs of the Society for Research in Child Development, 50*: 66–104.

Maslow, A. (1970). *Motivation and Personality (revised ed.)*. New York: Harper & Row.

Masterson, J. F. (1976). *Psychotherapy of the Borderline Adult: A Developmental Approach*. New York: Brunner/Mazel.

Masterson, J. F. (1981). *The Narcissistic and Borderline Disorders: An Integrated Developmental Approach*. New York: Brunner/Mazel.

McNeel, J. R. (1976). The parent interview. *Transactional Analysis Journal, 6*: 61–68.

Mellor, K., & Andrewartha, G. (1980). Reparenting the parent in support of redecisions. *Transactional Analysis Journal, 10*: 197–203.

Mikulincer, M., Florian, V., & Tolmatz, R. (1990). Attachment styles and fear of personal death: A case study of affect regulation. *Journal of Personality and Social Psychology, 58*: 273–280.

Miller, A. (1981). *The Drama of the Gifted Child: The Search for the True Self*. R. Ward (Trans.). New York: Basic Books.

Miller, J. B. (1986). What do we mean by relationships? *Work in Progress, No. 22*. Wellesley, MA: Stone Center for Developmental Services and Studies, Wellesley College.

Miller, J. B. (1987). *Toward a New Psychology of Women*. Boston, MA: Beacon.

Mitchell, S. A. (1993). *Hope and Dread in Psychoanalysis*. New York: Basic Books.

Moursund, J. P., & Erskine, R. G. (2004). *Integrative Psychotherapy: The Art and Science of Relationship*. Pacific Grove, CA: Thomson: Brooks/Cole.

Muller, R., Sicoli, L., & Lemieux, K. (2000). Relationship between attachment style and posttraumatic stress symptomatology among adults who report the experience of childhood abuse. *Journal of Traumatic Stress, 13*: 321–332.

Nathanson, D. (1992). *Shame and Pride: Affect, Sex and the Birth of the Self.* New York: W. W. Norton.

Neimeier, G. J. (1995). The challenge of change. In: R. A. Neimeyer & M. J. Mahoney (Eds.), *Constructivism in Psychotherapy* (pp. 111–126). Washington, DC: American Psychological Association.

Neimeyer, R. A., & Wogrin, C. (2008). Psychotherapy for complicated bereavement: A meaning-oriented approach. *Illness, Crisis, Loss, 16*: 1–20.

Nelson, E. E., & Panksepp, J. (1998). Brain substrates of infant–mother attachment: Contributions of opioids, oxytocin, and norepinephrine. *Neuroscience and Biobehavioral Reviews, 22*: 437–452.

Novellino, M. (1984). Self-analysis of countertransference in integrative transactional analysis. *Transactional Analysis Journal, 14*: 63–67.

Novellino, M. (2003). Transactional psychoanalysis. *Transactional Analysis Journal, 33*: 223–230.

Olders, H. (1989). Mourning and grief as healing processes in psychotherapy. *Canadian Journal of Psychiatry, 34*: 271–278.

Orange, D. M., Atwood, G. E., & Stolorow, R. D. (1997). *Working Intersubjectively: Contextualism in Psychoanalytic Practice.* Hillsdale, NJ: Analytic Press.

O'Reilly-Knapp, M. (2001). Between two worlds: The encapsulated self. *Transactional Analysis Journal, 31*: 44–54.

O'Reilly-Knapp, M., & Erskine, R. G. (2010). The script system: An unconscious organization of experience. In: R. G. Erskine (Ed.), *Life Scripts: A Transactional Analysis of Unconscious Relational Patterns* (pp. 291–308). London: Karnac.

Parkes, C. M. (1972). *Bereavement: Studies in Grief in Adult Life.* London: Tavistock.

Parkes C. M., & Weiss, R. S. (1983). *Recovery from Bereavement.* New York: Basic Books.

Perls, F. S. (1944). *Ego, Hunger and Aggression: A Revision of Freud's Theory and Method.* Durban, South Africa: Knox.

Perls, F. S. (1967). Gestalt Therapy: Here and Now. Chicago Training Workshop, September 21–24, 1967. Chicago, IL.

Perls, F. S. (1969). *Gestalt Therapy Verbatim.* Lafayette, CA. Real People Press.

Perls, F. S. (1973). *The Gestalt Approach and Eye Witness to Therapy.* Palo Alto, CA: Science & Behavior Books.

Perls, F. S., & Baumgardner, P. (1975). *Legacy from Fritz: Gifts from Lake Cowichan*. Palo Alto, CA: Science & Behavior Books.

Perls, F. S., Hefferline, R., & Goodman, P. (1951). *Gestalt Therapy: Excitement and Growth in the Human Personality*. New York: Julian.

Perls, L. (1977). Conceptions and misconceptions in Gestalt Therapy. Keynote address, European Association for Transactional Analysis Conference, July 7–9, 1977. Seefeld, Austria.

Perls, L. (1978). An oral history of Gestalt Therapy, Part I: A conversation with Laura Perls, by Edward Rosenthal. *The Gestalt Journal, 1*: 8–31.

Piaget, J. (1936). *The Origins of Intelligence in Children*. M. Cook (Trans.). New York: International Universities Press, 1952.

Piaget, J. (1954). *The Construction of Reality in the Child*. New York: Basic Books.

Piers, C. (2005). The mind's multiplicity and continuity. *Psychoanalytic Dialogues, 15*: 239–254.

Putnam, F. W. (1992). Discussion: Are alter personalities fragments or figments? *Psychoanalytic Inquiry, 12*: 95–111.

Rapaport, D. (1967). *The Collected Papers of David Rapaport*. M. Gill (Ed.). New York: Basic Books.

Redecision Therapy (1987). 110 minute video featuring Bob Goulding, M.D. & Mary Goulding, MSW. San Francisco, CA: International Transactional Analysis Association.

Reich, W. (1945). *Character Analysis*. New York: Farrar, Straus & Giroux.

Reik, T. (1948). *Listening with the Third Ear: The Inner Experience of a Psychoanalyst*. New York: Pyramid, 1964.

Rogers, C. R. (1951). *Client-Centered Therapy: Its Current Practice, Implications, and Theory*. Boston, MA: Houghton Mifflin.

Schacter, D. L., & Buckner, R. L. (1998). Priming and the brain. *Nevron, 20*: 185–195.

Schore, A. N. (2002). Advances in neuropsychoanalysis, attachment theory, and trauma research: Implications for self psychology. *Psychoanalytic Inquiry, 22*: 433–484.

Siegel, D. J. (1999). *The Developing Mind: Toward a Neurobiology of Interpersonal Experience*. New York: Guilford.

Siegel, D. J. (2003). An interpersonal neurobiology of psychotherapy: The developing mind and resolution of trauma. In: M. Soloman & D. J. Siegel (Eds.), *Healing Trauma* (pp. 1–56). New York: W. W. Norton.

Siegel, D. J. (2007). *The Mindful Brain: Reflection and Attunement in the Cultivation of Well-being*. New York: W. W. Norton.

Slap, J. (1987). Implications for the structural model of Freud's assumptions about perception. *Journal of the American Psychoanalytic Association, 35*: 629–645.

Steiner, C. (1971). *Games Alcoholics Play: The Analysis of Life Scripts*. New York: Ballantine.

Stern, D. (1985). *The Interpersonal World of the Infant: A View from Psychoanalysis and Developmental Psychology*. New York: Basic Books.

Stern, D. (1995). *The Motherhood Constellation: A Unified View of Parent–infant Psychotherapy*. New York: Basic Books.

Stolorow, R. D., & Atwood, G. E. (1989). The unconscious and unconscious fantasy: An intersubjective developmental perspective. *Psychoanalytic Inquiry, 9*: 364–374.

Stolorow, R. D., Brandschaft, B, & Atwood, G. E. (1987). *Psychoanalytic Treatment: An Intersubjective Approach*. Hillsdale, NJ: Analytic Press.

Stuntz, E. C. (1972). Second order structure of the parent. *Transactional Analysis Journal, 2*: 59–61.

Sullivan, H. S. (1953). *The Interpersonal Theory of Psychiatry*. New York: W. W. Norton.

Surrey, J. L. (1985). The "self-in-relation": A theory of women's development. Work in Progress, No. 13. Wellesley, MA: Stone Center for Developmental Services and Studies, Wellesley College.

Suttie, I. D. (1935). *The Origins of Love and Hate*. London: Free Association, 1988.

Tasca, G. A., Balfour, L., Ritchie, K., & Bissada, H. (2007). The relationship between attachment scales and group therapy alliance growth differs by treatment type for women with binge-eating disorder. *Group Dynamcs: Theory, Research and Practice, 11*: 1–14.

Thelen, E., & Smith, L. (1994). *A Dynamic Systems Approach to the Development of Cognition and Action*. Cambridge, MA: MIT Press.

Tomkins, S. (1962). *Affect, Imagery, Consciousness. The Positive Affects (Vol. 1)*. New York: Springer.

Tomkins, S. (1963). *Affect, Imagery, Consciousness. The Negative Affects (Vol. 2)*. New York: Springer.

Trautmann, R. L., & Erskine, R. G. (1999). A matrix of relationships: Acceptance speech for the 1998 Eric Berne Memorial Award. *Transactional Analysis Journal, 29*: 14–17.

Tronick, E. Z., & Gianino, A. F., Jr. (1986). The transmission of maternal disturbance to the infant. In: E. Z. Tronick & T. Field (Eds.), *New Directions for Child Development: Vol. 34. Maternal Depression and Infant Disturbance* (pp. 5–11). San Francisco, CA: Jossey-Bass.

Tustin, F. (1986). *Autistic Barriers in Neurotic Patients*. London: Karnac.

van der Kolk, B. A. (1994). The body keeps the score: Memory and the evolving psychobiology of posttraumatic stress. *Harvard Review of Psychiatry, 1*: 253–265.

Wallin, D. J. (2007). *Attachment in Psychotherapy*. New York: Guilford.

Watkins, J. G. (1978). *The Therapeutic Self*. New York: Human Sciences.

Watkins, J. G., & Watkins, H. H. (1997). *Ego States: Theory and Therapy*. New York: W. W. Norton.

Weinberg, M. K., & Tronick, E. Z. (1998). The impact of maternal psychiatric illness on infant development. *Journal of Clinical Psychiatry, 59* (Suppl. 2): 53–61.

Weiss, E. (1950). *Principles of Psychodynamics*. New York: Grune & Stratton.

Wetherell, J. L. (2012). Complicated grief therapy as a new treatment approach. *Dialogues in Clinical Neuroscience, 14*: 159–166.

Wheeler, G. (1991). *Gestalt Reconsidered*. New York: Gardner.

Winnicott, D. W. (1965). *The Maturational Process and the Facilitating Environment: Studies in the Theory of Emotional Development*. New York: International Universities Press.

Winnicott, D. W. (1974). Fear of breakdown. *International Review of Psychoanalysis, 1*: 103–107.

Wolf, E. S. (1988). *Treating the Self: Elements of Clinical Self Psychology*. New York: Guilford.

Woolams, S. J. (1973). Formation of the script. *Transactional Analysis Journal, 3*: 31–37.

Yontef, G. M. (1993). *Awareness, Dialogue and Process*. Highland, NY: Gestalt Journal Press.

INDEX